WINES AND WINERIES OF CALIFORNIA'S CENTRAL COAST

WILLIAM A. AUSMUS

WINES
& WINERIES
of California's Central Coast

A COMPLETE GUIDE FROM MONTEREY TO SANTA BARBARA

University of California Press BERKELEY LOS ANGELES LONDON

University of California Press, one of the most distinguished
university presses in the United States, enriches lives around the
world by advancing scholarship in the humanities, social sciences,
and natural sciences. Its activities are supported by the UC Press
Foundation and by philanthropic contributions from individuals
and institutions. For more information, visit www.ucpress.edu.

University of California Press
Berkeley and Los Angeles, California

University of California Press, Ltd.
London, England

Library of Congress Cataloging-in-Publication Data
Ausmus, William A.
   Wines and wineries of California's Central Coast : a complete
guide from Monterey to Santa Barbara / William A. Ausmus.
      p.   cm.
   Includes bibliographical references and index.
   ISBN 978-0-520-24437-5 (pbk. : alk. paper)
   1. Wine and wine making—California.   I. Title.
TP557.A96   2008
641.2'2097947—dc22   2007027906

Manufactured in the United States of America
17   16   15   14   13   12   11   10   09   08
10   9   8   7   6   5   4   3   2   1
The paper used in this publication meets the minimum
requirements of ANSI/NISO Z39.48-1992 (R 1997)
(Permanence of Paper).

To my family

In vino veritas (In wine is truth).

ALCIBIADES IN PLATO'S *Symposium*

In vino sanitas (In wine is health).

PLINY THE ELDER

Wine can be considered with good
reason as the most healthful and
the most hygienic of all beverages.

LOUIS PASTEUR

CONTENTS

MAPS

ACKNOWLEDGMENTS

I dedicate this work to my family. My mother, Helga, loved her German Rieslings and shared them with others in the same way she shared her convivial personality. She introduced me to wine. My father, Bill Ausmus, has continued to expand and educate his palate over the years, thereby introducing me to some excellent wines and keeping me on my toes to try new styles and varieties. My brothers, Eric and Mark, have spent many hours with me in stimulating company as we enjoyed the wine that often makes for ribald and hilarious conversation. My uncles, Erich and Roland Russel, brought me into wine culture, carefully guiding and looking after the education of their young charge.

Nancy Ann Clark, my partner in life and in wine, promised me that the move to California's Central Coast might have some unexpected surprises in store. She is largely responsible for the genesis of this book and has been my steadfast and unwavering supporter for its entirety, knowing that it would require my attention seven days a week from beginning to completion over the course of more than three years. Without waiting for me to ask, she volunteered her help, taking on the role of my personal liaison to everyone interviewed for the profiles. She made the calls, set the appointments, had all my materials ready at the door, and provided briefings and directions as I hit the road. On days and weekends when her work schedule permitted, she took her free time and accompanied me, using her substantial charm, wit, intellect, and formidable palate to facilitate and contribute to the interview process. Although I have said this once and publicly, I will say it again with encouragement from Nancy: the woman is an organizational genius. Cal Poly is lucky to have her. I shudder to think what this book would have become without her highly competent assistance, her unflagging good humor, and perhaps most important, her unshakable trust that I could pull this off. How lucky I am to have a family with whom I can share my passion for life and wine at the table. I drink to their health, one and all. *In vino sanitas!*

My sincere and genuine thanks go to all the owners, winemakers, and staff at the wineries who gave so generously of their time, shared their passion and enthusiasm, and often went to great lengths to accommodate my requests for interviews and tastings. I owe a special debt of gratitude to A. John Berardo of AJB, Catherine Faris of Tablas Creek, Robert Hall of Robert Hall Winery, Rich Hartenberger at Midnight Cellars, and Carol and Gino Perata of Fratelli Perata. They were gracious enough to speak for me and support this project when it was still at the proposal stage. To Douglas Braun at Presidio, Gary Eberle of Eberle Winery, Brett Escalera at Consilience, Michael Giubbini at Rotta, Ed Holt at Rancho Sisquoc, Dr. Tom and Sheila Morgan of Casa de Caballos, and Kenneth Volk of Kenneth Volk Vineyards and Winery, my thanks for the loan and use of research materials. To Jim and Mary Dierberg of Dierberg Vineyards, a special thanks for taking such good care of my Iowa guests; and to Traudl and Norman Huber at Huber Winery, thank you for your kindness and hospitality. To Drs. Terry Weinbrenner and Christine Shea, thanks for the many nights you opened your home to us and shared so generously your knowledge and the wines of the Central Coast. Steve Doty and Marlene Ciorba, my fishing and hunting buddies, have pushed me and encouraged me and let me know in no uncertain terms that I could accomplish this task. Last, to the handball players at the San Luis Obispo County YMCA: thanks for feigning your interest in the project as you waited patiently for me to shut up, stop talking about wine, and serve the ball.

In all, I reiterate without exaggeration that the people with whom I worked to accomplish this monumental task made it a pleasure indeed, even as my energies began to flag a bit in the final days and my tongue began to dry out. The very last thank you, of course, is reserved for Blake Edgar, my editor, and his excellent team, whose sure and steady guidance has sustained me throughout the life of this project. Any errors that appear in the book are certainly my responsibility but are attributable in their entirety to the wine.

PART ONE

Introduction

Introductions are important in social life because they serve as openings to conversations. In books, they serve a similar purpose: they initiate the communication between reader and author. That said, I dislike long-winded introductions in person and in print. I do want to share with you a quick overview of the scope of the book, the pleasure I had in writing it, and perhaps a little bit about myself in order to lessen my anonymity. I begin with a question you might have in mind as you read these pages: Why this book?

When an author gets an idea for a nonfiction work such as this, the first step is to research what has already been written on the topic—in this case, the wines and wineries of the Central Coast of California. I started this project by reading every book about California wine that I could get my hands on (more than forty). To my amazement, although there are excellent books available on California wine in general, only one book, *Central Coast Wine Tour from San Francisco to Santa Barbara* by Richard Paul Hinkle and William Henry Gibbs, focuses specifically on the wines of the Central Coast. Written more than thirty years ago, it is now out of date, though I cherish it as a stepping-stone to this work. This allows us to modify the question slightly to read: Why this book now?

In part, one of the things I discovered in my research was that there exists an ocean of verbiage paying homage to the wine regions of Napa and Sonoma, and justifiably so. In the vast archipelago of California wine, however, the Central Coast is very much an undiscovered island, known mostly to the locals and some island hoppers. I hope to change that. There is a real need for this book. As I introduced myself and my project, over and over wine consumers, vintners, grape growers, and winemakers looked at me with a wry smile and said while shaking my hand, "What took you so long?" Good question.

In my defense, I didn't know the region well until I came to California's magnificent Central Coast in 2001 to begin my teaching appointment at the California Polytechnic State University (Cal Poly) in San Luis Obispo. Nancy A. Clark, my sweetheart and fellow wine aficionado, is also at the university, and we bought a house together in Paso Robles, where we can see vineyards in the distance. Nancy, a driving and supportive force behind the organization and execution of this work, loves to go wine tasting. At the time, I had no idea of the splendors of the area or the quality of the wine. We learned quickly. After sampling the best that Paso Robles had to offer, we ventured south to the Edna Valley, and then on into Santa Barbara County. I was astounded by what I saw and, perhaps more important, by what I tasted. As a young wine consultant more than twenty years ago, I was not enamored of California wines in general; this was due, no doubt, to my European bias. After six years of tasting and taking notes, I am now thoroughly convinced. In part, this book is my attempt to persuade others of the same. The talent is here, the money is here, the right grapes are in the right ground, and the accolades from wine critics in both the local and national press are pouring in. So where is the book telling the story of this remarkable region, still relatively undiscovered and capable of producing world-class wines? I hope you have it in your hand.

I structured the book to achieve a series of related and specific purposes. I conducted interviews and let the winemakers and owners tell their stories. I want to share with you these personal stories of the people behind the wonderful wine of our region. Accordingly, every winery with a tasting room open to the public that agreed to an interview has a narrative profile that describes its history and how it got where it is. Hearing and learning these individual histories also gave me a sense of the place and the history of the region. The relationships among the winemakers and owners are manifold and wonderful. For instance, in Paso Robles, Gary Eberle, Nils Udsen, Ken Volk, Justin Baldwin, and Chuck Ortman are renowned not merely for producing outstanding wines, but also for mentoring and encouraging other outstanding wine professionals. The same can be said for Brian Talley in Arroyo Grande, Bryan Babcock in the Santa Rita Hills, and the Fess Parker and Zaca Mesa wineries in Santa Barbara County. In Monterey County, Doug Meador has been and continues to be an impressive influence not only for young winemakers, but also for the new viticultural practices he has championed and instituted. These intertwined and interrelated stories allowed me to write short histories of each of the viticultural areas for this book and for the Central Coast in general.

I am not the first person to believe in the enormous potential of this region. Excellent wine was made here from the mid-nineteenth century until Prohibition reared its ugly moralistic head. To cite a brief example, in Paso Robles the famous Polish pianist Ignacy Paderewski made award-winning wines in the 1920s. In the early '70s of the past century, as the United States and the California wine industry recovered from the debilitating effects of the Prohibitionists, Richard Sanford and Michael Benedict grew Pinot Noir grapes capable of challenging some of the best Burgundies. The critics began to take notice—sometimes begrudgingly, because as many of the winemakers hereabouts will tell you, the wine press can display a bias, and that indicator of bias often points north. The shared secret that some whisper is that not a few of the great wines produced north of our region were and are made from grapes grown south of their region, meaning here on the Central Coast. We might even say that it is not a very well kept secret that the reputation of some of California's finest commercial producers was made on the backs of the Central Coast viticulturists who sent their production trucking north. Now the internationals are here too: Foster's Group and Diageo, Constellation and Kendall-Jackson and Gallo, to mention a few that have established a tenacious foothold in our soils. The French are here, and the Italians, the Swiss, the Germans, the Portuguese, and the Australians are all growing or making wine on the Central Coast.

Wine writers in newspapers and magazines dedicated to critiquing wine for the consumer have also taken notice. *Decanter,* the *Wine Spectator,* and *Wine & Spirits,* to mention a few, are all doing features on the wines or winemakers of the region. Perhaps the most influential wine critic in the world, Robert M. Parker Jr. of the *Wine Advocate,* now makes yearly trips to the Central Coast, convinced that it is capable of being one of the world's truly great wine regions.

The last answer to the question "why this book" is more personal and involves telling you a little bit about myself. I am by training a scholar and work as a university professor, but wine has been part of my life for nearly as long as I can remember. I was born in Germany of a German mother and an American father and grew up below the Bavarian Alps. I have fond memories from my teenage years of yearly tasting tours *(Weinproben)* with my father and uncles Erich and Roland. We tasted across Germany's great wine regions along the Mosel and Rhine rivers. Wine is part of my culture and has been an abiding interest of mine ever since I took a sip of my first Riesling Spätlese, a golden wine that seemed to capture some of the color of the sun, tasted in the small village of Piesport next to the banks of the Mosel River. I went to Oregon to start my university studies and discovered there the birth of fine northwest

CHAPTER I

The Lay of the Land

The book is divided into two sections. In the first I provide a general history of the region, designed to be read with a glass of your favorite wine at hand. I briefly describe the early days of the Spanish missionaries who trekked north from Mexico past San Francisco, planting the seeds of Christianity and crops as they established missions along the way. For those of you who enjoy reading about the geology of the place where the grapes are grown, I include a chapter that treats the geological origins of the region, going all the way back to the plate tectonics that produced the stones, rocks, and soils that contribute to the totality of *terroir*. There is also a chapter outlining the American Viticultural Areas, or AVAs, the officially designated wine-growing areas within the Central Coast. In that chapter, I offer an argument for revising the Central Coast AVA into a more manageable territory. I use the basis for that argument to structure the second section of the book, starting with the wines and wineries of Monterey County and moving on to cover those of San Luis Obispo County and Santa Barbara County.

The second section features both a listing of all the wineries I could include within the limitations of time, and profiles of those wineries that agreed to answer my questions. In addition, prior to the profiles I write about the early pioneers of wine production in each of the three counties in an effort to leave a lasting chronicle that memorializes those men and women who had the foresight, courage, and good fortune to make it here. I also include a more localized treatment of the factors that contribute to the *terroir* within the counties.

I personally visited each winery for which a profile was written, conducted the interviews, and tasted through the wines to find my and the owners' recommendations. The two wines featured for each winery are intended to serve as an entrée to the wine list. Their descriptions are designed to give you a sense of what the winery is trying to achieve and tell you something about specific wines so that you can ask for them by name, if you so choose. The purpose behind the recommendations is to guide you to at least two wines that you can buy with confidence. They represent the best of what the winery has to offer. If the vintage is sold out, do not despair. Move up to the next year available for sale and compare notes for yourself.

Each profile contains all the contact information you need to find the winery and start your tastings. If you cannot visit personally, I provide all listed phone numbers, Web sites, and information about wine clubs. Not all the wineries have profiles: some owners did not wish to be interviewed, and I honored that wish. Some wineries do not have a tasting room open to the public, but I have listed them with contact information. Although my desire was to make this book as comprehensive as possible, some wineries opened during the time I needed to finish my writing. I include information about them as well and hope to visit, interview, taste, and write profiles for those good people if a revised edition of this book is produced.

All the wineries profiled in the book are capable of producing good wines of interest to the consumer. Winemaking expertise and technology are such that very few, if any, poorly made or seriously flawed wines are brought to market. In the past, however, this was not always the case. The Central Coast also has the advantage of *terroir*—that is, the combination of climate and soils capable of consistently producing high-quality grapes. Unlike other wine regions around the world, the variation among vintage years is not as profound as it is in France's Bordeaux region, for example. When variation does occur, it might affect some grape varieties but others not so much. This is an added strength of the region. It is capable of producing a diversity of grape varieties of interest to the diverse palates of wine consumers.

I structured the winery ratings in the following manner: All the wines in the "Recommended" sections are worthy of seeking out. They will give much drinking pleasure. I adopted a five-star rating system to give some sense of the relative quality of the wines made at a particular winery; the significance of the stars is explained at the start of part II. In terms of overall quality by county, Santa Barbara has a slight edge over San Luis Obispo, with Monterey currently third. In general, the white wines of Santa Barbara County can be excellent to outstanding, with Chardonnay paramount. The Pinot Noir can be world-class, and Syrah is emerging as an important variety. More and more Italian grape varieties are being produced here as well. In the southern region of the county, Cabernet Sauvignon and Merlot seem to flourish in Happy Canyon, where it is warmer. I predict that San Luis Obispo County, powered by the energy and dynamism coming out of the Paso Robles–Templeton area, will emerge as the leader in the near future when more of its vineyards mature, an advantage currently held by Santa Barbara County. As more vintners develop and practice the art of blending, overall quality should also improve. I am impressed by the eclecticism of the San Luis Obispo County wines. The county's reputation, in part, was made on the back of Zinfandel, which can be world-class, but Cabernet Sauvignon and Merlot can be superb too, on both sides of the Salinas River. Rhône varieties also have top potential, but the reds are generally ahead of the whites. This quality is celebrated yearly in the international Hospice du Rhône festival held in Paso Robles. In addition, Italian and Spanish grape varieties are flourishing in San Luis Obispo County and will contribute to the area's eclectic offerings. Monterey County has fewer producers than its big brothers to the south but is making rapid progress overall. In an area once known primarily for its white wines, high-quality Pinot Noir is now being produced in the mountains bordering the Salinas Valley, and Syrah is gaining a foothold as a potentially excellent variety. In the mountains around the Carmel Valley some wonderful Cabernet Sauvignon and Merlot is being produced.

For the most part, all three counties have benefited from the lessons learned from past mistakes and now have the right grapes in the right growing conditions with the talent and money in place to take full advantage of the growing conditions and the *terroir*. This speaks well for future improvement in the quality of the wines from the Central Coast. An important factor in the region's continued upward climb is a clear, sustained focus and vision for the wines within the areas. I strongly suggest that fewer wineries try to be all things to the wine consumer; I urge them to narrow their lines and emphasize what they do best. I am convinced that this specialization, combined with the focus on regional flavors that emerge as a function of distinctive *terroir,* will result in raising the overall quality levels for wines on the Central Coast. The Central Coast AVA will then comfortably take its place alongside some of the truly great wine-producing regions of the world. The astute wine consumer will be ahead of the pack, cellars stocked with representative examples of these fine wines, many of which represent extraordinary values given the current price/quality ratio for wines from other world-class regions.

CHAPTER 2

Central Coast Wine History

EARLY HISTORY

The wine history of California in general, and its Central Coast region specifically, predates the formation of the United States by a few years and California's entry into statehood by more than eighty years. Neither the French, the Germans, the Italians, the Portuguese, nor even the Spanish explorers who first came to California did so with the intent to grow grapes and produce wine. In time, however, all made significant contributions; but the Russians, unlikely as it seems, played a pivotal, albeit indirect, role at the forefront of California's long and noble wine history.

When Russian explorers crossed the Bering Sea in their movement south through Alaska in the eighteenth century, they made the New World delegates of King Carlos III of Spain very nervous. Czar Peter the Great sent Danishborn navigator Vitus Bering to explore the north Pacific as part of the Great Northern Expedition, and Bering left his boot prints on Alaskan soil before 1741. Spanish officials feared that the intrepid Russian explorers, and the fur traders who would inevitably follow, would continue their push south into the territories first visited by Spanish explorers and claimed in the name of their king. Uncertain of Russian motivations, the Spanish understood that the British and the French, two other contending forces they needed to reckon with, also had designs on their holdings. Given their previous experiences with the British and the French, the Spaniards could not afford to take the chance that the Russians would recognize and then act beneficently toward Spanish claims. However, such knowledge and foresight could do little good if there were no one in place to substantiate and defend the sovereign's claims against the coming of the usurpers. The Spanish had to act fast or learn to drink vodka.

In 1768 the Spanish king Charles III sent an expedition to Alta (Upper) California in an effort to secure the Spanish right to California and augment established strongholds and settlements in Baja (Lower) California. The Sacred Heart Expedition came north by land and by sea. Don Gaspar de Portolá, newly appointed governor of Baja California and charged by King Charles with expelling the Jesuits from Baja, led the military arm; the religious arm fell under the jurisdiction of Franciscan Father Junípero Serra, later known as the Apostle of California. The purpose of the expedition was threefold: to establish presidios (forts) to protect the interests of Spain and the settlers who would follow; to establish missions and bring Christianity to the heathen natives; and to establish settlements with an agricultural economy to support the presidios, the missions, and the settlers. In January 1769 two expeditions by land and two by sea moved north and set about the task of building missions along the way. In July of that year the four expeditions met in San Diego.

The Spanish conquistadors were required to carry grapevines wherever their explorations took them. They brought the first plantings of the noble *Vitis vinifera* grape to California from Spain via Mexico. Deemed essential to their cultural mission, grapes grown from these cuttings were used by the Spanish padres to make wine for the administration of the Sacraments. Hernán Cortés, after his invasion of Mexico in the early sixteenth century, found native grapes growing near Mexico City. The Spanish conquistadors tried to make wine from them but had little success. A devout and pious man unwilling to forgo the rituals of the Church because of lousy-tasting wine, in 1522 Cortés asked his father, Martín, to send cuttings from Spain. From that point on, Cortés decreed, Spanish grapes were to be grown in every Spanish settlement in the New World. Father Serra, true to the decree more than 250 years later, continued the planting of grapevines at the newly erected missions. Once a cross was raised and a new mission stood on the newly conquered lands, he made sure that grapes were planted.

Traveling together, Don Gaspar de Portolá and Father Serra also found wild grapevines *(Vitis girdiana)* growing in Alta California and recognized that the Mission grape too could flourish in those soils. In the garden of that first mission at San Diego, they planted figs and olives for the table and Mission grapes for wine and Catholic service. After the establishment of the mission at San Diego, the determined missionaries moved relentlessly northward and blazed a trail that runs through California from San Diego to just north of San Francisco. This trail is known as El Camino Real, or the Royal Way (also the King's Way), and followed approximately the route now taken by Highway 101. In fact, as you drive the highway you might notice fifteen-foot-high poles with mission bells along the sides of the road. These commemorate the original trail of the early Spanish explorers as they moved northward to establish their missions.

By 1773 the grapes at the San Diego mission were being made into wine. Historical records also indicate that a vineyard was planted at Mission San Juan Capistrano by 1779. Cork Millner writes in *Vintage Valley* that given the success of the vines, "Padre Serra and his followers planted vineyards at all twenty-one missions. It was the only wine made in California for the next sixty years." However, grapes most likely were not planted at all the original locations of the missions. For example, on June 3, 1770, Serra started building the first mission on the Central Coast (second in the sequence of twenty-one total), San Carlos Borromeo de Carmelo near present-day Monterey. Unfortunately, the site was unsuitable for growing crops, and the mission was relocated a few miles south of the city of Carmel in the beautiful Carmel Valley. From his headquarters at San Carlos Borromeo de Carmelo, Serra dispatched missionaries to San Antonio de Padua, about a day's travel south. The new mission, established in 1771, was forced to move in 1773 to take advantage of a better water supply. In an effort to close the distance between himself and the mission at San Diego, Serra also sent two missionaries farther south to build the mission at San Gabriel Arcángel, near present-day Montebello. The next mission on the Central Coast, San Luis Obispo de Tolosa, was built in 1772; it was here, most likely, that the first grapes for sacramental wine were grown on the Central Coast. Historian Dan Krieger believes that the first grapevines planted in San Luis Obispo were propagated from a cutting from the *viña madre,* or "mother vine," at San Gabriel Arcángel. By 1830 there were at least three vineyards in San Luis Obispo County, two at Mission San Miguel and one at Mission San Luis Obispo de Tolosa in what is now the center of town. Paul Kocher *(California's Old Missions)* believes the latter was the second-largest vineyard in the mission system, with almost 45 acres of grapes. The planting of grapes at missions stretching the length of the Central Coast established this region as the vanguard of California's extensive viticulture, which now produces nearly two-thirds of all wine sold in the United States.

THE MISSION GRAPE

According to Maynard Amerine, professor of wine at the University of California, Davis, the Mission grape, first brought to California by the mission fathers, remained the principal grape in the state until about 1870. Similar to a variety called the Negra Corriente of Peru, the black Pais of Chile, and the Criolla Chica (the Argentine name for the Pais), the Mission grape was used mostly for dessert wines such as sherry and port. The light-red and purple grapes were late ripening and took well to the heat of Southern California. Unfortunately, they produced table wines that lacked color and acidity. Wine made from these grapes reputedly did not to have much of a bouquet either. In other words, Mission grapes made a thin, flat, bland wine.

In the sixteenth century, the Spanish had already planted the Criolla grape south of Mexico City. Amerine and Vernon Singleton suggest in *Wine: An Introduction* that "the Criolla, then, is the same as or closely related to the variety we call Mission in California." After the grape was planted at the numerous missions along El Camino Real, vineyard failures were recorded in Santa Cruz, San Francisco, and Santa Clara, where the climate was simply too cool for the grape to mature. Even when the Mission grape did ripen, it produced poor, low-acidity wines that quickly spoiled. For this reason, these grapes were better suited to the making of Angelica, a fortified dessert wine. Angelica, sometimes conflated with the grape it is made from, is a "medium golden-colored, fruity, very sweet dessert wine" that was popular in the early days of California, according to Amerine and Singleton.

In 1804 the Spanish Franciscans came to the Santa Ynez Valley and founded the Santa Inés mission, seventeenth of the twenty-one in the chain. When the Mexican Congress passed the Act for the Secularization of the Missions of California in 1833, life at the missions changed, and without Indian laborers to work the fields, the vineyards perished. But misfortune for the Franciscans became opportunity for private enterprise, and a new commercial wine industry took root and flowered. At the Santa Barbara Presidio, a non-mission-related vineyard was planted just prior to secularization. Felipe Goycoechea, *commandante* of the fort from 1784 to 1802, planted vines to the west. In 1843 Pascual Botiller, a Frenchman, acquired the property, planted additional vines, and produced wine. Ernest Penimore and Sidney Greenleaf write in their *Directory of California Wine Growers and Wine Makers in 1860* that Botiller was said to have a wine press and most likely was the first in the region to crush his grapes by a process other than traditional treading. By 1848 Spain had lost the coastline from Baja northward to the United States. The Mission grapes, left untended and unused, withered and died.

The first vines from France were introduced by an aptly named Frenchman from Bordeaux, Jean-Louis Vignes, who planted them in what is now downtown Los Angeles. By 1840 he was bottling and selling wine to settlers as far north as San Francisco. Dan Krieger writes that Vignes was so impressed by the quality of the wine he was producing in the New World that he wrote to his French relatives and friends extolling the virtues of the *terroir* in his new country. After nearly thirty years lying nascent, the California wine industry was again flourishing. For example, by 1860 Los Angeles County produced nearly 163,000 gallons of wine. At about the same time, Agoston Haraszthy, a Hungarian nobleman, arrived and founded his Buena Vista estate in Sonoma. This widely recognized milestone in California wine history occurred more than ninety years after the Spaniards began growing wine grapes on the Central Coast.

NATIVE PEOPLES AT THE MISSIONS

Native peoples have lived on the Central Coast for more than ten thousand years. When the Spanish missionaries encountered the Ohlone (Muwekma) in the Monterey and San Francisco Bay areas, they called these peoples the *costeños,* which has been transliterated to Costanoan and means "coast people." When the Spanish military expeditions, and the Franciscan missionaries who followed, marched north from Mexico through California, they ravaged the native peoples with disease and brought them to their knees with religion.

Mission life could be brutal for the natives, who often greeted the explorers with curiosity, kindness, and trust. In return, according to the *New Catholic Encyclopedia,* many of the natives were recruited to Christianity at the point of a gun and forced to work in the vineyards. In this regard, they played an early and integral role in the emergence of viticulture on the Central Coast. Wine was an essential part of mission life: it was a required part of church services and likely served as a hygienic and ready replacement for the local drinking water.

In addition to the Costanoan, there were at least two other important peoples living in the Central Coast region, the Salinan and Chumash Indians. The thermal springs around Paso Robles, already noted in 1795, were an attraction not only for the native peoples in the region, but for the missionaries who settled there as well. Although the Salinan and Chumash peoples were present on the Central Coast long before the arrival of the Spanish, there is no evidence that they cultivated the natural grape varieties growing in the region. As they were converted to Christianity, they contributed their labor to the establishment and caretaking of the vineyards required by the padres.

In 1925, when A. L. Kroeber first published the *Handbook of the Indians of California* as Bulletin 78 of the Bureau of American Ethnology of the

Smithsonian Institution, fewer than forty Salinan Indians remained. These native peoples were "named" by the Spanish after the river that runs through most of their territory. The headwaters of the Salinas River arise near Santa Margarita. The Salinan territory extended northward to Santa Lucia Peak and southward to below Soledad, from the Pacific Ocean to the main crest of the Coast Ranges. In 1769 they were encountered by Gaspar de Portolá's expedition. In the area between today's towns of San Luis Obispo and Monterey, the expedition reported seeing ten towns with about twelve hundred inhabitants; however, that first early census also included Esselen, Costanoan, and Chumash populations. The Salinan were bitter enemies of the Costanoan (Ohlone), located north of Soledad. Unfortunately, their conflict with the Salinan peoples was the least of the Ohlone's worries. When the Spanish missionaries came to Monterey Bay in 1769, about twenty thousand Ohlone populated the surrounding area, but by 1809 their numbers had been reduced to less than two thousand, and virtually no Ohlone villages remained. Estimates indicate that more than 70 percent of the population died from smallpox and measles brought by the Spanish, to which the local people had no inherited immunity.

The Yokuts to the east were trading partners of the Salinan tribe, but the Chumash, living south of present-day San Luis Obispo, were too far removed for trading, separated by the geographical division of the Cuesta Grade. The Chumash were predominantly a coastal people and held the three northern large islands of the Santa Barbara archipelago. They lived from Malibu to Point Conception, west and north from Estero Bay. They were held in high esteem by the Spanish, who considered them superior to other California tribes they encountered. At the time they encountered the Spanish, the Chumash were primarily hunters and gatherers and had no cultivated lands. The Chumash took their fruit sugar from toyon and elderberries. They also ate the fruits of prickly pear cactus and manzanita. They made beverages by soaking the berries, but the Chumash were not known to use fermented beverages. According to Krieger, they "were more likely to become intoxicated by drinking an infusion of jimpson [sic] weed." They made bead money, called *anchum,* from small disks of a marine snail called the purple olive shell *(Olivella biplicata).* Because *anchum* and *Chumash* are related words, *Chumash* most likely means "bead money makers," according to the Santa Barbara Museum of Natural History. However, another possible meaning is "islander," as there were both island and mainland Chumash.

When the Spaniards arrived in the Santa Ynez Valley, there were approximately twenty thousand Chumash. Over time, the Spanish settled them in and among five missions: San Buenaventura, Santa Bárbara, Santa Inés, La Purísima Concepción, and San Luis Obispo. Like the Ohlone tribes, in fewer than two hundred years the Chumash tribes nearly perished from the diseases brought by the Spaniards. Measles, for example, decimated the Chumash during the Spanish colonization as many of the Chumash were converted to Christianity and began working with the Spanish missionaries to cultivate the gardens, fields, and vineyards necessary to sustain the outposts. Ignacio Tomás, the last full-blooded Chumash, died in 1952; Fernando Librado Kitsepawit, born in 1839 and the last known full-blooded island Chumash, had died in 1915.

Looking back over the long and venerable early history of wine production on the Central Coast, a tip of the wine glass is in order to acknowledge the contributions of the mission fathers who brought the first semblance of wine culture to California. Motivated by the expansion of the French, British, and Russian explorations of the New World, the Spanish pressed north from Mexico to secure their lands and interests. Grapes were planted, cultivated, and made into wine, firmly establishing the fact that the *Vitis vinifera* grapevine could grow and flourish in the *terroir* of the Central Coast. To the native peoples, acknowledgment is due for their service and, often, servitude. Without their contributions, the vineyards would have withered. They provided the energy and labor required for planting, pruning, weeding, and harvesting the grapes. As any good vintner worth his or her weight in wine will tell you, wine culture could not exist without agriculture, and the native peoples working in the mission vineyards established the first instance of viticulture on the Central Coast.

CHAPTER 3

Central Coast *Terroir*

Galileo once said, "Wine is sunlight, held together by water." In the wine region of the Central Coast you will discover a diversity of terrain, wind, water, soils, climate, fog, and sunlight, all combining to produce wines capable of competing with the best in the world. This consilience contributes to what the French call *terroir*, an essential element that, in conjunction with skilled winemaking, can result in the production of world-class wines. For the French, *terroir* ("tair-*wahr*") has near-mythical importance. It describes the natural components necessary for growing premium-quality wine grapes. Recently, various scholars have tried to scientifically quantify those components in an effort to move the concept from a vaguely defined term to one that has a highly specific meaning. P. Laville considers *terroir* indispensable for the protection and elaboration of the French appellation of origin classification scheme, the basic classification system for French wines. Borrowing from Laville's work, I see *terroir* as the combination of the following natural factors:

- *Geology:* the physical and chemical characteristics of the soil
- *Hydrology:* water and its relation to the soil
- *Topography:* the lay of the land in terms of aspect, altitude, and slope; in other words, the terrain
- *Sunlight:* hours of bright sunlight
- *Climate:* rain, temperature, the influence of ocean fog, and wind

In the sections to follow, I provide a brief overview of the factors that have contributed to the Central Coast's distinctive topographical features. Next,

I briefly discuss the types of soils in which premium grapes are grown. I also include information on the general climate, but I do not go into detail about microclimates. These elements enable the Central Coast to grow and sustain a wide variety of high-quality grapes.

GEOLOGY

The suitability of the region's soils for growing high-quality grapes is due to its distinctive geological history, a history shaped by plate tectonics, the mechanism by which the Earth's surface transforms itself through time.

The outer "shell" of the Earth is the lithosphere, composed of about twelve segments called plates that move over the Earth's surface at a rate of about an inch or more a year through the process of continental drift. The plates of the Earth's lithosphere continue their drift to this day. Continental drift produced some of the geological conditions necessary for the topography and soils that contribute to the *terroir* of California's Central Coast appellation, and it also causes earthquakes (among them the 6.5 earthquake that struck Paso Robles in December 2003).

The Central Coast has a series of mountain ranges that resulted from the cataclysmic thrust and uplift of earth when three massive plates collided eons ago. The Coast Ranges are part of the North American cordillera, a mountain belt extending from Alaska to Guatemala. The cordillera is the result of a complex interaction among three tectonic plates: the Farallon, the Pacific, and the North American. About 200 million years ago, the Farallon Plate, which at the time occupied most of the eastern Pacific Ocean, moved eastward toward the North American Plate, which was moving westward. This movement, called convergence, resulted in the oceanic plate—in this instance the Farallon—subducting under a continental plate, the North American. This convergence occurs because continental plates typically are lighter than oceanic crust. The Farallon Plate is mostly gone now, consumed by the great North American (Continental) Plate making up most of the United States, but two small remnants remain: the Juan de Fuca and Cocos plates. The Juan de Fuca remnant, trapped between the Pacific and North American plates, produced the Cascade Range of active volcanoes and caused the devastating eruption of Washington State's Mount St. Helens in 1980. In an amazing process of recycling the Earth's materials, when the Farallon Plate burrowed below the North American Plate, it pushed up thick layers of ocean sediment and deposited them onto the Continental Plate. This helps explain the fact that some of the vineyards on the Central Coast are covered in a layer of diatomaceous earth, composed mostly of calcium carbonate from the dissolved shells of unicellular organisms, called diatoms, living in the ocean.

The cordillera emerged through a process called accretion, and produced some of the highest mountain ranges on the continent, including the Coast Ranges of California. Accretion occurs when one plate subducts beneath an overlying plate and geologic material then is thrust upward and onto the overlying plate. About 30 million years ago another plate, the great Pacific Plate, crept eastward and crashed into the North American Plate. Largest of all the Earth's tectonic plates, the Pacific Plate did not subduct below the North American Plate. Instead, in a process that produces great seismic energies and heat, it slides along the North American Plate at transform-fault boundaries. The San Andreas Fault is a prime example of a transform-fault boundary on land. As the North American Plate encroached northward and westward, it dragged along a section of the early Sierra Nevada, replete with plutonic and metamorphic rock. This section is called the Salinan Block and underlies most of the Central Coast. A second massive section called the Nacimiento Block tore away from the North American Plate and joined the Salinan Block in its inexorable journey north and west. The Salinan Block forms the core of the Santa Lucia Highlands. It is composed mostly of granitic rock forged below the Earth's mantle and metamorphic rock formed by partial melting of the ocean floor. The Nacimiento Block consists largely of sandstone, shale, chert, and blue schist and underlies the southern interior of the Santa Lucias and most of the coast.

The San Andreas Fault, which runs through Parkfield east and north of Paso Robles, marks the dividing line between the Pacific Plate and the North American Plate. The rest of California and most of North America are on the east side of the fault. On the western side sits the Central Coast, riding atop the Pacific Plate, which gives the region its geological distinctiveness. For example, as the result of accretion, in the southern part of the Central Coast, the Santa Ynez and San Rafael mountains run northwest and southeast instead of north and south, as do most other North American ranges (visualize the Rockies). André Tchelistcheff, a Russian émigré who became one of California's pioneering winemakers and consultants, believed great wines could be produced within the valleys and on the slopes of such transverse ranges. Their orientation allows the cooling oceanic winds and fog to penetrate inland.

The composition of the Pacific Plate soils is also ideal for growing premium grapes. Soil scientists are still debating whether the characteristics of the soil in which grapes are grown contribute directly to the flavor of the wine. For instance, the smoky taste and minerality of fine German Riesling is attributed to slate soils in which the Riesling grape grows, and the complexity and structure of a French Merlot, to the iron-rich clay subsoil *(crasse de fer)* of the Pomerol region. The debate continues and gave rise to the French term *goût de terroir,* the tastes and flavors that result from the combined factors previously discussed. What we do know, according to Oz Clarke and Margaret Rand, is that "the most important aspect of soil is its water-holding capacity, and how easily the vine can access that water." Vines seem to prefer soils that drain well, yet retain just enough water to sustain the plant. In locations where rainfall is insufficient, plants can be watered by carefully metered irrigation.

Soil provides nutrients necessary to the vine's survival. Ironically, soils deemed rich in nutrients might produce lesser-quality wine. In this instance, too many nutrients prevent the vine from being sufficiently stressed. Winemakers argue that a stressed vine often produces a better-quality grape. Soil nutrients are composed of the soil's minerals, organic matter, and natural pH— that is, the relative acidity or alkalinity of the ground. The grapevine is generally planted in dirt, but not always. In some instances on the Central Coast, plantings are made directly into limestone. In such cases, bore holes are driven into the rock to allow the vine to set its roots. A vineyard can comprise various layers from topsoil to alternating layers of subsoil and layers of rock. The depth to which the vine shoots its roots depends on a variety of factors, among them the fertility of the soil and the amount of water in the ground. A twenty-year-old vine might drop roots as deep as 15 feet. In fertile soils, vines tend to root sideways. Infertile or poor soils force the vine to dig deeper in an attempt to find the nutrients and water it needs to survive.

Usually a vineyard is planted in an admixture of soil and rock, giving us a variety of soil types. Below I list the most common types and their characteristics. Following the schema developed by Clarke and Rand in *Oz Clarke's Encyclopedia of Grapes,* the list offers an overview of the types of soils one might find in a vineyard on the Central Coast.

- *Alluvium:* soils deposited by oceans, rivers, deltas, or estuaries. Alluvial soils consist of silt, mud, sand, or gravel and are very fertile. Stone-and-sand alluvium is preferred for grape growing.

20 *ఔ* CENTRAL COAST *TERROIR*

- *Argillaceous soils:* clays, marls, and shales.
- *Calcareous soils:* typically alkaline soils, whose name derives from *calcaire*, the French word for limestone. Such soils consist of calcium and magnesium carbonates; typically they are water-retaining soils that result in high acidity in the grapes. *Argilo-calcaire* is a mix of clay and limestone.
- *Chalk:* a special type of pure white limestone, soft and crumbly, that results in excellent drainage and has good alkalinity.
- *Clay:* acidic, small-particle, poorly drained soil. A mixture of clay and loam (clayey-loam), or ferruginous clay (containing iron), is preferred to solid clay.
- *Granite:* coarse plutonic rock composed mostly of quartz and feldspar. Gneiss is a type of granite.
- *Gravel:* infertile, low-acid soil composed mostly of pebbles, providing excellent drainage.
- *Limestone:* a harder rock made of calcium carbonate and magnesium carbonate; not easily penetrated by root systems.
- *Loam:* a fertile soil consisting of clay, silt, and sand and high in organic materials. If too rich, loam can produce vines that grow too vigorously.
- *Marl:* a crumbly combination of calcareous limestone and clay that gives wines high acidity.
- *Sand:* freely draining, though relatively infertile, fine-grained soil that provides some measure of protection against the phylloxera root louse. Sandy loams are preferred over simple sand in the vineyard.
- *Sandstone:* a sedimentary rock of sandy particles, usually quartz; might contain some calcium carbonate to form calcareous sandstone.
- *Schist:* coarse, crystalline rocks that can split into thin layers and crumble.
- *Shale:* dark, rich clay-grade sediment.
- *Slate:* a fissile, fragmented rock derived from clay, shale, or other fine-grained sediments that produce heat-radiating, well-drained soils.

CLIMATE

Generally, as one nears the Pacific Ocean, one experiences moderate temperatures and less fluctuation from daytime highs to nighttime lows. For example, parts of Monterey County, the Edna Valley, and the Santa Rita Hills typically see 15- to 20-degree differences between high and low temperatures. This results in cool, long growing seasons and contributes to what viticulturists call "long hang times" for the grapes—that is, the grapes are slower to ripen. As one moves inland and away from the moderating effects of the ocean and fog (locals call it the marine layer), daily temperature swings can be as great as 60 degrees on the east side of Paso Robles and about 50 degrees in the Happy Canyon region of Santa Barbara County. Temperatures in Paso Robles, however, are influenced by maritime fog that moves up and through the Templeton Gap between the Cypress and Black mountains along Highway 46. Differences in rainfall totals between east and west Paso are extreme. The western hills can receive upwards of 25 to 50 inches annually, whereas the eastern plains are happy to count 8 to 13 inches during a good year. Droughts and El Niño years, of course, skew these averages toward their extremes. During the 2004–5 rainy season in Paso Robles, for instance, the region received more rainfall than Seattle. This led grape growers and vintners in the area to forecast an extraordinary vintage year for 2005, on par with 1997, and it appears their predictions were correct. The grapes achieved physiological ripeness at a lower Brix level (a scale for measuring concentration of grape sugars), which results in lower levels of alcohol in the wine, but with no diminution in perceived sweetness. In contrast, the spring of 2006 was generally cool and rainy, with a scorching July followed by an unusually cool August, which most likely saved the grapes. A moderate autumn allowed some vineyards in San Luis Obispo County to delay picking until mid-October, leading to long hang times and assuring ripe grapes. Monterey County reported warm days and cool nights into the picking season with good yields, and Santa Barbara County reported near-perfect conditions for ripeness and maturity of the grapes. At this writing, it seems another excellent vintage year is in the offing.

The overall climate in the region is similar to a Mediterranean climate from May to October, thanks to the infiltration of a large semipermanent high-pressure system called the North Pacific High-Pressure Belt. In the summer, the pressure system moves north and blocks storms from hitting California. In the winter, the system again drops southward and storms infiltrate the Central Coast. Toward the end of October, the rainy season begins and lasts until early spring. When the circulation patterns change and moisture-laden air arrives from the south and east, chains of storms often move in, dropping torrential amounts of rain, which inevitably causes flooding. For this reason, as much of the rest of the country is either covered with snow or lies dormant, the Central Coast enjoys a rejuvenation of soils and flora. The tops of the highest mountains might be dusted with snow, as happened in the late winter of 2006–7, but elsewhere the grasses are already green and flourishing. Cool northwesterly winds blow during this time of year, affecting San Francisco,

Monterey, and San Luis bays. In January, however, if the winds shift and blow from the east to the west (an offshore wind), San Luis Obispo can reach temperatures in the high nineties. The Santa Lucia Mountains paralleling the coast can also block the normal maritime cooling. The warmer San Joaquin Valley to the east also affects temperatures during the growing season. As valley temperatures soar, heated air rises and creates a vacuum that pulls cooling coastal air off the ocean and into the vineyards. In concert, warm days and cool nights contribute to the outstanding acidity levels and excellent color of the grapes.

The North Pacific High-Pressure Belt also has a profound effect on the ocean currents of the Pacific, thus contributing to climatic changes on the Central Coast. As a steady flow of air streams down from the northwest, it affects the flow of the great California Current, driving it southward and along the shore. A process called upwelling pulls deeper and cooler water toward the surface. In the northern part of the coast, the water temperature varies from about 49 degrees in the winter to 55 degrees in the summer. Farther south, temperatures range from 57 to 65 degrees winter to summer. For this reason, it is much more comfortable in the summer to surf in San Diego waters than in those near San Francisco. Surprisingly, water temperature near the coast can be up to 10 degrees colder than waters 200 miles offshore during the summer. As warm masses of Pacific air drift over the cold current, banks of marine fog form. The fog is blown inland by the prevailing northwesterly winds that emerge from the Pacific high-pressure system. This inland movement of the marine layer contributes significantly to moderating temperatures in many of the Central Coast's grape-growing regions, such as the Templeton Gap near Paso Robles and the Santa Rita Hills in Santa Barbara County, where excellent Pinot Noir grapes are grown. In the absence of rainfall, it also provides life-sustaining, moisture-laden air to the vines.

When the Spanish missionaries first planted grapes in the soils of the Central Coast, they knew not what they had. We now know that the Central Coast has a variety of soils and climates conducive to growing many types of wine grapes, including Spanish, French, German, Italian, and Portuguese varieties. Its varied geography includes mountain slopes, hillsides, benchlands, and valleys. In some areas—the mountains on the west side of Paso Robles, for instance—enough rain falls during the year to support dry farming of vineyards. In areas that see a surfeit of rain, drip irrigation provides a remedy. Some areas experience an overabundance of sunlight and heat, but cool ocean winds and fog help moderate daytime temperatures. Killing frosts, with an occasional exception, are a rarity. Cool evening temperatures result in good acidity levels in the grapes, and abundant sunshine helps the grapes achieve physiological ripeness. In some instances, very ripe grapes produce wines of relatively high alcohol, but such wines do not come across as "hot" because they are nicely balanced.

In the past twenty years or so, viticulturists and vintners, through trial and error, observation, and research, have discovered which grapes are best suited to which soils. The growing practices that have evolved allow growers and winemakers to take full advantage of the Central Coast's soils and climate. All the elements of Central Coast *terroir,* combined with appropriate farming practices and successful winemaking processes, give rise to consistently excellent wines, many of which rival the world's best.

CHAPTER 4

The Central Coast
American Viticultural Area

As you might imagine, anyone writing a book about the wines and wineries of the Central Coast must first understand what constitutes an American Viticultural Area (AVA). As I began my research, I encountered confusion where, naively, I expected clarity. To say the least, California's Central Coast AVA is an expanding and dynamic designation that covers an extraordinary amount of territory. The size, however, is only one problem. Another problem lies in the fact that the designation continues to grow and change over time as new petitions for AVA status within the region are presented to the federal government. Unfortunately, such requests are not always the result of a logical argument grounded in a uniform and identifiable geology, or distinct *terroir*. In some cases, just the opposite is true. Another problem I faced is that wine writers and critics sometimes use the official designation rather loosely and, in some instances, ignore the government's classification altogether, replacing it with their own conception of what the Central Coast AVA should be.

In an effort to bring some clarity and coherence to the confusion, in the following sections I present three ways of addressing the situation: (1) I discuss the AVA as an official designation as determined by the federal government and provide some historical context behind its establishment. (2) I offer two possibilities for redefining the Central Coast, and present an argument for adopting my choice. (3) Based on my redefinition of the Central Coast, I focus the book on the wines and wineries within Monterey (and a few in San Benito), San Luis Obispo, and Santa Barbara counties. This decision more closely coheres with the original intent and classification of the Central Coast AVA during its revision in 1983.

An AVA is an official designation described by the United States Treasury Department's Alcohol and Tobacco Tax and Trade Bureau (TTB), formerly the Bureau of Alcohol, Tobacco, and Firearms (BATF). The BATF approved the first Appellations of Origin in this country in regulation 27 CFR, Part 9, issued in 1980, which covers the fifty states and their counties. However, AVAs are established as the result of a petition drafted by interested parties and submitted to the TTB for consideration and approval. To create a viticultural area appellation of origin, the labeled area must be approved under U.S. regulations, specifically 27 CFR, Part 9. Under this provision, for a bottle to refer to a viticultural area of origin on its label, not less than 85 percent of the volume of the wine must be derived from grapes grown within that area. Within the state of California, there are now more than 90 AVAs listed.

Unfortunately, the establishment of AVAs is not always based on well-defined geographic considerations that help define a distinctive grape-growing area. In some instances, petitions for a new AVA are submitted for political rather than "vinological" reasons. Therefore, the Central Coast AVA, to some degree, is a hodgepodge of appellations and subappellations. In addition, as new appellations such as the San Bernabe AVA and the San Antonio Valley AVA in Monterey County are added, the region requires redefinition. For example, the second edition of James Laube's excellent work *Wine Spectator's California Wine* (1999) lists fifteen AVAs within the Central Coast. Ken Volk, in a presentation to the International Food and Wine Festival, counted twenty-six subappellations in 2000. The addition of the San Antonio Valley AVA to the Central Coast AVA raises the total to twenty-eight in 2007. At the time of this writing, there is a petition on file with the TTB that would establish a subappellation within the Paso Robles AVA. It is designated as the Paso Robles Westside, and encompasses about one-third (almost 180,000 acres) of the Paso Robles AVA. Happy Canyon in Santa Barbara County has also applied for designation as an AVA.

HISTORICAL CONTEXT

Prior to the establishment of federal laws defining appellations, it was legal to use the designation "Central Coast Counties" on wine labels if the grapes were grown within the counties of Sonoma, Napa, Mendocino, Lake, Santa Clara, Santa Cruz, Alameda, San Benito, Solano, San Luis Obispo, Contra Costa, Monterey, or Marin. After January 1, 1983, the BATF redefined the Central Coast as the coastline between the cities of Santa Cruz and Santa Barbara. This new ruling brought some clarity to the situation. On July 11, 1984, in response to a petition by Taylor California Cellars of Gonzales, the BATF established the Central Coast Viticultural Area. Sarah's vineyard, Mirassou Vineyards, and Wente Vineyards requested an extension of the appellation, effectively extending the appellation's northern boundaries. The owner of Sarah's vineyard, John Otteman, petitioned to include his vineyard within the northern boundary and, as a result, a large portion of Santa Clara County was admitted, based on Otteman's argument that it too is under marine climate influence. The establishment of the San Francisco Bay AVA in 1999, after a petition was presented by a consortium of seventy-five growers and vintners led by Wente Vineyards, California's oldest family-owned winery, further complicated the Central Coast AVA. The petition, following the same line of reasoning advanced by Otteman, asked that vineyards located in Livermore Valley also be included within the northern boundary of the Central Coast. The vast San Francisco Bay AVA alone covers more than 1.5 million acres and "encompasses the counties of San Francisco, San Mateo, Santa Clara, Contra Costa and Alameda, as well as parts of San Benito and Santa Cruz counties. . . . The appellation also includes San Francisco Bay itself and the City of San Francisco," according to appellationamerica.com. Based on those petitions the BATF changed the northern boundaries to their current location and approved the revised Central Coast appellation on October 24, 1985.

THE OFFICIAL DESIGNATION

By any measure, the AVA known as California's Central Coast is an enormous region. It currently covers approximately 4 million acres, making it one of the largest in the United States (one Texas appellation runs to 9 million acres). The geographic boundaries run from just north of San Francisco and Richmond to its northernmost edge near Vine Hill in Contra Costa County, east to the Diablo Mountains, and down to the boundary of Los Padres National Forest. The southern border is in Santa Barbara County, terminating at the creek of Toro Canyon, which flows into the Pacific Ocean, and extends from the Pacific Ocean in the west back up to San Francisco. However, not all land within the greater Central Coast AVA is under cultivation to grapevines. Currently, about 90,000 acres are planted to grapevines. Those areas within the region where vineyards are planted and that have petitioned for and received status as AVAs are so designated. The Central Coast AVA at present comprises the following ten counties: Alameda, Contra Costa, Monterey, San Benito, San Francisco,

San Luis Obispo, San Mateo, Santa Barbara, Santa Clara, and Santa Cruz. In appendix B I list the counties granted appellation of origin status within the Central Coast AVA and their subappellations, if any.

As noted previously, instead of being organized along meaningful geological or climatic criteria, the boundaries of the Central Coast AVA are complicated by politics and influence. For example, in a recent discussion about subdividing the Paso Robles AVA in San Luis Obispo County, Stephan Asseo, winemaker and owner of L'Aventure, stressed that such decisions should be "based more on scientific parameters than political parameters." Another factor contributing to the confusion is that in some instances the designated AVA is both a county and a subappellation, where the subappellation is a smaller grape-growing region nested within the larger appellation. Confusion is furthered when we see that other appellations often overlap subappellations, or a smaller appellation is fully contained within a larger appellation. For instance, the Santa Rita Hills AVA is located within both Santa Barbara County and the Santa Ynez Valley AVA.

WINE WRITERS WEIGH IN

In spite of the official designation of the Central Coast AVA by the TTB, writers within the wine industry frequently offer their own definitions of and rationales for what constitutes the Central Coast AVA. Noted wine historian Charles L. Sullivan defines the Central Coast AVA only in terms of counties that lie within the AVA. In his indispensable encyclopedia, *A Companion to California Wine,* he defines the AVA to include "the wine growing areas of Alameda, Santa Clara, Monterey, San Benito, San Luis Obispo, and Santa Barbara counties, and part of those in Santa Cruz County." As another example, noted wine critic Robert M. Parker Jr., writing in the August 31, 2004, edition of the *Wine Advocate,* loosely defines the Central Coast "as the area from Paso Robles south through Santa Barbara, with Monterey and Santa Cruz to the north separate entities." Hugh Johnson and Jancis Robinson's comprehensive *World Atlas of Wine* (2001) includes an entry for what they call the South Central Coast, starting just north of Paso Robles, but everything north of there is under the heading "South of the Bay." Other writers such as Oz Clarke divide the massive region into two zones, the North- and the South-Central Coast, with the South-Central Coast generally coinciding with Parker's definition of the area running from Paso Robles to Santa Barbara.

PROPOSAL FOR A NEW DIVISION
OF THE CENTRAL COAST

In keeping with the liberties taken by the wine press, I suggest at least two new possibilities for dividing the Central Coast AVA. If we examine a map of California's counties, we can make a case for dividing the Central Coast into thirds. This division is based solely on the need to parse the enormous Central Coast region into manageable parts. The rationale here is not merely enological; rather, it is a function of size and geographic location. I offer the following sections: the North-Central Coast, to consist of Alameda, Contra Costa, San Francisco, San Mateo, Santa Clara, and parts of San Benito and Santa Cruz counties; the Mid-Central Coast, comprising San Benito County, Monterey County, and San Luis Obispo County down to the Cuesta Grade; and the South-Central Coast, covering San Luis Obispo County south of the Cuesta Grade and including Santa Barbara County. I know that this coheres with the wishes expressed to me by numerous vintners in the region, who have the knowledge and expertise to see the logic of the division. Using the demarcation line of the 1,500-foot-high Cuesta Grade places the Paso Robles AVA in the Mid-Central Coast, which is defensible for geographical and climatic reasons.

THE SCHEME FOLLOWED IN THE BOOK

Another possibility for organizing the layout of the Central Coast, and my personal favorite, is the following: Take what I called above the North-Central Coast out of the official designation and make it a separate and distinct region. There is precedent for this idea. In the late '80s and early '90s, according to Carolyn Wente, president of Wente Vineyards, some in the wine industry considered dividing the Central Coast into San Francisco Bay, Monterey, and Santa Barbara. I suggest we designate this new area as the San Francisco Coastal region, made up of Alameda, Contra Costa, San Francisco, San Mateo, Santa Clara, and parts of San Benito and Santa Cruz counties. This leaves Monterey County as the new North-Central Coast. San Luis Obispo County then becomes the Mid-Central Coast. For the South-Central Coast, we have Santa Barbara County. This line of reasoning is practical in terms of the land area covered by the counties in each of the three segments and coheres more readily with the original intent of defining the Central Coast in the early '80s as south of Santa Cruz and north of Santa Barbara.

I have used this organizational scheme as the rationale for selecting the wineries to include in part II of the book. Making use of the new organizational scheme listed below, I describe the North-Central, Mid-Central, and South-Central Coast regions and their official AVAs, and include winery profiles. I conceived this strategy in order to complete the book in a timely manner and keep it from weighing a hundred pounds. Unfortunately, we are stuck with the current official layout of the AVAs. In the three counties, only the Chalone AVA crosses county lines. It straddles the border between Monterey and San Benito counties.

CALIFORNIA'S NEW CENTRAL COAST

The North-Central Coast (Monterey County)

Arroyo Seco AVA 1983	San Antonio Valley AVA 2006
Carmel Valley AVA 1983	San Bernabe AVA 2004
Chalone AVA 1982	San Lucas AVA 1987
Hames Valley AVA 1994	Santa Lucia Highlands AVA 1992
Monterey AVA 1984	

The Mid-Central Coast (San Luis Obispo County)

Arroyo Grande Valley AVA 1990	Paso Robles AVA 1983
Edna Valley AVA 1987	York Mountain AVA 1983

The South-Central Coast (Santa Barbara County)

Santa Maria Valley AVA 1981	Santa Ynez Valley AVA 1983
Santa Rita Hills AVA 2001	

PART TWO

CHAPTER 5

Introduction to the Winery Listings and Profiles

This section of the book is designed to provide the information you might need to contact a winery and purchase its wines, or to visit the tasting room and taste the wines. Some of the wineries listed are not profiled, for a variety of reasons. A few of the owners contacted did not wish to be interviewed, and I honored those wishes. Some, despite my persistence, simply did not return calls. Most of the nonprofiled wineries with tasting rooms came into existence after the cutoff date for completing this book. For instance, in the time I was working in Santa Barbara and Monterey counties, approximately thirty new wineries emerged in Paso Robles. My fear was that I would spend the rest of my writing life trying to catch up with each new winery that opened, like a dog chasing his tail. Some of the newly opened wineries do not have tasting facilities open to the public, and in those instances I included all the contact information provided for purchasing the wines directly from the winery, if that is an option. Wherever possible, telephone and fax numbers, a Web address, and the street address of the winery are listed.

The majority of the wineries listed have full profiles if a tasting room is available for the consumer to visit and explore the wine list. Those persons who were gracious enough to meet with us (Nancy, my partner, accompanied me whenever she could) sat down for a face-to-face interview. Most were extraordinarily generous with their time and their stories, and I hope I have done them justice. After the interviews I tasted the wines in an effort to get a sense of the winemaker's philosophy and style and the expression of the different grape varieties used in the wines. Once I had tasted through the list and taken notes, I asked for a recommendation from the winery. Next, I selected a wine

I could recommend to you; both wines are described in the "Recommended Wines" section of the profiles, and are worthy of seeking out as excellent to outstanding examples of the winery's offerings. I describe the wines using a tasting form I developed that incorporates the best elements of the work done by world-famous professor of wine Émile Peynaud of France and by Michael Broadbent, one of England's foremost experts on the tasting and sensory evaluation of wine.

In conducting the tastings, I looked for the visual appeal of the wine—that is, the color, clarity, and depth of the wine in the glass. I describe to the best of my ability the predominant flavor notes in its aromatics (also called the nose or the bouquet). I share with you the taste of the wine in the mouth, focusing on the balance and integration of all its elements. I talk a bit about its finish. Last, I share with you my assessment of its drinkability—in other words, whether it is ready for the table now or needs to wait. If wines are ageworthy, I also predict how long I think they will continue to evolve in the bottle for peak drinking. My estimates of a wine's peak drinking years look forward from 2008, not from the time I tasted the wines. For example, if I say a wine will drink best over the next two to three years, I have 2010–12 in mind. These recommendations are, at best, estimates designed to help you. I mention the vintage year in which the wine was produced merely to give you a reference. I invite you to compare my tasting notes with your own perceptions. In all, well over two thousand wines were tasted to arrive at the recommended wines.

My express wish is that you use these recommendations as an entrée to the list provided by the winery as you explore and taste the selections of interest to you. Taste responsibly, have fun, and remember that wine is more than just a food or a beverage; it can be used for facilitating communication, for socializing, and ultimately, for culture. I hope that this book will assist you in adding not only to your enological knowledge of the Central Coast, but also to your store of personal wine adventures and the stories that emerge as a result.

I adopted a five-star rating system to give readers some sense of the relative quality of the wines made at a particular winery. One star indicates that one or more wines in the list is competently made and of interest. These are good, drinkable wines. Two stars suggest that the line has an additional dimension of interest, be it bouquet, flavor, or potential to age. These wines are very good. Three stars say that the wines are consistently very good across the list and include some excellent examples. Four stars indicate that among the excellent wines in the list, you will find some that are outstanding. A five-star rating denotes that the list includes examples that are superb. Such wines are comparable to other world-class wines. An arrow between star ratings, for example two → three, indicates that the winery is moving toward the higher level of quality. Please understand that the star ratings are based on my palate and my subjective assessments. They are intended as a comparative guide to give you a reference point as you conduct your own evaluations and ratings.

CHAPTER 6

The North-Central Coast
(Monterey County)

At the start of each chapter of winery listings and profiles by county, I provide a brief overview of the area's more recent wine history to provide a sense of its place within the larger context of Central Coast wine history. I also give a description of the *terroir* that helps define the wines of the county.

WINE HISTORY

We know that Father Junípero Serra planted the first wine grapes in Monterey County at San Antonio de Padua after he established the mission in 1771, west of what is now King City. According to *Wine Style Monterey County,* some of those vines "still survive at Mission San Antonio," although they most likely are cultivars of the originals. The Spanish mission system was already suffering from neglect and lack of funds from Spain in the early nineteenth century, but its death knell tolled when Mexico overthrew Spanish rule and became a republic. After the missions were secularized in 1833, the Ohlone natives working in the missions of Monterey County were set free, the monks drifted away, and with no one to cultivate the vineyards, most perished from neglect. This series of events opened opportunities for commercial wine production in each of the three counties. By 1858 Monterey County had more than 50,000 vines under cultivation, according to Philip Woodward and Gregory Walker, authors of *Chalone: A Journey on the Wine Frontier.*

The history of commercial winemaking in Monterey County is reflected in the history of the Chalone winery and vineyard. Woodward and Walker write that around the turn of the twentieth century Frenchman Lucien Charles Tamm planted olives and the first vines for commercial use in what became the Chalone AVA. In 1912 John C. Dyer bought the Lindgren family ranch, a benchland property about three miles east of the Tamm property and 1,800 feet above the Salinas Valley. In 1921 Dyer sold to Francis William Silvear and four partners. Silvear, inspired by the excellent soils on the property and the plantings of his neighbor to the west, Tamm, decided to grow premium grapes for wine. This vineyard eventually became the famous Chalone vineyard. Although he made no wine for himself during the early years of production, he sold his grapes to other vintners, including Wente Brothers and Almaden. However, in 1936 he received a bond for a winery in Watsonville, which he called Cima. Without disclosing his reasons, Silvear petitioned the government in 1939 to cease production and close winery operations. In the meantime, his grapes were achieving recognition for their excellence. In 1938, according to Woodward and Walker, Will Silvear met André Tchelistcheff, then working as winemaker for Beaulieu in Napa. The owner of Beaulieu, Georges de Latour, who established the initial contact, used Silvear's Pinot Noir grapes in his wines. After Will's death in 1955—he fell out of a redwood tree—his wife, Agnes, sold the benchland vineyard. In 1957 Dr. Edward Liska and John Sigman bought the property, and they established Chalone, Inc., in 1961, with Philip Togni as the winemaker. Richard Graff took the winery to national and international prominence after working at the winery in the mid-'60s.

After Louis Benoist acquired Almaden in 1941, he planted near Paicines what would eventually become the largest premium vineyard of its time (1956), but the San Bernabe vineyard in Monterey County now holds that honor, with more than 9,000 acres under cultivation. In the mid-'50s, Almaden also started plantings nearby. In 1960 Professor A. J. Winkler from UC Davis published work that classified grape-growing districts by climate. He designated Monterey County as Region I and II, making it similar to Napa, Sonoma, Burgundy, and Bordeaux. This opened the door for the invasion of major growers such as Almaden, Wente, Masson, Mirassou, Kendall-Jackson, Mondavi, and others who established vineyard properties in the area during the '60s and '70s, particularly after new tax laws favored such partnerships and enterprises. The Mirassous came to Soledad in 1961 and planted grapes. The Wentes, who first established their vineyards in Livermore, moved south into Monterey County, planting 270 acres in the '60s, according to wine historian Charles Sullivan. Paul Masson, before it became part of Canandaigua Industries, expanded its presence into Monterey County at about the same time, building a winery in 1966. William Durney, beginning in 1967–68, established the first vineyard in Carmel Valley, and after her husband died, Dorothy Durney ran the operation before selling it to the Heller family in 1993–94. Jerry Lohr came from South Dakota and planted in the Arroyo Seco AVA in 1972, eventually branching southward to Paso Robles.

Credit must go to Doug Meador of Ventana for the second major contribution to Monterey County wine history. Fresh from service as a fighter pilot, Meador bought land with partners and established a vineyard in 1972. When that partnership dissolved, he bought 300 acres for himself and established the world-famous Ventana vineyard. Doug set both academic and conventional wisdom on its ear by breaking from the accepted viticulture perspectives of the time in order to develop his own. Because of his personal research into the growing conditions and climate of the Monterey County area, Doug determined that the wrong grape varieties were being grown in the wrong places, using inappropriate methods. His work revolutionized thinking about growing practices and grape varieties and has benefited everyone willing to listen to his presentations and read his technical works. Soon after Doug figured out his winning formula, his wines, and wines that other vintners made from his grapes, won worldwide acclaim.

A bit farther south, Alfred Scheid and a group of partners planted what became Scheid Vineyards in 1972. Over time, the Scheid company, now run by his son, developed into a major player in the production of premium-quality grapes in the Monterey County appellation, and Scheid, like Chalone, is now a publicly traded company. Paraiso Vineyards, established a year later by Richard Smith and his family, is also a major grower in the Arroyo Seco area. And physician Mark Lemmon planted vines in the Santa Lucia Highlands area in 1975 and released wines under the San Saba Vineyards label.

The 1980s saw further growth when the Hahn family bought Smith & Hook Vineyards around 1979–80 and started the Hahn Estates Winery. In 1982 Oklahomans Dick and Jeannette (Joullian) Sias bought property near the old Durney vineyards and established the Joullian Vineyards winery. That same year Robert Talbott and his family started the famous Diamond T vineyard. Bob and Patty Brower started Château Julien Wine Estate in the Carmel Valley in 1982 and built their beautiful winery a year later. Also in 1983, the Galante family planted vineyards on its ranch. Boyer released its first wines in 1985 while its owner, Rick Boyer, was still winemaker at Ventana. Bernardus planted grapes in 1989 and saw the release of its first wine four years later.

In the early 1990s, Derek and Courtney Benham founded Blackstone Winery, noted for its Merlot. The Cotta brothers built Baywood Cellars in 1997, the same year Gary Sinnet established Château Sinnet. The Pessagno label, founded in 1999, opened the door to its winery in 2004. In 2001, Joel Burnstein released his first wine under the Marilyn Remark label.

Given the quality of the grapes produced in each of the AVAs within Monterey County, one would expect more wineries to develop there, particularly if one casts a glance south to Paso Robles, where they seem to pop up like mushrooms on a forest floor. The difference is that Paso Robles has set the standard for providing leadership at the governmental level and passes laws that are friendly to and assist new winemaking enterprises. Monterey would do well to look to Paso for guidance, and a movement is currently under way to streamline the process for new applications. One welcome addition would be the formal establishment of a wine corridor running along River Road below the Santa Lucia Highlands.

TERROIR

The Monterey AVA (1984) funnels through the Salinas Valley from north of the town of Salinas near the Pajaro River to the southern edge of Monterey County at the San Luis Obispo County line. The huge region contains six smaller AVAs and ranks behind only Sonoma and Napa in total cultivated acres. On its northwestern edge, Monterey Bay sends cooling winds off the ocean in the afternoon, often replacing morning fog in the region. In Monterey County you will find fewer wineries, but more vineyards, than in San Luis Obispo and Santa Barbara counties.

As Monterey County flattens out, it is extremely fertile and far-reaching. The Salinas Valley is heavily planted, particularly around King City. The hot Central Valley sucks in cold air off Monterey Bay and produces a cold, often violent wind. As the winds blow deeper inland and farther from the ocean, they begin to warm. By King City, the warming effect of the wind permits grapes to ripen, but just west of King City, the wind is often too cool to permit sufficient ripening. Fewer than 10 inches of rain fall here, and the sunshine is nearly endless, giving the area around King City one of the longest, if not the longest, ripening periods in the world.

The Salinas River, often called the "upside-down river," is the largest underground river in California. Even during periods when the river appears to be dry topside, under the soil it continues to run. It also claims the idiosyncrasy of being one of a few rivers worldwide to flow south to north. It drains the Santa Lucia, Gabilan, and Diablo ranges, and it can vary from a dry riverbed in drought years to a raging tumultuous flood after heavy rains. At the base of the drainage, soils tend toward silt and sandy loam. Near and into the

Santa Lucia Highlands, the soil is composed of granitic gneiss and schist, ideal for growing Pinot Noir grapes.

Fewer than 300 acres are under cultivation in the Carmel Valley AVA (established 1983). It lies 5 miles inland from Carmel, and the vines grow on the terraces of steep granitic slopes. Most of the vineyards, which produce red Bordeaux varieties, are above 1,000 feet and the influence of marine fog and wind, but the region also grows white grapes.

The Santa Lucia Highlands AVA (1992) is in the western hills of the Salinas Valley and produces high-quality Chardonnay and Pinot Noir grapes. Many of the vineyards are planted above the fog line on north-south–oriented alluvial terraces up to 1,200 feet above the valley floor. The lee side of the mountains protects the grapes from cool winds.

Chalone AVA (1982) is nearly 2,000 feet above the Salinas Valley in the Gabilan Mountains and has fewer than 300 acres planted. If you were to ask a Burgundian *vigneron* at, let us say, Domaine de la Romanée-Conti the secret for growing great Pinot Noir, most likely he would shout, "C'est la craie-calcaire!" (It's the limestone!). At present-day Chalone, 1,800 feet up into the Gabilan range and below the Pinnacles, a Frenchman, the aforementioned Lucien Charles Tamm, not surprisingly, found limestone and planted the first vineyard. Twelve miles north at Mount Harlan, Josh Jensen of Calera Wine Company also has limestone. Both produce excellent Pinot Noir, and the French nod knowingly, if not warily. Because of the altitude above the fog, the climate is arid but generally warmer than other Monterey County vineyards. The soils there are mostly limestone and decomposed granite. The area is famous for Pinnacles National Monument, which serves as its magnificent backdrop.

In the center of Monterey County's Salinas Valley, Arroyo Seco AVA (1983) is south of Soledad and near the mouth of a dry riverbed—hence its name, which means "dry creek." The soils are sandy, rocky riverbed with gravelly loam, and vineyards are planted on the benchlands above the river. Mostly white-wine grapes are grown here, with Riesling and Chardonnay the dominant varieties. The grapes benefit from a long growing season and sunlight that reflects off the large stones known as Greenfield Pebbles. Cooling afternoon winds blow into the area off Monterey Bay. A smaller western section cuts a gorge into the Santa Lucia Mountains, and in this warmer section Zinfandel, Bordeaux, and Rhône varieties are planted on steep terraces.

The Hames Valley AVA (1994) lies at the southern end of Monterey County just above the border with San Luis Obispo County and is the warmest of the

Monterey appellations. During the summer, high temperatures often reach triple digits. Here Bordeaux varieties flourish in the shale and loam soils. In the warmer southern section grow the grapes traditionally used to make port, including Touriga Nacional and Tinta Cão.

The San Lucas AVA (1987) lies in the historic cattle country of southern Monterey County. The southern end of Monterey's Salinas Valley is relatively hot, but vineyards between 500 and 1,200 feet experience broad temperature swings from day to night. A large piece of the northern section, now the San Bernabe AVA, was granted status in August 2004 after a petition by Delicato Family Vineyards. At the base of the Santa Lucia Mountains and mostly on the southwestern side of the Salinas River, vineyard soils range from loam to well-drained sandy loam. The San Bernabe vineyard is so large that temperatures can differ by five degrees from its northern to its southern ends. An astounding twenty-one grape varieties are grown there.

The San Antonio Valley AVA, added in July 2006, is also at the southern end of the county. This too is a relatively hot region, although nearby Lake San Antonio does provide some cooling fog to the vineyards, and afternoon breezes off the Pacific Ocean help moderate daytime temperatures. The soils are mostly gravelly loam and clay, and like its neighbor to the south, Paso Robles, San Antonio Valley produces some excellent Cabernet Sauvignon, Cabernet Franc, and Syrah grapes.

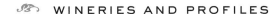 WINERIES AND PROFILES

Bargetto Winery

OWNERS: Bargetto family

WINEMAKER: Michael Sones

TASTING ROOM: Yes

DAYS/HOURS: Daily 10:30 A.M.–6 P.M.

ADDRESS: 700 Cannery Row, Ste. L, Monterey, CA 93940; 831-373-4053; 831-373-4803 (fax); bargetto.com

WINES/GRAPE VARIETIES: Bianca (blend), Cabernet Sauvignon, Chardonnay, Carignan, La Vita (blend), Merlot, Pinot Grigio, Pinot Noir, Zinfandel

WINE CLUB: Yes

TASTING ROOM AMENITIES: Merchandise

REGION: Monterey County AVA

Baywood Cellars

OWNER: John Cotta

WINEMAKER: John Cotta

TASTING ROOM: Yes

DAYS/HOURS: Call for hours

ADDRESS: 381 Cannery Row, Ste. C,
Monterey, CA 93940;
800-214-0445; 831-645-9345 (fax);
baywood-cellars.com

WINES/GRAPE VARIETIES: Cabernet Franc,
Cabernet Sauvignon, Chardonnay,
Gewürztraminer, late-harvest Symphony,

Malbec, Merlot, Pinot Grigio,
Pinot Noir, port, Sangiovese, Symphony,
Syrah, Tempranillo, Zinfandel

WINE CLUB: Yes

TASTING ROOM AMENITIES: Merchandise

REGION: Monterey County AVA

The Cotta family has been associated with the wine industry since 1925, when Joe Cotta Sr. founded Cotta Properties for the purpose of growing wine grapes and other agricultural products. Portuguese by heritage, the family expanded into wine production in 1986 when grandsons John and James Cotta started their Las Vinas label in the Central Valley's Lodi region. Las Vinas became Baywood Cellars in 1997 with the intent to produce affordable premium wines from Central Coast grapes.

In 1992 they made an award-winning Cabernet Sauvignon from Napa fruit. Over time Napa fruit became more and more expensive, so Baywood relies now on grapes from Paso Robles and Monterey County. Fruit is also sourced from the original Cotta vineyards in Lodi, where the climate is similar to the Douro region in Portugal, famous for producing outstanding port. Not surprisingly, the Baywood Cellars Vintage Port is made from Lodi grapes. John Cotta is the winemaker in charge of the grapes, and at one time, as vineyard manager, brother James made certain John got the best possible grapes from the family's more than 1,000 acres. John serves now as both president and winemaker, as James has gone on to pursue other ventures.

Staying true to his Portuguese heritage, John prefers an old-world style of winemaking where the focus is on the production of premium varietal wines. Given his family's presence in the California wine industry, he has the resources either to grow or to source the best possible grapes for the Baywood line. The tasting room is on Cannery Row, not far from Monterey Bay.

RECOMMENDED WINES: I tasted under the able direction of Ray Worsley, manager of the tasting room. Ray recommends the Cabernet Franc, a blend of Lodi and Paso Robles grapes. We tasted the 2000, an opaque, red-purple wine with hints of roses, cherries, red currants, and spice in the nose. The wine shows excellent balance between its acidity and tannin and the lovely ripe fruit. In this wine, drinking at its apex, you'll find a great nose above sweet fruit and a lingering finish.

I suggest the Symphony, a new grape for me and a wonderful find. The Symphony, a white grape developed at UC Davis in 1948 by Dr. Harold Paul Olmo, is the result of combining two French varieties, Grenache Gris and Muscat of Alexandria. The Muscat contributes to the flower and fruit in the nose, and the Grenache lends acidity and structure. I know of only one other winery currently using this variety. Ray and I tasted the 2002 Late Harvest, a double gold medal winner at the California State Fair. The nose is sweet and honeyed with gooseberries; orange peel and lemon zest are in evidence, but the flavors on the palate resolve to apricots and peaches. Although the residual sugar stands at 17 percent, there is enough acidity in this lemon-gold wine to keep it fresh and vibrant on the tongue. Drinking beautifully now, it will easily last another six to eight years. It is a great find and an outstanding 100 percent botrytis-affected sweet wine in the French Sauterne style.

RATING: One star (would like to see more focus on late-harvest wines and fewer varieties)

Bernardus Winery and Vineyard

OWNER: Bernardus Marinus Pon

WINEMAKER: Dean De Korth

TASTING ROOM: Yes

DAYS/HOURS: Daily 11 A.M.–5 P.M.

ADDRESS: 5 W. Carmel Valley Rd., Carmel Valley, CA 93924; 831-659-1900; 831-659-1676 (fax); bernardus.com

WINES/GRAPE VARIETIES: Cabernet Sauvignon, Chardonnay, Marinus (blend), Marsanne, Merlot, Pinot Noir, Sauvignon Blanc

WINE CLUB: Yes

TASTING ROOM AMENITIES: Merchandise

REGION: Carmel Valley AVA

Bernardus "Ben" Marinus Pon was born in Amersfoort, Holland, and owns the oldest wine distribution house in the Netherlands. He is a connoisseur of Bordeaux wines, collecting them for his personal cellar and for his business. Ben was a driver for Team Porsche and drove at Le Mans six times. A man of many and diverse talents, he represented Holland in skeet shooting during the 1972 Olympic Games. As an aside, Ben's father imported the first Volkswagen Beetle to America and designed the VW van.

Following his father's heritage of bringing things European to the States, Ben began looking for properties here in the late 1980s. He found undeveloped land in the Cachagua region of Carmel Valley, on which were planted 37 acres of Cabernet Sauvignon and Merlot vines. Robert Talbott sold him a white-wine winery, which he tore down and rebuilt in a traditional French winery design with the intent to focus on producing red wines. A vineyard was planted in 1989. As luck would have it, the Bernardus Chardonnay became a prizewinner. Despite his winery's growing reputation for fine white wines, Ben is determined to produce the finest French-style reds possible, wines capable of standing up to the best in the world. Along the way, he wants to make a little money and have lots of fun to keep things in their proper perspective. The first harvest at Bernardus was in 1993, and by 1997 the winery stabilized, producing white and red wines. Ben now has 220 acres of land for the Marinus, Jamesburg, and Featherbow Ranch vineyards. Ben and his wife, Ingrid, also own the famous Bernardus Lodge, a favorite getaway spot for folks wanting to visit Carmel Valley.

The winemaker is Dean De Korth, an American trained in France's Burgundy region, where he earned degrees in viticulture and enology at the *lycée* in Beaune and the University of Burgundy in Dijon. Carole Forest, a longtime friend of Bernardus, is the CEO.

RECOMMENDED WINES: Carole recommends the Marinus, a Bordeaux blend of mostly Cabernet Sauvignon and Merlot. The 2001 is black on black in color and admits no light to the stem of the glass. The nose is a heady perfume of cherries, boysenberries, black currants, and walnuts.

The wine is wonderful in the mouth, showing excellent ripe fruit and fine integration of all its elements. The finish lasts nearly a minute, and my notes suggest that given the gorgeous fruit in the wine, it should last eight to ten years in the bottle.

I recommend the Rosella's Vineyard Pinot Noir. The 2003 is a black cherry color and lies dark in the glass. The nose is black cherries, black currants, wild strawberries, and chocolate. The tannins are excellent in this wine, giving it strength and structure to support the excellent fruit. The wine is drinking beautifully now and should hold for the next two to six years.

RATING: Three stars (very good to excellent wines in both whites and reds)

Blackstone Winery

OWNER: Pacific Wine Partners (part of Constellation Brands)

WINEMAKER: Dennis Hill

TASTING ROOM: Yes

DAYS/HOURS: Daily 10 A.M.–5 P.M.

ADDRESS: 800 S. Alta St., Gonzales, CA 93926; 831-675-2481; 831-675-2611 (fax); blackstonewinery.com

WINES/GRAPE VARIETIES: Cabernet Sauvignon, Chardonnay, Dolcetto, Gewürztraminer, Malbec, Malvasia Bianca, Merlot, Pinot Grigio, Pinot Noir, Port, Riesling, Sauvignon Blanc, Syrah, Tannat, Teroldego, Viognier, Zinfandel

WINE CLUB: Mailing list

TASTING ROOM AMENITIES: Lakeside picnic area, merchandise, fine art gallery

REGION: Monterey County AVA

Most of us have seen the movie *Sideways* by now and are familiar with the main character's abhorrence of Merlot and his preference for seeking out and drinking the fine Pinot Noirs of the Central Coast. The character, Miles, though he expresses a dislike for Merlot, for some reason reveres his Château Cheval Blanc, a famous Bordeaux wine that is made from about 50 percent Merlot. In fact, outstanding wines are being produced on the Central Coast that feature Merlot as the principal variety. Blackstone developed its reputation as a winery making fine, value-priced Merlot at a time when the wine consumer could not drink enough of it. Brothers Derek and Courtney Benham founded Blackstone in 1990 and grew it into a 400,000-case brand. This attracted the attention of Pacific Wine Partners, now the owner of Blackstone Winery. PWP was first established in 2001 as a joint venture between Constellation Brands of New York and BRL Hardy of Australia. BRL Hardy had the reputation of being one of Australia's oldest and most renowned wine companies, second in size only to Southcorp. It became part of Constellation during the company's acquisition of the Hardy Wine Group in 2003. Currently, PWP operates as an independent branch of Constellation Wines U.S., part of Constellation Brands, which recently bought Mondavi.

The original winery was built in the early 1990s as a producer for private and control labels (wines sold through a particular retailer who may not own the brand), as well as producing numerous brands. At the time, Blackstone also gained a reputation for its excellent Merlot. In 1994 Dennis Hill became the winemaker for Blackstone, further cementing its reputation for high-quality Merlot at a value price. Hill makes no bones about his goal: trying to perfect California Merlot. With access to Mondavi assets, economies of scale resulting from acquisitions, and excellent Monterey County fruit, he just might pull it off. Blackstone Merlot has now become the most popular Merlot in the country.

Dennis grew up amid the wine culture of Sonoma. He is a graduate of San Jose State, where he fell in love with art and architecture. This passion took him to Europe for five months in 1971, where he visited museums, sketched buildings, and further immersed himself in the wine culture of Europe. In the early '70s he took his first job at Seghesio, where he worked to learn. In the meantime, he took chemistry courses at UC Davis. He spent three years building his store of knowledge at Seghesio before going on to Alexander Valley Vineyards, where he worked for nine years. After tours in Europe spent learning traditional winemaking techniques, he became the winemaker and general manager at De Lorimer Winery in the late 1980s. He spent five years at Mill Creek Winery, where he learned about and began to focus on Merlot, winning the prestigious Louis Benoist Award for winemaking in 1993. Blackstone, under the stewardship of Dennis Hill's winemaking, now produces more than 1 million cases of Merlot a year.

RECOMMENDED WINES: Dennis recommends the Cabernet Sauvignon. The 2002 is dark in the glass and black cherry and purple in color. The nose is reminiscent of cherries, vanilla, blackberry, and white pepper. The wine is nicely balanced and wonderful in the mouth. The fruit is forward but well supported by the ripe tannins, leading to a pleasing and long finish. Drink this wine now and over the next two to five years.

I recommend the Reserve Pinot Noir from Santa Lucia Highlands grapes. The 2002 is almost opaque in the glass and a dark cherry color. The nose is plums, leather, roses, dark chocolate, and stone. This is a rich and complex wine with extra layers of interest from the ripe, luscious fruit and the fine tannins. The finish is velvety and smooth, lasting nearly a minute. Drink now, but this wine will continue to improve over the next two to five years.

Dennis is doing some wonderful things with Tannat, a red grape grown in Madiran in the southwest of France, and Teroldego, a northeastern Italian grape that Jim Clendenen at Au Bon Climat says California should have planted instead of Barbera and Merlot.

RATING: Two → three stars (reds ahead of the white program)

Boëté Winery

OWNERS: John and Jana Saunders

WINEMAKERS: John Saunders and wine consultant Dave Coventry

TASTING ROOM: At Valley Hills Wine Tasting

DAYS/HOURS: Friday–Monday 11 A.M.– 5 P.M.

ADDRESS: 7156 Carmel Valley Rd., Carmel Valley, CA 93923; 831-659-7563; 831-659-8471 (fax); boetewinery.com

WINES/GRAPE VARIETIES: Cabernet Sauvignon, Cabernet Franc

WINE CLUB: Online ordering

REGION: Carmel Valley AVA

Boyer Wines

OWNER: Rick Boyer

WINEMAKER: Rick Boyer

TASTING ROOM: Planned

DAYS/HOURS: Saturday–Sunday 11 A.M.–5 P.M.

ADDRESS: 655 River Rd., Salinas, CA 93908;
831-455-1885; 831-455-8019 (fax)

WINES/GRAPE VARIETIES: Chardonnay, Pinot Noir, Riesling, Syrah

WINE CLUB: No

TASTING ROOM AMENITIES: Herb gardens, organic education room

REGION: Monterey County AVA

Rick Boyer played football while at UC Davis and after graduation got a job working for Gallo as a field representative on the Central Coast. He met and had the pleasure of working with Julio Gallo himself, who would take Rick with him as he visited the Central Coast, the Central Valley, Lodi, and other places where Gallo owned vineyards. One of the things Julio impressed on him was that for all the romance associated with winemaking and wine culture, it is a business first. He worked for Gallo through five harvests before Ventana Vineyards in Monterey County offered him a position. At Ventana he was exposed to a new perspective: he got to work with the iconoclast and trailblazer Doug Meador, who encouraged him to think through theories of viticulture, try out new ideas in the cellar, and implement a new process of high-density planting in 1983 and 1984. This technique for planting vines close together was already being used with great success in the vineyards of Europe, but there was no equipment here sized for closer plantings, so they had to import it. During his eleven years at Ventana, they experimented with different varieties, trellis designs, and clonal variations. In the meantime, Rick made his own wines under the Boyer label starting in 1985. In 1994 he moved to Jekel Vineyards, where he was responsible for everything from winemaking to sales to finances. He worked there for ten years until Jekel closed and was put up for sale.

Rick is currently making his wines at the Paso Robles Co-op until his permits to build a winery come through. His business plan includes opening a tasting room on the property, and he hopes to produce about 5,000 cases a year. He makes wines that are more European than Californian, meaning more acidity, less oak, and worthy of laying down.

Rick has a love for plants, and this passion will be shared with wine consumers as he develops the property where the tasting room will stand. He envisions pick-it-yourself herb gardens and self-guided trails through gardens that will allow visitors to stop and touch and enjoy the beauty of nature.

RECOMMENDED WINES: Rick recommends the Riesling. The 2004 is a lovely green and gold in the glass with a honeyed nose of apples, gooseberries, tropical fruit, and fine minerality. Rick leaves the barest perception of sweetness in the wine to balance the excellent acidity. The wine has a clean, refreshing finish and is ready for drinking now and over the next three years—that is, if you can get past sniffing the wonderful aromatics and actually start drinking.

I recommend the Chardonnay. The 2002 is a golden yellow in the glass with an attractive nose of vanilla, buttered cinnamon toast, pineapple, pears, and tangerines. The wine presents a lively acidity to the tongue, supporting the wonderful ripe fruit. The wine has the elegance and minerality of a fine Chablis. Drink now and over the next three to five years.

RATING: Three stars (whites are very good to excellent)

Carmichael Vintners

OWNER: Mariposa Wine Company

WINEMAKER: Michael Leven

TASTING ROOM: At A Taste of Monterey

DAYS/HOURS: Daily 11 A.M.–6 P.M.

ADDRESS: A Taste of Monterey, 700 Cannery Row, Monterey, CA 93940;

800-946-3039, 559-673-6372; 559-673-4788 (fax); carmichaelwine.com

WINES/GRAPE VARIETIES: Grigio e Bianco (blend), Sa Vini (blend), Sangiovese, Sur le Pont (blend)

WINE CLUB: Yes

REGION: Monterey County AVA

Chalone Vineyard

OWNER: Chalone Wine Group (part of Diageo)

WINEMAKER: Dan Karlsen

TASTING ROOM: Yes

DAYS/HOURS: Saturday–Sunday 11:30 A.M.– 5 P.M., Monday–Friday by appointment

ADDRESS: Hwy. 146 E. at Stonewall Canyon Rd., Soledad, CA 93960; 831-678-1717;

831-678-2742 (fax); chalonevineyard .com

WINES/GRAPE VARIETIES: Cabernet Sauvignon, Chardonnay, Chenin Blanc, Grenache, Pinot Noir, Syrah, Viognier

WINE CLUB: Yes

TASTING ROOM AMENITIES: Merchandise

REGION: Chalone AVA

Chalone Vineyard is the oldest bonded winery in Monterey County and is located at the base of the Pinnacles, remnants of the old Neenach volcano that died 23 million years ago near present-day Lancaster. Located on the San Andreas Fault, the volcano was split by earthquakes, and portions carrying the Pinnacles gradually crept north through the eons.

The first plantings near Chalone were made by Frenchman Lucien Charles Tamm 1,800 feet above the Salinas Valley in the Gabilan Mountains in what is now the Chalone AVA. In the early '20s, a property east of Tamm's vineyard, then owned by the Dyer family, was sold to William and Agnes Silvear of Watsonville. Silvear planted 15 acres prior to Prohibition and 15 acres again in the 1940s, focusing on Chardonnay, Pinot Blanc, Chenin Blanc, and Pinot Noir. These are the vineyards that over time have become the famous Chalone vineyard, named after the Native American people living there, known as the Chollen tribe.

In the '60s Richard Graff discovered and bought the property, producing his first vintage in 1966. Dick was among the first to use new French oak barrels and malolactic fermentation for his Chardonnay wines. Phil Woodward joined in 1971 and took over management of the winery, becoming president in 1974. He and his partners created the Chalone Wine Group, which in 1980 partnered with Paragon Vineyard to start Edna Valley Vineyard in San Luis Obispo County. It also has relationships with partners in Bordeaux and was the first California wine company to invest in Washington State. In 1984 it became the first wine company to be publicly traded, and it was recently purchased by Diageo.

Dan Karlsen, a graduate of Sonoma State in marine biology, is the winemaker at Chalone. He is proud of the fact that he has learned while on the job and mostly from deranged mentors, as he likes to say. His early dreams were to make beer and open his own microbrewery, but after graduation he went to work for the U.S. Forest Service. His first exposure to the wine industry came in 1980, when he was hired as a carpenter to help build Dry Creek. After working the harvest of 1981, he stayed on for four years. In 1985 he was hired as assistant winemaker at Dehlinger, where he worked under the tutelage of Tom Dehlinger, who taught him the importance of making wine based on flavors, not chemistry. He next moved to Domaine Carneros, part of the French Champagne house of Taittinger, where he gained additional experience with Chardonnay and Pinot Noir grapes, both used in sparkling wines. In 1992 he was promoted to head winemaker. Five years later he moved to Estancia and in January 1998 came aboard at Chalone as general manager and winemaker. Dan believes that California has a nearly perfect climate for grape growing, but this creates the problem of overripe grapes. For this reason, he advises against thinking too much about Burgundy and its methods. He focuses instead on the climate and soils of the region, and makes wine based on what the vineyards give him. Accordingly, he depends on flavors that are the product of either underripe, ripe, or overripe grapes. Underripe grapes, according to Dan, tend to have vegetal flavors; overripe grapes taste of prunes or raisins if the fruit is desiccated. But his prized grapes are physiologically ripe grapes that taste sweet. This sweetness can be preserved even when no residual sugar is left in the wine.

RECOMMENDED WINES: Dan recommends the Wente clone Chardonnay. Tasted from the barrel, the 2004 is already showing gold in the glass and has a wonderful nose of spiced apples, gooseberries, sweet pineapple, cinnamon, and minerals. The acidity and minerality in the wine are outstanding and provide a superb backbone to the lovely, ripe fruit. The finish is fresh and clean and enlivens the tongue. In every regard, this is an outstanding Chardonnay that should drink beautifully over the next two to five years.

I recommend the Pinot Noir. The 2004 is almost opaque in the glass when tasted from the barrel and a gorgeous dark garnet color. The wine is showing soft vanilla and cream with cherries, blackberries, plums, earth, and cinnamon spice. Thanks to the lovely ripe tannins, the wine is already wonderful in the mouth, and the plush finish lasts nearly a full minute. This is an elegant, lush Pinot Noir that speaks to Dan's extraordinary talents as a winemaker.

RATING: Four stars (reds are excellent to outstanding; whites are very good to excellent)

Château Christina

OWNER: Frank Joyce

WINEMAKER: Frank Joyce

TASTING ROOM: At A Taste of Monterey

DAYS/HOURS: Daily 11 A.M.–6 P.M.

ADDRESS: A Taste of Monterey, 700 Cannery Row, Monterey, CA 93940; 831-659-0312 (phone and fax); chateauchristinawines.com

WINES/GRAPE VARIETIES: Cabernet Sauvignon, Chardonnay, Merlot, Pinot Noir, Syrah

WINE CLUB: Yes

REGION: Carmel Valley AVA

Château Julien Wine Estate

OWNERS: Bob and Patty Brower

WINEMAKER: Bill Anderson

TASTING ROOM: Yes

DAYS/HOURS: Monday–Friday 8 A.M.–5 P.M., Saturday–Sunday 11 A.M.–5 P.M.

ADDRESS: 8940 Carmel Valley Rd., Carmel, CA 93923; 831-624-2600; 831-624-6138 (fax); chateaujulien.com

WINES/GRAPE VARIETIES: Cabernet Sauvignon, Chardonnay, Merlot, Pinot Grigio, Sangiovese, Sauvignon Blanc, Syrah, Zinfandel

WINE CLUB: Yes

TASTING ROOM AMENITIES: Patio area, merchandise, tours

REGION: Monterey County AVA

One of the benefits of moving between two continents is the exposure it brings to new ideas and new vistas of the mind. Travel presents the opportunity to see things beyond a local perspective. Another positive benefit is that when you do return home you have an entirely new appreciation for what is possible where you are. After I returned from my last trip to various European vineyards and wine estates, I was more convinced than ever of the potential for greatness of Central Coast wines.

Bob and Patty Brower, former natives of New Jersey, sold their company in the petroleum industry and came to Carmel in 1978. They enjoy taking wine excursions in France, and after one such trip, they brought home a greater understanding of Monterey County's vast potential as a high-quality winegrowing region. In 1982 they got a bond and a year later started building Château Julien in Carmel Valley. Since its inception, Bill Anderson, now also vice president, has been the winemaker.

Bill's first foray into winemaking occurred at a rather early age when the aspiring and precocious winemaker used apricots and Fleischmann's yeast to brew up a batch of fruit wine. Even then he loved the aromatics of the wine. He went away to college at Stanford and worked at Stanford Hospital as a blood-gas technician. He continued to make wine at home as he furthered his studies in math. After graduation, he started working toward a master's degree at UC Davis and was almost finished when he got a job instead. He went to Mount Eden Vineyards in Saratoga for a couple of years and worked with Chardonnay, Cabernet Sauvignon, and Pinot Noir. There he also received exposure to fine wines and got to taste some of the great French releases. He was offered a position at Château Julien in 1983 and started as assistant winemaker. Six months later he assumed the lead position. From the beginning, Château Julien received accolades for its excellent Merlot.

The vineyards now run to about 250 acres, and the emphasis is on producing the best-quality grapes possible from that acreage. Nestled behind the Santa Lucia Mountains, which serve as a spectacular backdrop, the château is modeled on a home the Browers saw on one of their visits to the border between France and Switzerland. It contains a grand fireplace, a great hall, and an 18-foot mahogany table for tasting. In 1998 the Chai was added, a facility for storing wines built one story underground.

RECOMMENDED WINES: Bill recommends the Private Reserve Merlot. The 2001 is purple in the glass and opaque to the stem. The wine exudes chocolate aromas, bing cherries, black currants, and some crème de cassis. The fully ripe fruit is complemented by the great tannic grip, which gives the wine an excellent structure. The lovely acidity in the wine leads to a tart and lively finish. The wine is ready for the table now but will easily hold and improve over the next five to eight years. This is truly a fine Merlot.

I recommend the Estate Syrah. The 2002 is black-purple in color and opaque to light in the glass. The aromatics show blueberries, sage, violets, crème brûlée, and ripe blackberries. This wine shows wonderful integration of all its elements: the lovely ripe fruit, the ripe tannins, and the bracing acidity. The wine is so well integrated that it seems velvety in the mouth and lasts almost a full minute on the tongue. This too is a keeper and will continue to evolve for the next five to eight years. In all, it is an outstanding example of what Monterey County Syrah can be.

RATING: Four stars (reds are excellent to outstanding across the board)

Château Sinnet

OWNER: Gary Sinnet

WINEMAKERS: Gary Sinnet, Mike Walters, and
   Alexandre Andrieux

TASTING ROOM: Two

DAYS/HOURS: Daily 11 A.M.–6 P.M.

ADDRESS: 13746 Center St., Carmel Valley, CA
   93924; 1182 Broadway, Seaside, CA 93955; 831-
   659-2244 (Carmel Valley),
   831-394-6090 (Seaside); 831-659-2171 (fax);
   chateausinnet.com

WINES/GRAPE VARIETIES: Cabernet Franc, Cabernet Sauvignon, Chardonnay, Merlot, port, Sangiovese, sparkling wine, specialty fruit wines, Zinfandel

WINE CLUB: No

TASTING ROOM AMENITIES: Merchandise

REGION: Monterey County AVA

Gary Sinnet's grandfather relocated from Russia to the United States, so there is travel in the family's blood. Gary says you should pronounce the *t* in the family name, but if you want to give his wine the French cachet it truly deserves, pronounce it "sin-a." Sinnet, with the *t,* grew up in Manhattan on the Hudson River across from a park, his nearest and only involvement with nature at the time. He knew even as a youngster that he loved nature; he just didn't have access to it. After university at Plattsburg State, he knew he couldn't settle in New York, so he took his accounting degree and, like his grandfather before him, headed west. In Texas, he was pulled over for being non-Texan and asked to keep moving, which he did. He kept driving until he had an accident in San Jose, back in the days before Silicon Valley became prominent, and figured it was as good a place as any to stop. He found work with an accounting firm and was one of the first to help customers do taxes via computer. He started specializing in out-of-state returns and became much sought after as a result. He got his CPA license in 1982 and began working for himself.

Gary loves to scuba dive, and this passion first brought him to Monterey and Carmel. He is always in the process of building something, be it his CPA business, a tasting room, or a wonderful vineyard and garden below his house, where he has seventy different banana plants (who knew there were so many varieties?) along with pineapples and mangoes. He has traveled extensively across Europe and has always liked wine. In 1995 Gary constructed his building with the intention of renting it to a bank, as there were no banks in Carmel Valley then. When no bankers came calling, he rented the building to the Durney family, which bonded it as a winery and stayed for five years. Bernardus set up shop across the street, and Château Julien soon followed with tasting rooms. Gary, a keen observer, decided he wanted a winery too, and after Durney left, he created Château Sinnet on the premises, offering his first wines for tasting February 1, 2002. After reading every book he could get his hands on, Gary took on the winemaking, but his vineyard manager is Buster Goodwin, who has about forty years of expertise behind him. Gary then set out to acquire more vineyards so he could control the quality of the fruit. Recently, Gary acquired the Jolon vineyards in southern Monterey County, previously owned by Goodwin. Gary has the help of winemaker Mike Walters and sommelier Alexandre Andrieux. The three work closely together to make adjustments as needed and decide on the various blends. Château Sinnet's first release was in 1997. The next step is to build a new tasting room on his vineyard property.

RECOMMENDED WINES: Gary recommends the Private Cuvée Champagne. This sparkling wine is lemon and gold in the glass with a nose of peaches, apricots, mangoes, and bananas. The wine is dry and has a fine backbone of acidity to support the ripe fruit in the middle. It is refreshing on the palate and has a clean, creamy finish. It represents an excellent value.

I recommend the Cabernet Franc. The 2002 is almost opaque in the glass and has a pretty brick-red color. The wine has lovely aromatics of cherries, blueberries, red currants, and red roses. The tannins are ripe and contribute to a well-balanced structure below the fine fruit. Drink now and over the next four years. This wine also represents a good value.

RATING: Two stars (very good values in the reds and sparkling wines)

Cima Collina

OWNER: Richard Lumpkin

WINEMAKER: Annette Hoff

TASTING ROOM: By appointment only

ADDRESS: 3344 Paul Davis Dr., #6, Marina, CA 93933; 831-384-7806; 831-384-7850 (fax); cimacollina.com

WINES/GRAPE VARIETIES: Chardonnay, Hilltop Red Wine (blend), Merlot, Petite Sirah, Pinot Noir

WINE CLUB: Yes

REGION: Monterey County AVA

Clos LaChance Winery

OWNERS: Bill and Brenda Murphy

WINEMAKER: Stephen Tebb

TASTING ROOM: Yes

DAYS/HOURS: Daily 11 A.M.–5 P.M.

ADDRESS: 1 Hummingbird Ln., San Martin, CA 95046; 408-686-1050; 408-686-1052 (fax); clos.com

WINES/GRAPE VARIETIES: Cabernet Sauvignon, Chardonnay, dry rosé, Grenache, Merlot, Petite Sirah, Pinot Noir, Sauvignon Blanc, Syrah, Viognier, Zinfandel

WINE CLUB: Yes

TASTING ROOM AMENITIES: Picnic area, merchandise, boccie court

REGION: Central Coast AVA

Bill Murphy, with his wife, Brenda, is the owner and founder of Clos LaChance. He sees the business as a true family enterprise and hopes that it will eventually become multigenerational. He knows from experience that the great wineries in Europe were almost always family enterprises. Bill describes his emergence in the wine business using the metaphor of a book unfolding. Chapter 1 of the saga opens with the young Murphy studying engineering as an undergraduate at Tufts. (He also has an MBA from San Diego State.) He started his first career as a software engineer for Hewlett-Packard, rising through the ranks to become a top corporate executive. During the time the Murphys lived in Saratoga, they developed a love and appreciation for fine wine. Bill and his family had a home near the Santa Cruz Mountains and had to disk part of the property as a safeguard against fire danger. He saw some old vineyards in the area and got the idea to put a small vineyard on the property in 1987. Once the grapes came in, he decided to make wine as a hobby. That hobby grew substantially when he realized he was making up to 160 cases of Chardonnay, half of which he would give away to friends. He knew it was time to come up with a label and selected Clos LaChance (LaChance is Brenda's maiden name). The hummingbird on the label honors the little flitters in the vineyard who, because they are so territorial and protective of their nectar sources, help keep other birds away. After their children left home, Bill and Brenda, a teacher, were interested in starting a small business; they decided to turn their hobby into that business. At first, Bill put a small company together called CK Vines in 1996 to help people with vineyards smaller than 10 acres manage those properties. This gave him access to their fruit, and afforded him control of the growing practices in the vineyards even as the Murphys were growing their own wine business.

Chapter 2 opens with the Murphys in the wine business for real. Bill met one of the developers of the CordeValle golf resort, which you can see across the valley from the winery tasting room. As part of the agreement to build the golf course, the developer was required to leave 1,700 acres for open space and agricultural uses. In fact, some vines left over from the Spanish missionaries were on the property, and parcels of the land were required to remain dedicated to viticulture. Bill recognized the synergy between his needs and the needs of the developer and leased the land for seventy-five years. After months of walking the valley, he planted the vineyard and saw that the current location was perfect for the winery and hospitality center.

The winemaker is Stephen Tebb, a graduate of UC Davis, hired after a series of interviews involving the entire staff in which Tebb was noted as the winemaker everyone wanted to work with. There are currently more than a thousand members in the wine club, a testament to Tebb's winemaking skills. Clos LaChance offers the consumer three levels of wine: Hummingbird Series, Estate Series, and Special Selection Series.

RECOMMENDED WINES: Bill recommends the Biagini Vineyard Pinot Noir. The 2004 is almost opaque in the glass and a pretty garnet-red. The nose is dark toast, leather, roast meats, cherries, red currants, and spice. The wine is outstanding in the mouth, with fine balance, and has sensational fruit. It is luscious on the tongue and lasts nearly a minute in the finish. This is an outstanding Pinot Noir and will evolve further over the next six to eight years.

I recommend the Sauvignon Blanc, a blend of that variety, Sémillon, and a touch of Muscat. The 2004 is lemon and green in the glass with a lovely nose of lemons, grapefruit, and honey and a brace of minerality under the fruit. The wine is well balanced between the ripe fruit and the lively acidity, which leads to a crisp, tart finish. This is a fine drinker and ready for the table. Drink now and over the next two years.

RATING: Two stars (three stars for Special Selection Series)

De Tierra Vineyards

OWNER: Tom Russell

WINEMAKER: David Coventry

TASTING ROOM: At A Taste of Monterey

DAYS/HOURS: Daily 11 A.M.–6 P.M.

ADDRESS: A Taste of Monterey, 700 Cannery Row, Monterey, CA 93940;

831-484-2557; 831-484-9843 (fax); detierravineyards.com

WINES/GRAPE VARIETIES: Chardonnay, Ekem (late-harvest Sauvignon Blanc), Merlot, Pinot Noir, Syrah

WINE CLUB: No

REGION: Monterey County AVA

Escafeld Vineyards

OWNERS: Steve and Elsbeth Wetherill

WINEMAKER: Steve Wetherill

TASTING ROOM: At A Taste of Monterey

DAYS/HOURS: Daily 11 A.M.–6 P.M.

ADDRESS: A Taste of Monterey, 700 Cannery Row, Monterey, CA 93940; 831-385-4960 ext. 12; no fax; escafeld.com

WINES/GRAPE VARIETIES: Merlot, Petit Verdot, Zinfandel

WINE CLUB: Yes

REGION: San Antonio Valley AVA

Figge Cellars

OWNER: Peter Figge

WINEMAKER: Peter Figge

TASTING ROOM: By appointment only

ADDRESS: 3348 Paul Davis Dr., Ste. 101, Marina, CA 93933; 831-384-4149; 831-384-4159 (fax); figgecellars.com

WINES/GRAPE VARIETIES: Chardonnay, Pinot Noir, Syrah

WINE CLUB: Online ordering

REGION: Carmel Valley AVA

Galante Vineyards

OWNER: Jack Galante

WINEMAKER: Greg Vita

TASTING ROOM: Yes

DAYS/HOURS: Daily 11 A.M.–6 P.M.

ADDRESS: Dolores between Ocean and 7th Ave., Carmel-by-the-Sea, CA 93921; 831-624-3800; 831-624-3200 (fax); galantevineyards.com

WINES/GRAPE VARIETIES: Cabernet Sauvignon, Merlot, Petite Sirah, Pinot Noir, Sauvignon Blanc

WINE CLUB: Yes

TASTING ROOM AMENITIES: Merchandise

REGION: Carmel Valley AVA

Jack Galante has an impressive great-grandfather—one J. Frank Devendorf, who, with his partner, Frank Powers, founded the town of Carmel in about 1900. He also built the famous Highlands Inn, a landmark on the Central Coast. In 1969 Jack's parents purchased the current 700-acre property in upper Carmel Valley for cattle ranching, and young Jack grew up working as a cowboy on the ranch. In 1983 the family decided to grow premium wine grapes on part of the land, making them one of the earliest in the appellation. (The Durney vineyards were already in place at that time, but that vineyard is no longer owned by the family.) Jack got a hands-on introduction to viticulture as he helped his dad plant the vineyard on the slopes of their Carmel Valley ranch.

Jack went away to study geology at the University of the Pacific in Stockton. After graduation he became the operations and field manager at Galante Vineyards. He went back east to Penn State to get a master's degree in geography, and after graduation in 1986 went to work as an environmental analyst and planner. He has also taught cartography and geography at the college level. In 1991 he assumed the general management position over the property; owing to his love of wine and interest in home winemaking since the mid-1980s, he decided in 1993 to build a winery. The winery was completed the next year and now produces about 6,000 cases, with the focus on vineyard-designated Cabernet Sauvignon.

Greg Vita is the winemaker and brings more than twenty years of experience to Galante, where he has been since its inception. The vineyard property runs from 700 to 2,200 feet in elevation, with the Pinot Noir growing at 1,800 feet. When Jack researched the Pinot Noir vineyard, he found that at one time about 130 to 140 years ago it had been planted to red grapes. In fact, Jack has found some of the original grower's old bottles.

RECOMMENDED WINES: Jack recommends the fine Red Rose Hill 100 percent Cabernet Sauvignon. The 2003 is a classic black-purple in the glass and opaque to light. The nose delivers soft vanilla, black currants, violets, earth, and a hint of sandalwood. Black cherry and black currant fruit engages the palate and there are enough tannins in the wine to suggest a long life ahead. The ripe fruit starts softly in the mouth but ends with a big finish because of the ample tannins, making this wine amenable to bottle-aging.

I recommend the Pinot Noir. At the time of this writing, it is the only Pinot Noir grown in the Carmel Valley appellation. The 2003 is black and purple in the glass and dark to the stem. One could easily mistake it for a Cabernet Sauvignon. The wine's aromatics suggest black plums, black cherries, black currants, leather, and Moroccan spice. The fruit is lovely, the tannins are ripe and plush, and the wonderful nose is complemented by the long, silky finish. Drink now and over the next four years. A wine of this quality suggests that the hills and *terroir* of the Carmel Valley are conducive to the production of excellent Pinot Noir. In the future, we may very well see more ground given over to the production of that grape variety.

RATING: Three stars (reds are excellent)

Hahn Estates / Smith & Hook Winery

OWNERS: Nicolaus and Gaby Hahn

WINEMAKER: Adam LaZarre

TASTING ROOM: Yes

DAYS/HOURS: Daily 11 A.M.–4 P.M.

ADDRESS: 37700 Foothill Rd., Soledad, CA 93960; 831-678-2132; 831-678-0557 (fax); hahnestates.com

WINES/GRAPE VARIETIES: Cabernet Franc, Cabernet Sauvignon, Chardonnay, Meritage (blend), Merlot, Pinot Noir, Syrah

WINE CLUB: Yes

TASTING ROOM AMENITIES: Picnic area, merchandise

REGION: Santa Lucia Highlands AVA

Swiss businessman Nicolaus "Nicky" Hahn and his wife, Gaby, first discovered California wines while living in England. Hahn is trained in economics and started his career in Paris as an arbitrageur before working as a credit analyst in New York. During his time in London, he served as the chairman of a leading international software company. In the mid-1970s Hahn first brought his family to Monterey County, and he was convinced that the region had the potential to produce world-class wines. After two years of searching, he and Gaby purchased two ranches in 1974, planted vineyards, and established the Smith & Hook Winery in 1980 on the old Smith Ranch. The Smith Ranch had been used for raising horses, while the neighboring Hook Ranch had been used for grazing cattle. Located in the Santa Lucia foothills, the two properties were ideal for the establishment of vineyards.

The first wine made from those vineyards' fruit, a Cabernet Sauvignon, was released in 1979. In 1991 Nicky created the Hahn Estates label to share accessible and value-priced wines with the consumer. The combined operation, taking fruit from the two vineyards and other properties that have been acquired by the Hahn family, is now known as Hahn Estates/Smith & Hook Winery. In 2000 both the vineyards and the winery underwent an $8 million renovation under the direction of Hahn's longtime associate Bill Legion, who was appointed president in 2001.

That same year Adam LaZarre took over as winemaker, moving from Jekel. LaZarre discovered his passion for wines during his six years' service in the navy. He was stationed at Alameda, took numerous trips to Napa during shore leave, and decided he would become a winemaker after his service. He graduated from Fresno State before taking jobs at Elliston Vineyards and Jekel.

The move led by Bill Legion has been one primarily of transitioning from growing grapes on a contract basis to producing estate wines from the renovated vineyards. The focus is now on Bordeaux varieties, Pinot Noir, and Syrah grown on the winery's holdings of about 1,000 acres. Recently, Hahn added 67 acres on the western side of Paso Robles to its portfolio. This allows the company to focus on Pinot, Syrah, and Chardonnay in the Santa Lucia Highlands region, while the Paso vineyard has all the Bordeaux varieties and Syrah.

According to Andy Mitchell, vineyard manager and a Cal Poly graduate, it was once thought that the Smith & Hook vineyards sat atop alluvial fans and glacial moraines, but a recent geological survey indicates that the soils are derived from the rocks of the Sierra de Salinas Mountains, the easternmost ridge of the Santa Lucia Highlands. The two primary rocks from these mountains are metamorphic schist and gneiss, formed 600 million to a billion years ago 10 miles below the surface of the earth. Add the marine influence and you have a *terroir* considered ideal for growing wine grapes. In fact, Nicky Hahn and Rick Smith were instrumental in achieving AVA status in 1992 for the Santa Lucia Highlands.

RECOMMENDED WINES: Adam recommends the Meritage, a Merlot-based blend with Cabernet Sauvignon, Malbec, Petit Verdot, and Cabernet Franc. The 2003 is black cherry in color and opaque to light in the glass. The aromatics are wonderful, recalling black cherries, vanilla, caramel, plums, and cinnamon spice. The tannins are ripe and rounded, leading to a silky feel in the mouth. The finish is long and lasts almost a full minute. In all, this is a fine Bordeaux blend that will give great pleasure now, but if you can wait another six to eight years, it will be even better as it matures.

I recommend the Reserve Cabernet Sauvignon. The 2003 is opaque in the glass and a pretty black and purple color. In the nose I found black currants, cherries, vanilla spice, cedar, and a hint of sweet tobacco. The wine shows excellent integration of all its components, making it wonderful in the mouth, and it resolves to a long and luscious finish. The tannins and the superb fruit at the time of my tasting suggest that this wine is probably ready now and will continue to improve over the next six to eight years.

RATING: Two stars (four stars for reserve wines)

Heller Estate

OWNERS: Heller family

WINEMAKER: Rich Tanguay

TASTING ROOM: Yes

DAYS/HOURS: Monday–Friday 11 A.M.–5:30 P.M., Saturday–Sunday 11 A.M.–6 P.M.

ADDRESS: 69 W. Carmel Valley Rd., Carmel Valley, CA 93924; 831-659-6220; 831-659-6226 (fax); hellerestate.com

WINES/GRAPE VARIETIES: Cabernet Sauvignon, Chardonnay, Chenin Blanc, Merlot, Merlot port, Pinot Noir, Riesling

WINE CLUB: Yes

TASTING ROOM AMENITIES: Merchandise

REGION: Carmel Valley AVA

The Heller Estate vineyards are planted at an altitude of 1,200 to 1,500 feet on slopes overlooking the Cachagua region of Carmel Valley. In Spanish *agua* means "water," and in French *cacher* means "hidden or concealed." Cachagua is thus the Indian derivative for "hidden waters." In this spectacular region William and Dorothy Durney planted vineyards in 1968. The first wines were released in 1976. Looking to expand his business interests beyond raising cattle, Durney had a vision for the Cachagua Valley, deciding that the soils and climate were ideal for grapes. In fact, some of the locals still refer to him as the Mondavi of the valley. He planted some 80 acres of fifteen varieties. Of course, not all of these prospered in the specific *terroir* of the region. Through trial and error in the vineyard, he selected Cabernet Sauvignon and Merlot, the two Bordeaux varieties that flourished in these soils. At the time, one of the critiques of many Monterey County–grown Cabs was that they were too vegetal, a taste often characteristic of underripe grapes. A touch of bell pepper might add to the wine's flavor complexity, but when overdone it is considered a flaw. That is not a problem in the Cachagua hills, where the growing season, with its fairly long hang times, sufficient exposure to sunlight, and cool nights, is amenable to ripening Cabernet and Merlot. Knowing what he had, Durney decided to separate himself from the perceived image of vegetal Monterey reds by having a new AVA approved—Carmel Valley—with help from UC Davis in 1982–83. When Durney decided to sell, the Hellers bought the 1,000-acre estate.

The Hellers were looking for vineyard properties around the world. After a return from Tuscany, they saw the Durney vineyard and fell in love with it during a drive through the Carmel Valley. In 1993–94, with a consortium of European investors, they bought the property. The Durneys had made a commitment to farming as organically as possible, and the Hellers have honored that commitment. The vineyards are now certified 100 percent organic. In an effort to serve loyal Durney wine consumers, the Hellers kept the Durney label as long as possible, and only in the past three years or so have they relabeled the wines. After they upgraded the winery and buildings and renovated the vineyards, Rich Tanguay was brought in as winemaker. Rich has a French-Italian heritage; in fact, his father served in the French Foreign Legion, and it was his father's wine cellar that introduced Rich to wine culture. After coming west to California from the East Coast, Rich worked on a chemistry degree at Sonoma State but left to take his first job as a lab tech at Buena Vista. He rose to the position of winemaker's assistant, went to Napa for a time, and then worked for Topolos in the Russian River Valley. In 2001 he came to Heller at the family's request.

RECOMMENDED WINES: Rich recommends the Estate Cabernet Sauvignon. The 2001 is black and purple in the glass and opaque to light. The main notes in the lovely aromatics are black currants, black plums, earth, cinnamon spice, and peppermint. This is a highly concentrated wine thanks to the lovely ripe fruit, which lends the wine a sense of sweetness on the tongue. The tannins too are ripe and serve as the structural backbone to the excellent fruit. This is an outstanding Cabernet Sauvignon that should last eight to thirteen years, though it is ready for drinking now.

I recommend the Estate Merlot. The Hellers call this their Pétrus, and this wine is not far off the mark. The 2001 is black-purple and blocks all light. The nose is cedar, leather, vanilla spice, black cherry, anise, black currants, and earth. The fine, ripe tannins support the great ripe fruit, and there is an exquisite hint of sweetness in the wine that French wines achieve only during exceptional vintages. This wine too will last another eight to ten years in the bottle. In all, given the breadth, depth, concentration, and integration of all its components, it is truly a superior Merlot.

RATING: Three → four stars (reds are excellent to outstanding)

J. Lohr Vineyards & Wines

See chapter 7.

Joullian Vineyards

OWNERS: Dick and Jeannette Joullian Sias

WINEMAKER: Ridge Watson

TASTING ROOM: Yes

DAYS/HOURS: Daily 11 A.M.–5 P.M.

ADDRESS: 2 Village Dr., Ste. A, Carmel Valley, CA 93924; 831-659-8100; 831-659-8102 (fax); joullian.com

WINES/GRAPE VARIETIES: Cabernet
Sauvignon, Chardonnay, Merlot,
Sauvignon Blanc, Syrah, Zinfandel

WINE CLUB: Yes

TASTING ROOM AMENITIES: Merchandise

REGION: Carmel Valley AVA

Dick and Jeannette (Joullian) Sias, of Oklahoma City, Oklahoma, are the owners of Joullian, and as delightful a couple as one could hope to meet. In the late 1970s and early '80s, Dick's principal business was in the oil and gas industry, and he was looking to diversify his interests. Dick and Jeannette have always appreciated fine wines, and this was the time when California wines were developing a national reputation. Dick started his research, and as he was interested in some form of an agricultural investment, he found that land was available at fairly reasonable cost in Monterey County.

In 1981 current winemaker Raymond "Ridge" Watson teamed with the Joullian and Sias families to help them locate a suitable property in the Carmel Valley. Ridge knew Bill Durney, who agreed to help them out, and they identified some suitable properties. They were close to buying the neighboring Bloomquist Ranch when they found the current property. In its original configuration, the ranch was about 655 acres but was divided into thirteen parcels. When Jeannette's brother (and half-owner) fell ill, Dick bought his share but kept the Joullian name for the winery. Dick personally planted the first Zinfandel in Carmel Valley, Ridge brought in new clones for the Bordeaux varieties, and the winery opened its doors in 1991.

General manager and winemaker Ridge Watson is originally from Kansas City but came west to take his first degree at Stanford. He spent almost four years in the Peace Corps working in Thailand, where he met his Australian-educated wife, a native of Thailand and an outstanding cook. They were married in Carmel Valley in 1972. Ridge furthered his education with a master's degree from Fresno State, followed by apprenticeship in France and Australia.

RECOMMENDED WINES: Ridge recommends the Zinfandel. The 2002 is black cherry in color and opaque to light. The nose is chocolate, raspberry, spice, and a whiff of rose petals thanks to the addition of some Grenache. The acidity is fine and the tannins ripe, leading to a softer and more flowery Zinfandel than most people might be used to. The fruit is lovely and contributes to the wine's sense of elegance in the mouth. Drink now and over the next two to four years.

I recommend the Family Reserve Sauvignon Blanc. The 2003 is a blend of mostly Sauvignon Blanc and some Sémillon. The wine is light gold in color and has a lovely nose of lime, pineapples, gooseberries, lemongrass, and minerality. Its ample acidity serves as a backbone to the ripe lush fruit. The wine is ready for drinking at the table but will age in the bottle another three to five years. This is an excellent Sauvignon Blanc.

The Cabernet Sauvignon at Joullian, too, has the potential to be terrific.

RATING: Four stars (both whites and reds are excellent to outstanding)

Lakeview Vineyards/Ronan Cellars

OWNERS: Ron Frudden and Nanci Bernard

WINEMAKERS: Ron Frudden and Nanci Bernard

TASTING ROOM: By appointment only

ADDRESS: Call for details; 805-434-9159; 805-434-9152 (fax); ronancellars.com

WINES/GRAPE VARIETIES: Belle Cuvée (blend), Cabernet Franc, Cabernet Sauvignon, Petite Sirah, Syrah, Zinfandel

WINE CLUB: Yes

REGION: San Antonio Valley AVA

Lockwood Vineyard

OWNERS: Paul Toeppen, Phil Johnson, and Butch Lindley

WINEMAKER: Larry Gomez

TASTING ROOM: At A Taste of Monterey

DAYS/HOURS: Daily 11 A.M.–6 P.M.

ADDRESS: A Taste of Monterey, 700 Cannery Row, Monterey, CA 93940; 800-753-1424, 831-642-9200; 831-644-7829 (fax); lockwood-wine.com

WINES/GRAPE VARIETIES: Cabernet Sauvignon, Chardonnay, Meritage (blend), Merlot, Sauvignon Blanc, Syrah

WINE CLUB: Yes

REGION: Monterey County AVA

Manzoni Estate Vineyard

OWNERS: Manzoni family

WINEMAKER: Mark Manzoni

TASTING ROOM: Yes

DAYS/HOURS: Saturday–Sunday 11 A.M.– 5 P.M.

ADDRESS: 30981 River Rd., Soledad, CA 93960; 831-675-3398; 831-675-8951 (fax); manzoniwines.com

WINES/GRAPE VARIETIES: Chardonnay, Pinot Noir, Syrah

WINE CLUB: Yes

REGION: Santa Lucia Highlands AVA

Marilyn Remark Winery

OWNERS: Joel Burnstein and Marilyn Remark

WINEMAKER: Joel Burnstein

TASTING ROOM: Yes

DAYS/HOURS: Saturday–Sunday 11 A.M.– 5 P.M.

ADDRESS: 645 River Rd., Salinas, CA 93908; 831-455-9310; 831-455-9291 (fax); remarkwines.com

WINES/GRAPE VARIETIES: Grenache, Marsanne, rosé de Saignée, Roussanne, Petite Sirah, Pinot Noir, Syrah

WINE CLUB: Yes

TASTING ROOM AMENITIES: Merchandise

REGION: Monterey County AVA

Joel Burnstein's university degree is in business, and he wanted to be a stockbroker after graduation. For a short time he managed a Radio Shack to get business experience before becoming a stockbroker. Living in Fresno, he was introduced to people who had an appreciation for wine. He left his successful job and bought a seat on the Pacific Stock Exchange in San Francisco. This move afforded him the opportunity to visit Napa and Sonoma and gain further exposure to wine culture. At age thirty-eight he quit his job on the exchange and went back to school, earning a degree in enology at Fresno State, from which he graduated in 1991. Before graduation he was required to do an internship. Steve Pessagno, then winemaker at Jekel, interviewed him, but he was offered a position at Sterling as assistant research enologist, which allowed him to make experimental wines and see and do just about everything an intern could dream of. Steve called again after his own intern did not work out and offered Joel a job, which he took after his professors offered to let him test out of his courses to finish his degree. When Steve moved on to Lockwood, Joel had to take over as default wine-maker. He became the full-time winemaker, but when Bill Jekel sold the winery to Brown-Foreman, Joel had no interest in becoming a corporate winemaker. His next job took him to San Saba, a smaller winery that had just been built.

In the spring of 2001 he and Marilyn took a trip through the Rhône valley in France, one that changed their lives forever. Although they originally went for the ruins and not the wines, Joel and Marilyn were able to taste some of the great wines from the superb 1998 and 1999 vintages, and he fell forever in love with Grenache. When they returned, the two set out to acquire the licenses they would need to start their own winery, with a focus on Rhône varieties.

Marilyn Remark, a Minnesota native, was raised on a farm. She has degrees in so-cial work and moved in 1985 to Monterey County, where she works with the elder-ly as a social-work supervisor. She saw Joel in a charity "bachelor auction" brochure but, too shy to bid, asked her sister to arrange a meeting. That was more than ten years ago. It also helps explain why her name is on the label. It does have a nice ring to it.

RECOMMENDED WINES: Joel recommends the Grenache, the variety that won Best of Show at the L.A. County Fair "Wines of the World" competition for the 2001 vintage. The 2002 is black cherry in color and almost opaque in the glass. The wonderful aromatics suggest blue-berries, plums, sweet vanilla cream, hot cinnamon spice, raspberry, smoke, and a hint of chocolate. The well-integrated tannins and the outstanding aromatics complement the lovely ripe fruit. The finish is long and plush. The wine is ready now but will evolve in the bottle over the next three to seven years. This is a full-bodied and outstanding Grenache, one of the best I've tasted on the Central Coast. I tasted the 2001 also, and I believe the 2002 may sur-pass it in time. This wine also won a gold medal and the Chairman's Award at the Orange County Fair.

I recommend the Petite Sirah. The 2003 was tasted after only ten days in the bottle, but the potential was already beginning to show. The wine was pushing its oak heritage ahead of the fruit this early in its life, but the fruit is of outstanding quality, with elements of grape jelly and blackberries, with white pepper spice to follow. The ripeness is superb, the wine already shows beautifully in the mouth, and the finish is long and plush. Give this wine a year in the bottle, and then watch all the medals start piling up. In fact, it recently scored 90 points in the *Wine Enthusiast.* It will continue to evolve over the next four to eight years.

RATING: Four stars (outstanding potential among the reds)

Miura Vineyards

OWNER: Emmanuel Kemiji

WINEMAKER: Byron Kosuge

TASTING ROOM: At A Taste of Monterey

DAYS/HOURS: Daily 11 A.M.–6 P.M.

ADDRESS: A Taste of Monterey, 700 Cannery Row, Monterey, CA 93940; 707-566-7739; 707-566-7788 (fax); no Web site

WINES/GRAPE VARIETIES: Cuvée Kemiji and Portay (blends)

WINE CLUB: Yes

REGION: Monterey County AVA

Morgan Winery

OWNERS: Dan and Donna Lee

WINEMAKERS: Dan Morgan Lee and Gianni Abate

TASTING ROOM: At A Taste of Monterey

DAYS/HOURS: Daily 11 A.M.–6 P.M.

ADDRESS: A Taste of Monterey, 700 Cannery Row, Monterey, CA 93940; 831-751-7777; 831-751-7780 (fax); morganwinery.com

WINES/GRAPE VARIETIES: Chardonnay, Pinot Gris, Pinot Noir, Sauvignon Blanc

WINE CLUB: Online sales

REGION: Santa Lucia Highlands AVA

Paraiso Vineyards

OWNERS: Rich and Claudia Smith

WINEMAKER: David Fleming

TASTING ROOM: Yes

DAYS/HOURS: Monday–Friday 11 A.M.–4 P.M., Saturday–Sunday 11 A.M.–5 P.M.

ADDRESS: 38060 Paraiso Springs Rd., Soledad, CA 93960; 831-678-0300; 831-678-2584 (fax); paraisovineyards.com

WINES/GRAPE VARIETIES: Chardonnay, Pinot Noir, Riesling, Syrah

WINE CLUB: Yes

TASTING ROOM AMENITIES: Picnic area, merchandise

REGION: Santa Lucia Highlands AVA

Graduates of UC Davis, Rich and Claudia Smith arrived in Monterey County in 1973 in a borrowed pickup truck and an old Plymouth Valiant, eager to put their training to work. At the time they arrived, the Salinas Valley had not changed much since the time of Steinbeck and was primarily oriented toward growing vegetables and fruit. Major wineries had come from outside the region to plant enormous vineyards and take advantage of the fertile growing conditions, but their grapes were sent elsewhere for blending. Rich and Claudia saw the potential in the *terroir* of the Santa Lucia Highlands and planted their first vineyard in 1973, managing the property for a group of investors. When that investor group moved on, the Smiths bought the property in 1987. Over time the Smith family came to oversee 3,000 acres of grapes around Monterey County, and in 1988 they began releasing their own wines under the Paraiso label. They took the name from the Spanish word for "heaven," which they first learned from Steinbeck's *East of Eden*. Their efforts resulted in the designation of the Santa Lucia Highlands as an official AVA.

Rich grew up in the Bay Area and went to Davis (his brother, also at the winery, had attended previously) with the intention of becoming a veterinarian. He wound up in soil science instead. His first job was as a lab tech in Santa Clara County for farm customers who needed soil, water, and leaf sampling. In 1972 that job brought him down to the current property to do soil and water work. His boss at the time worked at Asgrow Seeds, but when his boss left, Rich took over. He became the manager in 1975 and shortly thereafter started his own consulting and management company. In 1977 he bought a harvester and did contract harvesting. Eventually he acquired twelve harvesters for work on more than 6,000 acres. The monies from that business allowed the Smiths to buy their current property. They started their own winery because there simply weren't enough in Monterey County at the time.

Paraiso remains very much a family operation. Son Jason is the vineyard manager. Daughter-in-law Jennifer Murphy-Smith is hospitality manager. Son-in-law David Fleming is the winemaker, although he was well on his way to becoming a minister when he met and fell in love with Rich's daughter Kacy. Rich and Claudia Smith deserve their reputation as two of the most respected and influential growers and vintners on the Central Coast.

RECOMMENDED WINES: Rich recommends the Santa Lucia Highlands Syrah. The 2001 is opaque in the glass and black-purple in color. The nose is vanilla spice, tar, black currants, pepper, blackberries, and cherries. The tannins are soft and rounded under the luscious ripe fruit. The finish is long and lovely. Ready for drinking now, the wine will continue to evolve over the next three to five years.

I recommend the Santa Lucia Highlands Pinot Noir. The 2002 is opaque to light and blood-ruby in color. The nose is black cherries, vanilla spice, smoke, forest floor, truffles, and black currants. The sweet, ripe fruit shows excellent integration with the warm, ripe tannins, leading to a seamless structure. The wine is silky in the mouth and ready for drinking. It should evolve further over the next three to eight years. In all, this is a fine example of Pinot Noir from the Santa Lucia Highlands.

RATING: Three stars (quality throughout the line, but reds slightly ahead of the whites)

Parkfield Vineyards

OWNERS: Harry and Roger Miller

WINEMAKER: Jon Korecki

TASTING ROOM: By appointment only

ADDRESS: Call for details; 805-441-6546

WINES/GRAPE VARIETIES: Cabernet Sauvignon, Chardonnay, Merlot, Sauvignon Blanc, Syrah, White Zinfandel, Zinfandel

WINE CLUB: No

REGION: Monterey County AVA

Parsonage Winery

OWNERS: Bill and Mary Ellen Parsons

WINEMAKER: Bill Parsons

TASTING ROOM: At Valley Hills Wine Tasting

DAYS/HOURS: Friday–Monday 11 A.M.–5 P.M.

ADDRESS: 7156 Carmel Valley Rd., Carmel Valley, CA 93923; 831-625-5040; 831-659-2215 (fax); parsonagewine.com

WINES/GRAPE VARIETIES: Cabernet Sauvignon, Merlot, Syrah

WINE CLUB: Yes

REGION: Carmel Valley AVA

Pavona Wines

OWNER: Richard Kanakaris

WINEMAKER: Aaron Mosley

TASTING ROOM: At A Taste of Monterey

DAYS/HOURS: Daily 11 A.M.–6 P.M.

ADDRESS: A Taste of Monterey, 700 Cannery Row, Monterey, CA 93940; 831-646-1506; 831-649-8919 (fax); pavonawines.com

WINES/GRAPE VARIETIES: Chardonnay Blanc (blend), Petite Sirah, Pinot Noir, Syrah, Zinfandel

WINE CLUB: Yes

REGION: Monterey County AVA

Pessagno Winery

OWNER: Stephen Pessagno

WINEMAKER: Stephen Pessagno

TASTING ROOM: Yes

DAYS/HOURS: Friday–Sunday 11 A.M.–5 P.M., Monday–Thursday by appointment only

ADDRESS: 1645 River Rd., Salinas, CA 93908; 831-675-9463; 831-675-1922 (fax); pessagnowines.com

WINES/GRAPE VARIETIES: Chardonnay, Pinot Noir, port, Syrah, Zinfandel

WINE CLUB: Yes

TASTING ROOM AMENITIES: Merchandise

REGION: Santa Lucia Highlands AVA

Stephen Pessagno grew up in the Bay Area and can remember spending summers in the Santa Clara Valley with his grandfather Anthony Escover on his walnut ranch. At age sixteen, Steve and his grandfather made small vats of Zinfandel. That effort, more fun than successful, convinced him he probably had a better chance at pursuing a different career, his Portuguese and Italian heritage notwithstanding. He selected mechanical engineering at Santa Clara University for his major and went on to study for a master's degree in alcohol fuel combustion, but did not finish. Instead he went to Brazil, where he got involved in the biomass and ethanol fuels business. After he returned to the United States and continued his successful career as a mechanical engineer, he read wine books and made wine at home. Deciding he no longer wanted to live in Silicon Valley, he took a leave of absence from his job in 1982 and worked at a small winery in Gilroy called Kirigin Cellars. They liked his work so much that they asked him to stay on as assistant winemaker. Shortly thereafter he called Fresno State and the Department of Viticulture and Enology invited him to visit the campus, which he did, wife and infant in the car. He sat down across a desk and spoke with the department head, and after his interview found himself accepted to the enology program. (An old and very wise professor of mine once said that the fewer requirements and hoops an academic program makes you jump through, the stronger the program.)

After graduation in 1986, Jekel offered him a job during a very difficult time in the wine industry. He accepted and ran Jekel as vice president and winemaker until 1991, taking it from about 12,000 cases a year to over 100,000. A new winery called Lockwood was then starting up and invited him onboard to direct its growth and winemaking, given his previous success at Jekel. He accepted that challenge. In 1999, Steve and two of his closest friends started the Pessagno label, and in July 2004 the partners bought the current property, then a winery in name only. They acquired the permits, bought the necessary equipment, and established the business by early 2005.

Steve is convinced that we have just scratched the surface of the Santa Lucia Highlands for high-quality Syrah and Pinot Noir. In fact, he believes it has the same potential for Pinot Noir as the Santa Rita Hills farther south in Santa Barbara County, and will soon surpass what Oregon has to offer.

RECOMMENDED WINES: Steve recommends the Garys' Vineyard Pinot Noir. The 2001 is almost opaque in the glass and a beautiful ruby-garnet color. The nose is redolent of blackberry fruit, truffles, roast beef, black currants, and cinnamon spice. The wine is full in the mouth, given the silky, ripe tannins. The finish is long and recalls the excellent ripe fruit. Although it's ready for drinking now, the fine tannins in this wine suggest it will improve further over the next five years.

I suggest the Idyll Times Syrah. The 2001 is opaque in the glass and a deep and beautiful purple. The nose gives up a touch of vanilla oak, black plums, blackberries, and black currants. Teeth-coating tannins that will allow it to age for another four to ten years in the bottle support the lovely fruit. The wine is currently full and lush in the mouth with wonderful integration of all its elements, including a finish that lasts almost a full minute. After tasting these two wines, I think Pessagno may be right in his predictions about the potential of the Santa Lucia Highlands.

RATING: Three → four stars (the reds are excellent to outstanding)

Pianetta Winery

OWNERS: Pianetta family

WINEMAKER: John Pianetta

TASTING ROOM: By appointment only

ADDRESS: 75751 Indian Valley Rd., San
Miguel, CA 93451; 805-467-3830;
805-467-2522 (fax); pianettawinery.com

WINES/GRAPE VARIETIES: Cabernet
Sauvignon, Sangiovese, Shiraz-Cabernet
(blend), Syrah

WINE CLUB: Yes

REGION: Monterey County AVA

San Saba Vineyard

OWNERS: Mark and Barbara Lemmon

WINEMAKERS: Jeff Ritchey and Sabrine
Rodems

TASTING ROOM: Two

DAYS/HOURS: Tuesday–Sunday 11 A.M.–
5 P.M.

ADDRESS: 19 E. Carmel Valley Rd., Carmel
Valley, CA 93924; 35801 Foothill Rd.,
Soledad, CA 93960; 831-659-7322 (Carmel
Valley); 831-678-2992 (Soledad);
831-659-3725 (Carmel Valley fax);
831-678-2525 (winery fax); sansaba.com

WINES/GRAPE VARIETIES: Cabernet
Sauvignon, Chardonnay, Merlot,
Sauvignon Blanc, Pinot Noir

WINE CLUB: Yes

TASTING ROOM AMENITIES: Picnic area,
merchandise

REGION: Monterey County AVA

SAN SABA® Estate
2006
Sauvignon Blanc
Monterey

750 ML   ALCOHOL 13.5% BY VOL

Dr. Mark Lemmon's father was an architect in Dallas, Texas. An ardent Francophile, he took the family on frequent vacations to Europe, where young Mark received his early exposure to wine culture. His father photographed architectural details for upcoming projects while Mark took photos in the wine regions of France. These experiences formed the basis for his early appreciation of fine food and wine. After service during World War II and Korea, Mark returned to Texas, where he became chief of staff at Gaston Episcopal Hospital in Dallas and became renowned for pioneering the modern face-lift procedure. While still a practicing cosmetic surgeon in Texas, Mark looked for other interests to occupy his time and energies after retirement, forming partnerships with other physicians looking to invest in vineyards. When he came to Monterey County and saw the surrounding Santa Lucia Highlands, he was struck by the similarities to regions he had visited in France as a young man. After viewing the current River Road property, he struck out on his own and took a chance, buying it with his wife, Barbara, in 1975, a purchase that made him one of the earliest of the modern growers in the county, along with Rich Smith at Paraiso and Doug Meador at Ventana. From his years of tasting and appreciating fine wines from around the world, he knew he had a good palate and decided to trust it. Mark retired from medical practice in 1995, and he and Barbara now devote their attention to the day-to-day business of the winery. The first Cabernet Sauvignon grapes from the San Saba vineyard were made into wine by McFarland (now Blackstone) in 1981 and released in 1984. After McFarland was bought out, Steve McIntyre, the viticulturist at Smith & Hook, started the Monterey-Pacific vineyard management company, and Mark was his first client; they maintain their relationship to this day.

In those early years Cabernet Sauvignon was the only wine produced, and Mark literally sold it by hand, taking it around to stores and restaurants. Convinced of the quality of the grapes coming out of the vineyard, he knew he needed a full-time winemaker and hired Joel Burnstein in 1994. Joel strengthened the label by adding Chardonnay and Merlot and starting Bocage, the second label at San Saba. For nine years Joel did it all, and his efforts were rewarded with critical acclaim. In fact, for a time San Saba was rated one of the top wineries in the region, producing world-class Chardonnay. In 2002 Mark decided it was time to renovate the vineyards and take the winery in a new direction. Joel left to start Marilyn Remark, and Jeff Ritchey came aboard. He has a master's degree from UC Davis and formerly worked at Buena Vista, Gundlach Bundschu, and Clos LaChance. Sabrine Rodems, after a short time with Gloria Ferrer, joined San Saba in 2004. She also holds a master's degree from Davis. Jeff and Sabrine work together to produce wines from one of the oldest vineyards in Monterey County. The new state-of-the-art winery and hospitality center are now open and ready for business.

RECOMMENDED WINES: Managing Director Claire Marlin recommends the Bocage Chardonnay. The 2004 was tasted from the tank and showed a light green color in the glass—expected from a white wine still in its infancy. The nose showed grapefruit, citrus peel, lemon juice, and hints of mango. The lovely ripe fruit presents intimations of sweetness on the tongue, but is well balanced by the acidity in the wine. The finish is crisp and clean in this unoaked wine. Drink now and over the next two to three years.

I recommend the San Saba Chardonnay. The 2004 was tasted from the barrel and had already developed a lovely gold hue. The wine's aromatics are lovely with minerality present, soft vanilla from the oak, and a honeyed sweetness to the fruit of apples, pears, mangoes, and a touch of field-ripened pineapple. This wine comes alive in the mouth, with excellent minerality and acidity supporting the lush fruit. The finish is long and creamy. After a year in the bottle this Chardonnay will be very good and continue to improve over the next two to four years. This wine was recently named the third-best Chardonnay in the world under $15 by *Wine Enthusiast*.

RATING: Two stars (three stars Bocage; whites represent a fine value)

Scheid Vineyards

OWNERS: Scheid family and stockholders

WINEMAKER: Dave Nagengast

TASTING ROOM: Yes

DAYS/HOURS: Daily 11 A.M.–5 P.M.

ADDRESS: 1972 Hobson Ave., Greenfield, CA 93927; 831-386-0316; 831-386-0127 (fax); scheidvineyards.com

WINES/GRAPE VARIETIES: Cabernet Sauvignon, Chardonnay, claret, Gewürztraminer, Merlot, Pinot Noir, Riesling, Sauvignon Blanc, Syrah

WINE CLUB: Yes

TASTING ROOM AMENITIES: Picnic area, merchandise

REGION: Monterey County AVA

In the six years I have lived in Paso Robles, more than fifty wineries have opened or earned building permits there. In that same time just two wineries opened in Monterey County, a statistic that Scott Scheid says has to change. Scott is currently a director of the Monterey County Vintners and Growers Association (MCVGA) and, more important, is now the president and CEO of Scheid Vineyards, which has nearly 6,000 acres under management and cultivation. From those acres about 5,000 cases of wine are produced for Scheid wines, and the rest, totaling more than 2 million cases, go to supply other wineries. Scott is adamant about the county adopting a new general plan that includes a River Road Wine Corridor, but that will require changing current land-use policies. If the county commits, new artisanal wineries can be established, which will benefit everyone, including wine tourists, the wineries, and Monterey County.

Scheid Vineyards got its start growing grapes in 1972 thanks to Scott's father, Alfred, and coinvestor E. F. Hutton & Co. In those early days the grapes were sold primarily to Almaden. In 1988 Al, who holds a graduate degree from Harvard Business School, bought out the Hutton & Co. interests and became sole owner. Al is also a founder of the California Association of Winegrape Growers and the MCVGA, and Scott serves on both as a director. Scott, a graduate of Claremont Men's College, holds a degree in economics and started as an options trader with Hutton in New York. He came to Scheid in 1986 to serve as vice president and became the CEO in 2002. Scheid is a publicly traded company and has state-of-the-art technology in the vineyards it manages, such as VitWatch, which provides wireless access points for weather stations, moisture gauges, and cameras. This system gives the winemaker, Dave Nagengast, real-time data on conditions in the vineyards.

RECOMMENDED WINES: Scott recommends the Chardonnay. The 2003 is gold in the glass, with a nose of citrus, apple, pears, toast, and minerals. The wine has excellent acidity and lies wonderfully on the tongue. The fruit is fine, the finish is fresh and clean, and the wine is ready for the table now but will give an additional two to four years of fine drinking. This is very competently made Chardonnay.

I recommend the Syrah. The 2002 is almost opaque in the glass and a pretty cherry-red color. The aromatics suggest blackberries, black cherries, black currants, earth, and smoke. The wine shows a wonderful balance and integration of all its elements, but the joy here is the lovely ripe fruit. The ripeness is excellent, the mouthfeel wonderful, and the finish is elegant and long. Drink now and over the next three to six years.

RATING: Two stars (competently made whites and reds)

Silver Mountain Vineyards

OWNER: Jerold O'Brien

WINEMAKER: Jerold O'Brien

TASTING ROOM: Yes

DAYS/HOURS: Daily 11 A.M.–6 P.M.

ADDRESS: 381 Cannery Row, Ste. Q, Monterey, CA 93940; 831-644-9609; 831-644-9608 (fax); silvermtn.com

WINES/GRAPE VARIETIES: Alloy (Bordeaux blend), Chardonnay (organically grown), Pinot Noir, Zinfandel

WINE CLUB: Yes

TASTING ROOM AMENITIES: Merchandise

REGION: Monterey County AVA

The Air Force brought Jerold O'Brien, now a retired pilot, to Monterey. He started his education at community college but at age nineteen decided he needed to pursue other activities. He ran away to join the military and entered the cadet program for pilot training in 1960. At that time in the service, adult beverages were "mandatory," and since Jerold liked wine better than beer, his interest in that beverage was piqued. As he traveled, he broadened his knowledge by trying wines from different countries, and when he returned to San Francisco he met people in the wine industry, including Joe Swan from Sonoma and Dick Graff at Chalone. He was impressed by their ethos, wherein a man could still make a deal on the basis of a handshake and help other vintners in need.

In the 1970s Jerold invested in silver commodities, made some money, and used his profits as the down payment on his vineyard property, an abandoned orchard with no access road. Jerold built a house and planted grapes. He received his bond in 1979, converting the barn to a winery. In 1980 he retired from the Air Force and focused his attention full-time on winemaking and grape growing. As fate would have it, the winery was located two miles from the epicenter of the October 17, 1989, Loma Prieta earthquake, at the time the most costly natural disaster in the history of the United States. The winery was destroyed, his house was severely damaged, and he lost three years of production. He put together a new business plan, secured loans from FEMA, and started the long and arduous process of rebuilding his winery and his life. It took six years, but in 1995 the new winery was in place and production started again. Jake O'Brien, his son, now manages the tasting room and all IT for the winery operation.

RECOMMENDED WINES: Jerold recommends the Estate Chardonnay. The 2001 is a lovely gold in the glass. The nose is soft vanilla, pineapple, guava, and honeyed fruit. The fine, ripe fruit leaves impressions of sweetness on the tongue but is nicely balanced by the acidity in the wine. The hint of vanilla oak gives additional structure. If you are a fan of Chardonnay that has a touch of honeyed sweetness, drink this one now and over the next three years.

I suggest the Alloy, a blend of Bordeaux varieties such as Merlot, Cabernet Sauvignon, and

Cabernet Franc. I tasted the 1997, almost opaque in the glass and a pretty black cherry color. The nose is black cherries, cinnamon spice, vanilla from the oak, and black currants. The wine shows fine integration of the fruit and tannins, making it ready for the table. Drink now and over the next two years.

RATING: One star (good, drinkable wines)

Talbott Vineyards

OWNERS: Robb and Cynthia Talbott

WINEMAKER: I. C. Balderas

TASTING ROOM: Yes

DAYS/HOURS: Daily 11 A.M.–5 P.M.

ADDRESS: 53 W. Carmel Valley Rd., Carmel Valley, CA 93924; 831-659-3500; 831-659-3515 (fax); talbottvineyards.com

WINES/GRAPE VARIETIES: Chardonnay, Pinot Noir

WINE CLUB: Yes

TASTING ROOM AMENITIES: Picnic area, merchandise

REGION: Santa Lucia Highlands AVA

In 1950 Robert F. Talbott, formerly an investment banker, and his wife, Audrey, a former model, started a small business in Carmel producing some of the finest neckwear and silk accessories in California. Audrey sewed the ties and Robert sold them out of the back of his station wagon up and down the coast. During trips to Europe to visit silk mills and buy silk, they became interested in French and Italian wines. They incorporated wine into their family life at home, serving wine with the evening meal. As the business grew, they moved to Cannery Row, but a fire in the early 1970s brought them back to Carmel; it also brought son Robb home from teaching to help reestablish the business.

Their many trips to Europe convinced Robb that the Europeans had it right when it came to winemaking techniques. He believed that UC Davis–influenced winemakers were straying too far from proven European winemaking. In 1982 Robb and his wife, Cynthia, planted the 24-acre Diamond T estate vineyard with Chardonnay vines at their home in Carmel Valley, using Burgundian techniques. In the same year they started construction on a winery in the Cachagua area of Carmel Valley. That facility was eventually sold to Bernardus in 1988, paving the way for the current facility. After great success with their initial Chardonnay, the 1984 vintage proved problematic and, because it did not meet the Talbott family's high standards, was never released. In 1985 I. C. ("Sam") Balderas came to the winery to lend his expertise, and as his skills became evident, he was offered the position of winemaker and has remained to this day. In fact, the 1985 vintage, on which he worked, was released to high critical acclaim. Over time, the Talbotts have added acreage to their vineyard holdings. The new winery was built in 1990, and in 1994 the Sleepy Hollow vineyard in the Santa Lucia Highlands was purchased. As a result, since 1994 all wines released from Talbott feature fruit exclusively from Talbott estate vineyards.

Lee Codding, a graduate of Cal Poly's Communication Studies Department, is the director of marketing and sales. In addition to the Talbott line, there are three labels named after the children: Case, Logan, and Kali Hart.

RECOMMENDED WINES: Lee recommends the Sleepy Hollow Chardonnay. The 2001 is gold in the glass. The nose shows vanilla oak, pineapple, apples, pears, citrus, and minerals. The acidity supporting the lovely fruit is crisp and tart. The nose is refined in the Burgundian fashion. The oak in this wine will carry it another five to seven years, but it is showing beautifully now.

I recommend the Case Pinot Noir. The 2000 is almost opaque in the glass and a bright cherry-red color. The wine has wonderful aromatics of red cherry, red currants, blackberries, lavender, and raspberries. The fruit is lush and ripe, with a wonderful, elegant presence in the mouth. The finish is outstanding, and the generous, ripe tannins in this wine suggest a long life ahead. Drink now and over the next six to eight years.

RATING: Three stars (Estate wines four stars)

Ventana Vineyards/Meador Estate

OWNERS: Douglas and LuAnn Meador

WINEMAKERS: Douglas Meador, Reggie Hammond, and Miguel Martinez

TASTING ROOM: Yes

DAYS/HOURS: Daily 11 A.M.–5 P.M.

ADDRESS: 2999 Monterey-Salinas Hwy., Monterey, CA 93940; 831-372-7415; 831-655-1855 (fax); ventanawines.com

WINES/GRAPE VARIETIES: Beaugravier (blend), Cabernet Franc, Cabernet Sauvignon, Chardonnay, Chenin Blanc, Due Amici (blend), Dry Rosado (blend), Gewürztraminer, Grenache, Magnus (blend), Merlot, Orange Muscat, Pinot Noir, Riesling, Sauvignon Blanc, Syrah

WINE CLUB: Yes

TASTING ROOM AMENITIES: Merchandise

REGION: Arroyo Seco AVA

Wenatchee, Washington, home to the Apple Blossom Festival, is also the hometown of Doug Meador. Son of an apple orchardist, Doug attended the University of Washington, then joined the Navy and flew A4s during two combat tours of duty in Vietnam. After his service, he formed a limited partnership in 1972 to plant 2,500 acres of vineyards in Monterey County. He would give that project about three years to succeed, then return home to Wenatchee and take up life again as an apple baron. In the meantime, he was making money off his pals in dice games and sending it home to his father to buy more land for orchards. The tax laws of that era were conducive to partnerships for grape growing, but when the laws were changed investors took their money elsewhere. This afforded Doug the opportunity in the late 1970s to take 300 of those original acres and turn them into Ventana Vineyards. He was convinced that the area could become a world-class producer of wine grapes, and went to work to prove his case.

Doug knew what he had in terms of his soils, climate, and cool growing conditions. It didn't take him long to figure out that most of the viticultural practices then being used were flat-out wrong for the area: the spacing between vines was wrong, the trellising was wrong, the wrong clones were growing in the wrong soils, and so on. He saw the situation as French mythology filtered through British writings. Moreover, he found the wine scholarship of the time to be useless for his needs. He did his own research, changed the growing practices for his *terroir,* and started winning medal after medal. In fact, his vineyard has won more gold medals than any other single vineyard in the United States. As a result, other vintners in the area noticed his success and changed their farming practices.

Currently, he sells about 70 percent of his grapes to other wineries, holding back the rest for his own wines. Doug readily shares his new ideas and practices, thus fostering the rise and development of Monterey County viticulture and winemaking. For example, his clonal research to develop the correct Sauvignon Blanc grape for the area resulted in wines that no longer had a characteristic vegetal or overly herbaceous taste. He was by ten years the first to grow Syrah in the county. He was the first to introduce the great Spanish grape Tempranillo, which he believes has a great future in the region. His wife, LuAnn, will tell you that in spite of his trailblazing efforts, Doug still hasn't gotten all the credit he deserves, a claim that Kendall-Jackson and Mondavi heartily agree with.

Doug and LuAnn met more than twenty years ago when she was in the banking business and he was recently divorced. One dinner together and a partnership flourished. She has been instrumental in developing the idea of agricultural hospitality in the county. The Meador Estate line of wines—the result of Doug's *terroir* studies— are aged longer and produced in limited quantities; they are sold at the winery, high-end retail stores, and restaurants. The winemaking is done by the team of Douglas Meador, Reggie Hammond, and Miguel Martinez.

RECOMMENDED WINES: LuAnn recommends the Magnus, a Bordeaux blend of Cabernet Sauvignon, Merlot, and Cabernet Franc. The 2001 is almost opaque in the glass and purple and black in color. The nose is black cherries, cassis, cinnamon spice from the French oak barrels, raspberries, and blackberries. This is a superb blend, and the wine shows wonderful integration of all its elements. The fine ripe fruit and excellent tannic grip give it complexity and structure. The finish lasts nearly a minute. Drink now, but the tannins in this wine suggest that it will improve with age over the next five to eight years.

I suggest the Block 9 Chardonnay. The 2001 is liquid gold in the glass. The nose is a classic show of apples, pears, honeycomb, mangoes, minerals, and cinnamon toast. The wine is superb in the mouth, given the ripe, luscious fruit. The excellent acidity pairs beautifully with its minerality to make for a complex, well-integrated wine. Drink now and over the next two to four years.

RATING: Three stars (Meador Estate line merits four stars)

Wines of Carmel

OWNERS: Paul Stokes and Lynn Sakasegawa Stokes

WINEMAKER: Lynn Sakasegawa Stokes; Paul Stokes is the vineyard manager.

TASTING ROOM: At A Taste of Monterey

DAYS/HOURS: Daily 11 A.M.–6 P.M.

ADDRESS: A Taste of Monterey, 700 Cannery Row, Monterey, CA 93940; 831-659-0750 (phone and fax); winesofcarmel.com

WINES/GRAPE VARIETIES: Chardonnay, Cabernet Sauvignon

WINE CLUB: Yes

REGION: Carmel Valley AVA

CHAPTER 7

The Mid-Central Coast
(San Luis Obispo County)

WINE HISTORY

The Cuesta Grade, which passes through the La Panza range of the Los Padres National Forest at about 1,500 feet, divides San Luis Obispo County into north and south. A southerly descent from the summit provides breathtaking vistas of the hills unfolding in the valleys below. The county derives its name from the San Luis Obispo de Tolosa mission, which also gave its name to the city, home of California Polytechnic State University (where I teach). The city also holds the distinction of being one of the first areas in the county to produce wine.

In 1772 Father Junípero Serra established the mission in what is now downtown San Luis Obispo and there received plantings of Mission grapes. By the 1820s, according to Cal Poly historian Dan Krieger, Father José Sánchez was making 400 barrels of wine a year. In what is now Mitchell Park in San Luis Obispo, Father Luis Antonio Martínez produced 100 barrels of wine per year from a vineyard near the Dallidet Adobe. After the vineyards were abandoned because of the secularization of the missions, Pierre Hypolite Dallidet restored them to vigor in the 1860s, and the wine trade flourished for a time in the area, with other growers following his lead by planting vineyards. For example, after buying property in 1878, Henry Ditmas and his wife, Rosa, planted the first vineyard near Lopez Lake (in today's Arroyo Grande Valley AVA) in 1879. The remote Ditmas vineyard, which lies to the south and east of San Luis Obispo in the upper reaches of the Arroyo Grande Valley, allegedly produced wine throughout Prohibition despite the best efforts of federal agents, who were unable to find it.

Some of the Zinfandel vine stock there dates back to the first plantings by the Ditmases in the 1880s, making it among the oldest on the Central Coast. Bill Greenough, the current owner of the property, told me that the Ditmas family moved to the 560-acre ranch in 1878 and a year later planted Zinfandel and Muscat. Greenough purchased the land, originally called Rancho Saucelito after the many willows on the property, in 1974 from the grand-daughters of the owners and founders of the vineyard.

Abram B. Hasbrouck came to California in 1866 from the East Coast via Colorado and later moved next to the Ditmas family. He bought Rancho Arroyo Grande, a spread of 4,437 acres, in 1883 and established Rancho St. Remy. The property, originally a Spanish land grant, supported the mission at San Luis Obispo de Tolosa. St. Remy was already renowned for its cattle and cheese, but Hasbrouck, impressed with neighbor Ditmas's vineyard, planted about 40 acres of the vast dairy ranch to vines. He built a winery that processed wines from grapes grown at his ranch and at Rancho Saucelito and eventually garnered a reputation for his estate-bottled wines. After Rosa divorced Henry Ditmas, she hopped the fence and married neighbor Hasbrouck. In 1915 phylloxera, the root louse, destroyed the St. Remy vineyard, but Rosa kept the winery going with Rancho Saucelito grapes. Faced with the difficulties of running a winery by herself during Prohibition, Rosa eventually closed the winery and leased the Rancho Saucelito property to tenants who maintained the vineyard and wine production into the 1940s, after which it was abandoned. When Rosa died in 1927, her son Cecil Ditmas inherited both properties. He sold St. Remy but passed Rancho Saucelito on to his daughters, who sold to the Greenough family in 1974. Bill and Nancy Greenough learned that the vineyard had Zinfandel vines dating back to the 1880s. In a remote canyon 5 miles west of Arroyo Grande, they planted the Saucelito vineyard in 1982 from Zinfandel cuttings taken from the historic original vineyard.

In the early 1970s the Paragon and Chamisal vineyards were planted in the Edna Valley AVA, with Andy MacGregor's vineyard following in 1975. In 1982, at the mouth of the valley, the famous French house Champagne Deutz selected Arroyo Grande for Maison Deutz, its new American venture for the production of sparkling wines. In 1997 Jean-Claude Tardivat purchased the winery and named it after his daughter, Laetitia, changing the focus from sparkling wines to Burgundy-style wines. John Alban came to the valley in 1989 and planted the first vineyard in the United States dedicated to the Rhône-style varieties Viognier, Syrah, Roussanne, and Grenache. In so doing, he revolutionized thinking about which grape varieties from the south of France could grow and flourish on the Central Coast. He firmly established the region's reputation as an outstanding location for growing and producing Rhône-style wines.

About 25 miles north of the Cuesta Grade, the small town of El Paso de Robles also grew in size and in its reputation for water and wine. The early inhabitants of the Paso Robles area were the Salinan Indians, attracted by the natural hot springs there. Both the mission fathers, who arrived next, and their congregations took thermal baths in the waters. The Salinan Indians and the padres all referred to the area as Agua Caliente (hot water or springs). Father Fermín Lasuén established the mission at San Miguel Arcángel in 1797, about 8 miles north of El Paso de Robles. The Mexican land grant El Paso de Robles (one of ten) consisted of approximately 26,000 acres and was awarded originally to Pedro Narváez, then captain of the port of Monterey, in 1844. An absentee owner, he passed the ranch to Petronilo Ríos, who filed a claim for the land with the U.S. government in 1852. He received the patent for the land only in 1866, some nine years after he had sold it in its entirety to James H. Blackburn, Daniel Drew Blackburn, and Lazarus Godehaux.

When Southern Pacific extended the railroad from San Miguel to Templeton in 1886, it caused a building and population boom. A site for the town of Paso Robles was mapped around the hot springs. The town officially incorporated as a city on March 11, 1889. The main spring for the thermal baths supplied water for a bathhouse in 1864, and this became the site of the first hotel, Hotel El Paso de Robles, started in 1891 and completed in 1900. Due to its abundance of almond orchards, Paso Robles earned the nickname "Almond City." Outlying ranches that once harbored horses and cattle or grew grains or fruit have largely been converted to vineyards.

Arriving from Indiana, Andrew York established the first commercial winery in 1882 in the hills west of Templeton. He planted Mission grapes, Zinfandel, and Alicante Bouschet in a former apple orchard. He also built a small stone winery near a plot of grapevines that came with the land and called it Ascension Winery. Some of the original stone walls are still in place, and the winery, now called York Mountain Winery, is the oldest in San Luis Obispo County. It also has its own AVA. James R. Anderson had a small winery next to York Mountain around 1882, north of the Cuesta Grade and west of Paso Robles.

Another Paso Roblan important in the early history of grape growing in the area, Gerd Klintworth, emigrated from Germany in 1883 and moved to Paso Robles in 1886. Before his arrival, he had lived in Orange County, where he worked on a 360-acre vineyard. He brought his knowledge of viticulture north with his wife, Ilsabe, and the two bought land in the Geneseo/Linne area southeast of Paso Robles, where they planted almonds, a fruit orchard, and a vineyard. His granddaughter Violet Ernst remembers that her grandfather's small winery had a dirt floor but produced good wine: he sold Zinfandel, claret, port, and the white wine called Angelica. Klintworth's son Henry took over the winery at the turn of the century. Although the land remains in the family, the vineyard is no longer producing.

The next important vintner in the history of the area is Adolphe Siot, a Frenchman who planted Zinfandel grapes west of Templeton. He arrived from France with his wife, Paulina, in 1890, planted the vineyard, and established a small winery. In 1908 he sold the winery to the Rotta family, whose descendants own it today. In 1907 Mel Casteel planted the Casteel vineyards of Willow Creek. A vineyard present on the property that he purchased south and west of Paso Robles still grew some of the old Mission grapevines. According to local historian Cindy Rankin, the Casteel vineyard is also reputed to have some of the oldest Zinfandel clones in California. Ten years later, Lorenzo and Cesarina Nerelli planted a vineyard at the foot of York Mountain. After Prohibition was repealed, the Nerellis' Templeton Winery was the first in the region to resume winemaking. Frank Pesenti, who worked for the York brothers, planted Zinfandel grapevines in 1923 near the Rotta Winery with cuttings from his neighbor Adolphe Siot, and he established the Pesenti Winery in 1934. The Pesenti and Nerelli families ultimately intermarried and merged their businesses. Frank Nerelli, following in the footsteps of his father, Aldo Nerelli, and his grandfather Frank Pesenti, now produces wines at Zin Alley, not too far from the family's original winery.

The Zinfandel grape and classical music combined to thrust Paso Robles into early international prominence as a winegrowing region with the arrival of Polish pianist Ignacy Jan Paderewski. During a West Coast tour in 1913, pain in his right arm forced him to cancel several appearances. A fellow musician told him about Paso Robles and its curative mud baths. Paderewski acted on his friend's suggestion, booked passage to Paso Robles, and stayed for three weeks. One day while Paderewski was in repose, immersed up to his neck in the soothing mud baths, the physician in attendance at the Paso Robles Hotel, where the great pianist was staying, convinced him to buy land in the area. According to Paderewski, "I could not protest, I could not resist, and he never gave up. I must add in justice, however, that I was a quite willing victim, for I really loved the place and was very grateful besides." He showed his gratitude by buying a 2,000-acre mountain ranch in the Adelaida area, west of Paso Robles. He named the place Rancho San Ignacio after himself and planted it with almond trees.

A virtuoso pianist, Paderewski's concert schedule required him to be largely an absentee landlord, but in the early 1920s, after serving as Poland's prime minister for a year, he returned to the ranch. This time, he decided to plant a vineyard. His friend and noted viticulturist of the time, University of California at Berkeley professor Frederic Theodore Bioletti, helped him establish the vineyard. Bioletti recommended that Paderewski plant Petite Sirah grapes on the eastern slopes of his ranch and reserve the highest section for Zinfandel. After several years of producing disappointing wines, Paderewski the pianist took the matter in hand and became Paderewski the winemaker. He trucked a load of Zinfandel grapes to his neighbors at the Ascension Winery, where he and Andrew York crushed the grapes. Four years later, he transferred his wine in the bottle to the vault at Rancho San Ignacio for storage. The Eighteenth Amendment had signaled the arrival of Prohibition in 1919, but fortunately, the Volstead Act permitted production of 200 gallons per year for personal use. The Twenty-first Amendment repealed the Eighteenth, and after Prohibition Paderewski sent a sample of his personally made Zinfandel to the California State Fair, where it won first prize in its class.

As early as the 1920s, Amedeo Martinelli came to Templeton from Milan, Italy, and planted a new vineyard of Zinfandel and other red grapes. Sylvester and Caterina Dusi planted the now-renowned Dusi vineyards and heralded the arrival of several other Italian immigrants to the area, such as the Bianchi, Vosti, and Busi families, all of whom established vineyards there. In the late 1960s, following advice from renowned winemaker André Tchelistcheff, Dr. Stanley Hoffman planted Pinot Noir, Cabernet Sauvignon, and Chardonnay in the hills of Adelaida. Hoffman Mountain Ranch became the first large-scale modern facility on the west side of Paso Robles. Bob Young started the first east-side large-scale winery on the Shandon heights (now Rancho Dos Amigos). Herman Schwartz planted the 500-acre Rancho Tierra Rejada in 1973, and Gary Eberle and his partners founded Estrella River Winery in 1977. In 1988 they sold the property, and new winemaker Chuck Ortman's wife changed the name to Meridian Vineyards. The Paso Robles and York Mountain AVA designations were granted in 1983 under the sponsorship of then-mayor Gary Stemper, now owner of Eagle Crest Winery.

TERROIR

The Paso Robles AVA is one of the larger appellations in the Central Coast AVA. It is the high point of the Salinas Valley, which runs north and west and up through Monterey County to the sea. The county line is about 8 miles north of Paso Robles. The Salinas River is the geographical dividing line between what are called the east and west sides of the Paso Robles winegrowing region. In fact, today there is talk of denominating the sections as separate appellations. Given the climatic conditions and the soils of the region, a good argument can be made for the separation. In fact, Doug Beckett, owner of Peachy Canyon Winery, leading a consortium of twenty-one wineries on the west side, presented a petition for a new Westside AVA to the TTB on November 23, 2005. If approved, the Westside AVA within the greater Paso Robles AVA would run from the Cuesta Grade in the south up to the Monterey County line. The Santa Lucia Mountains would demarcate the western border and the Salinas River the eastern edge, the only difference from the current Paso Robles AVA, which now runs eastward to the Kern County line.

The east side is much hotter than the west and receives less rain. On the west side, altitudes can reach 1,700 feet (for example, York Mountain Winery sits at 1,640 feet). The west side is influenced by fog coming through the Templeton Gap, but the fog can also move into the east side. Both sides experience large temperature swings from daytime to nighttime, more so on the east side as one moves farther inland, out of the hills and onto river terraces and hilly grasslands studded with oak trees. On the east side, there are more alkaline soils of sandy and clay loam. On the west, there is rich calcareous limestone and some montmorillonite, a porous clay mineral capable of slowing the progress of water through soils and other rocks and, to some degree, retaining water. Originally found in Montmorillon, France, it is the main constituent in a volcanic ash called bentonite.

The Paso Robles AVA is known for its outstanding Zinfandel, Cabernet Sauvignon, Merlot, and Rhône-style wines such as Syrah, Roussanne, Viognier, and Mourvèdre. An increasing number of growers and vintners are enjoying success with Italian varieties such as Barbera, Sangiovese, and Nebbiolo.

Located within the larger Paso Robles AVA, the York Mountain AVA (1983) is in the hills on the west side of Paso Robles, where the altitude provides for cooler temperatures and greater rainfall atop fairly shallow soils. This AVA was created to honor the York brothers and their original winery, Ascension, the oldest commercial winery in San Luis Obispo County. Also one of the smallest AVAs in California, York Mountain is home to only one winery. Max and Stephen Goldman, then owners of the winery, were the original petitioners. Most of the vineyards are at an altitude of some 1,500 feet on the eastern slopes of the Santa Lucia Mountains. Only 7 miles from the Pacific, the area is cooler than Paso Robles and receives much more rain atop the low-vigor soil on the steep slopes. Martin & Weyrich is currently the owner of this historic winery, which dates its inception to 1882.

As you travel south from Paso Robles over the Cuesta Grade and down into the city of San Luis Obispo and the neighboring Edna Valley, the temperature moderates. You can also see the famous Nine Sisters of San Luis Obispo, locally called the Morros, a series of nine volcanic plugs formed about 25 million years ago. They run from Islay Hill in San Luis Obispo to Morro Rock in Morro Bay. The Edna Valley AVA (1987) is south of San Luis Obispo and extends to the ocean. Bounded by mountains on one side, the valley is a pocket of land vented by Price Canyon, which admits fog off the ocean at nearby Pismo Beach, less than 5 miles away. A cooling afternoon wind from Morro Bay, about 15 miles away and to the northwest, helps give Edna Valley one of the longest growing seasons in all of California. As one would expect, the soils are rich black humus in addition to marine sediments, with pockets of decomposed granite and tufa, a type of limestone formed when calcium carbonates settle out of water as a solid. The east-west–oriented valley in the shadow of volcanic mountains has the distinct microclimate André Tchelistcheff predicted would be ideal for growing high-quality grapes. Here exists a transverse valley that opens to the ocean and admits the morning marine layer and the cool afternoon winds, and this area is particularly well suited to the growing of Chardonnay, Pinot Noir, and Rhône-style grapes.

Arroyo Grande Valley AVA (1990), the southernmost appellation in San Luis Obispo County, has light soil of marine deposits and some clay loam. The valley is about 16 miles long and runs east and northeast, permitting coastal fog and cool breezes to moderate the climate. The climate in the mountains tends to be warmer than the areas closer to the coast. South of Arroyo Grande and once again on Highway 101—El Camino Real—the wine traveler crosses the county border into Santa Maria and the start of Santa Barbara County.

 **WINERIES AND PROFILES**

Adelaida Cellars

WINERY OWNERS: Elizabeth and Don and Van Steenwyk

WINEMAKER: Terry Culton

TASTING ROOM: Yes

DAYS/HOURS: Daily 11 A.M.–5 P.M.

ADDRESS: 5805 Adelaida Rd., Paso Robles, CA 93446; 805-239-8980; 805-239-4671 (fax); adelaida.com

WINES/GRAPE VARIETIES: Cabernet Sauvignon, Chardonnay, dessert wine, Pinot Noir, Rhône varieties, Syrah, Viognier, Zinfandel

WINE CLUB: Yes

TASTING ROOM AMENITIES: Picnic area, merchandise

REGION: Paso Robles AVA

Terry Culton is the winemaker at Adelaida, though his first degree is in speech communication. This has prepared him rather nicely for dealing with wine writers and interviewers. His degree in psychology probably helps, too. For a time he put that degree to work in protective services, even as he worked the crush at Creston Manor. When Ken Volk, then at Wild Horse, offered him a job as a cellar rat, he saw the writing on the cellar walls. He went north for a time to Oregon's Willamette Valley Vineyards and took the training he got working with Volk into the Pinot Noir vineyards. By 2000 he was assistant winemaker at Calera. But let us backtrack a bit.

Paso Robles's renowned enology iconoclast John Munch and friend Neil Collins started Adelaida in the early 1980s. Collins now makes excellent wines for Tablas Creek, and Munch has established his unique presence at Le Cuvier. For a time, Jon Priest made the wines for Adelaida after the departure of the inimitable duo of Munch and Collins, so Terry blended the 2002s left in the barrel. He first placed his individual mark on the 2003 vintage. Terry remembers that while he was working for Volk at Wild Horse, the old Hidden Mountain Ranch vineyard—among Paso's earliest post-Prohibition—would sell its Pinot Noir fruit to Volk. Once the Van Steenwyk family took controlling interest of HMR and Adelaida, that fruit began to go into Adelaida wines.

As for the current owners, Don Van Steenwyk runs a worldwide high-tech company and generally leaves the operation of the winery to his wife, Elizabeth, a former broadcast journalist and a writer of children's books. When the Van Steenwyks hired Terry, he was allowed to bring in his own team. He loves the camaraderie at the winery and the fact that folks in the area continue to help each other. His connections with Volk, Collins, and Munch certainly help in that regard. Given his history and background, Terry hopes to elevate Pinot Noir at Adelaida and restore it to the preeminent position it enjoyed in the 1960s when Dr. Stanley Hoffman of HMR rocked the Pinot Noir world with his wines from the sticks of then little-known Paso Robles.

RECOMMENDED WINES: Terry suggests the HMR Pinot Noir from the vineyard planted in 1963. We tasted various barrel samples of what was to become the 2003 blend. The cherry and plum fruit shows excellent physiological ripeness, which contributes to a rich, velvety mouthfeel. The tannins are ripe and round, boding well for the wine's future. Once all the components are blended and married together, I expect this will become a heady, sensuous glass of Pinot Noir.

In the recently remodeled tasting room, I found the 2002 Syrah to be my favorite. Dropped into 100 percent French oak, this is an opaque black cherry–colored wine with a wonderful nose of truffles, café au lait, and roast lamb under the cherry fruit. Given the wine's aromatics and the lovely fruit, it is ready for drinking now but will give pleasure three years ahead.

RATING: Two → three stars (Terry Culton is revitalizing the line and improving the overall quality of the wines)

AJB Vineyards

WINERY OWNER: A. John Berardo

WINEMAKER: A. John Berardo

TASTING ROOM: Yes

DAYS/HOURS: Saturday–Sunday 12–5 P.M.

ADDRESS: 3280 Township Rd., Paso Robles, CA 93446; 805-239-9432; 805-239-1931 (fax); ajbvineyards.com

WINES/GRAPE VARIETIES: Nebbiolo, Super Tuscan (blend), Sangiovese, Syrah, Viognier, Zinfandel

WINE CLUB: Yes

TASTING ROOM AMENITIES: Picnic area, merchandise, rental apartment above the winery

REGION: Paso Robles AVA

First impressions are often deceptive: by looking at him, one wouldn't think that A. John Berardo was a successful Manhattan Beach dentist. Being a dentist is how John earned his living for many years in the same sense that his wife, Marilyn, now retired, dedicated her life to education. Then again, when meeting Dr. Berardo in the context of his vineyard and winery, his hair slicked back and curling at the nape of the neck, his brown, bowed legs sticking out of his work shorts, his feet covered by dust and sandals, one comes away with the impression that this is a winemaker. I don't think anything else suits him quite as well at this time in his life. There is certainly the family influence of an Italian heritage. His father and brothers, all ardent amateur winemakers, bottled wine at his grandmother's home. Young John would watch, fascinated and amazed at the activity that surrounded the pressing of the juice, the racking, the fining, the manipulation of the wine, the bottling, and the corking. His father went so far as to build the family's new house with a barrel room underneath. That can be taken only as amateur winemaking with serious intent.

John's father tried mightily to dissuade his son from a life spent among the vineyards and the barrels by convincing him to become a dentist—first. Ever the obedient son, and given the family predilection for orthodontics (one brother owns a dental lab), John went off to dental school, returned with a degree, and established a flourishing practice by the ocean. His métier afforded him a comfortable living and the resources that ultimately permitted him to realize his manifest destiny as an Italianate winemaker par excellence. You can see it now in his face: the art of wine is his passion and life.

About twenty years ago, true to the family heritage, he bought some grapes for personal use and made some wine. The first year wasn't bad, he admits, but the second year just didn't ring the bell. He hadn't done anything different in the process: only the quality of the grapes had changed. He learned therein an early and valuable lesson. His sister Joanne, who had worked as a receptionist for thirty-seven years in the dental offices of her father and her brother John, moved to Paso Robles in 1991 and now manages her brother and the tasting room at AJB. In 1992 Dr. Berardo bought land on the west side and planted AJB vineyards, realizing that more often than not, making wine that tastes good starts in the vineyard. The site selected, with its south-facing slopes, was originally part of a Mennonite community that had settled there more than a hundred years ago. Little did they know that the property was sitting on the equivalent of gold in the vineyard business: the soils were mostly limestone. In 1999 John and Marilyn bought some adjacent land, bringing their total acreage to just short of 40. In 1997 and 1998 a consultant was hired to make the wine, but, new bond in hand, John took on those duties thereafter.

The winery gives the Berardos the lifestyle they want. A jack-of-all-trades, John restored and refurbished the original buildings on the site. At this point in his life John is absolutely certain about what he can do and is very happy doing it. He will be the first to tell you that his wines are getting better with each passing year as the vines mature and take full advantage of the special soils and climate. His driving motivation currently is to make wines that he likes to drink, sell some of it to the good people who visit, and enjoy Paso Robles as long as he can.

RECOMMENDED WINES: John recommends the Sangiovese. The 2003 is opaque to the stem and black cherry in color. The nose is smoke, red currants, sweet raspberries, chocolate-coated raisins, and mocha. The wine is full and round in the mouth, well balanced and well integrated. The excellent fruit on the tongue recalls the lovely aromatics. The finish lasted nearly a minute. Give this wine a year to develop and drop some of its tannins and it will reward another five to six years of fine drinking. To my taste, this is one of John's best wines to date.

I recommend the Zinfandel. The 2003 is opaque and black cherry in color. The nose is black cherries, blackberries, black currants, and white pepper. The fruit is ripe and luscious in the mouth, leading to a wonderful mid-palate that recalls the perfume of the aromatics. The finish lingers nearly a minute. This wine is ready for the table now but will give another four to six years of drinking pleasure if you can wait.

I also tasted John's 2005 Viognier from the barrel, and I predict that this will be his breakthrough white wine. It is already excellent.

RATING: Three stars (Berardo's wines have jumped in quality and represent excellent values)

Alapay Cellars

WINERY OWNERS: Scott and Rebecca
    Remmenga

WINEMAKER: Scott Remmenga

TASTING ROOM: Yes

DAYS/HOURS: Daily 10:30 A.M–6 P.M.

ADDRESS: 415 First St., Avila Beach, CA
    93424; 805-595-2632; 805-595-1313 (fax);
    alapaycellars.com

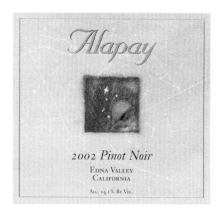

2002 *Pinot Noir*
EDNA VALLEY
CALIFORNIA
ALC. 14.1% BY VOL.

WINES/GRAPE VARIETIES: Beachtown Blush
(rosé Rhône blend), Cabernet Sauvignon,
Chardonnay, late-harvest Moscato,
Merlot, Pinot Noir, Syrah, Viognier,
Zinfandel, Zinfandel port

WINE CLUB: Yes

TASTING ROOM AMENITIES: Merchandise

REGION: San Luis Obispo County

Located in downtown Avila Beach (you can see the ocean from the tasting room), Alapay is the brainchild of Scott and Rebecca Remmenga. If you appreciate the ocean and wine, you have an opportunity to combine both at Alapay, a Chumash word for "heavenly world above." Scott is a native of Santa Barbara and came north to take his degree in graphic communication at Cal Poly in 1986. After working in Los Angeles for a time, he returned to San Luis Obispo, where he opened a print shop with his father. They focused on producing labels for wineries, and the business grew from two employees to twenty-five. He developed friendships with some of the winemakers who would ask for help on the design and printing of their labels. Scott decided he was in the right place at the right time (the Central Coast) to make the move from merely printing labels for bottles to actually filling them with his own wine.

About five years ago, the Alapay label was born. Rebecca handles all the marketing. Scott buys the best-quality fruit he can get his hands on and buys barrels from four coopers in an effort to match the right wood to the right varieties. If he doesn't like a wine, he won't bottle it. Scott emphasizes that he wants to offer his customers premium wines but also give them a great time as he takes care of them in the tasting room. That explains why so many of his customers come back for more. On some of the earlier vintages you might notice the raised dots on the label. Scott introduced the first Braille wine label in the United States. As you taste, take the time to admire the saltwater aquarium in the tasting room.

RECOMMENDED WINES: Scott recommends the Santa Barbara County Viognier. I tasted the 2003, a pale lemon wine with a nose of white peaches, apricots, and orange blossoms. This wine has an excellent mouthfeel, and the acidity makes for a fresh and lively taste on the tongue. The finish is nearly a minute. The wine is vinified dry, but the excellent ripeness of the fruit gives a delightful intimation of sweetness.

I suggest the Paso Robles Rebekah, a blend of Cabernet Sauvignon, Merlot, Cabernet Franc, and Malbec. This Bordeaux-style wine is almost opaque to the stem, showing dark red cherry color in the glass. The nose is cherries, black currants, and mocha coffee. The wine is wonderfully integrated, huge in the mouth, and the finish was more than a minute. This is a powerful but elegant wine that is drinking well now but will reward another six to eight years of age. The Rebekah (spelled the Chumash way), named after Scott's wife, has many gold medals ahead of it.

RATING: Three stars (whites and reds are both very good to excellent)

Alban Vineyards

WINERY OWNER: John Alban

WINEMAKER: John Alban

TASTING ROOM: No

ADDRESS: 8575 Orcutt Rd., Arroyo Grande,
CA 93420; 805-546-0305; 805-546-9879
(fax); albanvineyards.com

WINES/GRAPE VARIETIES: Rhône varieties
such as Grenache, Roussanne, Syrah,
Viognier

WINE CLUB: Mailing list

REGION: Edna Valley AVA

If you are a reader of any of the national wine publications, you are aware of a group of winemakers on the Central Coast called the Rhône Rangers. For those of you new to the term, a short explanation is in order. It just so happens that grape varieties from France's Rhône region grow exceedingly well in some parts of the Central Coast. More than any other, Gary Eberle was the motivational force for bringing Syrah to the area. His analysis of the *terroir* on the Estrella River bench suggested that the growing conditions were ideal for Syrah. When the Hospice du Rhône gathering was started by Mat Garretson and John Alban, bringing in aficionados of Rhône-style wines from around the world to Paso Robles, more and more people began to turn their attention to Rhône varieties coming out of the Central Coast. John Alban is one of the pioneers of this movement, his vineyard being the first in America to focus on Rhône varieties.

John's father, a physician, was fond of wine and made it integral to the evening meal. In fact, even then his father was so enamored of wine's health benefits that he prescribed it in responsible medicinal doses for his postoperative patients. In turn, he would receive the gift of wine from appreciative patients, which permitted John to broaden his knowledge of wine. He wanted to try everything and understand all there was to know about wine. He read voraciously, and when he tasted he kept notes, catalogued, and critiqued the wines. He was a bit nonplussed to find that the two wines he ran into most often were Chardonnay and Cabernet Sauvignon. He wondered why just those two, when so many other fabulous varieties were out there. At age fifteen, he knew he was destined for a life in wine.

He went to school at both Fresno State and UC Davis. His best friend had a birthday close to his own, and their habit was to exchange wines, hopefully something new to each. His friend brought a bottle of Condrieu (known for its great white wines), and after tasting it John could not sleep thinking about the possibilities for the Viognier grape in California. He read everything he could get his hands on about Condrieu and became a self-taught expert on that region. He learned that the wine was relatively expensive because it was made from the rare and fickle Viognier grape. So he moved to Condrieu to learn growing practices, soils, climate, and so on. After working up and down the Rhône valley, Alban was convinced of the grape's possibilities and came back to the United States with soil samples and meteorological data for comparison with the climate and soils of California. All the information pointed him to the Central Coast, where he zeroed in on the Edna Valley, which had a similar Mediterranean climate so essential to the Rhône varieties such as Grenache Blanc, Mourvèdre, Syrah, and, of course, Viognier. In addition, he introduced the varieties Grenache Noir and Roussanne to the United States. At the time John began his plantings of Viognier, there were only 40 acres of that variety grown in all the Rhône. In that year, with his plantation of 32 acres, John almost doubled the world's production and set certain regions within the Central Coast on the path to forging a new and unique identity. When John decided where he wanted to live, he built his house onto the winery. He lives where he works.

RECOMMENDED WINES: I had the pleasure of doing a barrel tasting with John. Tasting with him is equivalent to a master's seminar in the sensory evaluation of wine. We tasted two samples that were to be blended to become the 2005 Estate Viognier, a classic Alban wine. The aromatics of these two samples were simply outstanding. The wines showed honeysuckle, orange zest, sweet pineapple, mangoes, peaches, and crème brûlée. There is a wonderful viscosity that both underlies and broadens the superb ripe fruit in the wine. In tasting these samples, one would swear that residual sugar has been left in the wine, but this is an illusion of taste owing to the physiological ripeness of the grapes. This ripeness is balanced by fine minerality and lovely acidity. This is the best Viognier it has been my pleasure to taste on the Central Coast, and I am convinced that the 2005 will continue to push the envelope for what Viognier, in the capable hands of John Alban, can be. I expect that once released this wine will age another eight to ten years.

I recommend the 2004 Reva Vineyard Syrah, samples tasted from the barrel. The wine is opaque to the stem of the glass and stygian black. The superb nose is black currants, blackberries, asphalt, mocha, and café au lait. The wine is already extraordinary in the mouth, showing both breadth and complexity. Even at this early stage of its development, it shows potential for great elegance and finesse, given the ripeness of the tannins. The finish lasted more than a minute. This wine should live nobly in the bottle ten to fifteen years after release.

In sum, after having tasted these wines, I am thoroughly convinced that John Alban, responsible for the genesis of the Rhône movement on the Central Coast, will continue to make outstanding contributions to its exceptional future.

RATING: Five stars (one of the best line-ups on the Central Coast)

Anglim Winery

WINERY OWNERS: Steve and Steffanie Anglim

WINEMAKER: Steve Anglim

TASTING ROOM: Yes

DAYS/HOURS: Tuesday–Sunday 10 A.M.– 5 P.M.

ADDRESS: 740 Pine St., Paso Robles, CA 93446; 805-227-6813; 805-888-2717 (fax); anglimwinery.com

WINES/GRAPE VARIETIES: Grenache, Roussanne, Syrah, Syrah rosé, Viognier

WINE CLUB: Yes

REGION: Paso Robles AVA

Arroyo Robles Winery

WINERY OWNER: Robert Shore

WINEMAKERS: Robert Shore and Alex Brown

TASTING ROOM: Yes

DAYS/HOURS: Wednesday–Sunday 12–8 P.M.

ADDRESS: 739 12th St., Paso Robles, CA 93446; 877-759-9463; no fax; arroyorobles.com

WINES/GRAPE VARIETIES: Cabernet Sauvignon, Syrah

WINE CLUB: Yes

REGION: Paso Robles AVA, west side

Austin Hope Winery

WINERY OWNERS: Austin and April Hope

WINEMAKER: Austin Hope

TASTING ROOM: No

ADDRESS: P.O. Box 3832, Paso Robles, CA 93447; 805-227-2004; 805-237-2994 (fax); austinhopewinery.com

WINES/GRAPE VARIETIES: Roussanne, Syrah, Westside Red (blend)

WINE CLUB: No

REGION: Paso Robles AVA

B & E Vineyard/Winery

WINERY OWNERS: Jerry and Patricia Bello

WINEMAKERS: Jerry and Patricia Bello

TASTING ROOM: Yes

DAYS/HOURS: Friday–Sunday 11 A.M.– 5 P.M., Monday–Thursday by appointment only

ADDRESS: 10,000 Creston Rd., Paso Robles, CA 93446; 805-238-4815; 805-237-0805 (fax); bevineyard.com

WINES/GRAPE VARIETIES: Cabernet Franc, Cabernet Sauvignon, Merlot, red blend, Syrah

WINE CLUB: Yes

REGION: Paso Robles AVA

Baileyana Winery

WINERY OWNERS: Niven family

WINEMAKER: Christian Roguenant

TASTING ROOM: Yes

DAYS/HOURS: Daily 10 A.M.–5 P.M.

ADDRESS: 5828 Orcutt Rd., San Luis Obispo, CA 93401; 805-269-8200; 805-269-8201 (fax); baileyana.com

WINES/GRAPE VARIETIES: Chardonnay, Pinot Noir, Sauvignon Blanc (Tangent line), Syrah

WINE CLUB: Yes

TASTING ROOM AMENITIES: Merchandise, gourmet food items, picnic area

REGION: Edna Valley AVA

Two distinctive threads are woven together in the historical tapestry at Baileyana: one is a grandmother's story; the other, the winemaker who is the embodiment of the former's vision for world-class wines in the Edna Valley. Catharine Niven is the founder of Baileyana, named after the street where she first met her husband, Jack. Catharine was born to the racing-horse culture of Lexington, Kentucky, one of her many interests and passions. Jack introduced her to wine, and when the Nivens moved to the Edna Valley in the 1970s, they pioneered the planting of the now-famous Paragon vineyard. Fully involved with her new life on the Central Coast, Catharine planted 3.5 acres of grapes in her front yard. Determined to bring a little bit of Burgundy to the Edna Valley, she immersed herself in research into Burgundian techniques, right down to the details of spacing between vines and canopy management—all contrary to the conventional wisdom then being practiced in California. From those early beginnings, Baileyana emerged and is now in the capable hands of the third generation, grandsons Michael Blaney and John H. Niven.

In 1998 the Nivens hired veteran French winemaker Christian Roguenant, a graduate of the University of Dijon's enology program. Dijon is the capital of France's Burgundy region. In addition to growing the great Pinot Noir grape, among others, it is renowned as a medieval fortress city and is the center for the region's bountiful agricultural industry. And they make a pretty good mustard there. Roguenant, born in Dijon, learned of wine from his father, a banker who often took his son along during his visits to the local *vignerons.* Speaking of the culture of wine in France, Roguenant remembers an elementary-school teacher who would send young Christian to the store to procure his daily quota of two bottles of wine for drinking during the day. Christian delighted in being able to keep the change as payment for his duty in obtaining his teacher's wine.

After his early inculcation into wine culture, Christian graduated in 1982 from the university and went on for graduate work. Those enology degrees took him across five continents as a consultant and winemaker. In 1984 he became the enologist for the famous Champagne house of Deutz. In 1987 he helped South Korea make the official sparkling wines of the 1988 Seoul Summer Olympics. When Beringer became the managing partner of Maison Deutz in 1986, he joined the team as a senior winemaker, a move that brought him to California to make sparkling wines for Maison Deutz Winery in Arroyo Grande. From 1995 to 1999 he was winemaker and president at Laetitia, as Maison Deutz was renamed. In 1999 the Niven family approached Roguenant with their vision for a state-of-the-art winery, to become the home of Baileyana. He was given carte blanche, and the innovative, meticulously designed high-tech marvel he developed is geared to the production of Chardonnay, Sauvignon Blanc, Syrah, and the difficult Pinot Noir grapes. The production of Baileyana's wines from the estate Paragon and Firepeak vineyards under the direction of Christian Roguenant is the realization of the vision Catharine Niven brought to the Edna Valley in the '70s.

RECOMMENDED WINES: The tasting room is the old Independence Schoolhouse, built about 1909 and formerly the Seven Peaks Winery. After Christian offered to let me drive his Porsche, we tasted in the renovated schoolhouse—a deliciously coincidental setting given his elementary-school stories and the fact that his mother was a schoolteacher. Both he and John H. Niven recommend the Grand Firepeak Cuvée Chardonnay. The 2001 is an outstanding example, bright lemon in color with a nose of apples, lemons, pears, a touch of pineapple, and excellent minerality underlying the fruit. I love the acidity in this wine, balancing the lovely ripe fruit. The finish is smooth, long, and elegant. The wine is ready for enjoyment now but will easily give another five to six years of pleasure.

The easy recommendation for me would be one of Christian's wonderful Pinot Noirs or even the Syrah; nevertheless, I suggest the Sauvignon Blanc. The 2003 is a very young pale lime in color but already shows oodles of passion fruit, lemons, and grapefruit in the nose. The acidity is again a wonderful counterpoint to the ripe, luscious fruit. This is an outstanding Sauvignon Blanc and a testament to Christian's far-ranging knowledge as a winemaker. Don't despair if you find the wines are sold out. The 2005 vintage should be excellent. The Sauvignon Blanc will become the flagship wine under a new brand called Tangent, and the Baileyana Sauvignon Blanc will no longer exist.

RATING: Three → four stars (whites are outstanding and slightly ahead of reds)

Bella Luna Winery

WINERY OWNERS: Kevin Healey and Sherman Smoot

WINEMAKERS: Kevin Healey and Sherman Smoot

TASTING ROOM: Yes

DAYS/HOURS: Saturday–Sunday 10 A.M.– 5 P.M.

ADDRESS: 1850 Templeton Rd., Templeton, CA 93465; 805-434-5477; 805-434-5479 (fax); bellalunawine.com

WINES/GRAPE VARIETIES: Estate Riserva III (blend), Fighter Pilot Red (blend), Tempranillo

WINE CLUB: Yes

REGION: Paso Robles AVA, Templeton area

Bianchi

WINERY OWNER: Glenn Bianchi

WINEMAKER: Tom Lane

TASTING ROOM: Yes

DAYS/HOURS: Daily 10 A.M.–5 P.M.

ADDRESS: 3380 Branch Rd., Paso Robles, CA 93446; 805-226-9922; 805-226-8230 (fax); bianchiwine.com

WINES/GRAPE VARIETIES: Cabernet Sauvignon, Chardonnay, Merlot, Pinot Grigio, Pinot Noir, Sauvignon Blanc, Syrah, Zinfandel

WINE CLUB: Yes

TASTING ROOM AMENITIES: Lakeside picnic area, merchandise, deli, special event area, lodging

REGION: Paso Robles AVA

Glenn Bianchi has a brand-new state-of-the-art winery and tasting room in Paso Robles. However, this is no Johnny-come-lately to the wine scene. The Bianchi family has a long and proud history in wine, and the current endeavor is the culmination of more than thirty years' hard work in the industry. The Bianchi family can trace its winemaking roots back to the early days in Kerman, California, where patriarch Joseph Bianchi and son Glenn bought a shell of a winery in 1974 in Fresno County. At the time, they had a winery in name only until the Bianchi family turned the original facility around with new equipment purchases, established a 600-acre vineyard, and fostered some innovative and groundbreaking ideas. They produced wine coolers in a can, sold the airlines canned wine, and were among the first to sell a "bag in a box." In the late '80s, Glenn suggested to his father that Bianchi should begin to emphasize what he called the "fighting varieties." This required fighting for the best grapes, fighting for high-quality wines, and, ultimately, fighting for the shelf space to sell the wines. The change in emphasis worked. Bianchi became the thirty-seventh largest winery in the country, producing upwards of 2 million gallons of wine a year. But Glenn wasn't satisfied yet.

In the late '90s, he had the suspicion that the Central Valley appellation would not be able to take him in the direction he wanted to go, so he went instead. He went to Napa, he went to Sonoma, and in both places he took a long, hard look. Then he went to Paso Robles, found the acreage on Branch Road, and went no farther. The site had it all—the *terroir,* the beauty, and enough land to build the culmination of his dream: a 150,000-gallon premier winery capable of producing, in time, up to 35,000 cases a year. He loved the potential of the place and understood that his vision for making premium wines could best be realized there. The winery and the separate tasting room are a testament to his vision, and they allow him to demonstrate his appreciation for the area. You can sip wines on couches in front of the fireplace, view the surrounding vineyards, or even sail a model remote-controlled boat on the pond in front of the tasting room

To make premium wines requires first the fruit and then a winemaker of talent and experience to oversee the process. Enter Tom Lane, a graduate of UC Davis, who brings more than twenty years of experience in the business. In 1997 Tom won the prestigious Dan Berger Winemaker of the Year award. Tom and Glenn share a common goal for the new Bianchi winery: they want to have fun in a fun business, but they also want to produce top-of-the-line wines capable of winning gold medals. They understand the process that it takes to achieve that end point and are willing to do the things that will result in excellent wines of great value for the consumer.

RECOMMENDED WINES: Glenn recommends the 2004 Jack Ranch Chardonnay, which recently scored a 90 in the "Best of the Year" issue of *Wine Enthusiast.* Produced from Edna Valley grapes, the wine has a bracing acidity that supports flavors of lemons, mangoes, and bananas. It exhibits an underlay of crème fraîche and soft vanilla from the judicious use of oak.

I recommend the Syrah. The 2001 Signature Selection has a splendid nose of cherries, cinnamon, blackberry, and some cassis. The wine has excellent mouthfeel and a silky-smooth finish. Though quite drinkable now, it will reward an additional three years in the bottle.

RATING: Two stars (very good line, but keep an eye on Bianchi; will likely move up quickly in overall quality)

Brian Benson Cellars

WINERY OWNER: Brian Benson

WINEMAKER: Brian Benson

TASTING ROOM: At Dark Star Cellars

DAYS/HOURS: Friday–Sunday 10:30 A.M.–5 P.M.

ADDRESS: Dark Star Cellars, 2985 Anderson Rd., Paso Robles, CA 93446; 805-296-9463; 805-226-9467 (fax); brianbensoncellars.com

WINES/GRAPE VARIETIES: Cabernet
Sauvignon, Karma (red blend),
Merlot, Shop Truck Red (blend),
Syrah, Zinfandel

WINE CLUB: Yes

TASTING ROOM AMENITIES: Merchandise

REGION: Paso Robles AVA

Calcareous Vineyard

WINERY OWNERS: Lloyd Messer and Dana
Brown

WINEMAKER: Justin Kahler

TASTING ROOM: Yes

DAYS/HOURS: Daily 10 A.M.–6 P.M. (winter
5 P.M.)

ADDRESS: 3000 Peachy Canyon Rd.,
Paso Robles, CA 93446; 805-239-0289;
805-239-0916 (fax); calcareous.com

WINES/GRAPE VARIETIES: Cabernet
Sauvignon, Chardonnay, Pinot Noir,
Roussanne, Syrah, Viognier, Zinfandel

WINE CLUB: Yes

REGION: Paso Robles AVA, west side

Caparone Winery

WINERY OWNERS: Dave and Marc
Caparone

WINEMAKER: Dave Caparone

TASTING ROOM: Yes

DAYS/HOURS: Daily 11 A.M.–5 P.M.

ADDRESS: 2280 San Marcos Rd., Paso
Robles, CA 93446; 805-467-3827;
805-467-3827 (fax); caparone.com

WINES/GRAPE VARIETIES: Aglianico,
Cabernet Sauvignon, Merlot, Nebbiolo,
Sangiovese, Zinfandel

WINE CLUB: Yes

TASTING ROOM AMENITIES: Tours

REGION: Paso Robles AVA

Dave Caparone and son Marc have spent a number of years quietly flying under the
radar of the Paso Robles wine scene. Dave and Marc are both accomplished musicians
in the jazz and classical repertoires and are more interested in making wine and music
than in pursuing publicity. Their story, however, is worth memorializing, since Dave
is one of the early vintners to dig out a foothold for the Paso Robles wine industry. He
has also been instrumental in establishing Italian varietal grapes in Paso and made his
first Zinfandel in 1973. At that time Benito Dusi was selling his Zinfandel grapes to
Paul Masson up north. Rotta and Pesenti were making bulk wines from both local
grapes and those bought outside the area, and Max Goldman had purchased York
Mountain Winery. In fact, Merv Rotta of the Rotta wine family was a trucker and
helped bring out the stainless steel tanks for Dave's winery.

Even though he has been here quite some time, Dave is an expatriate from Southern California. After graduating from UCLA in the late 1960s with a degree in fine arts,
Dave took an interest in red wines after moving to Shell Beach, where he lived for thirteen years. His musical career as a trombonist allowed him to travel and buy wines for

his growing collection. At one point he decided to make wines for himself. He built a basement with a drain under his Shell Beach home, bought good-quality grapes from the few local growers, and started bottling wine. After outgrowing his garagiste operation, he sold the home, and the new owners transformed it into a money-making operation by installing a meth lab.

In 1973, when he first started making wines, Paso Robles was very much tied to cattle ranching and almond growing, and the rural, rustic region was not much given to wine appreciation. Dave saw the potential for growing high-quality grapes even then. In 1976 he got interested in the great Nebbiolo grape from northern Italy's Piedmont region. *Nebbia* means "fog" in Italian, and Nebbiolo is the principal grape in the great wines of Barolo and Barbaresco. His interest in Nebbiolo piqued, Dave researched the grape and found a study published in 1936. Interestingly, the study did not recommend the grape for California, but Montevina in Amador did some experimentation with the variety in 1971–72. Dave bought his current property in 1978, then a working cattle ranch. He planted 28 of the 98 acres over to vines (he still runs some cattle on the property). The land had not been farmed before and was primarily alluvial soils with some igneous and marine sedimentation. For years, Dave did the weed hoeing by hand, and to this day the Caparones do not have to spray for mold or mildew in the vineyards. They use very little water—less than a single-family home requires for a year—and they spray less than most certified organic farmers. The first Nebbiolo vines were planted in 1980, and 1985 saw the release of their first wine; they have been making it every year since. Dave believes that his Nebbiolo plantings might have been the first on the Central Coast. He also believes that it is the most difficult of all red grapes, and he grins when he says, "For winemakers who have mastered Pinot Noir, they can move on to the real challenge of Nebbiolo." Dave and Marc also have the distinction of owning the first winery in the United States to produce and market Sangiovese as a varietal wine.

Dave emphasizes that he is interested in achieving a natural and consistent varietal expression for his grapes. All his wines are unfined and unfiltered; in fact, he doesn't even own a filter. He has spent years matching the proper varieties to the climate and the soils of his vineyard. In every regard, this is very much a father-and-son operation. Son Marc, who has a degree in history from UC Davis, is following in his father's footsteps. Over the next few years they intend to drop production from about 10,000 cases per year (sold mostly to Trader Joe's) to 4,000, with continued emphasis on the production of high-quality red varieties. Dave believes that given the winemaking methods at Caparone, their wines have the potential to age fifteen to twenty-five years. For example, he poured a 1986 Caparone Zinfandel at the 2002 Paso Robles Zinfandel Festival, and the wine showed beautifully. I tasted the 1980 Merlot, but it had passed its prime, sadly. Nevertheless, the wine still showed elements that had given it a long and memorable life.

RECOMMENDED WINES: Dave suggests the 2001 Sangiovese, a fine, fruity wine with excellent ripeness in the grapes. This is a pretty red cherry–colored wine, light to the stem, with a nice balance of acidity and tannins. The wine is wonderful on the mid-palate and has a lingering finish. The nose shows cherries, red currants, and ripe raspberries. The wine is drinking nicely now but will last another two to four years.

I chose the 2001 Zinfandel, almost opaque in the glass and a deep cherry-red color. In the nose I found plums, figs, briars, and ripe blackberry fruit. The wine has a fine tannic grip, which suggests an additional three years of aging potential. Interestingly, Dave Caparone believes, as do I, that well-made Zins from Paso Robles are capable of aging.

If you are interested in taking the less-trodden wine path, try Dave's 2001 Aglianico (pronounced "ah-lee-ah-nee-koh"). Dave found this grape at UC Davis in the 1980s when he was doing research on grape varieties and cultivars. Reading Sheldon and Pauline Wasserman's book had interested him in growing Nebbiolo, Sangiovese, and Aglianico. He discovered that although Davis had the vine, no one at the time was doing anything with it. He saw the opportunity and took it. Since then, he has had the grape verified by a famous Italian ampelographer (a scientist who describes and identifies grape varieties). The grape was initially brought by the Phoenicians to Greece; from there it migrated to southern Italy, where it is establishing a reputation for high-quality wines. Known as *Vitis hellenica,* Aglianico stems from the Italian word for "Hellenic," *ellenico.* Dave is proud of the fact that he is able to continue the time-honored tradition for this little-known varietal. The grape produces a cherry-red wine, almost opaque in the glass, with a nose of plums, tobacco, earth, and black currants. The tannins are chalk-dry, with the ripe fruit contributing to an excellent mouthfeel and exotic taste. The wine will benefit from an additional three to five years of bottle age.

RATING: Two stars (Caparone is moving in the right direction and offers some fine values)

Carmody McKnight Estate Wines

WINERY OWNERS: Gary and Marian Conway

WINEMAKER: Greg Cropper

TASTING ROOM: Yes

DAYS/HOURS: Daily 10 A.M.–5 P.M.

ADDRESS: 11240 Chimney Rock Rd., Paso Robles, CA 93446; 805-238-9392, 800-282-0730; 805-238-3975 (fax); carmodymcknight.com

WINES/GRAPE VARIETIES: Bordeaux-style blends, Cabernet Franc, Cabernet Sauvignon, Chardonnay, dessert wines, late-harvest Cabernet Franc, Merlot, Pinot Noir, sparkling wine

WINE CLUB: Yes

TASTING ROOM AMENITIES: Picnic area, art gallery

REGION: Paso Robles AVA

Things are going very well for you artistically. The two series you starred in *(Burke's Law* and *Land of the Giants)* have established your celebrity in Hollywood. On an excursion to the Central Coast with friends, you fall in love with the natural beauty of the place. On the trip home, you and your wife, Marian, decide to buy a ranch near Paso Robles. A real-estate agent flies you over the area in a helicopter on your next visit north. You hover and watch the sun settle behind the Coastal Ranges as deer graze on the hillside; you are stunned by the sheer physical beauty of the place. The rotor of the helicopter clips a power line and you crash-land on the property. You and the pilot stagger away from the aircraft's burning hulk as the ranch owner runs down the hill to render assistance. Uninjured, you seek to allay his fears about you, the pilot, and the smoking hole augered into the ground. You reassure him: "Don't worry. I'm going to buy the place." And you do. True story. Even the folks back in Holly-wood are impressed.

Gary Conway (né Carmody) brings art to the things he touches: the land, the wines, the canvas. Beautiful things draw the eye; then the hand draws beautiful things. Marian Conway (née McKnight) can speak to beauty as well. A former Miss South Carolina, she went on to become a reigning Miss America. Their daughter, Kathleen Conway, grew up in the vineyard and has added her artistic touch to the making of the wines. Greg Cropper, now general manager and winemaker, was formerly part of a construction company that built wineries. About fifteen years ago, he became a cellar hand and worked his way up through the ranks, gaining experience in every aspect of the job. In 1997 he was introduced to the Conways and was hired to take control of the winery from vineyard to final production. It was a good fit for everyone concerned. Gary and Greg understand that great wine requires more than the artisan's touch. You can't neglect the science, and here the two have made an interesting discovery.

The geologics of Paso Robles are unique, but when you dig at Carmody McKnight the soil samples test out to be just about as good as one could hope. The limestone is here, and so is calcareous shale; igneous (volcanic) rock protrudes through the soil, and there is also montmorillonite, which contributes to the so-called wonder soil of the area. Montmorillonite is a type of clay with a special property: when water is absorbed by its crystals, they swell to several times their original volume. It tends to soak up water like a sponge. Accordingly, Cal Poly soil scientists are here doing research. John Deere Global Ag Services, in concert with Motorola and Earth Information Technologies, has selected Carmody McKnight for a scientific study of the components of *terroir.* Greg is contributing to that knowledge base by carefully gathering and recording data on the plantings given the location and soil types of this very special place. Gary, Marian, Greg, and Kathleen are a special family with a special vineyard, scientifically and artistically. They allow the vineyard to produce the best possible grapes for the exceptional *terroir.* The point is not to interfere and thus allow the grape varieties to express their characteristics.

At the winery you will find the tasting room, a remodeled farmhouse more than 130 years old. Take the time to view some of Gary's paintings: you'll see many of them represented on the labels. Take away a copy of his book *Art of the Vineyard,* and have him personally sign a copy. Then enjoy the wines, the pond of waterlilies and floating lotus, and the beautiful countryside that lured an artist and his family away from the city and brought down a helicopter.

RECOMMENDED WINES: Gary rhapsodizes over the Chardonnay. It is made entirely from free-run juice (pure juice that flows from the grapes even before they are pressed), with just a touch of oak lying beneath the fruit. There is a lovely nose of apples, pears, melons, and hint of fig at the bottom. This light gold wine is crisp and lively in the mouth and atypical of California Chardonnay—it is not about huge oak and butterscotch. It is vinified to show the fruit and the crisp acidity that makes it so appealing.

The 2000 Cadenza is my recommendation. It shows opaque black-purple in the glass. The fruit is currants and black cherries with a hint of mocha. The tannins make this wine drinkable now, but it will easily live another five to eight years in the bottle. This is an excellent example of blending Cabernet Franc (Greg's personal recommendation), Merlot, and Cabernet Sauvignon. The 1999 won Best Meritage in California.

RATING: Three stars (reds and whites are very good to excellent)

Casa de Caballos Vineyards

WINERY OWNERS: Tom and Sheila Morgan

WINEMAKER: Tom Morgan

TASTING ROOM: Yes

DAYS/HOURS: Daily 11 A.M.–5 P.M.

ADDRESS: 2225 Raymond Ave., Templeton, CA 93465; 805-434-1687; 805-434-1560 (fax); casadecaballos.com

WINES/GRAPE VARIETIES: Cabernet Sauvignon, Merlot, Pinot Noir, red blends, Riesling

WINE CLUB: Yes

TASTING ROOM AMENITIES: Arabian horse farm and horse viewing, merchandise, patio, barrel-room rental

REGION: Paso Robles AVA

Casa de Caballos combines the passions of two people: Sheila's love of fine Arabian horses and Tom's love of fine wines. Dr. Tom Morgan has been in Paso Robles since 1975 and has seen the number of wineries grow from five to more than a hundred. During his studies at Stanford, he visited wineries in the region, Beringer among them, and had the pleasure of being served by none other than Mrs. Beringer herself. During his travels to Germany, he discovered the great Rieslings of the Mosel district. He took a residency at Orange County Medical Center and in his spare time made wines from fruit and berries. He eventually settled in Templeton to work as a physician, but continued to experiment with wines as a hobby. He planted Riesling, reflecting his love of German wines, and Pinot Noir. He sought out Ken Volk, then at Wild Horse, for a critique. Volk liked what Morgan had in the bottle and offered his help and support. In 1982, the year after Sheila and Tom married, the first vines were planted at Casa de Caballos. There are currently 6 acres under cultivation. The winery was officially bonded in 1995.

Sheila Morgan has always had an appreciation for horses but was able to realize her dream of breeding and raising Arabians with the purchase of Casa de Caballos. While Tom pursued his hobby and made award-winning wines, she pursued hers and raised championship horses. Tom and Sheila decided to combine their interests, and the wine labels now feature the pictures and names of Sheila's award winners. She personally designs all the labels.

According to Tom, to make wine commercially it helps to have a background in chemistry, but successful winemaking is more than quantitative analysis: the senses must also come into play. It helps to have a little luck, too. After experiencing some difficulties growing his Zinfandel (a tricky variety), he grafted the rootstocks over to

Cabernet Sauvignon, better suited to the climate at Casa de Caballos. Shortly thereafter—you guessed it—he won a double gold medal for the Zinfandel. Tom understands *terroir,* but he is not a fanatic about it. He understands the necessity of matching the correct grape varieties to the proper soils and he emphasizes how important a good climate is—and Casa de Caballos has it. He also believes canopy management of the vines is crucial to his success. With 6 acres under his care, he keeps crop yields and case production low.

RECOMMENDED WINES: Tom recommends the Periwinkle Pinot Noir, and he makes an excellent example of the variety. I found a savory roasted meat flavor in the nose, most likely the result of the American oak barrels he uses. Cherries and violets lie next to the meaty flavor, and the wine has the soft, rounded tannins characteristic of a fine Pinot. In a Pinot Noir Shoot-out held in Sacramento, the 2002 Periwinkle finished in the top fifteen among more than 250 wines.

I recommend the fine 2002 Maggie Mae, a blend of Pinot Noir and Merlot. There is plenty of jammy cherry fruit here, with enough oak backbone to age the wine if you have the patience. You get all the characteristics of the Periwinkle Pinot Noir with the cherry from the Merlot for even more interest. After you try the wines and walk the grounds to see and perhaps pat the horses, don't forget to admire the spectacular views. They are among the most beautiful of the region.

RATING: Three stars (some nice surprises in the line)

Cass Wines

WINERY OWNER: Steve Cass

WINEMAKER: Dan Kleck

TASTING ROOM: Yes

DAYS/HOURS: Saturday–Sunday 11 A.M.–6 P.M., Monday–Friday 12–5 P.M.

ADDRESS: 7350 Linne Rd., Paso Robles, CA 93446; 805-239-1730; 805-227-2889 (fax); casswines.com

WINES/GRAPE VARIETIES: Cabernet Sauvignon, Cassa Nova Rosé Cuvée, Hacienda (red blend), Rockin One (red blend), Roussanne, Syrah, Viognier

WINE CLUB: Yes

TASTING ROOM AMENITIES: Gourmet food tasting, merchandise

REGION: Paso Robles AVA, east side

Castoro Cellars

WINERY OWNERS: Niels and Bimmer Udsen

WINEMAKER: Tom Myers

TASTING ROOM: Yes

DAYS/HOURS: Daily 10 A.M.–5:30 P.M.

ADDRESS: 1315 N. Bethel Rd., Templeton, CA 93465; 805-238-0725; 888-326-3463; 805-238-2602 (fax); castorocellars.com

WINES/GRAPE VARIETIES: Cabernet Sauvignon, Chardonnay, Chenin Blanc, Fumé Blanc, late-harvest Zinfandel, Merlot, Muscat Canelli, Pinot Noir, Syrah, Tempranillo, Viognier, White Zinfandel, Zinfandel

WINE CLUB: Yes

TASTING ROOM AMENITIES: Art gallery, merchandise, picnic area

REGION: Paso Robles AVA

Niels Udsen is very much a family man, and his winery reflects his values right down to offering alcohol-free Zinfandel grape juice for children while their parents taste. Although Niels grew up in Ventura, California, he has maintained contact with his Danish roots. His father, a successful farmer and businessman, immigrated to the United States in the late 1940s. On one of his first trips back to Denmark, Niels was introduced to Bimmer, who would later become his wife and partner at Castoro. At the time, he was eight and she was six. Niels seems to have no problem in making relational commitments: the partnership has endured, and the two take great pride in the family winery they established in Paso Robles in 1983. So why give the winery an Italian name instead of one in keeping with their Danish heritage?

Wine has always been part of the family culture in the Udsen home, and after graduation from high school Niels spent a year abroad in Italy, where he became fluent in the language. The translation of his nickname, Beaver, into Italian is Castoro—hence the motto on the labels, "Dam Fine Wine." Niels returned from Italy with an appreciation for the growing and making of wine. He took a degree at Cal Poly in agricultural business management, and one of his classmates was Ken Volk, who would go on to start Wild Horse. His first job was at Estrella River Winery, where he worked for winemaker Tom Myers. Under Myers's tutelage, he learned the business from the ground up, starting as a harvest hand. The relationship between the two men continues, with Myers working as head winemaker at Castoro since 1990.

In 1983, two years after their marriage, Niels and Bimmer started Castoro as a part-time operation: Niels made the wine and Bimmer sold it. After early and encouraging success, Niels left Estrella in 1985 to focus entirely on the wines of Castoro. To this day, Niels and Bimmer work together, their desks side by side.

In addition to starting an extremely successful winery, Niels had the foresight to predict the emergence of Paso Robles as a region capable of producing great wines. He established a custom-crush operation with a mobile bottling line that enables smaller wineries to do the work locally instead of sending their grapes to other parts of California. This decision was in keeping with the sense of camaraderie and the spirit of cooperation very much in evidence around Paso Robles. Castoro Cellars, now renowned and well respected, is still a family-owned winery. At this point in the evolution of the business, Niels and Bimmer are focusing more on growing the brand than on growing the winery.

Head winemaker Tom Myers has a master's degree in biology from Michigan State and a master's degree in food science from UC Davis, where he studied enology and viticulture. You won't find a bad wine at Castoro. If a wine shows a defect, they won't bottle it. Although Myers emphasizes the fruit character of the wines, he is not afraid of oak but uses it judiciously. Both men, in keeping with their shared values, prefer to offer affordable wines to the consumer. The more limited Reserve wines do cost more but still present value.

RECOMMENDED WINES: Niels recommends the Due Mille Due, a Reserve Bordeaux blend of Cabernet Sauvignon, Merlot, Petit Verdot, and Cabernet Franc. This is a purple and red wine that comes alive in the mouth. The vanilla oak is still forward, but as the wine ages, the tannins from the oak will resolve to allow the ample fruit to show itself more assertively. I smelled cherries and loganberries in the nose, with a lovely touch of chocolate below the fruit. The wine has an impressive and long finish to go with the excellent nose and mouthfeel. I had the pleasure of drinking this wine again at the home of friends, and we were impressed by its quality and the fact that it had survived a nearly 1,500-mile trip to Iowa. This bodes well for the wine's longevity.

My recommendation is the Reserve Viognier. The 2002 is lemon and gold, with a classic nose of flowers and fruit. Just the right touch of oak adds complexity, and the wine has enough acidity to invigorate the taste buds. The wine is rich owing to the excellent ripeness in the grapes at harvest and is a fine example of Viognier.

If you are a lover of Zinfandel, come to Castoro and spend the day sampling just the Zins. Better yet, call the winery and find out when they are doing a vertical tasting. It's not unusual for Niels and Tom to offer ten to fifteen vintage years for tasting.

RATING: Two stars (well-made wines across the line) → three stars (Reserve line is excellent)

Cayucos Cellars

WINERY OWNERS: Stuart and Laura Selkirk

WINEMAKER: Stuart Selkirk

TASTING ROOM: Yes

DAYS/HOURS: Wednesday–Monday 11 A.M.–5 P.M.

ADDRESS: 143 N. Ocean Ave., Cayucos, CA 93430; 805-995-3036; 805-995-2415 (fax); cayucoscellars.com

WINES/GRAPE VARIETIES: Cabernet Sauvignon, Chardonnay, Pinot Noir, red blend, Syrah, Zinfandel

WINE CLUB: Yes

REGION: San Luis Obispo County

Cerro Caliente Cellars

WINERY OWNER: Don Peters

WINEMAKER: Don Peters

TASTING ROOM: Yes

DAYS/HOURS: Friday–Sunday 12–5 P.M.

ADDRESS: 831-A Via Esteban, San Luis Obispo, CA 93401; 805-544-2842; 805-544-2842 (fax); cerrocalientecellars.com

WINES/GRAPE VARIETIES: Cabernet Franc, Cabernet Sauvignon, Chardonnay, Franciovese (blend), Merlot, Multi-Viscosity (blend), Pinot Grigio, Pinot Noir, Sangiovese, Syrah, Zinfandel

WINE CLUB: Yes

TASTING ROOM AMENITIES: Merchandise

REGION: Edna Valley AVA

If you want to have your oil changed or a tune-up done while you sit and taste wine in San Luis Obispo, Don Peters is your man. Pull the car into his garage and mechanic's shop, walk next door to the tasting room, and try the wines while you wait. Peters has managed to combine and consolidate his two areas of expertise under the same roof. His formal education is in mechanical engineering and automotive technology. Originally from Wisconsin, he served in the Air Force during the Vietnam War and, when he returned from duty, went to work doing what he loved most: repairing automobiles. In 1973 he opened his own gas station. Over the years he pursued his second love, wine, and trained his palate through tastings and study.

In 1990 he and a friend made wines in Paso Robles in the basement of the friend's house. The first effort, made from Thompson Seedless grapes, was okay at best, but a good foray into the process of making wine. His next effort, made from Cabernet Sauvignon grapes, convinced him to continue as a winemaker. Don bonded his winery in 1998. The name Cerro Caliente means "hot hill" (a reference to summers in Paso Robles) and was suggested to Don by his son-in-law, Pat Nuñez. Carol, his wife, is an accomplished cook and published cookbook author. In keeping with the theme of a winery as a family operation, she serves as the in-house chef and assists with many of the winery operations. Daughter Mitzi Nuñez runs the tasting room.

Case production is about 2,000 cases now, and Don's philosophy is to make flavor-driven wines for people who want to drink them right away. Because of his excellent contacts in both the automotive and the wine industries, he is able to get great fruit for his wines. He sees his strength as a blender, as evidenced in his premier marque, the Multi-Viscosity, a blend of different grape varieties and even different years in the grand European tradition. This wine features the artwork of Gene Francis on the label. Don's wines have won five international awards, and he has an excellent referral rate, not only as a top-notch, highly trained mechanic but also as a vintner.

RECOMMENDED WINES: Don recommends the Multi-Viscosity nonvintage blend. The wine is opaque to the stem of the glass and reddish-purple in color. The nose is black currants, cassis, and cherry, with an underlying hint of mocha. The ripe fruit leads to an excellent mouthfeel and a soft lingering finish lasting almost a minute. I tasted the wine again at the table, and it confirmed Don's desire to produce flavorful wines ready for drinking. Take this altogether excellent blend home, pull the cork, and drink it with confidence.

I suggest the 2003 Zinfandel, pulled from the barrel and made from Paso Robles fruit. This dark purple wine is opaque in the glass and has a wonderful nose of blueberries, black cherries, and nutmeg spice. The tannins are soft and although the wine was tasted while still on the oak; per Don's philosophy it is ready for drinking now. This is a very good Zinfandel, and, given the wonderfully ripe fruit in the wine, I expect that it will give pleasure over the next three years or so.

RATING: Two stars (very good wines, but overall quality is improving across the line)

Changala Winery

WINERY OWNERS: Jean and Heidi Changala

WINEMAKER: Heidi Changala

TASTING ROOM: New tasting room coming

DAYS/HOURS:

ADDRESS: Call for details; 805-238-0421;
805-237-1844 (fax); no Web site

WINES/GRAPE VARIETIES: Cabernet
Sauvignon, Chardonnay, Synergy (blend),
Syrah, Viognier, Zinfandel

WINE CLUB: Yes

REGION: Paso Robles AVA

CHANGALA

2000

Central Coast

SYRAH

ALC. 14.0% BY VOL.

Heidi and Jean Changala will offer their wines for tasting in a location soon to be determined, moving from their previous location in downtown Templeton. The Changalas (the name is of Basque origin) are in Templeton because they were interested in a rural lifestyle. Jean grew up in farming, and both attended Cal Poly and took degrees in electrical engineering. The move to establish a winery was in part due to Jean's wish to return to farming and growing grapes. Heidi started her career as an engineer in Los Osos. In 1987 Jean started a job as assistant winemaker at Martin Brothers Winery (now Martin and Weyrich) and in 1989 became the facilities engineer for Meridian, helping with its expansion plans. For a time, Heidi did marketing for HMR (Hidden Mountain Ranch Winery), and when an opportunity presented itself, they became partners at HMR, where they were making garage wines. The partnership with HMR began in 1997 and only recently ended when they sold their share of the business. While co-owners, the Changalas contributed to continuing a tradition started by one of Paso's original wine pioneers, Dr. Stanley Hoffman. Changala Winery officially opened its doors in the spring of 2001. Currently, Rich Hartenberger at Midnight Cellars provides the use of his facilities for their winemaking.

Because of his love for farming and the soil, Jean planted a small vineyard of Zinfandel and Cabernet Sauvignon grapes and does the vineyard work. He also stays in close contact with the other growers who provide fruit for Changala's wines. Heidi is the winemaker, and, in the true spirit of a family-owned operation, their daughters also make contributions to the business. Jean has a minimalist philosophy when it comes to his grapes and wants to showcase the quality of the fruit coming from the vineyard. Accordingly, Changala seeks to integrate work from the agriculture all the way to the actual selling of the wines.

RECOMMENDED WINES: Heidi suggests the Viognier, and I tasted the 2002. The wine is made from Zaca Mesa grapes in Santa Barbara County, and I found it to be pale lemon in color with a fruity nose of peaches and pineapples. The wine displays good mouthfeel and a lively back-bone of acidity. This is a fresh, fruity Viognier ready for drinking now.

Jean suggests the Paso Robles Zinfandel, a bright purple wine almost opaque to the stem of the glass. The blackberry fruit has a spicy component with very good mouthfeel. The tannins are rounded and well balanced with the acidity in the wine. The excellent ripeness of the grapes contributes a sense of sweetness to the wine, though it is vinified dry. I tasted the 1999.

I recommend the Cabernet Sauvignon, made from grapes purchased from the east side of Paso Robles. This black-purple wine is nearly opaque and has a lovely nose of ripe cherries above a layer of soft vanilla. The tannins are ripe and rounded, making this wine accessible now, but it will reward three years of aging. The excellent mouthfeel and the lingering finish show this to be a good example of an east-side Paso Cabernet Sauvignon. I tasted the 1999; if this wine is sold out, look for the now-released 2001.

RATING: One star (competently made wines)

Château de Deighton

WINERY OWNER: Mark Hutchenreuther

WINEMAKER: Mark Hutchenreuther

TASTING ROOM: No

DAYS/HOURS: By appointment only

ADDRESS: 2515 Lara Ln., Oceano, CA 93445; 805-489-0979; 805-489-0979 (fax); chateaudedeighton.com

WINES/GRAPE VARIETIES: Cuvée Blanc (blend), Cuvée Rouge (blend), Grenache, Histoire en Bouteille (blend), late-harvest Grenache, late-harvest Sémillon, Mourvèdre, Petite Sirah, Pink Nun (rosé blend), Pinot Noir, Zinfandel

WINE CLUB: No

REGION: Paso Robles AVA

Chateau Margene

WINERY OWNERS: Mike and Margene Mooney

WINEMAKER: Mike Mooney

TASTING ROOM: Yes

DAYS/HOURS: Saturday–Sunday 12–6 P.M.

ADDRESS: 4385 La Panza Rd., Creston, CA 93432; 805-238-2321; 805-238-2118 (fax); chateaumargene.com

WINES/GRAPE VARIETIES: Bordeaux blend, Cabernet Sauvignon, Chardonnay, late-harvest Merlot, Syrah, Zinfandel

WINE CLUB: Yes

TASTING ROOM AMENITIES: Picnic area

REGION: Paso Robles AVA

Margene Mooney lends her name to the winery she and Mike started in 1998 with the purchase of a property east of Paso Robles near Creston. Mike traveled the world as director of digital cinema for Christie Digital Systems, which he left in 2002. Margene runs the day-to-day operations of the winery, while Mike handles the winemaking duties. Jim Smoot is the vineyard consultant, and the irrepressible John Munch of Le Cuvier acted as winemaking consultant during the first three formative years. The results of these relationships are very much in evidence in the wines of Chateau Margene. As Munch says, Mike is an excellent student, and it didn't take him long to get it right. When you taste the quality of the wines, you know exactly what Munch means.

Mike and Margene Mooney have set their standards high: Chateau Margene is not about premium or even superpremium wines. They aspire to make a luxury cuvée, as evidenced in the Beau Mélange, their limited-release estate Bordeaux-style blend, which has the distinction of being the highest-priced wine in the AVA. This is one of the reasons they spent eight years looking for just the right property to start their venture. Once they located the current site, they planted vines. Their breakout year, 2000, established their style and was the culmination of Mike's early interest in wines, particularly Cabernet Sauvignon. For example, by age twelve, he already had visited Stony Hill in Saint Helena and loved that experience. As he grew older, he developed those early experiences into a lifelong appreciation for fine wines.

Mike makes no bones about his target audience: he markets to the sophisticated drinker. His goal is to produce world-class wines capable of aging at least five to ten years in the bottle. He is reaping the benefits of his passion for winemaking and his high expectations. In an international Cabernet Sauvignon competition with more than three hundred wines entered, Chateau Margene was ranked number seven. In another competition where wines were rated by experts and consumers, Margene won both tastings; and this was for the regular Cab, not the Reserve.

RECOMMENDED WINES: Although I initially tasted the 2001 and 2002 wines, they are sold out. A return trip to the winery allowed me to taste barrel samplings of the outstanding 2003 vintage. It's no surprise then that Mike recommends the 2003 Cab. This is a black-purple wine with a nose of cherries and chocolates and a floral note of violets. There is excellent ripeness in the grapes, and the tannins are sufficient for aging. The wine has gobs of fruit, and the judicious time spent on oak has added a dimension of elegance and finesse. Give this wine five to seven years to reach its full potential.

My recommendation is the 2003 Reserve Cab. We had to coax this recently bottled wine to open and show its marvelous potential. An inky black-purple wine, it has cassis, black currants, black cherry jam, and mint in the nose. The wine is superb in the mouth and has a touch more tannin than the regular Cab, but just as much ripe, luscious fruit. I expect this wine will show its best in another ten years or so. These wines are both superb examples of fine, ageworthy Cabs with elegance and finesse. If either one is sold out, don't despair. In personal communication with me, Mike says he believes that 2005 looks to be the vintage of the decade.

RATING: Five stars (Mike produces superb wines)

Christian Lazo Winery

WINERY OWNERS: Steve Christian and
Guadalupe Lazo

WINEMAKER: Steve Christian

TASTING ROOM: Yes

DAYS/HOURS: Saturday–Sunday
10 A.M.–5 P.M.

ADDRESS: 249 10th St., Ste. A,
San Miguel, CA 93451; 805-467-2672;
no fax; christianlazowines.com

WINES/GRAPE VARIETIES: Barbera, Petite
Sirah, Zinfandel

WINE CLUB: Yes

REGION: Paso Robles AVA

Chumeia Vineyards

WINERY OWNERS: Lee and Mark Nesbitt,
Eric Danninger

WINEMAKER: Lee Nesbitt

TASTING ROOM: Yes

DAYS/HOURS: Daily 10 A.M.–5 P.M.

ADDRESS: 8331 Hwy. 46 E., Paso Robles, CA
93446; 805-226-0102; 805-226-0104 (fax);
chumeiavineyards.com

WINES/GRAPE VARIETIES: Barbera,
Cabernet Sauvignon, Chardonnay,
Merlot, Pinot Noir, Sangiovese, Silver
Nectar (blend), Syrah, Viognier, Zinfandel

WINE CLUB: Yes

TASTING ROOM AMENITIES: Picnic area

REGION: Paso Robles AVA

Spend an afternoon with Lee Nesbitt of Chumeia Vineyards and you might come away thinking that David Lee Roth has retired from rock and roll and started a winery. Nesbitt and Roth share many of the same qualities: gregarious charm, a passionate interest in what they do, and a willingness to share that interest with others. Lee started at Cal Poly on a football scholarship and by graduation was good enough as linebacker to be drafted by the Minnesota Vikings. When not playing football, his agriculture business major got him access to the university's vineyard. Hands-on training familiarized him with every aspect of the industry, from growing grapes to marketing wine. Kristin, his wife, has the same degree, so Lee can't hide his mistakes.

In 1989 Lee had an internship at J. Lohr that evolved into a four-year stay. Jerry Lohr allowed him to arrange his time at the winery around his school schedule. As he got more experience, Jerry gave him permission to produce his own wine during his leisure time, what little there was, and in 1991 Lee made 250 cases of wine. Released in 1994, it sold out. He also spent seven years at Meridian learning everything he could about operating a winery. This gave him the last piece of the puzzle he needed to start on his own. Lee knew how to grow the grapes, and now he had confirmation that he could sell the wine. His mom gave him the name for the winery: Chumeia—Greek for "alchemy"—and the name fitted. Instead of turning base metals into gold, Lee Nesbitt set about the task of transforming soil, water, grapes, and light into wine.

Chumeia has two labels for the consumer. The White is designed primarily for supermarkets and is vinified in a "buy it, take it home, and drink it tonight" style. Lee believes the White label line supports a strong price-to-quality ratio. You get an excellent value at the store. The Black Label uses fruit exclusively from specific vineyards on the Central Coast. Although the Black Label line has a higher price point, the proportionally higher quality of the grapes maintains the value of the wines.

RECOMMENDED WINES: Lee will put his $12 Viognier up against others costing four times as much. I offer it as my White Label recommendation. This butterscotch-colored wine has a nose of apples, melon, peaches, and nectarines. A hint of minerality also comes through. The wine has just enough oak to carry the fruit and enough acidity to keep the fruit in balance. Though vinified to be dry, this is a luscious Viognier given the very ripe fruit and just a hint of residual sugar—in all, a fresh, lively wine with plenty of fruit and a satisfying finish. And when you remember what you paid for it, you'll be even more pleased.

From the Black Label wines, I selected the Pinot Noir. The 2001 is a potential prizewinner. Unfined and unfiltered, the wine is blood-red and almost opaque in the glass. There is a note of clean straw in the nose, and then violets and cherries emerge. The nose concludes with interesting notes of vanilla and cloves. The soft and rounded tannins give the wine an elegant feel in the mouth. An intriguing component is the kick at the finish: the lovely nose is followed by excellent fruit on the palate, and the finish seems to revitalize the taste of the wine for added, lingering pleasure.

Lee's favorite grape is Cabernet Sauvignon. He recommends the Black Label Cabernet Sauvignon from the 2001 vintage. This is a dense, black and purple wine with a nose of cassis, plums, and strawberry jam below the spiced oak. The wine is well balanced, and the tannins will support an additional three to eight years in the bottle: it has the complexity to reward aging, and an additional five years will allow the wine's finesse to emerge.

RATING: Two stars (White label); three stars (Black label)

Claiborne & Churchill Vintners

WINERY OWNERS: Claiborne Thompson and Fredericka Churchill

WINEMAKER: Claiborne (Clay) Thompson

TASTING ROOM: Yes

DAYS/HOURS: Daily 11 A.M.–5 P.M.

ADDRESS: 2649 Carpenter Canyon Rd., San Luis Obispo, CA 93401; 805-544-4066; 805-544-7012 (fax); claibornechurchill.com

WINES/GRAPE VARIETIES: Chardonnay, dry Gewürztraminer, dry Riesling, dry rosé, Orange Muscat, Pinot Gris, Pinot Noir, Runestone (blend), Syrah

WINE CLUB: Yes

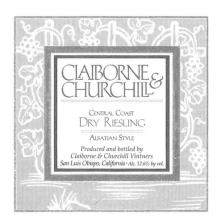

TASTING ROOM AMENITIES: Merchandise

REGION: Edna Valley AVA

Dr. Claiborne (Clay) Thompson, then professor of Old Norse languages and literatures and department head at the University of Michigan, once was invited to present a paper at a conference in California. Traveling with Fredericka Churchill, M.A., an instructor of German, he took some time between presentations and drove up and down the Central Coast, visiting wineries along the way. They tasted at Firestone in Santa Barbara and later visited the Edna Valley. The great poet Rainer Maria Rilke said that after looking upon the famous statue of the torso of Apollo, you must change your life, and so it was with Clay and Fredericka after seeing the Central Coast. Shortly afterward they left the ivy-covered brick walls of academe, came west in 1981 on a honeymoon train, and started life anew. Clay went to work as a cellar rat in a winery and Fredericka in a bookstore to help pay the bills as they set about gaining new experience and knowledge. As Clay developed his skills in the winery, he was encouraged to make his own wine. Dick Graff, the famous winemaker from Chalone who was then at Edna Valley, offered to help with space and information, and in 1983 Claiborne & Churchill celebrated its first crush.

Fredericka and Clay have always admired the dry white wines of Alsace. Their first vintage produced 565 cases of Gewürztraminer and Riesling from grapes grown at the famous Paragon vineyard. When the wines were ready for sale, the two would load up, drive the wines to San Francisco, and sell them from the back of their truck to restaurants and wine shops. They weathered the recession of the early 1990s and over time saw production increase to about 5,000 cases a year. With the growth in production and relative financial stability afforded by the excellent reception of the wines, it became time to establish their own facility, so they bought 6 acres on which to build the winery and tasting room. That facility, completed in 1995, is a straw-bale building, the first of its kind in California. And no, the big bad wolf's huffing and puffing won't blow the walls down, as they are 16 inches thick and made from bales of rice straw. An excellent example of environmental engineering, the straw bales provide enough insulation to afford a constant cellar temperature without the need for additional heating or cooling of the structure. The unique construction of the winery and the wines produced within alike attract visitors.

Now one of the oldest wineries in the Edna Valley, Claiborne & Churchill remains very much a family-oriented business. Throughout all the challenges and hard work over the years, Clay and Fredericka never took on additional investors, in an effort to remain true to their original vision of producing noteworthy white wines. They emphasize that the wines are very much a reflection of themselves and the pride they take in fashioning high-quality wines using the traditional techniques they learned under the tutelage of Dick Graff.

RECOMMENDED WINES: Clay and Fredericka suggest the dry Riesling. The 2003 is a light yellow- and lime-colored wine with a nose of honey, citrus, floral notes, and tropical fruit. A layer of minerality underlies the fruit, and there is enough acidity to balance the wine nicely. It is ready for drinking now.

I have found their Gewürztraminer to be among the best on the Central Coast, and it compares favorably with some of the excellent wines I have tasted in Alsace and in Germany. The 2003 is a pale yellow wine with grapefruit, lemon zest, and honey in the nose, although this wine is vinified to be completely dry. The lively acidity carries the lovely floral-scented fruit, and there is a touch of *Gewürz* ("spice") in the mid-palate. Drink now and over the next three years. And if you come across some Icelandic runes you need interpreted, Clay is the one to see.

RATING: Three stars (whites are very good to excellent)

Clautiere Vineyard

WINERY OWNERS: Claudine Blackwell and Terry Brady

WINEMAKER: Terry Brady

TASTING ROOM: Yes

DAYS/HOURS: Daily 12–5 P.M.

ADDRESS: 1340 Penman Springs Rd., Paso Robles, CA 93446; 805-237-3789; 805-237-1730 (fax); clautiere.com

WINES/GRAPE VARIETIES: Cabernet Sauvignon, Grenache, Mourvèdre, port, rosé, Rhône blends, Roussanne, Syrah, Viognier

WINE CLUB: Yes

TASTING ROOM AMENITIES: Mosaic World, metal sculptures, picnic area

REGION: Paso Robles AVA

The motto at Clautiere reads: "Live the best life you can." The tasting room invites you to do just that. Along the way, try on a wig or two from the extensive selection available as you taste the wines. A brash red on the outside and stunning periwinkle and silver inside, the building is awash in vibrant colors that shout at visitors to let their artificial hair down and not take wine so seriously. This is by design. When Claudine Blackwell and Terry Brady put the tasting room together, they decided to make it an extension of their attitude. They want tasters to have both a different and a memorable experience. That said, Claudine takes the growing of the grapes as seriously as Terry takes the winemaking. If you like Rhône-style wines, you have reason enough to visit. However, if, along the way, you want to try on a purple wig and get a little silly, what's the harm?

Terry and Claudine's interest in a European style of winemaking comes from six months living in Portugal in 1998. The couple bought a house in Madeira and became so caught up in making wine from the hundred-year-old vines on their property that they looked for a vineyard in the Alentejo region of southern Portugal, renowned for its cork oaks and concentrated red wines. However, given the remoteness of the place and the language barrier, they returned to Santa Monica and opened a restaurant called The Lobster. But the wine bug bites deeply, and so Claudine, a graduate of Cal Poly, began researching possible sites for relocation out of the city. In 1999 they found the current winery property in Paso Robles, already planted with ten-year-old vines. The year 2000 marked their first vintage, and in 2002 they opened the tasting room. As you taste the wines, you will see that Terry's winemaking style derives from his work with John Munch of Le Cuvier and Matt Trevisan of Linne Calodo. Munch brings an appreciation for the old-world style of winemaking, where Trevisan adds a young winemaker's approach. In all, Terry seeks to produce complex wines that emphasize flavors and intensity. A guiding principle is the pairing of the wine with food. In this sense, he is interested in achieving a "California version of the European style of wine-making." On the way out, don't forget to leave your wig and take a moment to admire the 240-foot wrought-iron sculpture that serves as a fence along the property. Claudine made that.

RECOMMENDED WINES: Terry recommends the 2002 Syrah. I tasted this wine only two weeks after bottling, and the vanilla oak was a little bit forward at the time—to be expected, given the wine's youth. In due time, the cherry and plum fruit will take precedence. The tannins are soft and nicely rounded and make the wine accessible but are sufficient to rewarding age. The wine is black cherry in color and opaque. Had Terry not chosen this wine for his recommendation, it would have been my first choice.

Next on my list was the excellent 2001 Mon Rouge, a blend of mostly Mourvèdre, some Syrah, and a touch of Cabernet Sauvignon. The wine is a pretty garnet-red in the glass with a nose of cherries and currants. This is a well-balanced wine with excellent mouthfeel. The fruit dominates, but there is enough oak to carry it to a pleasant finish. The wine is drinkable now but will reward another three years in the bottle.

RATING: Three stars (both reds and whites very good to excellent across the line)

Clayhouse Vineyard

WINERY OWNERS: Middleton family

WINEMAKER: Dave Frick

TASTING ROOM: No

DAYS/HOURS: By appointment only

ADDRESS: Call for details; 805-239-8989; 805-238-7247 (fax); clayhousewines.com

WINES/GRAPE VARIETIES: Cabernet Sauvignon, Malbec, Petite Sirah, Petit Verdot, Sauvignon Blanc, Syrah, Zinfandel

WINE CLUB: Yes

REGION: Paso Robles AVA

Dark Star Cellars

WINERY OWNERS: Benson family

WINEMAKER: Norm Benson

TASTING ROOM: Yes

DAYS/HOURS: Friday–Sunday 10:30 A.M–5 P.M.

ADDRESS: 2985 Anderson Rd., Paso Robles, CA 93446; 805-237-2389; 805-237-2589 (fax); darkstarcellars.com

WINES/GRAPE VARIETIES: Anderson Road (blend), Cabernet Sauvignon, Merlot, Ricordati (blend), Syrah, Zinfandel

WINE CLUB: Yes

TASTING ROOM AMENITIES: Merchandise

REGION: Paso Robles AVA

Norm Benson is a self-taught winemaker and a pragmatist. He went from not liking wine very much at all in 1992 to making a living from it by producing award-winning wines at Dark Star. In 1990 his parents bought and planted a vineyard and, in the act of selling their grapes, came to know and love the people in the wine industry around Paso Robles. With encouragement from new friends and the established winemakers among them, the Bensons decided to try their hand and crushed grapes in 1993 and 1994. They bought the current property, with its tasting room, in 1995. As with many of the wineries in Paso Robles, this is still very much a family operation. Susan, Norm's wife, runs the new tasting room, and son Brian is taking an active role in helping his father even as he establishes his own line of wines, Brian Benson Cellars. In fact, you can taste Brian's wines in what used to be the Dark Star tasting room (they have opened a new and more spacious facility next door). Norm received his training on the job as free labor for other winemaker friends early in his career. In so doing, he forged lasting relationships, and to this day it is not unusual for someone to call at midnight asking for help to fix a malfunctioning press during the middle of crush. He goes and helps because that's how it's done in Paso Robles.

Norm's philosophy can be summed up in this quote: "Grow the grape, ferment it, put it in the bottle." The key is in his relationships with his growers. He knows them and they know him. Price is not the primary concern. He treats the wine with care but prefers an unintrusive style; after pressing and fermentation, put on the kid gloves; save the hands-on for the fermentation process, and then only if adjustment is required. In this sense, despite all the technological advancements available to the winemaker, he prefers making wine the old-fashioned way, appreciating the fact that winemaking has a long history that we can learn from. One thing he knows for certain: the variation of the vintages is part of the beauty of making wine, and he will tell you in no uncertain terms that he has made better wines every vintage since that first crush in 1993.

RECOMMENDED WINES: Norm considers each of his red wines to be dark stars, but the Ricordati (Italian for "always remember" and a tribute to his late father), his Bordeaux blend, shines most brightly. The 2002 is a blend of 63 percent Cabernet Sauvignon, 30 percent Merlot, and the rest Cabernet Franc. The wine is almost opaque to the stem and a cherry-garnet color in the glass. It has a bouquet of cerise, leather, smoke, red currants, and violets. This lovely blend has excellent fruit above a fine tannic grip and is drinking wonderfully now. The finish is nearly a minute and recalls the fine ripe fruit. This wine should hold another three to five years in the bottle.

I suggest the Cabernet Sauvignon. The 2002 is almost opaque and a pretty cherry-red in the glass. The nose is cherries, cassis, smoked meats, briars, boysenberry, and cinnamon spice. The wine is well balanced and integrated, showing lovely fruit ahead of the ripe tannins. It lasted nearly a minute on the tongue. This excellent example will continue to improve over the next five to seven years.

RATING: Two → three stars (quality is improving)

Denner Vineyards & Winery

WINERY OWNERS: Ron and Marilyn Denner

WINEMAKER: Brian Denner

TASTING ROOM: Yes

DAYS/HOURS: By appointment only

ADDRESS: 5414 Vineyard Dr., Paso Robles, CA 93446; 805-239-4287; 805-239-1054 (fax); dennervineyards.com

WINES/GRAPE VARIETIES: Syrah, Viognier-Roussanne

WINE CLUB: Yes

REGION: Paso Robles AVA, west side

Doce Robles Winery & Vineyard

WINERY OWNERS: Jim and Maribeth Jacobsen

WINEMAKER: Jim Jacobsen

TASTING ROOM: Yes

DAYS/HOURS: Daily 10 A.M.–5:30 P.M.

ADDRESS: 2023 Twelve Oaks Dr., Paso Robles, CA 93446; 805-227-4766; 805-227-6521 (fax); docerobles.com

WINES/GRAPE VARIETIES: Barbera, Cabernet Sauvignon, Chardonnay, late-harvest Zinfandel, Robles Rojos (blend), Sunset Red (blend), Syrah, Syrificab (blend), Zinfandel

WINE CLUB: Yes

TASTING ROOM AMENITIES: Merchandise

REGION: Paso Robles AVA

The entrance to the tasting room at Doce Robles may be guarded by two German shepherds, Syrah and Zinny. As you step over them, be careful not to make too much noise, but if they do rouse, a quick scratch behind the ears and they are likely to fall back asleep, their duties done. Once in the tasting room, sidle up to the beautiful oak bar salvaged from the old Mission View Winery (now Pretty-Smith) with the oak storage cabinets behind it and meet owners Jim and Maribeth Jacobsen. Jim will tell you that his start in the wine business was the result of a train wreck—literally. In 1994 a train carrying thousands of bottles of wine derailed. Jim was hired to help unload it, and the train company let him salvage what he wanted. He invited friends over, and the fun was on.

If you press him further, Jim admits that he and Maribeth are both third-generation farmers from Fresno County, where their families grew almonds, peaches, raisins, and wine grapes. This background shapes Jim's viewpoint: "If you do it right in the field, you don't have to mess with it too much in the winery." The key is to grow good grapes from the start. They moved from the San Joaquin Valley to Paso Robles in 1997. After looking for properties in the area, they settled on 40 acres atop an oak-crowned hill on Twelve Oaks Drive and named the winery Doce Robles. They produced their first harvest in 1998. It is very much a family business; Maribeth's mother, Fresno artist Gail Hansen, created the label.

Growing good grapes is one thing—albeit a very important one—but making them into good wine is another. Jim knew he had a good palate (try tasting through a trainload of wine), but he also had good friends. Dan Panico at Dover Canyon and Vic Roberts at Victor Hugo gave him hands-on training, and his experience working with the winemakers at Grey Wolf and JanKris allowed him to build his knowledge base. In 1999 he started making his own wines. The very things that attracted him to this region—the location, the soils, and the people—have all contributed to his wine-making endeavors.

RECOMMENDED WINES: Maribeth offers the Robles Rojos as her recommendation. I tasted the 2000, a medal-winning blended red of Cabernet Sauvignon, Cabernet Franc, and Merlot. This reddish-purple wine is nearly opaque in the glass. The nose is berries and jam, with rounded tannins and a soft finish. The dominant element in the blend is the Cabernet Sauvignon.

Jim suggests the 2001 Merlot. The wine has plenty of fruit in the middle, and the soft tannins contribute to a supple mouthfeel. This red and purple wine has notes of cherry and mint in the nose. In all, a fine Merlot ready for the table now.

My recommendation is the late-harvest Zinfandel, and if the 2001 is a representative example of what Jim can do with this variety, the future bodes well for Doce Robles. This is a black cherry–colored wine almost opaque in the glass. The ripeness of the grapes gives it a touch of ruby port in the nose, but ripe figs are present too. The residual sugar in this wine is an enormous 40 percent, but thankfully, the acidity in the wine balances the sugar so it doesn't seem cloying. The Zinfandel fruit definitely has a chance to show its quality. This is another fine example of how good a late-harvest Zin from Paso Robles can be. I would load up the train with this one.

RATING: One → two stars (reds are ahead of whites)

Domaine Alfred

WINERY OWNER: Alfred "Terry" Speizer

WINEMAKER: Mike Sinor (until 2006), Fintan du Fresne

TASTING ROOM: Yes

DAYS/HOURS: Daily 10 A.M.–5 P.M.

ADDRESS: 7525 Orcutt Rd., San Luis Obispo, CA 93401; 805-541-9463; 805-546-2744 (fax); domainealfred.com

WINES/GRAPE VARIETIES: Chardonnay, Pinot Gris, Pinot Noir, red blend, Syrah

WINE CLUB: Yes

TASTING ROOM AMENITIES: Merchandise

REGION: Edna Valley AVA

Chamisal, the oldest vineyard in the Edna Valley, was originally planted by Norm Goss in 1972. He planted 68 acres of mostly Chardonnay grapes, along with some Cabernet Sauvignon. Interestingly, Norm was a world-class pianist who enjoyed the performances of another great pianist, Ignacy Jan Paderewski, who established his winery on the west side of Paso Robles. In 1994 current owner Terry Speizer purchased the dormant vineyard and ripped out all the vines save one, which you can see on display in front of the tasting room. Terry replanted 30 acres with Chardonnay and 30 acres of what most likely was the first large-scale planting of Pinot Noir in the Edna Valley. In

1999 Terry purchased about 63 acres next door to Chamisal and introduced other varieties such as Syrah, Grenache, and Pinot Gris. Where John Alban had proved that Rhône varieties grow beautifully in the Edna Valley, Terry was convinced that Pinot Noir could also flourish if the right clones were properly matched to the cool climate, excellent soils, and long growing season.

Terry made his first fame and fortune in the electronics world, but at one point in his life decided he wanted to make world-class wines. After attending an international wine festival at Oregon one year, he started working harvests and tasting wines and was seduced by the lifestyle of the *vigneron*. After his successful career at Atari, he made the jump and bought Chamisal. The inaugural vintage of Domaine Alfred was in 1998, with Terry also making the wines in 1999 and 2000. Mike Sinor then made the wines until May 2006, when he left to launch his own winery. The new winemaker is New Zealand native Fintan du Fresne, who has earned graduate degrees in viticulture and enology. Fin's hiring will allow Terry to focus his attention on the farming of the grapes. They both believe in the potential for biodynamics as part of their effort to make the best wines possible from the best grapes in the vineyards. Terry kindly and patiently takes small groups of tourists through the tasting room and out into the vineyards, answering all their questions and helping them through the tasting of the wines.

RECOMMENDED WINES: One example of the winery's potential is Terry's recommendation, the Domaine Alfred Red, or, as it's cleverly known, DA Red, pronounced "duh red." This is a wonderful blend, almost opaque in the glass, red-purple in color. The cherry and plum fruit of the Pinot Noir greets you, and the spice and pepper of the Syrah invites you back for another taste. The tannins are round and soft, making the 2002 ready for drinking. Quite simply, this is one of the best blends coming out of the Edna Valley today.

I suggest the Califa (an Indian name meaning "the prettiest one") Pinot Noir. The 2001 is a dark, blood-red wine nearly opaque in the glass. It has a nose of plums, black cherries, black currants, and an intriguing hint of pomegranate. This outstanding Pinot Noir lives in the mouth and lasts nearly a minute on the tongue. It has great fruit and excellent weight and is beautifully balanced. All in all, this is a wonderful example of Edna Valley's potential for Pinot Noir.

RATING: Four stars (reds are excellent to outstanding)

Donati Family Vineyard

WINERY OWNER: Ron Donati

WINEMAKER: Dan Kleck

TASTING ROOM: Yes

DAYS/HOURS: Daily 10 A.M.–6 P.M. (winter 5 P.M.)

ADDRESS: 2720 Oak View Rd., Templeton, CA 93465; 877-511-9463; (fax); no fax; donatifamilyvineyard.com

WINES/GRAPE VARIETIES: Current Mastantuono stock is being liquidated

WINE CLUB: No

TASTING ROOM AMENITIES: Picnic area

REGION: Paso Robles AVA, Templeton area

The former Mastantuono Winery was taken over by Ron Donati of Donati Family Vineyards in February 2007, after the retirement of Pasquale Mastantuono.

Donatoni Winery

WINERY OWNER: Hank Donatoni

WINEMAKER: Hank Donatoni

TASTING ROOM: Yes

DAYS/HOURS: Saturday–Sunday 12–5 P.M.

ADDRESS: 3225 Township Rd.,
Paso Robles, CA 93446; 805-226-0620;
no fax; donatoniwinery.com

WINES/GRAPE VARIETIES: Cabernet
Sauvignon, Chardonnay, Petite Sirah,
red blend, Sangiovese, Syrah, Zinfandel

WINE CLUB: No

REGION: Paso Robles AVA

Dover Canyon Winery

WINERY OWNERS: Dan Panico and Mary
Baker

WINEMAKER: Dan Panico

TASTING ROOM: Yes

DAYS/HOURS: Thursday–Sunday 11 A.M.–
5 P.M.

ADDRESS: 4520 Vineyard Dr., Paso Robles,
CA 93446; 805-237-0101; 805-237-9191
(fax); dovercanyon.com

WINES/GRAPE VARIETIES: Barbera,
Cabernet Sauvignon, Chardonnay, Che
Vita da Cane (blend), Merlot, Renegade
Red (blend), Roussanne, Syrah, Syrah
port, Viognier, Zinfandel, Zinfandel port

WINE CLUB: Yes

TASTING ROOM AMENITIES: Picnic tables

REGION: Paso Robles AVA

Dan Panico, known casually hereabouts as Dover Dan, is a Cal Poly alumnus with a degree in fruit science. Early in his career, Dan happened to meet Gary Eberle, owner of his eponymous winery and already becoming renowned as a steward of young talent, and the master took the pupil on. He kept a close eye on Dan's progress and noticed that he was organized, hardworking, and talented. Gary says that Dan was the first at his winery, other than the big boss himself, to be officially designated winemaker. Dan prospered under Gary's expert tutelage for six years before establishing Dover Canyon Winery. So must it ever be for great teachers.

Dover Canyon is much more than Dan Panico: Mary Baker plays a key role as partner. She started her odyssey in the Paso wine region at Martin Brothers (now Martin & Weyrich) before she went to Wild Horse and there managed the tasting room. After her time there, she moved on to become the business manager for Justin Baldwin at the Justin Winery. What started as a hobby in 1992 became a full-time vocation as Dover Canyon Winery in 1997.

Where Dover Dan makes the wines and tends to the vineyards they own, Mary does the marketing and sales in addition to managing the tasting-room operations. But you might also find her in the vineyard, hoe in hand, chopping out weeds growing in the cover crops between the vines. Or you might be fortunate enough to try her hand-crafted Sangiovese, if there is any left. Dan is very much a winemaker who believes that the quality of the fruit is dependent on the *terroir,* and Paso has that in spades. A pre-calcareous shale runs through the properties where he buys his grapes. There is also limestone in the hills behind the winery; the cooling breezes off the Pacific help moderate the temperatures, and sufficient yearly rainfall in the hills precludes the need to irrigate the plantings. Mary and Dan are careful stewards of the land they own. Dan prefers low-impact, largely organic farming practices, and Dover Canyon is an officially registered wildlife habitat where one can see owls, red-tailed hawks, and, at the right time of year, perhaps a cougar or two patrolling the hills.

RECOMMENDED WINES: Dan and Mary have made a considered decision not to grow the winery too fast or too large. This enables Dan to maintain the control he needs to produce hand-crafted superpremium wines that exhibit his distinctive style as a winemaker. The Syrah comes highly recommended. I tasted the 2002 and the 2001, and to my palate, at this time the 2001 is slightly better. This is a dark garnet wine opaque in the glass with a nose of plums, pepper, cloves, and ripe fruit. It exhibits a wonderful mouthfeel, and you can taste the quality of the fruit. This rich and luscious wine is finely balanced and has the tannic structure necessary to support the fruit. Drinking well now, it has at least five years ahead of it.

When I arrived in Paso Robles, friends and colleagues made a special point of taking me to Dover Canyon. Since then I have been an ardent fan of the Cujo Zin. I tasted the 2002, and this wine is somewhat lighter than in years past, most likely a result of the vintage. The red cherry color is bright and pretty in the glass but not opaque as in former years. The dominant notes in the nose are wild strawberries and fresh red raspberries, with sage and peppercorn undertones. The fine fruit and tannic structure contribute to a long, satisfying finish. Even though one noted wine publication considers Cujo the dog to be an ugly caricature for a wine label, I think he is a rather handsome brute and altogether worthy of gracing the label with his happy mug. When you learn the story of why Cujo has been so memorialized, decide for yourself, but don't let the quality of the wine influence your judgment.

RATING: Three stars (reds are very good to excellent)

Dunning Vineyards

WINERY OWNERS: Dunning family

WINEMAKER: Robert Dunning

TASTING ROOM: Yes

DAYS/HOURS: Thursday–Monday 11 A.M.– 5 P.M.

ADDRESS: 1953 Niderer Rd., Paso Robles, CA 93446; 805-238-4763; 805-238-4763 (fax); dunningvineyards.com

DUNNING VINEYARDS

2002
PASO ROBLES
SYRAH
WESTSIDE

GROWN, PRODUCED AND BOTTLED BY DUNNING VINEYARDS
PASO ROBLES, CALIFORNIA • ALCOHOL 14.3% BY VOLUME

WINES/GRAPE VARIETIES: Cabernet
Sauvignon, Chardonnay, Merlot, Syrah,
Vin de Casa (blend), Zinfandel

WINE CLUB: Yes

TASTING ROOM AMENITIES: Picnic area,
merchandise, bed-and-breakfast

REGION: Paso Robles AVA

When the Dunning family bought the old Niderer property of 80 acres back in 1960, it was primarily to give the family a rural escape from Malibu; Grandfather also admired the property for its bountiful population of deer and turkey. Much has changed in the interim, but you won't have to drive far from the property before you run into a flock of gobblers. During those early years there was some semblance of a wine industry in Paso Robles, with the likes of the Pesentis, the Rottas, and the Nerellis, but most of the farm properties were planted to barley or supported horse ranches or almond orchards. Shortly after Robert met his wife, Jo-Ann, in the late 1970s, they began to nurture a growing interest in wine. They had visited Napa on occasion and were intrigued by the possibility of planting some of the acreage over to grapes. When a nearby neighbor put in a vineyard, Robert's interest was piqued, so he started asking questions and read all the viticulture textbooks he could get his hands on.

As he got more education through extension courses and reading, he tried his hand at home winemaking on an experimental basis even as he was learning what it takes to run a vineyard. In the meantime, the neighbor's vineyard proved to be a wonderful hands-on apprenticeship for what was to come, and Robert learned his style there. The Dunnings decided to make the move into viticulture. In 1991 the first plantings were Chardonnay, Merlot, Cabernet Sauvignon, and Cabernet Franc. Over time, Robert has come to appreciate the four factors he considers essential for making authentic estate-grown wines: the site, the soil, the climate, and last on the list, the human impact of the winemaker. Sixteen acres of the original 80 are now under cultivation and permit Robert to express the *terroir* so crucial to the making of his wines. In 1996, with almost fifteen years of home winemaking behind him, Robert Dunning's wines won a gold medal for Merlot and bronzes for the Chardonnay and Cabernet Sauvignon, at the Orange County Fair.

The property, once bought as a family retreat in the country, now affords the Dunnings the lifestyle they have come to cherish. They farm the land and grow their own grapes; they produce handmade artisanal wines, and everything is family-owned. And in keeping with their vision for the development of the property, the Dunnings have included a bed-and-breakfast facility called Dunning Vineyards Country Inn, now open year-round. A picture of that house adorns the label. Their intent is to make a contribution to agri-tourism, already popular in Europe, in which visitors can come to a family farm—or, in this case, a farm, vineyard, and winery—to enjoy a splendid rural setting far from the hustle and daily grind of city life. Visitors can spend the night, sit under the canopy of oaks and admire the forested hills where the turkeys still roost, stroll among the vineyards, and take it all in over the rim of a wineglass.

RECOMMENDED WINES: Robert suggests the Cabernet Sauvignon. I tasted the 2001, a blend of 80 percent Cab and the rest Merlot. The wine is brick-red and almost opaque to the stem. The nose is reminiscent of chocolate truffles, ripe cherries, and cassis. The tannins are ripe and rounded and do not overpower the fruit. The finish is long, with the taste of currants reemerging. This wine is ready for the table now and is vinified to be a food wine. It will drink well over the next three to five years.

I enjoyed the Syrah. The 2002 is a very lightly colored cherry-red that shows ripe raspberry fruit with a touch of mocha and a hint of smoke. The tannins are in good evidence, providing fine structure and the potential for another five years in the bottle. Despite the atypical color for the variety, this is a very attractive Syrah capable of aging.

RATING: Two stars (very good and competently made wines)

Eagle Castle Winery

WINERY OWNERS: Gary and Mary Lou Stemper

WINEMAKER: Gary Stemper

TASTING ROOM: Yes

DAYS/HOURS: Daily 10:30 A.M.–5:30 P.M.

ADDRESS: 3090 Anderson Rd., Paso Robles, CA 93446; 805-227-1428; 805-227-1429 (fax); eaglecastlewinery.com

WINES/GRAPE VARIETIES: Cabernet Sauvignon, Chardonnay, late-harvest Viognier, late-harvest Zinfandel, Merlot, Muscat Canelli, Petite Sirah, Royal Red (blend), Syrah, Syrah rosé, Viognier, Zinfandel, Zinfandel port

WINE CLUB: Yes

TASTING ROOM AMENITIES: Merchandise, 8,000-square-foot castle

REGION: Paso Robles AVA

If you take a trip to Germany's great wine regions along the Rhine or Mosel rivers, in addition to seeing vineyards climbing up the steep sides of the hills you will see ancient castles. Or, if you want to save on the airfare, visit Gary and Mary Lou Stemper's Eagle Castle instead. You'll see full suits of armor inside, and now that construction is completed, you will cross a moat to the towers. Gary's home might figuratively be his castle, but his winery, located off Highway 46 West, literally is one.

Gary knows Paso Robles, and he knows his wines. In fact, the former mayor has the distinction of having established Paso Robles as a wine appellation. However, he did not travel the usual road to becoming a winemaker and the king of his castle (Mary Lou will tell you who has the real power). During his early years in construction, he was busy paving roads. Many of the roads leading to Paso Robles wineries were built and finished by Gary and his crew. That is how he met Gary Eberle, then at Estrella River Winery. When Eberle started his own winery, Stemper got the bid to do the site work and construction. In addition to his partnership with Eberle over the years, Stemper also invested in Treana, now Summerwood.

His associations, personal and professional, with people in the industry led him to try his hand at home winemaking. He began production in his garage. Keep this in mind when you visit his new facility and tour the castle—the dirt roads of the early years have transformed into a royal carpet. It is also apparent that Gary put his many years in politics to good use at the winery. He understands the power of a theme to bring people into the winery, and he knows the benefits of surrounding himself with knowledgeable, competent associates. For example, Vic Roberts has served as wine consultant, but in the grand political tradition of Harry Truman, Gary has the final say as he oversees the winemaking.

RECOMMENDED WINES: Gary told his investors that the goal at Eagle Castle was to produce balanced and drinkable wines; otherwise, the "wine doesn't go in the bottle." The 2000 Cabernet Sauvignon is a good representation of Gary's philosophy as winemaker. This is a dark red, almost black Cab, opaque in the glass. The nose is redolent of loganberry, Juicy Fruit gum, and cassis. The tannins are soft and add to the wine's elegance in the mouth, but are sufficient to help the wine age. It has already won two California state competition gold medals.

My recommendation is the 2001 Zinfandel, a dark cherry-colored wine of ripe plums and a hint of smoke. The wine is well balanced and has the complexity of fruit and oak to reward aging, but is accessible now.

I also want to mention the 2003 Late Harvest Viognier. The wine is nearly gold in color, with a wonderful nose of fruit and flowers. The residual sugar is 11 percent, but the acidity in the wine nicely balances the sweetness. Drink this as a fine example of a sweeter Viognier.

RATING: Two → three stars (reds ahead of whites)

Eberle Winery

WINERY OWNER: Gary Eberle

WINEMAKER: Ben Mayo

TASTING ROOM: Yes

DAYS/HOURS: Daily 10 A.M.–5 P.M. (summer 6 P.M.)

ADDRESS: 3810 Hwy. 46 E., Paso Robles, CA 93446; 805-238-9607; 805-237-0344 (fax); eberlewinery.com

WINES/GRAPE VARIETIES: Barbera, Cabernet Sauvignon, Chardonnay, Côtes-du-Rôbles (Rhône blend), Full Boar Red (blend), Muscat Canelli, port, Roussanne, Sangiovese, Syrah, Syrah rosé, Viognier, Zinfandel

WINE CLUB: Yes

TASTING ROOM AMENITIES: Picnic area, merchandise, cave tours

REGION: Paso Robles AVA

One would have no problem calling Gary Eberle "Professor" or designating his winery the Wine University of Paso Robles. He has both the theoretical training and the experience to make it work. All that is missing is a toga above his ever-present sandals.

It is also a well-known fact that some of the area's well-established winemakers got their start working for the professor either at Estrella, his first venture, or at Eberle, home of the little boar statue that sits out front. I like to pet him for good luck (watch the tusks) before I taste or take the tour of the caves below the wonderful tasting room. The panorama from the patio is breathtaking as you take in the surrounding hills and vineyards. But to become a professor, you first have to be a good student and have a strong desire to excel.

Intelligence and athleticism made Gary Eberle a prize college recruit. A high-school all-American football player, Eberle was spared the heat and toil of the blast furnaces in the steel mills of Pittsburgh, Pennsylvania, where he was born, when Joe Paterno offered him a full ride to play on the gridiron of Penn State. Paterno pushed him not only on the field but in the classroom as well. He took those lessons to heart and after graduating with a degree in biology was accepted as a graduate student in cellular genetics at Louisiana State University.

Gary also has an abiding love of classical music, which he discovered in the eighth grade. After his first hearing of Beethoven's Ninth, with its stupendous Chorale, he was hooked. The Impressionists, particularly Grofé's *Grand Canyon Suite,* also left their mark. He wanted to sing in a choir but was told he did not have the voice for it. Undaunted, he pursued his interest in music on his own. He cobbled together a respectable library of LPs during his playing days in Happy Valley and took his collection south to LSU. There he discovered a professor who shared his appreciation for opera. Eberle's professor introduced the young scholar to some of the finest Bordeaux wines in his collection as they listened to Richard Tucker sing the role of Canio in *Pagliacci* and drank Château Latour. Ever the curious student, Eberle found his interest again piqued, and he read everything about wine that he could find. He discovered the pioneering work being done at UC Davis in enology and was compelled to visit. The chair of the department was so impressed with his credentials (Eberle had already published two papers as a graduate student) and his desire to become a winemaker that Eberle was admitted into the doctoral program without taking the qualifying exam.

In the 1970s his professors at Davis were touting the potential of Paso Robles for growing outstanding Cabernet Sauvignon. California was in the beginning of its second great wine boom (all his classmates got jobs as winemakers). Eberle had walked the land near what became Estrella with his professors as they took soil samples. In fact, Eberle wrote and published one of the first monographs on the calcareous soils of the area, the chalky ground so well suited for the Cabernet Sauvignon grape. As fortune would have it, a half brother wanted to start a cattle ranch in the area, but as these things go they planted the 500 acres of ground with grapevines on the Estrella River plains east of Paso Robles instead. In 1973 he and partner Cliff Giacobine built the Estrella River Winery, now Meridian Vineyards. After seeing the winery grow to 200,000 cases annually, he was ready to start his eponymous label in 1982.

Gary has given the winemaking duties over to Ben Mayo. Together they continue to follow the dictates of Professor Maynard Amerine, who said do as little damage as possible in bringing the grape to the glass. This philosophy has resulted in the production of world-class Cabernet, which Gary says he will put in double-blind tastings against the best in the world anytime, anywhere. With the likes of Justin Baldwin, Jerry Lohr, John Munch, Chuck Ortman, and Ken Volk, Gary is considered one of the first among the modern wine pioneers of Paso Robles. Recently he earned the honor of being named a Top Ten Gold Medal Award Winning Winery in the United States. Joe Pa would have expected nothing less.

RECOMMENDED WINES: Professor Eberle's recommendation is the 2001 Cabernet Sauvignon, which I tasted first in the barrel and then in the bottle, confirming my excitement for this wine. This wine is an opaque black cherry color. The nose is redolent of black cherries, blackberries, vanilla spice, truffles, and crème fraîche. The wine is stuffed with ripe, luscious fruit that sits atop an excellent balance of tannins and acidity. The finish is nearly a minute, and this wine will easily last another six to eight years. It is a wonderful example of Paso Robles east-side Cabernet Sauvignon.

I suggest the 2002 Steinbeck Syrah. Opaque and black cherry in color, the wine exhibits blackberries, cherries, spice, and sweet, smoky oak in the nose. The tannins are sufficient for aging another three to five years, and the wine has a lush, well-rounded mouthfeel.

Do take the time to try Eberle's Muscat Canelli. It is consistently the finest in the area, and the 2003 is a particularly good example (and one of my father's favorites).

RATING: Four stars (consistently excellent whites and outstanding reds)

Edna Valley Vineyard

WINERY OWNERS: Paragon Vineyard
Company (owned by the Niven family)
and Diageo Chateau & Estate Wines

WINEMAKER: Harry Hansen

TASTING ROOM: Yes

DAYS/HOURS: Daily 10 A.M.–5 P.M.

ADDRESS: 2585 Biddle Ranch Rd., San Luis
Obispo, CA 93401; 805-544-5855;
805-544-0112 (fax); ednavalleyvineyard
.com

WINES/GRAPE VARIETIES: Cabernet
Sauvignon, Chardonnay, Merlot, Pinot
Gris, Pinot Noir, Sauvignon Blanc, Syrah

WINE CLUB: Yes

TASTING ROOM AMENITIES: Banquet room,
patio, merchandise, tours

REGION: Edna Valley AVA

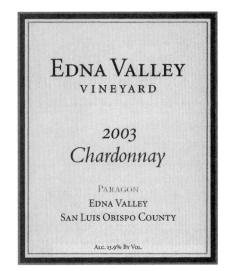

EDNA VALLEY
VINEYARD

2003
Chardonnay

PARAGON
EDNA VALLEY
SAN LUIS OBISPO COUNTY

ALC. 13.9% BY VOL.

When my partner, Nancy, and I first came to the Central Coast, members of her department at Cal Poly decided to take a tour of the Edna Valley wineries. They rented a van, designated a driver, and invited me along as the resident wine expert. Even then I was impressed with the beauty of the Jack Niven Hospitality Center, a 5,000-square-foot facility named after the founder of the famous Paragon vineyard. Edna Valley Vineyard takes its name from the small community of Edna, founded about 1883. In 1974 the Niven family of what is now Baileyana planted the Paragon vineyard. In 1979, after the droughts of 1976 and 1977 caused supply problems in Monterey County, Chalone Vineyard, whose founders were Dick Graff and Phil Woodward, joined with the Nivens in a partnership that led to the establishment of Edna Valley Vineyard. Edna Valley was known for its long and, more important, cool growing season, conducive to producing fine Chardonnay and Pinot Noir. The Chardonnay fruit has generally been judged excellent, but the Pinot Noir has proved more troublesome—problems attributable to the clones planted at that time. The original plantings of almost 100 percent Martini clones now comprise only 3 percent of the vineyard. The majority of the Pinot Noir fruit is grown from Dijon clones and some Oregon variations. Accordingly, with up to six clonal selections planted, all carefully selected to match the soils and the climate, the Pinot Noir fruit is now producing wines that are winning accolades.

Harry Hansen, winemaker at Edna Valley Vineyard since 2001, loves Pinot Noir. He compares the difficult grape to "the beautiful girl you always admired in high school but were too shy to ask out." In other words, it takes a certain amount of courage to deal with this high-maintenance grape, but Harry will tell you this beauty is ultimately worth the time and trouble. Where the Chardonnay plantings can be dated back to the 1970s, the new Pinot Noir clones first went in about 1997. Harry, a graduate of UC Davis, earned a bachelor's degree in genetics in 1982, followed by his master's degree in enology in 1986. This no doubt helps explain his expertise in selecting the correct clones for planting in the vineyard. After receiving his degree at Davis and working at Buena Vista for a time, he decided to forgo a career in genetics and focus on wine instead. Originally from Santa Rosa, he moved to Gloria Ferrer in Sonoma shortly after finishing his education and was eventually promoted to associate winemaker. Ferrer is noted for producing some of the best California sparkling wines using the *méthode champenoise,* and Harry developed his expertise with Chardonnay and Pinot Noir, the two principal grapes of great Champagne, during his time there. As circumstance would have it, Harry's sister went to Cal Poly, and the family often took vacations near San Luis Obispo on the Central Coast. He greatly enjoyed the community and the hospitable people and saw the potential for the area's wine industry. When Edna Valley Vineyard offered him the position of head winemaker, he accepted.

RECOMMENDED WINES: Harry recommends the Paragon Vineyards Chardonnay. We tasted the 2002, a pretty lemon-yellow wine that shows peaches, vanilla, caramel, and butterscotch to the nose. It has an excellent mouthfeel, and the peaches come forward on the tongue. The wine is beautifully balanced between the lovely fruit and the crisp acidity, but the pleasure is in the luscious middle. Ready for drinking now, it will give another three to five years of pleasure.

My recommendation is the single-vineyard Pinot Noir. The 2002 is nearly opaque in the glass and black cherry in color. In the nose I found a wonderful bouquet of plums, cherries, currants, smoke, and a hint of raspberry. The tannins are ripe, soft, and rounded, adding structure and additional dimensionality to the fruit. The finish lasted longer than a minute. Drink now and over the next five years. This wine can stand as an exemplar for the quality of the Pinot Noir fruit now being grown in the Edna Valley Vineyard.

RATING: Three stars (both reds and whites very good to excellent)

Edward Sellers Vineyards & Wines

WINERY OWNER: Edward Sellers

WINEMAKER: Edward Sellers

TASTING ROOM: Yes

DAYS/HOURS: Thursday–Monday 12–7 P.M.

ADDRESS: 1220 Park St., Paso Robles, CA 93446; 805-239-8915; 805-239-8312 (fax); edwardsellers.com

WINES/GRAPE VARIETIES: Grenache, Mourvèdre, red Rhône blend, Roussanne, Syrah, Viognier, white Rhône blend

WINE CLUB: Yes

REGION: Paso Robles AVA

Eos Estate Winery

WINERY OWNERS: Jeff Hopmayer, Sapphire Wines LLC

WINEMAKER: Leslie Melendez

TASTING ROOM: Yes

DAYS/HOURS: Daily 10 A.M.–6 P.M. (winter 5 P.M.)

ADDRESS: 5625 Hwy. 46 E., Paso Robles, CA 93446; 805-239-2562; 805-239-2317 (fax); eosvintage.com

WINES/GRAPE VARIETIES: Cabernet Franc, Cabernet Sauvignon, Chardonnay, French Connection (blend), Fumé Blanc, late-harvest Moscato, Merlot, Moscato, Petite Sirah, Pinot Grigio, Sangiovese, Sauvignon Blanc, Synergy (blend), Zinfandel, Zinfandel port

WINE CLUB: Yes

TASTING ROOM AMENITIES: Merchandise, race-car exhibit, deli, meeting room, self-guided tour, rose garden, picnic area

REGION: Paso Robles AVA

The history of Eos-Arciero begins with the history of an Italian family, the Arcieros. Giovanni Arciero came to the United States from Montecassino, Italy, south of Rome, in 1914, and by 1948 the family had relocated, with brothers Frank and Phil moving on to California. The brothers arrived with a dream of becoming movie stars in Hollywood, despite being penniless and unable to speak English. Their dreams were grounded when they found work digging ditches and eventually started a small cement contracting business. As they prospered, they moved into land development and had a role in building Los Angeles International Airport and parts of Marina del Rey. On weekends in the late 1950s, their success now assured, they raced Ferraris. The Arciero racing team has featured some of the sport's greatest drivers, including Mario Andretti, Dan Gurney, and Al Unser. At the tasting room you can pause to admire the race cars showcased there.

With a family heritage of winemaking in southern Italy, the Arcieros decided to get into the wine business. After researching the area in 1982, they purchased 160 acres in Paso Robles and opened a winery in 1985. There are now more than 700 acres of estate vineyards planted, 500 of them in nearby Shandon. Nebbiolo and Sangiovese grapes are included among the many varieties in the vineyards. The winery is more than 100,000 square feet and has a production capacity of 400,000 cases. The beautiful facility is modeled after a famous Benedictine monastery near the Arcieros' home village in Italy.

Kerry Vix joined the Arciero family as a partner in 1993, adding his more than twenty years of experience in management positions at major wine corporations. In 1997 Vernon Underwood, a family friend of the Arcieros and a successful distributor, came aboard with the intent of maximizing the winery's potential. The new team started with a fresh sheet of paper and essentially remade the winery. Steve Felton was hired as winemaker. To commemorate and reflect the dawning of their new enterprise, they renamed the winery Eos, after the Greek goddess of the dawn. The release of their first vintage Chardonnay came in 1996.

The Arciero family sold the winery to Jeff Hopmayer of Sapphire Wines LLC in August 2007. Kerry Vix continues as general manager.

After Felton left, Leslie Melendez was appointed the winemaker. She initially went to work in a hospital but soon became dissatisfied. She saw an advertisement for a harvest lab technician at the winery and decided, why not? She loved the work so much that in 1993 she took a quarter off from her studies at Cal Poly. Once she completed her degree in nutrition, with its emphasis in food science and chemistry, she worked in almost every position available at the winery, including compliance. She became lab manager, then enologist, then (under the tutelage of her mentor Steve Felton) assistant winemaker, and then staff winemaker, and she was appointed senior winemaker in 2004. Leslie enjoys making elegant and fruit-forward wines and takes a hands-on approach to the winemaking. This philosophy allows her to realize the production of handcrafted wines one would typically see in a smaller winery. In one sense, this is a large winery run as a family operation where everyone knows one another and the crews take pride in their work. The June 2002 issue of *Wine and Spirits* magazine listed Eos as a "Value Winery of the Year."

RECOMMENDED WINES: Leslie recommends the Eos Reserve Petite Sirah. I tasted the 2000, a black-purple wine of lovely sweetness in the nose atop soft oak, plums, cherries, and a touch of black pepper. The wine presents ample ripe fruit to the mid-palate and finishes with a smooth, long-lasting aftertaste. This is a wonderful example of Petite Sirah, and my barrel tasting of the 2001 suggests that it will surpass the 2000.

The Cupa Grandis is the top line at Eos, and my recommendation from this group is the 2001 Cupa Grandis Petite Sirah. This wine shows essentially the same dark purple color as the Reserve, and the nose is redolent of black fruit and spice. But the judicious use of heavy-toast Mercier French oak adds an extra dimension to the wine's structure and complexity. The wine is wonderful and rich in the mouth and has a long, ripe, luscious finish. This is one of the best Petite Sirahs in the region.

RATING: One star (Cupa Grandis line three stars)

Firestone Vineyard (Paso Robles)

WINERY OWNERS: Firestone family

WINEMAKER: Kevin Willenborg

TASTING ROOM: Yes

DAYS/HOURS: Daily 10 A.M.–5 P.M.

ADDRESS: 2300 Airport Rd., Paso Robles, CA 93446; 805-591-8050; 805-686-1256 (fax); firestonewine.com

WINES/GRAPE VARIETIES: Cabernet Franc, Cabernet Sauvignon, Chardonnay, Merlot, Sauvignon Blanc, Syrah

WINE CLUB: Yes

TASTING ROOM AMENITIES: Picnic area, merchandise, tours

REGION: Paso Robles AVA

For details on Firestone Vineyard, see chapter 8.

Four Vines Winery

WINERY OWNERS: Susan A. Mahler, Christian Tietje, Bill Grant

WINEMAKER: Christian Tietje

TASTING ROOM: Yes

DAYS/HOURS: Thursday–Monday 11 A.M.– 6 P.M. (winter 5 P.M.)

ADDRESS: 3750 Hwy. 46 W., Templeton, CA 93465; 805-237-0055; 805-227-0863 (fax); fourvines.com

WINES/GRAPE VARIETIES: Anarchy (blend), Chardonnay, Petite Sirah, Syrah, Zinfandel

WINE CLUB: Yes

REGION: Paso Robles AVA, Templeton area

Fratelli Perata

WINERY OWNERS: Gino and Joe Perata

WINEMAKER: Gino Perata

TASTING ROOM: Yes

DAYS/HOURS: Saturday–Sunday 10 A.M.–
5 P.M., Monday–Friday by appointment
only

ADDRESS: 1595 Arbor Rd., Paso Robles, CA
93446; 805-238-2809; call for fax;
fratelliperata.com

WINES/GRAPE VARIETIES: Bambino Grande
(blend), Cabernet Franc, Cabernet
Sauvignon, Merlot, Montepulciano, Petite
Sirah, Petit Verdot, Sangiovese, Tre Sorelle
(blend), Zinfandel

WINE CLUB: Yes

TASTING ROOM AMENITIES: Picnic area

REGION: Paso Robles AVA

In the grand Italian tradition, the Perata brothers, Joe and Gino, have established a winery that is very much a family enterprise. Gino's wife, Carol, will tell you that the winery is much more than a business for the Perata family; it is a lifestyle. That lifestyle has Italian roots that reach back through Gino's father, Giuseppe Perata, who brought his father's winemaking skill with him to California. On the maternal side, Bambino Diorio came to Colorado from Belmonte di Sanno, Italy. In 1977 the Perata family purchased a 40-acre parcel of land on which barley was grown. Gino and Carol built a home atop the hill in 1978, and the vineyard was started two years later. The winery was bonded in 1987, a date to remember for the family because their third daughter was born the day they pressed their first wine.

Gino and Joe share the duties in the vineyard and in the cellar, and Carol oversees the day-to-day operation of the winery, which includes pulling corks in the tasting room. Given the history of winemaking that runs through the family, it is not surprising that the Perata brothers believe in stressing the plants in order to produce lower crop yields. In some instances, the yields are deliberately held below 1.5 tons per acre, resulting in fruit with intensely focused flavors. Gino's hands-on experience as winemaker is supplemented by his academic work at UC Davis. Daughter Catherine, most likely to become the next-generation winemaker at Fratelli Perata, attended UC Davis, where she majored in enology and viticulture.

The view from the winery takes in the rolling hills to the south and east. It is a breathtaking vista of golden meadows, dark oak forests, and older and more recently planted vineyards. The tasting room is crowded with barrels of wine in the making, and it is not unusual for Carol to offer visitors wine samples while one great Italian tenor or another sings on the stereo. The polish and pizzazz of million-dollar tasting rooms might not be in evidence here, but you will not notice it once the wines are poured. The richness is in the Perata family and in the wines they produce.

With the advice and support of Ken Volk, an early trailblazer among the Paso Robles wine producers, Gino and Joe made both a Merlot and a Cabernet Sauvignon, the varieties recommended for Paso Robles by André Tchelistcheff. Their 1990 Merlot won gold at the Los Angeles County Fair and was mistaken for a Château Pétrus, one of Bordeaux's most famous wines. The Cabernet Sauvignon Riserva is hand-harvested, and the dry-farmed, deep-rooted vines produce small clusters of tiny berries. The wine rests in French oak from Bordeaux, which imparts a smooth silkiness and adds vanilla undertones. The Riservas have been consistent gold-medal winners. In 1997 Joe and Gino produced their first Bordeaux blend, Tre Sorelle, named in honor of the three Perata sisters.

In addition to producing what I consider the best Sangiovese and Nebbiolo in the region, a family so firmly rooted in the traditions of Italian winemaking has to produce a Zinfandel, especially after fifty years of family history with the grape. The *terroir* of Paso Robles and Zinfandel are made for each other, and some of the finest Zinfandel in the world is made in this region. Gino and Joe take only the best fruit and the ripest berries for the wine. The more neutral wood of old oak is preferred because it preserves the essential fruitiness of the grape. After spending seventeen months in the barrel, the wine is bottled relatively young for a Perata wine. It is one of my favorites and exemplifies what Fratelli Perata is all about. The winery is a labor of love, a labor shared by the family, and the fruits of that labor are manifest in the wines. They make wine because that is what they enjoy doing, and they release it only when they believe the wine is ready. The superb wines of Fratelli Perata can be enjoyed now, but in keeping with the tradition of great French and Italian wines they will become even greater over time.

RECOMMENDED WINES: Gino and Carol recommend the Sangiovese. Like the 1999, the 2000 spent an amazing four and a half years in the barrel. The wine is a pretty cherry color with a touch of orange but is somewhat lighter in the glass because Cabernet Sauvignon has not been blended in, as it was in years past. The aromatics are wonderful: cherries, mulberries, red currants, flowers, and vanilla spice regale the nose. The fruit is ripe and lush, lending to an expansive mouthfeel. The finish lasts nearly a minute. This wine is similar to a superb Chianti Classico Riserva, and though drinking beautifully now will hold another six to eight years.

I recommend the sensational Merlot. The 2002 is opaque to the stem and black cherry in color. The nose is a wonderful palette of cherries, cranberries, chocolate, mocha, leather, and red currants. The wine is broad and deep, filling the mouth with ripe fruit and tannins; it shows superb integration and complexity. The rich, multidimensional finish lasts well over a minute. Give this wine a year in the bottle and then drink over the next ten to twelve years. And don't forget to open your Perata wines at least an hour before drinking in order to taste the subtle but splendid transformation that takes place in these remarkable wines.

RATING: Five stars (superb wines across the line)

Garretson Wine Company

WINERY OWNERS: Mat and Amie Garretson

WINEMAKER: Mat Garretson

TASTING ROOM: Yes

DAYS/HOURS: Daily 11 A.M.–5 P.M.

ADDRESS: 2323 Tuley Court, Ste. 110, Paso Robles, CA 93446; 805-239-2074; 805-239-2057 (fax); garretsonwines.com

WINES/GRAPE VARIETIES: Dry rosé, Grenache, Grenache Blanc, Mourvèdre, red table wine, Rhône-style blends, Roussanne, Syrah, Viognier

WINE CLUB: Yes

TASTING ROOM AMENITIES: Merchandise

REGION: Paso Robles AVA

When Mat Garretson was a senior in high school in Atlanta, he worked as a clerk in the beer and wine section of a local grocery store; he was permitted to sample the wines (in service to his position, please understand), and developed a lifelong appreciation of their differences. While attending the University of Georgia, he rose to the position of manager at the store and ultimately opened his own wine shop after he graduated. In 1982 he was already making homemade wine and in 1988 began to sell his bottlings. By then, his taste had turned to the wines of the Rhône after a fellow retailer had given him a birthday present of a bottle from Condrieu (a Viognier) in 1983. In the meantime, he noticed California shift in the mid-1980s to the production of the very same Rhône varieties he enjoyed so much. He decided to popularize them by founding the Viognier Guild in 1991. Shortly thereafter, he realized that his passion in life would have to include not just popularizing Rhône varieties but also making them. He decided to leave the South and head for California.

Considering the popularity of his new enterprise, he had numerous offers to work in Napa and Sonoma, but he found Paso Robles during one of his travels and decided that there, best of all, Rhône varieties could flourish. Then, in 1994, Gary Eberle called to offer him a position as sales and marketing director, and since the position was an ideal fit, he took it. The Viognier Guild grew by leaps and bounds, and he ultimately renamed it Hospice du Rhône (started with friend John Alban), a clever variation on the theme of Hospices de Beaune. He was bitten by the bug to make his own wines while continuing to build the popularity of the Rhône program at Eberle and started Garretson Wine Company in 1997. In 1998 trying to do both became too much, so he left Eberle and worked for a time with Ken Volk, who allowed him to make Garretson wines at Wild Horse free of charge. By 2000, Hospice du Rhône had become the preeminent international celebration of Rhône varieties, held each year at the Mid-State Fair in Paso Robles; the Equus (Rhône-style) wines at Wild Horse were established; and his case production was nearing 3,000 and rapidly garnering excellent reviews. At one point the *Wine Spectator* anointed him "Mr. Viognier."

In 2001 he moved his operation to the current tasting room, and production increased to about 5,000 cases. All he ever wanted was to remain unpretentious and nonconformist. In fact, "what started as a cathartic release has become a business plan," Mat says. He sticks with a noninterventionist philosophy when it comes to the wine. He lets it be what it's going to be. This means his wines will not see a polish filtration, so you may see a bottle that looks a little cloudy. Don't let it put you off: Garretson prefers his wines to have maximum flavor, even if it means they are not polished to gleaming perfection, which risks stripping flavor and nuance. Garretson gives his wines Gaelic names, and he will be more than happy to help you with their pronunciation.

RECOMMENDED WINES: Not surprisingly, Mat suggests the Viognier, and I had the pleasure of tasting the 2001. The wine shows gold already and has a perfumed nose of kiwi, melons, tangerines, and oranges. It fills the mouth with body, and the neutral oak is just enough to provide a backbone to the layers of fruit. The wine is excellent now but will reward another three years or so in the bottle.

I recommend the 2001 Reliquary (a vessel that holds a sacred object), a blend of mostly Syrah, with some Counoise, Mourvèdre, and Viognier. The wine is opaque to the stem and a lovely lampblack color. The nose is licorice, figs, black cherries, blackberries, blueberries, earth, and spice. The wine is wonderful in the mouth owing to its seamless integration and rounded tannins. The finish lasted nearly a minute. This fine blend should reward another five to six years of age.

RATING: Four stars (outstanding Rhône-style wines)

Gelfand Vineyards

WINERY OWNERS: Leonard and Jan Gelfand

WINEMAKER: Leonard Gelfand

TASTING ROOM: At Wines on Pine

DAYS/HOURS: Wednesday–Sunday 11 A.M.–7 P.M.

ADDRESS: Wines on Pine, 1244 Pine St., Paso Robles, CA 93446; 805-239-5808; 805-239-1507 (fax); gelfandvineyards.com

WINES/GRAPE VARIETIES: Cabernet Sauvignon, Cabyrah, Menage a Bunch (blend), SFR (blend), Petite Sirah, port, Quixotic (blend), Sophie, Syrah, Zinfandel

WINE CLUB: Yes

REGION: Paso Robles AVA

Grey Wolf Cellars

WINERY OWNERS: Barton family

WINEMAKER: Joe Barton

TASTING ROOM: Yes

DAYS/HOURS: Daily 10:30 A.M.–5:30 P.M.

ADDRESS: 2174 Hwy. 46 W., Paso Robles, CA 93446; 805-237-0771; 805-237-9866 (fax); grey-wolfcellars.com

WINES/GRAPE VARIETIES: Cabernet Sauvignon, Chardonnay, Fumé Blanc, Meritage (blend), Merlot, Muscat Canelli, red table wine, Syrah, Zinfandel

WINE CLUB: Yes

TASTING ROOM AMENITIES: Picnic area, merchandise

REGION: Paso Robles AVA

Joe and Shirlene Barton thought long and hard about the symbol they would use to represent their wine and, ultimately, their family. No stranger to the notion of the alpha leader, Joe decided on the metaphor of the wolf pack, which symbolizes the ideals of family and working together toward a common goal—the primary values that drive the Bartons in their approach to family and business. The labels depicting Joe's vision are often drawn by renowned western artist Larry Brees, a native of Paso Robles. About once a year, if you time your visit properly, you might arrive to see real wolves and wolf hybrids on the grounds, brought there to help raise funds for the local shelter dedicated to helping abandoned or abused animals.

Originally from Bakersfield, the Bartons sold a restaurant they owned in Steamboat Springs, Colorado, moved back to California, and bought a house in Cambria in 1992. Joe and Shirlene brought along an understanding of and appreciation for fine wines. With their connections in the restaurant business, they frequently toured and tasted, getting a sense of what was possible for California wines. Joe settled on Paso Robles for his venture into the wine business because the people he met there fitted very nicely into his value system of community and friendship—to say nothing of the area's potential to produce great wines.

In 1994 Grey Wolf Cellars was established at what is now the Penman Springs property when Joe and Shirlene bought in as partners, taking full control by 1996. The first Grey Wolf release was a 1994 vintage. Joe got to see the release of that vintage in 1997 but then passed the mantle of alpha Barton to his son Joe Jr. in 1998. A graduate of Cal Poly with a degree in fruit science, Joe Jr. had given quite a bit of thought to a career after university; seeing his father's interest in wines, he proposed that he should become a winemaker. A careful businessman after his experience in the restaurant and construction fields, Joe Sr. considered it from the perspective of a business opportunity for the family. To get the ball rolling, he bought some grape juice and let son Joe have a go at it. At about that time Joe and Shirlene finalized the purchase of the Penman Springs property, thus guaranteeing a supply of grapes. In 1996 they planted new ground and moved the operation to the property at Green Valley with its then-sixty-year-old farmhouse (on hundred-year-old foundations), which is now the tasting room. Joe Sr. passed away in 1998, but by then Joe Jr. was already moving among a pretty good circle of friends, all fellow winemakers—Toby Shumrick of Tobin James, Art Norman of Norman Vineyards, and Dan Panico of Dover Canyon, just to drop a few names. Old Joe had been right all along in his vision: a place is more than just geography; it's about friends helping friends. In fact, Joe Jr. and neighbor Rich Hartenberger at Midnight Cellars did their first crushes together in 1998, and Joe Sr. was the general contractor who helped build the Justin winery for Justin Baldwin. Joe Sr. might have had the early vision, but Joe Jr. and the rest of the Barton family have helped realize it in the same way that they restored and refurbished the old Porter farmhouse at Green Valley. The health of Grey Wolf Cellars is a testament to Joe's original vision of the family pack.

RECOMMENDED WINES: Son Joe has spent enough time in his position as winemaker to see the potential for Rhône varieties, Zinfandel, and Cabernet Sauvignon in Paso Robles. Joe believes that although excellent Cabs are being produced from both west and east sides, the west side produces wines of higher acidity because of the different growing conditions. Accordingly, he builds his line around the Meritage, a blend of Cabernet Sauvignon, Merlot, and Cabernet Franc.

He suggests the Lineage Meritage, and we sampled the 2001, just two weeks in the bottle. This is a dark black and purple wine, completely opaque in the glass. The wine teases the nose with soft vanilla scents, then gives way to ripe cherries, cassis, and a brush of violet perfume. The tannins are sufficiently soft for drinking now but give the wine an essential structure for another five years of aging. The finish is lovely and long now, but this should be an outstanding wine in two years.

I am a fan of the Zinful Cab, an excellent bargain, but the 2002 Zinfandel is my recommendation. The black-purple color makes this wine opaque to light. The dominant note in the nose currently is oak, but this will submerge beneath the fruit of raspberries and strawberries. The tannins are soft and rounded, giving the wine a wonderful mouthfeel and an elegant structure. There is a sense of finesse in the lingering finish. The wine has enough fruit, tannin, and oak to age another four years, if you can wait that long.

RATING: Two → three stars (quality improving every year)

Halter Ranch Vineyard

WINERY OWNER: Hansjorg Wyss

WINEMAKER: Steve Glossner

TASTING ROOM: Yes

DAYS/HOURS: Friday–Sunday 11 A.M.–5 P.M.

ADDRESS: 8910 Adelaida Rd., Paso Robles, CA 93446; 805-226-9455; 805-266-9668 (fax); halterranch.com

WINES/GRAPE VARIETIES: Cabernet Sauvignon, Cabernet Franc, Cinsaut, Counoise, Grenache, Malbec, Merlot, Mourvèdre, Petit Verdot, Roussanne, Sauvignon Blanc, Syrah, Viognier, Zinfandel

WINE CLUB: Yes

TASTING ROOM AMENITIES: Picnic area, merchandise, tours

REGION: Paso Robles AVA, west side

Hansen Vineyards

WINERY OWNER: Bruce Hansen

WINEMAKER: Bruce Hansen

TASTING ROOM: Yes

DAYS/HOURS: Friday–Sunday 11:30 A.M.–5:30 P.M.

ADDRESS: 5575 El Pomar, Templeton, CA 93465; 805-239-8412; 805-226-9023 (fax); hansenwines.com

WINES/GRAPE VARIETIES: Cabernet Sauvignon, Merlot, Syrah, Viognier, Zinfandel

WINE CLUB: Yes

TASTING ROOM AMENITIES: Picnic area

REGION: Paso Robles AVA, Templeton area

Harmony Cellars

WINERY OWNERS: Charles and Kimberley
Mulligan

WINEMAKER: Charles Mulligan

TASTING ROOM: Yes

DAYS/HOURS: Daily 10 A.M.–5:30 P.M. (winter
5 P.M.)

ADDRESS: 3255 Harmony Valley Rd., Harmony,
CA 93435; 805-927-1625; 805-927-0256 (fax);
harmonycellars.com

WINES/GRAPE VARIETIES: Cabernet
Sauvignon, Chardonnay, Harmonie (blend),
Merlot, port, Quartet (blend), Syrah, White
Riesling, White Zinfandel, Zinfandel

WINE CLUB: Yes

TASTING ROOM AMENITIES: Picnic area,
merchandise, gourmet foods

REGION: San Luis Obispo County, near Paso
Robles AVA

Chuck and Kim Mulligan are the owners of Harmony Cellars thanks to a fortuitous experience at Zaca Mesa Winery early in their relationship when, very much in love and still in the giddy thrall of their honeymoon, the young couple was touring and tasting there. Chuck was impressed with the wines and the facility and mentioned aloud how he could see himself owning a winery and making his own wine during his retirement. The pragmatic guide there asked, "Why wait? You can get your degree in enology from Fresno State or Davis." This made eminent sense to the young man, and shortly thereafter, in 1983, he started in the degree program at Fresno State while Kim worked on her MBA. Chuck had a job lined up even before he graduated and started his new life in wine at Estrella River Winery, working with winemaker Tom Myers. After Estrella was sold to Beringer in 1988 (to be renamed Meridian), he continued as assistant winemaker. During his tenure at Meridian he took consulting work as well and got to know the industry and the region.

It just so happened that wife Kim's great-grandfather Giacomo Barloggio was one of the founders of the old creamery cooperative in Harmony, and Giacomo (don't be surprised) made wine in his basement. In a perfect example of the acorn not rolling very far from the oak, the current winery sits on land that has been in Kim's family for four generations. In 1989 the Mulligans founded Harmony Cellars and sold the first wines out of the old creamery. By 1993, after considerable negotiation with the Coastal Commission as to the best use of the land, Harmony Cellars was built, and the tasting room was added in 1998. Technically not in the Paso Robles AVA, they are members of the Paso Robles Wine Country Alliance.

RECOMMENDED WINES: Chuck and Kim are interested in producing wines at reasonable prices. They can keep their wines affordable because they do all the work. They maintain excellent relationships with the growers of their fruit, thus maintaining the consistency of its quality. Chuck has established a reputation for excellent Chardonnay, and Kim recommends her husband's Diamond Reserve Chardonnay. The 2001 is a clear lemon-gold wine with a nose of melted butter, vanilla, and lemons. The wine is wonderful in the mouth and shows fine balance. The wine has a long, satisfying finish and will age another four years.

I offer the Cabernet Sauvignon as my recommendation. The 2001 is almost opaque in the glass and black cherry in color. There is a touch of black olive in the nose, followed by licorice, cassis, and ripe cherries. The wine has an excellent mouthfeel and shows an excellent balance between the acidity and the refined tannins. The ripe fruit rewards the palate with a long, lingering finish. This wine will easily reward another five years in the bottle, but it is drinking very nicely now.

As an aside, a group of women in the tasting room loved the Quartet, a blend of Chenin Blanc, Riesling, and Muscat Canelli, with a splash of Zinfandel for color. The wine has about 3 percent residual sugar, with enough acidity to keep the sweetness balanced. You can't beat the price on this interesting blend. Sip a glass or two as you take in the bucolic scenery overlooking the little town of Harmony.

RATING: One → two stars (very good reds, ahead of whites)

Harrow Cellars

WINERY OWNER: Steve Harrow

WINEMAKER: Steve Harrow

TASTING ROOM: Yes

DAYS/HOURS: By appointment only

ADDRESS: 1800 Calle Joaquin, San Luis Obispo, CA 93405; 805-544-1467; 805-544-1470 (fax); harrowcellars.com

WINES/GRAPE VARIETIES: Chardonnay, Merlot, Pinot Noir

WINE CLUB: Yes

REGION: San Luis Obispo County

Hice Cellars

WINERY OWNERS: Eric and Bettina Hice

WINEMAKER: Eric Hice

TASTING ROOM: Yes

DAYS/HOURS: Friday–Saturday 12–7 P.M., Sunday 12–5 P.M., Monday–Thursday by appointment only

ADDRESS: 821 Pine St. Unit D, Paso Robles, CA 93446; 805-237-8888; 805-237-0181 (fax); hicecellars.com

WINES/GRAPE VARIETIES: Alicante Bouschet, Cabernet Sauvignon, Chardonnay, Porto Robles (port), Syrah, Tre Blanc (white blend), Vintners Blend (red blend)

WINE CLUB: No

REGION: Paso Robles AVA

Hug Cellars

WINERY OWNER: C. I. Hug

WINEMAKER: C. I. Hug

TASTING ROOM: Yes

DAYS/HOURS: Thursday–Monday 11 A.M.–5:30 P.M.

ADDRESS: 2323 Tuley Court, Ste. 120D, Paso Robles, CA 93446; 805-226-8022; 805-237-9051 (fax); hugcellars.com

WINES/GRAPE VARIETIES: Encantada (blend), Pinot Noir, Syrah

WINE CLUB: Yes

TASTING ROOM AMENITIES: Merchandise

REGION: Paso Robles AVA

When you first meet C. I. "Augie" Hug, don't be surprised if he has just stepped off a plane on his return from, say, the Timor Sea off the coast of Australia. You see, Augie is an oilman born and bred, with more than thirty years in the business now. He started at the bottom of an oil rig and, over a period of seventeen years, worked his way up to foreman. For the past four years or so he has worked as a consultant to oil companies all over the world, which explains why he often has to get on the next plane to distant and exotic locales. But that's only a part of what Augie does.

In the mid-1980s, he had a steak house up north where he was the chef, but his interest in wines predates his professional work in the restaurant. He has always appreciated a good glass of red paired with the right entrée. His work at the restaurant forced him to learn about wines as he made the buying decisions for the restaurant's wine list. A short time later he and Raquel Mireles Rodriguez bought a wine shop and tasting room in Harmony, just over the mountains from Paso Robles. There he met and became friends with two pretty good winemakers in their own right, Mat Garretson and John Alban. Shortly thereafter, Garretson and Alban founded the Hospice du Rhône in celebration of the great grape varieties coming out of France's Rhône region, grapes that also flourish around Paso. Augie and Raquel made a point of featuring small boutique wines made from the Rhône varieties, and the store developed a following for those wines in particular.

With a little shove from Alban, Augie made eighty-seven cases of Syrah in 1994, the first commercial release for Hug Cellars. Under Alban's guidance and mentoring, Augie fleshed out his practical experience with extension courses at UC Davis and Cal Poly. As his wines began to receive accolades, Raquel and Augie decided to leave the retail side of the business and take the plunge, focusing their efforts on developing Hug Cellars. Garretson shared his own facilities, which he has done time and again for up-and-coming winemakers. Given his connections and his emerging talent, it was time for Augie to bring that gusher in, and in 2000 Hug Cellars formed a cooperative wine tasting room called Coastal Vintners with Per Bacco Cellars, Orchid Hill Vineyard and Winery, and Silver Stone Wines. Over the years Augie has secured grapes from some of the finest grape growers in the region, including the Bassetti vineyard near Cambria for Syrah; Rancho Ontiveros in the Santa Maria Valley for Pinot Noir; the Gill vineyard for west-side Paso Syrah; and Mike Schenkhuisen's vineyards, also a part of the co-op as Orchid Hill, for Pinot Noir. These vineyards provide the type of grapes he needs, such as intense, cool-climate Syrah with plenty of acidity to balance the ripe fruit for a more European-style wine perfect for pairing with food.

RECOMMENDED WINES: Augie and I tasted his wines from the barrel, and he recommends the 2003 Bassetti Vineyards Syrah. The 2002 is a tough act to follow, having received a 92 from Robert M. Parker Jr., but I think the 2003 is potentially better. This is an opaque, purple and violet wine with a fruity and floral nose of violets, spice, blackberries, black currants, and plums. The wine, owing to the excellent ripeness of the grapes, has a wonderful feel in the mouth, the lovely fruit supported by a fine tannic structure. Even from the barrel the wine had a finish that lasted more than a minute. The wine will benefit from aging another five to seven years.

I enjoyed the 2004 Pinot Noir from the Ontiveros vineyards near Santa Maria. This is an intensely dark Pinot, opaque in the glass and almost a black-purple in color. The nose is a perfume of black cherries, smoke, crème de cassis, and spice. The wine shows excellent balance between the acidity and the tannins and provides a fine structure to the wonderful fruit. It has both finesse and delicacy in the mouth, leading to a long, satisfying finish. This wine should be accessible shortly after bottling but will reward at least three years of age.

RATING: Three → four stars (excellent to outstanding wines across the line)

Hunt Cellars

WINERY OWNERS: David and Debby Hunt

WINEMAKER: David Hunt

TASTING ROOM: Yes

DAYS/HOURS: Daily 10 A.M.–5:30 P.M.

ADDRESS: 2875 Oakdale Rd., Paso Robles, CA 93446; 805-237-1600; 818-718-8048 (fax); huntcellars.com

WINES/GRAPE VARIETIES: Cabernet Sauvignon, Chardonnay, Sangiovese, Sauvignon Blanc, Syrah, Zinfandel

WINE CLUB: Yes

TASTING ROOM AMENITIES: Picnic area, merchandise

REGION: Paso Robles AVA, west side

J. Lohr Vineyards & Wines

WINERY OWNER: Jerry Lohr

WINEMAKER: Jeff Meier

TASTING ROOM: Yes

DAYS/HOURS: Daily 10 A.M.–5 P.M.

ADDRESS: Paso Robles Wine Center, 6169 Airport Rd., Paso Robles, CA 93446; San Jose Wine Center, 1000 Lenzen Ave., San Jose, CA 95126; 805-239-8900 (Paso Robles); 408-288-5057 (San Jose); 805-239-0365 (Paso Robles fax); 408-993-2276 (San Jose fax); jlohr.com

WINE CLUB: Yes

TASTING ROOM AMENITIES: Patio, picnic area, event and meeting facilities, full kitchen, merchandise

WINES/GRAPE VARIETIES: Cabernet Sauvignon, Chardonnay, Cuvée Series blends, Merlot, Pinot Noir, Riesling, Sauvignon Blanc, Syrah, Valdiguié, White Zinfandel, Zinfandel

REGION: Paso Robles AVA; Arroyo Seco AVA; Napa Valley

Jerry Lohr grew up on a South Dakota farm and graduated from South Dakota State University in 1958. An exceptionally bright man who wears the dust on his boots with pride, he went on to graduate school at Stanford, where he got a master's degree in 1959 and completed all his coursework and passed his oral exams for a Ph.D. in civil engineering. He joined the Air Force, and Captain Lohr was posted to NASA's Ames Research Center from 1961 to 1964, where he worked as a research scientist. After his service, he opened a land development business and built custom homes.

His partner in the building business, Bernie Turgeon, introduced him to good French wine. In the late '60s, calling on his background in farming, he began intensive research into grape-growing regions in California. He found Monterey County in 1971 and the next year planted his first vineyard in Arroyo Seco to Chardonnay and Riesling grapes. Jerry understood that wine is climate first, then soils, then people with a passion for what they do. He also read everything he could get his hands on, including the work of Professors Amerine and Winkler, taking courses on the side. His holdings in Monterey now number about 1,000 acres. In 1986 he sought out the Paso Robles area and became convinced of its potential for growing Bordeaux varieties such as Cabernet Sauvignon and Merlot. His holdings there approximate 2,000 acres. The J. Lohr Winery was established in 1974, and J. Lohr Vineyards & Wines is the largest producer in Paso Robles.

Ever the scientist, Jerry continues to do research in the vineyards designed to benefit the entire region because he believes that the Central Coast is one of the most dynamic wine regions in the world. He is convinced that its story needs to be told, and he is more than happy to help tell it. Jerry firmly believes that the region has "world-class potential, if not yet world-class vision." With men like him in the vineyards, that vision will emerge. In the meantime, Jerry is interested in helping build the region's wine culture. To that end, he is a generous supporter of wine education and is certain that the more people learn about wine and its benefits, the more enjoyment it will bring to them. Through the manifold contributions he has made to wine culture in Monterey and Paso Robles, Jerry is truly one of those men who can walk the walk through the vineyards and the winery.

RECOMMENDED WINES: Jerry recommends the J. Lohr Cuvée Pau, a Bordeaux blend of Cabernet Sauvignon and Merlot. The 1999 vintage is opaque in the glass thanks to its inky black-purple color. The nose is violets, cherries, black currants, bread dough, and crème de cassis. The wonderful ripe fruit makes the wine huge in the mouth, but it has extraordinary balance and integration. The finish lasted well over a minute. Drink now and over the next ten to twelve years. This is a superb blend that speaks volumes about the potential for Paso Robles and Bordeaux varieties.

I recommend the Hilltop Vineyard Cabernet Sauvignon. The 1999 is opaque in the glass and more reddish-purple than the J. Lohr Cuvée Pau. The nose is redolent of hot sweet blackberry pie, blueberries, violets, cedar, and dark chocolate. The wine is superb in the mouth, given its wonderful balance and integration, and the finish lasts nearly a minute. This wine is still very young and lively in the bottle and will likely reward another seven to nine years of age. Once again, Jerry Lohr has hit the nail squarely on the head with this excellent Cabernet.

RATING: Three stars (excellent values); four stars (Cuvée line)

Jack Creek Cellars

WINERY OWNERS: Doug and Sabrina Kruse

WINEMAKER: Doug Kruse

TASTING ROOM: No

DAYS/HOURS: By appointment only

ADDRESS: 5265 Jack Creek Rd., Templeton, CA 93465; 805-226-8283; 805-226-8285 (fax); jackcreekcellars.com

WINES/GRAPE VARIETIES: Chardonnay, Pinot Noir, Syrah

WINE CLUB: Yes

REGION: Paso Robles AVA, Templeton area

JanKris Winery

WINERY OWNERS: Gendron family

WINEMAKER: Mark Gendron

TASTING ROOM: Yes

DAYS/HOURS: Daily 11 A.M.–5 P.M.

ADDRESS: 1266 Bethel Rd., Templeton, CA 93465; 805-434-0319; 805-434-0905 (fax); jankriswinery.com

WINES/GRAPE VARIETIES: Cabernet Sauvignon, Chardonnay, Crossfire (blend), Merlot, Picaro (blend), port, Riatta (blend), sparkling almond, sparkling raspberry, Syrah, Viognier, Zinfandel

WINE CLUB: Yes

TASTING ROOM AMENITIES: Inside and outside picnic area, merchandise

REGION: Paso Robles AVA

Mark and Paula Gendron were looking for a change. Their real-estate development company in Ventura County was going gangbusters, but three years of traveling had become a bit too much. Mark noticed that many of his employees were buying homes in the Nipomo area; it seemed everyone in the south was interested in moving north. Paula researched the schools and discovered Templeton in San Luis Obispo County. One day while out driving and looking at properties, they noticed an agent nailing a "For Sale" sign on the fence of a property. After taking a look, they bought it. It just so happened that Penny Baldwin, Justin Baldwin's wife at the time, had a boutique winery with a tasting room on the grounds. They figured, why not? The acreage was large enough for the horses their daughters were crazy about, and there would be enough land left over to keep the existing vineyard. They also kept the tasting room, transferred the bond, and were in the wine business full-bore by 1990.

After two years of working both jobs, Mark decided he wanted to farm the vineyard and make wine instead of building houses. Paula enjoyed the management of the tasting room, and Mark loved the agricultural side of the venture. They sold most of the grapes to other wineries, with some held back for the wines in the tasting room. In the meantime, daughters January and Kristin pursued their love of horses through junior high, high school, and college rodeo, and both eventually went on to ride and compete professionally. After both daughters graduated from college, there was a time in the late 1990s when Mark considered selling the winery. Jan and Kris would not hear of it and asked to take over the operations gradually—with Mom and Dad's help from time to time, of course.

In addition to shepherding his daughters through the rough going in the business, Mark was instrumental in developing a marketing group for Paso Robles wines that eventually became the PRVGA (now known as the Paso Robles Wine Country Alliance). He still grows the grapes and makes the wine, trusting his palate, and uses consultants if and when adjustments are needed. Mark prefers fruit-forward wines that are approachable now, because the last time he looked there weren't too many houses around with cellars for wine storage. He is to this day a grower first and thus wants to emphasize the fruit in his wines, not the tannin or the oak.

RECOMMENDED WINES: Mark recommends the Crossfire, a blend of Cabernet Sauvignon, Merlot, and some Syrah. The wine is nearly opaque in the glass, showing dark cherry colors and a nose of plums, blackberries, chocolate, and spice. The 2002 is a well-integrated wine with an appealing long finish. It has enough tannin to last another three to five years but is vinified for drinking now.

I suggest the Chardonnay. The 2001 is a light yellow wine that has an appealing nose of butter and tropical fruit with excellent ripeness to the grapes. If you like fruit-forward Chards with enough acidity to give the wine structure, this one is for you. As a side note, I might also mention that the Zinfandel program is improving by leaps and bounds at JanKris. The Zin port is very good, and the 2003 Zinfandel is simply an excellent value. After enjoying the views of the surrounding hills and vineyards, taste the wines and have lunch in the adjoining indoor picnic area.

RATING: One → two stars (quality is improving across the line)

Justin Vineyards & Winery

WINERY OWNERS: Justin and Deborah Baldwin

WINEMAKER: Fred Holloway

TASTING ROOM: Yes

DAYS/HOURS: Daily 10 A.M.–5 P.M.

ADDRESS: 11680 Chimney Rock Rd., Paso Robles, CA 93446; 805-238-6932; 805-238-7382 (fax); justinwine.com

WINES/GRAPE VARIETIES: Cabernet Sauvignon, Chardonnay, Isosceles (blend), Justification (blend), Malbec, Mourvèdre, Obtuse (blend), Orange Muscat, Petit Verdot, Sangiovese, Sauvignon Blanc, Syrah, Tempranillo

WINE CLUB: Yes

TASTING ROOM AMENITIES: Inn and restaurant, picnic area, merchandise, cave tours

REGION: Paso Robles AVA

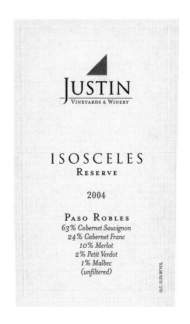

Deborah and Justin Baldwin have made an impressive contribution toward firmly establishing the reputation of the Paso Robles AVA. Their Isosceles blend of Cabernet Sauvignon, Merlot, and Cabernet Franc rocked the wine world in 1994 and finally put little-known Paso Robles on the map of great wine regions of the world. That particular vintage won the Pichon Longueville Comtesse de Lalande trophy for Best Blended Red Wine Worldwide at the London International Wine & Spirit Competition. In addition, the 1997 Isosceles was ranked sixth best wine out of the top hundred in the world by the *Wine Spectator* in 2000.

Deborah hails from Washington State and chose a career in mortgage banking in Los Angeles. Justin was raised in San Francisco and made his mark as an international investment banker. For a time he lived and worked in England and very much liked his weekend getaways to the country. This planted the seed of his desire eventually to leave the city, open his own business, and create a product he could share with people. When he became a family man, he wanted to raise his family in an environment more conducive to realizing his dreams, and since the banking industry had changed radically and was moving in a direction he was unwilling to go, he and Deborah relocated to the beautiful west side of Paso Robles, in the Adelaida Valley. There they purchased 160 acres of land in 1981 from Gary Conway, owner of Carmody McKnight, and planted a vineyard the following year. Justin has always admired Bordeaux wines, and after reading every book he could get his hands on, planted the vineyard to Cabernet Sauvignon, Merlot, Cabernet Franc, and Chardonnay. The winery was built in 1985, and the first release of 100 percent estate wines followed in 1987.

The Baldwins bring a shared expertise to their business: they most certainly understand the financial side of the enterprise and the importance of marketing their brand. To that end, Justin wines quite possibly enjoy the widest distribution of all Paso Robles wines, with the exception of the larger Meridian label. Justin Baldwin takes great pride in ownership and staffs his winery with the best and brightest help available, including students from nearby Cal Poly. The Baldwins have built an inn for tourists wanting the complete wine experience, and a restaurant at the winery, Deborah's Room, opened in 1998. More recently, a new facility called the Isosceles Center, featuring caves as an additional attraction, has opened to the public, and I had the pleasure of being one of the first to see this impressive edifice. It is certainly worth touring.

RECOMMENDED WINES: Justin recommends the Isosceles. I have had the pleasure of doing a vertical tasting of this wine, thanks to the generosity of my friends and colleagues Terry Weinbrenner and Christine Shea. The earlier examples were justifiably great wines. Unfortunately, I noticed a drop in the quality of the wine after the sensational 1997, and I came away disappointed by some of the later offerings. I am pleased to say that the 2001 Isosceles will most likely restore the blend to its lofty position as one of the best blended wines coming out of the Paso Robles AVA, even understanding that the overall quality of Paso Robles Cabernet-based wines has improved remarkably in the past five to seven years. Robert M. Parker Jr. gave the 2002 Isosceles a score of 95, further evidence that the important and justifiably famous Isosceles is once again the great wine that it can be.

The 2001 example of Baldwin's flagship wine is a reserve blend of 73 percent Cabernet Sauvignon, 13 percent Cabernet Franc, 5 percent Merlot, and some Petit Verdot and Malbec to round out the wine. Though almost opaque to the stem, this black cherry blockbuster is a touch cloudy because it is unfiltered. The nose shows both perfume and fruit: black cherries, plums, black currants, and cassis form a lovely layer above dark chocolate and vanilla, with additional notes of spice and incense. The soft and elegant tannins contribute to a voluptuous feel in the mouth. The lush, ripe fruit contributes to a long and multilayered finish. This wine will easily age another ten years and is a fine example of what the Isosceles is capable of.

I suggest the 2001 Syrah Reserve. This is a purple and black wine almost opaque to the stem with a nose of blackberries and peppery spice. The fine tannins are complemented by enough acidity to give it a wonderful texture in the mouth. The wine has a long, deep finish and is drinking beautifully now but will easily reward another three to five years in the bottle. These two wines alone are enough to reaffirm my opinion of the high quality of Justin's line.

RATING: Four stars (reds can be excellent to outstanding)

Kelsey See Canyon Vineyards

WINERY OWNERS: Kelsey family

WINEMAKER: Harold Osborne

TASTING ROOM: Yes

DAYS/HOURS: Daily 11 A.M.–5 P.M.

ADDRESS: 1947 See Canyon Rd., San Luis Obispo, CA 93405; 805-595-9700; 805-595-7459 (fax); kelseywine.com

WINES/GRAPE VARIETIES: Apple Chardonnay, Apple Merlot, Cabernet Sauvignon, Chardonnay, late-harvest Zinfandel, Merlot, Orange Muscat, Sauvignon Blanc, Syrah, White Zinfandel

WINE CLUB: Yes

TASTING ROOM AMENITIES: Merchandise

REGION: San Luis Obispo County

One of the most attractive features of living on the Central Coast is access to the Big Blue, the magnificent Pacific Ocean. The Kelsey family, including Dick and Dolores, originally took their living from the sea before establishing their vineyard and winery. At the winery you will see pictures of Dolores's father, Tony, an abalone diver out of Avila Beach. Her father's family, the Sylvesters, came from the Azores and are Portuguese. Tony Sylvester was a driving force in the family and an authentic self-made man. Circumstances forced him to start work early in life, and he became a businessman at the tender age of ten, buying and reselling fish from island to island.

Once in California, Tony and his brother Joe started an abalone diving business in 1937. Dick worked as a line tender during Tony's last year of diving. In those days, a diver could bring aboard as many as one hundred abalone a day. Two of Tony's brothers, Manuel and Albert, ran sport-fishing boats out of Avila. After Tony quit his abalone business he made money by selling fish to the local Portuguese population and later went into the tugboat business with Joe, running crew boats and tugs to service the offshore oil industry. In the meantime, in the early 1950s, Dick's family bought the property where the winery now stands. Dick originally built the barn to store his antique cars and to work on boat engines. When it came time for Dick to retire in 1998, he decided the place had potential to become a winery.

The winemaker is the renowned Harold Osborne, the first winemaker at Maison Deutz, which became Laetitia. He also made wine for twelve years at Cambria, in addition to his consulting work. Dick and Dolores know they have an excellent winemaker and, working together, intend to keep the winery a small, family-run business, much the way Tony did some fifty years ago when he owned his abalone diving business. Dick is a wonderful storyteller: he says he uses the massive 90-foot length of chain (called a shot) in the parking lot to tie up his dog, and when that doesn't hold, he adds the anchors from the old sailing ships that brought lumber into Port Hartford (Port San Luis) and took out wheat grown in Paso Robles. I've seen the dog, and between you and me, the chain should suffice.

RECOMMENDED WINES: Dick and Dolores suggest the late-harvest Zinfandel. We tasted the 2002, a red cherry–colored wine, light to the stem. The nose is raspberries, red currants, chocolate, and dates. The wine is sweet but not overly so, with a residual sugar of 4.7 percent. It has enough acidity to balance the sweetness of the ripe fruit. This is a well-made wine that will offer pleasure to those who like their wines on the sweeter side.

In keeping with the theme of well-made sweet wines, I suggest the late-harvest 100 percent Zinfandel port, made in the ruby port style. The wine was tasted from the barrel and showed black-purple colors in the glass, making it opaque to the stem. Blackberries, purple plums, and a touch of pepper enliven the nose. The wine has a wonderful balance between the ripe fruit and the acidity necessary to keep it from cloying on the palate. I am certain that Tony Sylvester, given his Portuguese heritage, would have given this wine his stamp of approval.

RATING: One → two stars (quality is improving across the line; late-harvest wines are very good to excellent)

Kynsi Winery

WINERY OWNERS: Don and Gwen Othman

WINEMAKERS: Don and Gwen Othman

TASTING ROOM: Yes

DAYS/HOURS: Thursday–Monday 11 A.M.–
5 P.M.

ADDRESS: 2212 Corbett Canyon Rd., Arroyo
Grande, CA 93420; 805-544-8461;
805-544-6181 (fax); kynsi.com

WINES/GRAPE VARIETIES: Chardonnay,
Merrah (blend), Pinot Noir, Syrah,
Zinfandel

WINE CLUB: Yes

REGION: Edna Valley AVA

Upon first tasting Kynsi's Merrah blend, then just released, in 2001, I though it had wonderful potential. At Kynsi—the Finnish world for "talon"—I also met for the first time engineer, inventor, and winemaker Don Othman and his wife, Gwen. Don came to San Luis Obispo in 1975 after he decided to trade working in the space industry for the rural life on the Central Coast. Using his extensive knowledge of exotic metals and stainless steel, he started Bulldog Welding and Manufacturing, servicing the growing number of wineries in San Luis Obispo and Santa Barbara counties.

As he saw and understood the equipment needs of the winemakers, he put his talent for innovative design and manufacturing to work. In the 1980s he invented a tool called the bulldog pup, now an indispensable piece of equipment used in wine cellars around the world. Usually, when a delicate grape such as Pinot Noir is transferred from tank to barrel, for example, the wine is pumped from one location to the other. Unfortunately, this process typically adds oxygen to the wine and agitates it, reducing the complexity and nuances of the wine. Don solved the problem by inventing a gas pressure wand that uses the inert gas nitrogen to move the wine gently from tank to barrel, barrel to barrel, or barrel to bottle. By using his bulldog pup, winemakers avoid beating up the wine and achieve an exceptionally clean racking as the wine is gently pushed instead of pumped. A clean racking is indispensable for wines that will not be fined or filtered, again helping to maintain the inherent quality of the fruit.

Don and Gwen started Kynsi in 1995, taking their inspiration for the name from the resident owls that roost in the barn next to the winery. In 2001 a vineyard was planted on the ranch, and wines are now being produced from those grapes. Currently, vintages are rounded out with grapes purchased from such famous vineyards as Paragon, Bien Nacido, and Barn Owl in the Adelaida hills west of Paso Robles. All the wines, including the Pinot Noir, are transferred using the bulldog pup, of course. And if there is ever an equipment failure in the winery, Gwen knows whom to call.

RECOMMENDED WINES: Don recommends the Pinot Noir from Bien Nacido fruit. We tasted the 2002, newly bottled, and it was already excellent. This is a luscious dark cherry wine, almost opaque in the glass, and jammed full of sweet cherry fruit with undertones of black currants and spiced plums. It is rich and luxurious in the mouth with a wonderfully long and pleasing finish. This wine has at least five years of great drinking ahead.

I recommend the Syrah. We tasted the 2000, a worthy successor to the 1999, voted Best California Syrah at the Sacramento State Fair. This is an opaque wine of black and red plum colors. The nose is blackberries, plums, violets, and a hint of cardamom spice next to the smoke flavor. Black pepper emerges in the finish. The French oak is well integrated with the opulent fruit and leads to a long, satisfying finish. The wine is drinking beautifully now but should hold another three years.

Don't forget the blend of Merlot and Syrah called the Merrah, one of my favorites. I also had the pleasure of tasting Don and Gwen's 2003 vintage from the barrel, and the Pinots, Syrahs, and especially the Zinfandel show excellent potential.

RATING: Three stars (reds ahead of whites and very good to excellent)

Laetitia Vineyard & Winery

WINERY OWNERS: Selim Zilkha and Nadia Zilkha Wellisz

WINEMAKERS: Dave Hickey and Eric Hickey

TASTING ROOM: Yes

DAYS/HOURS: Daily 11 A.M.–5 P.M.

ADDRESS: 453 Laetitia Vineyard Dr., Arroyo Grande, CA 93420; 805-481-1772; 805-481-6920 (fax); laetitiawine.com

WINES/GRAPE VARIETIES: Brut cuvée, brut de blanc, brut de noir, brut rosé, Chardonnay, late-harvest Riesling, Pinot Blanc, Pinot Gris, Pinot Noir, Syrah

WINE CLUB: Yes

TASTING ROOM AMENITIES: Picnic area, merchandise, tours

REGION: Arroyo Grande Valley AVA

When the famous Champagne Deutz was looking to expand its production of sparkling wine in the New World, it turned to the Arroyo Grande Valley of the Central Coast, having deemed its soils and climate similar to those of its native Épernay. In 1982 it planted 185 acres of Pinot Noir, Chardonnay, and Pinot Blanc, the principal grape varieties for classic Champagne, in one of the coolest climates for growing grapes in all of California. For the next thirteen years, the California branch of Champagne Deutz, branded Maison Deutz, produced some of the best sparkling wines in the United States made according to the *méthode champenoise*. When Jean-Claude Tardivat purchased the winery and the vineyards in 1997, he named it after his daughter, Laetitia. By that time, experimentation had determined that Pinot Noir could be excellent not merely as Champagne-style wine, but as an individual varietal wine, and the focus began to shift from sparkling wines to still. A year later a partnership led by Selim Zilkha bought the winery, and by 2001 Zilkha remained as the sole proprietor. Laetitia now is also the parent company of Avila Winery and Barnwood Vineyards.

The success of Maison Deutz was shepherded by Christian Roguenant (see his profile under Baileyana, where he now works). When Roguenant left Laetitia, the sparkling-wine production was handed over to Dave Hickey, with still wine made by his son Eric. Dave was originally trained as a journeyman electrician and for a time ran his own janitorial company. When Maison Deutz built its winery in 1982, he was contracted to do the cleanup work. The winemaker at that time—Harold Osborn, formerly of Schramsberg and Cambria—hired Dave in 1985 to continue at the winery. After Harold moved on and Roguenant came in, Dave assisted with the sparkling-wine production for the next twelve years. In 1998 he took over the task of making the sparkling wines. Dave's son Eric started working at the winery as a sixteen-year-old, helping with harvests and learning at his father's side. By 1994 he was promoted to cellar master. He learned his skills working with Roguenant and his father, and as production shifted to include more still wine, he traveled and studied under French, Australian, and American winemakers in addition to taking courses at UC Davis. His hard work and hands-on training were rewarded in 2002 when he was named head winemaker. With his father handling the sparkling wines and mom Carmen in the tasting room, Laetitia remains very much a family-run operation. Wines from Santa Barbara County's Barnwood Winery can be tasted here, too.

RECOMMENDED WINES: Once known primarily for sparkling wines, Laetitia is now making a name for itself with the release of high-quality Pinot Noir. But the sparkling wines are still very good, and Dave and Eric suggest the brut cuvée, a traditional blend of Pinot Noir, Chardonnay, and Pinot Blanc. This is a classic golden-yellow brut with a nose of apples and pears and a hint of freshly baked bread from the yeast. It is a medium-bodied Champagne-style wine, with the Chardonnay fruit presenting itself ahead of the Pinot Noir. The finish is clean and refreshing, making the wine a fine complement to food at the table.

I suggest the Estate Pinot Noir. We tasted the 2002, but the 2001 Reserve was also excellent. The 2002 is a blend of grapes, 40 percent from old vines, 60 percent from new. The wine is almost opaque in the glass, brick-red in color with violet and purple hues. The fruit is cherries and plums, with raspberries also present. There is some earth and a touch of tobacco as well. This is an elegant Pinot Noir, well balanced and with a long, velvety finish. The wine will reward at least another five years in the bottle.

RATING: Two stars (very good line with reds ahead of whites; both improving)

L'Aventure Winery

WINERY OWNERS: Stephan and Beatrice Asseo

WINEMAKER: Stephan Asseo

TASTING ROOM: Yes

DAYS/HOURS: Thursday–Sunday 11 A.M.–4 P.M.

ADDRESS: 2815 Live Oak Rd., Paso Robles, CA 93446; 805-227-1588; 805-227-6988 (fax); aventurewinery.com

WINES/GRAPE VARIETIES: Côte-à-Côte, Estate Cuvée, Optimus (blends), Roussanne, Syrah

WINE CLUB: Yes

REGION: Paso Robles AVA

TASTING ROOM AMENITIES: Some merchandise

The call to the soil may start in a mother's garden, if you have a love for the land and the sensibility of a poet. In Paris, a boy of sixteen had to decide early the direction to take his future. He chose to go to school, visit farmers, do an internship in the Loire, spend two years in Burgundy, learn to prune, and graduate from enology college, where he worked with professional growers and vintners, not merely academicians. But he never gave up the call to poetry and, before beginning the real work of making a life, spent three years in French Polynesia just to be certain that he was taking the correct life path.

The Asseo family bought its first winery, Domaine de Courteillac, in Bordeaux in 1982, and when the call came from his parents inviting him to see the new property, Stephan Asseo was ready to return. However, his three years abroad left him unprepared for what he saw. Fresh off the plane and barefoot in shorts and sunglasses, he surveyed the chaos of the property: an ancient castle in ruins, outbuildings in shambles, a jungle of vines in the vineyard. Two choices occurred to Stephan: catch the next flight back to the sand and sun and the easy life, or buy some boots and a machete and start swinging. Adventure is not always about travel; sometimes it's in the challenge of standing and facing down the turmoil that confronts you. He stayed, and the poet became a *vigneron*.

Vigneron does not translate readily into English because it embodies a variety of roles: landowner, farmer, grape grower, winemaker, poet. Stephan became firmly established as a winemaker and consultant in the Bordeaux region of Entre-Deux-Mers. His wines earned accolades from both European and American critics. It took him nearly twenty years to create order from the initial chaos of the property. The passion that brought him to poetry and to the land was directed to the production of fine wines crafted like poems. He learned that if you work the land diligently with dedication and creativity, the honors and respect will follow. Over time, he added the properties of Château Robin and Château Fleur Cardinale, a Saint-Émilion Grand Cru. As his reputation grew, Stephan was called on to consult as winemaker at other properties in the region. During this period of his life in France, Stephan honed his craft in the vineyards, developed his vision and philosophy, and refined his style of winemaking. In the meantime, he fought the stultifying rules and regulations of France's other great contribution to the social order, bureaucracy. Like a poet forced to write only in rhyming couplets, Stephan chafed under the onerous restrictions. He decided he'd had enough and looked to the west to begin the search anew.

Stephan traveled the world looking for the right combination of climate, soils, and freedom. His odyssey took him to the far reaches of Australia, to South Africa, back to Spain, and then to California's Napa, Sonoma, and Santa Barbara counties. In 1997 the journey came to an end in Paso Robles, near the Templeton Gap, where he was stopped again, but not by shock or surprise. This time he was suffused with the flush of genuine excitement. He felt the *terroir* of the place, and it was a beautiful place indeed. He knew that with a few exceptions like the Médoc, it takes a beautiful place to make a beautiful wine. He and his father and mother bought 126 unplanted acres where the morning fog and cooling winds of the evening moderate the warm, sunny days of Paso's west side. He thought of his wife, Beatrice, back in Entre-Deux-Mers. How would she feel about trading the castle for a trailer? But he knew her: she would help bring the best of Bordeaux to this new place. For them both, there was the additional romance of starting anew, adventure in the courage of beginning again.

His search for a new property was also the search for the freedom to pursue his creative vision as a winemaker. That vision required finding and identifying the requisite climate and *terroir* for the production of premium-quality wines. Then the right grape varieties could be planted to match the potential offered the fruit. By 2001 *Wine Spectator* magazine declared that Stephan was producing "California's best Rhône-style wines." Not surprisingly, Asseo called his new venture L'Aventure.

In addition to the requirements of planting his rootstocks in the proper *terroir* necessary to sustain and nurture them, Stephan firmly believes in the need to limit production. Grapes already have a hard time growing in the substrate of limestone, clay, and even some quartz, but less fruit results in greater intensity of flavor. To stress the fruit further, he plants more than 2,000 vines per acre but takes less than 2 tons of fruit. In contrast, yields in some parts of Napa can be as high as 6 to 8 tons. After pressing, the wine rests in French oak barrels, which do not require the same toasting as other types. L'Aventure produces two lines of wine: Stephan Ridge and L'Aventure.

RECOMMENDED WINES: The flagship wines are the renowned Optimus, a blend of Cabernet Sauvignon, Syrah, Petit Verdot, and Zinfandel; and the Estate Cuvée, sort of an inverse Optimus of Cabernet Sauvignon, Petit Verdot, and Syrah. These are wines that owing to regulations could not have been made in France. The blending of these grapes makes the wines and gives them a flavor profile that owes allegiance to French origins while at the same time remaining true to the spirit and freedom of Stephan's winemaking philosophy. Stephan calls them his signature blends because he believes that the combination of Cabernet and Syrah will contribute to the establishment of a distinct identity for red wines from Paso Robles.

The wine most reflective of Stephan's winemaking philosophy is the Estate Cuvée, and it is his recommendation. The 2003 wine is unfiltered and unfined and spent fourteen months in French oak. It is opaque in the glass and a brilliant purple and black color. The nose suggests black cherries, boysenberry, plums, violets, and spice. The wine is outstanding in the mouth, given the ripe, luscious fruit and the fine, ripe tannins. It shows just a touch more elegance and refinement than the Optimus, and the remarkable finish lasts well over a minute. The wine is drinkable now, but that would be a shame. Let it rest a year or so, then drink it with pleasure over the next ten to fifteen years.

The other flagship wine is the Optimus, my recommendation. The 2003 is also opaque in the glass and the same pretty purple-black color. Now the nose is blackberries, smoke, leather, cherry jam, cassis, anise, and spice. The wine is superb in the mouth and explodes with flavors as air is brought into it. This wine too has a finish that lasts well over a minute. Be patient with this one; let it rest a year and then drink this hedonistic pleasure of a wine over the next ten to twelve years. I also had the good fortune to taste the 2004 Syrah from the barrel, and it too has extraordinary potential.

Is this property capable of producing Rhône-style red wines that rank among the best in the world? I am convinced that the Estate Cuvée, the Optimus, and the Syrah have that much potential. Although the competition is fierce, Stephan Asseo has the courage, skills, and determination to become first among equals.

RATING: Five stars (one of the best wine programs on the Central Coast)

Le Cuvier Winery

WINERY OWNERS: John Munch and Mary Fox

WINEMAKER: John Munch

TASTING ROOM: Yes (for wine club members and their guests only)

DAYS/HOURS: By appointment only

ADDRESS: Call for details; 805-238-5706; 805-237-0577 (fax); lcwine.com

WINES/GRAPE VARIETIES: Cabernet Franc, Cabernet Sauvignon, Chardonnay, Pinot Noir, Sangiovese, Syrah, Zinfandel

WINE CLUB: Yes

TASTING ROOM AMENITIES: Merchandise, black light in toilet

REGION: Paso Robles AVA

John Munch is revered as the iconoclast of Paso Robles winemaking. Born in Costa Rica, he is one of those unique individuals who has traveled and studied broadly, and the man and, ultimately, his winemaking style are informed and shaped by these disparate experiences. At one time John was planning to study law, but that didn't work out. He then worked for a time on a master's degree at San Francisco State in history, but he didn't finish because he was restoring a Victorian house and made too much money on the project. He met his late wife, who was French, in 1967. One day a friend visiting at Cambria said the region reminded him of France's Provence. In 1980 a group of investors from Champagne was interested in starting a winery in California. They wanted to make sparkling wines in the Champagne style with the intent of shipping and selling the wines to France (this has to be very much like selling refrigerators to the Aleuts or sand to the Saudis). John searched Paso Robles for grapes suitable to make sparkling wines. He called his friend Gary Eberle, then at Estrella River Winery, and asked him for help; a trial batch was made there. They sent the juice to France's Champagne region for blind tasting. The results were so good that John made a long-term contract with Estrella and set up his operations there. Eberle had Munch make the sparkling wines for his operation as well and allowed John the use of his facilities as he began developing his own label, Adelaida, in 1981.

John bought land on the west side of Paso Robles and by 1982 was producing his own wines. Shortly thereafter, he was discovered by wine writer Anthony Dias Blue. Unfortunately, when Estrella closed its doors and Eberle went on to other ventures, John was locked out. Niels Udsen, founder of Castoro Cellars, was also at Estrella then, and the two formed a temporary consortium. Although the group from France decided to abandon the California venture, John eventually took over the sparkling wine and sold it under the Adelaida label. He also established his Le Cuvier brand in

1981 and produced both Cabernet Sauvignon and Syrah under that label. In the meantime, Udsen took his operation to the J. Lohr Winery, and John followed him there for a year before going to Wild Horse. Then he teamed up with the Van Steenwyck family to keep Adelaida as a growing concern, but sold his interest in that venture to the Van Steenwycks in 1998, although he continued at Adelaida as the winemaker until the harvest of 1999. By then, his reputation for making extraordinary old-world-style wines firmly established, he continued to work as a consultant even as he put the plans together for Le Cuvier Winery; the name means "little barrel room" in French.

After the death of his first wife in 1998, John moved his winery to a newly built facility on the Ramage Ranch, far out on Adelaida Road. There he formed a partnership with Mary Fox, an organizational psychologist with a Ph.D. from Columbia University. Mary wanted to establish a small business in the Paso Robles area, and John told her about the potential for building a tasting-room business at the Ramage place, which John was already leasing. The two have since teamed up, with Mary directing business operations and John focusing on winery and vineyard operations. The success of their wine club (the Elliptical Society) was such that Mary and John were forced to close the tasting room because of a shortage of wine. At the winery, tasting is available now to club members and their guests only. John is still very much in demand as a teacher and consultant: he has consulted for Justin and Clautiere, for instance, and Neil Collins, now the winemaker at Tablas Creek, was once an assistant to John at Adelaida Cellars. Anytime anyone speaks of John, they smile. If you have the pleasure of meeting him, you will discover why.

RECOMMENDED WINES: I tasted all of John's wines in the barrel, and I was taken with the quality of the 2002 Chardonnay. The wine is already showing a beautiful gold color and has a nose of orange peel, mango, and pineapple. The wine has great layers of fruit but enough acidity to provide a fine balance. It is as soft as velvet in the mouth and has an extraordinarily long finish. This is a wonderful and atypical example of Chardonnay that emphasizes the quality of the fruit and not the oak.

John suggests the 2001 Cabernet Sauvignon, which is an inky-black wine completely opaque in the glass. I found cassis in the nose, black currants, some tobacco notes, and blackberry fruit. The wine shows lovely soft tannins with great layers of fruit and a long finish. It will easily age another eight years.

I also have to recommend the 2000 Zinfandel, which John will most likely keep in the barrel one more year. This is another dark, dense wine of red-purple color, opaque in the glass. It has an intriguing nose of passion fruit, cranberries, and a hint of white pepper under the fruit. The wine is already superb in the mouth, well balanced between the oak and the acidity. I was impressed by both the fruitiness of this young wine and the tannins that will allow it to age. The hand of the master in evident in this wine, a blend of grapes from five vineyards.

RATING: Three → four stars (quality has improved substantially across the line)

Linne Calodo Cellars

WINERY OWNERS: Matt and Maureen
Trevisan

WINEMAKER: Matt Trevisan

TASTING ROOM: Yes

DAYS/HOURS: Friday–Sunday 11 A.M.–5 P.M.

ADDRESS: 3845 Oakdale Rd., Paso Robles,
CA 93446; 805-227-0797;
805-227-4868 (fax); linnecalodo.com

WINES/GRAPE VARIETIES: Cherry Red
(blend), Contrarian (white Rhône
blend), Leona's (red blend), Nemesis red
Rhône (blend), Outsider (red blend),
Problem Child (red blend),
Rising Tide (red Rhône blend), Slacker
(red blend), Sticks & Stones (red Rhône
blend)

WINE CLUB: Yes

TASTING ROOM AMENITIES: Some
merchandise

REGION: Paso Robles AVA

The tasting room at Linne Calodo Cellars (named for a stratum of the rocky calcare-ous soil on the west side of Paso Robles) is located within the new building that houses the winery where Matt and Maureen Trevisan produce their wine. During my visit, I had the pleasure of watching Matt climb four and five barrels high, glass in one hand, wine thief for pulling samples from the barrels in the other. Matt is also climbing the mountain of recognition in the wine world. When Robert M. Parker Jr. gave his 2001 Sticks and Stones and the Nemesis Syrah both a 95 rating, the phone rang off the wall.

Unfortunately, those wines are long gone. However, I had the opportunity to sample many of the varieties for upcoming releases directly from the barrel. After we sampled each of the components of his blended wines, I watched enthralled as he put the wines together in the glass to give an approximation of what the blends would eventually look and taste like. It was indeed an honor to watch him work as he moved with skill and agility up and down the rows of oak barrels stacked to the ceiling. One barrel in particular was under-going malolactic fermentation. Matt popped the plastic bung out of the barrel and we put an ear to it. The wine crackled and popped like rice cereal in a breakfast bowl.

Matt knows his way around wine the way he knows his way around the barrel room at Linne Calodo. He is a graduate of Cal Poly with a degree in biochemistry. A super-visor in the lab at Poly told him to look into getting a job at a winery, and since he had once helped a roommate's parents during a harvest party, he liked the idea. He sent a résumé to Justin Vineyards on a Friday and had a job by Tuesday. At Justin they worked him like a slobbering cellar dog up to seventy hours a week in the summer of 1995. He stayed for two years learning everything possible, and then went to Wild Horse in the summer of 1997. In four years at Wild Horse he did everything from cleaning pipettes to driving the forklift for moving barrels in the warehouse, which he managed. Ken Volk, then the owner of Wild Horse and as gracious as ever, allowed Matt and his partner, Justin Smith, to make their own wines after hours, giving them access to all the facilities and equipment. The first vintage bottling of Linne Calodo was in 1998. Justin Smith went on to establish his own line at Saxum.

Because Linne Calodo is very much a family-owned and -run winery, Maureen Tre-visan plays a vital role in the day-to-day operation of the business. She administers all the accounts, looks after distribution, and takes care of sales and the tasting room while Matt makes the wine. In fact, she worked at Turley for a time just to gain firsthand experience in running and managing a tasting room.

The building that houses the tasting room and the barrels was built in 2002. If you have the good fortune to meet Matt, take a quick look at his pants. His jeans or shorts will be pockmarked with tears in the fabric. That means he has been working, climbing up among the barrels. Sometimes nail heads used to fasten the metal wraps around the staves catch the fabric. That's one way to tell you are talking with an authentic cellar man.

RECOMMENDED WINES: Matt recommends the Rising Tide; the 2003 is a blend of Syrah, Grenache, and Mourvèdre. The wine is opaque in the glass and dark purple-red in color. The wine shows boysenberry, blackberry, cassis, and black currants to the nose. It is wonderfully well integrated and shows beautifully on the tongue. The ripe fruit, fine tannins, and long, satisfying finish combine to make this a truly outstanding blend. The wine should last another ten to twelve years.

I suggest the Nemesis; the 2003 is a blend of Syrah, Grenache, and Mourvèdre, making it opaque to light and a reddish-purple color. The nose is boysenberry, crème de cassis, black cherry, and white pepper spice. The wine is opulent in the mouth, given the luscious ripe fruit and wonderful balance of tannins and fruit. The finish lasted nearly a minute. It is a superb wine of outstanding texture and depth that will last another ten to fifteen years. The tastings from the bottle confirmed the outstanding potential of the unblended varieties tasted from the barrel.

RATING: Five stars (wines outstanding to superb)

Locatelli Vineyards & Winery

WINERY OWNERS: Louis and Raynette Gregory

WINEMAKER: Louis Gregory

TASTING ROOM: Yes

DAYS/HOURS: Friday–Sunday 11 A.M.–4 P.M.

ADDRESS: 8585 Cross Canyon Rd., San Miguel, CA 93451; 805-467-0067; 805-467-0127 (fax); locatelliwinery.com

WINES/GRAPE VARIETIES: Aurelia Dolce (blend), Cabernet Sauvignon, Cielo Rosso (blend), Luminous (blend), Merlot, Petite Syrah, Viognier

WINE CLUB: Yes

REGION: Paso Robles AVA, San Miguel area

Lone Madrone

WINERY OWNERS: Neil Collins, Tom Vaughan, and Jackie Meisinger

WINEMAKER: Neil Collins

TASTING ROOM: At Sycamore Farms

DAYS/HOURS: Daily 11 a.m.–5 p.m.

ADDRESS: Sycamore Farms, 2485 Hwy. 46 W., Paso Robles, CA 93446; 805-238-0845; 805-238-0845 (fax); lonemadrone.com

WINES/GRAPE VARIETIES: Albariño, Barbera, Cabernet Sauvignon, Chardonnay, Chenin Blanc, Mourvèdre, Nebbiolo, Petite Sirah, Pinot Grigio, port, red blend, rosé, Roussanne, Syrah, Tannat, Viognier, white Rhône blend, Zinfandel

WINE CLUB: Yes

REGION: Paso Robles AVA

Madison Cellars

WINERY OWNERS: Jon L. and Margie Korecki

WINEMAKER: Jon L. Korecki

TASTING ROOM: At Parkfield Wine and Produce

DAYS/HOURS: Monday–Saturday 9 A.M.–7 P.M., Sunday 10 A.M.–5 P.M.

ADDRESS: Parkfield Wine and Produce, 1761 Ramada Dr., Paso Robles, CA 93446;

805-237-7544; 805-237-7798 (fax); maidsoncellars.com

WINES/GRAPE VARIETIES: Merlot, Syrah, Syrah rosé

WINE CLUB: Yes

TASTING ROOM AMENITIES: Gourmet market, merchandise

REGION: Paso Robles AVA

Maloy O'Neill Vineyards

WINERY OWNER: Shannon O'Neill

WINEMAKER: Shannon O'Neill

TASTING ROOM: Yes

DAYS/HOURS: Friday–Saturday 10 A.M.–5 P.M., Sunday 12–5 P.M., or by appointment

ADDRESS: 5725 Union Rd., Paso Robles, CA 93446; 805-238-7320; 805-226-8412 (fax); maloyoneill.com

WINES/GRAPE VARIETIES: Cabernet Sauvignon, Chardonnay, Enzo (blend), Gioi (blend), late-harvest Muscat, Lexicon (blend), Merlot, Petite Sirah, Pinot Gris, Pinot Noir, Syrah, Syrah port, Syrah rosé, Zinfandel

WINE CLUB: Yes

TASTING ROOM AMENITIES: Picnic area, merchandise

REGION: Paso Robles AVA

The O'Neill family purchased 180 acres of ranch land east of Paso Robles in 1980. By 1982 they had planted 27 acres over to Chardonnay. Nine years later, 40 acres of Cabernet Sauvignon were planted. Over the years they purchased more acreage and introduced other varieties. The high-quality fruit was sent to some local wineries, but also to Napa, Sonoma, Mendocino, and Lake county companies. By 2000 they had started a winery producing small-lot wines. The next year, Maloy O'Neill won its first gold medal for the 2000 Syrah Private Reserve.

Although his family might have given him the impetus to become a winemaker, Shannon O'Neill, a prodigal son in the sense of the wanderer come home, took the long and winding road during his return. The initial leg of his journey away started with promise. In 1983 his sister was already a student at UC Davis and encouraged her brother to attend. After all, what better path to follow for siblings whose family owns high-quality vineyards? Following his sister's advice, he graduated in 1991 with a degree in fermentation science, meeting his wife, Maureen Maloy, while at university. During his time at Davis he took internships with Chevron and ARCO for the opportunity to work in their chemistry labs. At that point his path began to diverge. Not to lose sight of his original trail, however, he continued to work harvests back home and in the cellars of local wineries. He continued his work for Chevron after graduation and ventured farther afield to a Palo Alto biotechnology firm doing fermentation and enzyme research applicable to the beer and wine industry. But in 1998 he did an about-face and traveled the road home to become the winemaker for his family. Not surprisingly, he had been experimenting with winemaking since 1984. He took the job with the express purpose of showcasing the excellent quality of the fruit produced in his family's vineyards. Then came the gold.

His experiences away from home, combined with his technical education and years of making wine as a hobby, gave Shannon the requisite tools for crafting extraordinary wines. As a scientist he remains a student of his craft; in fact, he has an outstanding library of books on winemaking and California wines. He is a purist at heart and wants to maintain a high level of control over his wines to ensure optimal quality in every aspect of the wine's production, from grape growing in the vineyards to finished wines in the bottle. That quality was readily apparent in each of the wines I tasted.

RECOMMENDED WINES: Shannon recommends the Private Reserve Syrah, and for good reason. This wine has now won three gold medals in a row. The 2003 is a dark purple with a black core that makes it opaque to the stem. In the nose the wine presents subtle vanilla and spice notes next to cherry and raspberry fruit. The intriguing aspect of the wine is its wonderful breadth in the mouth. The tannins, while still present, are soft enough to contribute to the wine's elegance. The wine has a long, lingering finish that brings you back for more of the generous ripe fruit. In five to eight years, as it drops its tannins, this wine will show its inherent finesse as well.

I suggest the 2002 Lexicon, a blend of Syrah, Cabernet Sauvignon, Merlot, and Zinfandel. This wine too is an inky dark purple. The vanilla notes are present in the nose alongside the raspberry and cherry fruit and a hint of black currants. It is a well-balanced wine, drinkable now but capable of rewarding patience. The finish is noticeably long and smooth, as the wine wants to live in the mouth. It will age beautifully another seven to eight years. These two wines are representative of Shannon's attention to detail and his goal of creating superpremium wines that remain excellent values when compared to other wines costing twice or even three times as much.

RATING: Four stars (a rising star on the Central Coast)

Martin & Weyrich Winery

WINERY OWNERS: David and Mary Weyrich

WINEMAKERS: Alan Kinne and Craig Reed

TASTING ROOM: Yes

DAYS/HOURS: Sunday–Thursday 10 A.M.–5 P.M., Friday–Saturday 10 A.M.–6 P.M.

ADDRESS: 2610 Buena Vista Dr., Paso Robles, CA 93446; 805-238-2520; 805-238-6041 (fax); martinweyrich.com

WINES/GRAPE VARIETIES: Cabernet Etrusco, Cabernet Sauvignon, Chardonnay, Insieme red (blend), Matador Rosé, Moscato Allegro, Nebbiolo, Pinot Grigio, Pinot Noir, Sangiovese, Sauvignon Blanc, Zinfandel

WINE CLUB: Yes

TASTING ROOM AMENITIES: Picnic area, merchandise, deli snacks

REGION: Paso Robles AVA

The Martin Brothers Winery was originally established in 1981 with the intention of producing Italian wines such as Nebbiolo, Sangiovese, and Pinot Grigio. Brothers Tom and Dominic, with the help of sisters Mary and Ann, bought an 83-acre dairy farm that year a few miles northeast of Paso Robles and set about the task of transforming it into an estate winery. Mary Martin married David Weyrich, and they became the sole owners of Martin Brothers in 1998; hence the name change to Martin & Weyrich. The winery claims two firsts to its credit: it is one of the first modern growers and producers in the United States of Nebbiolo, the noble red grape grown in the famous Piedmont region of Italy. (My research indicates that David Caparone of Caparone Winery planted a Nebbiolo cultivar taken from UC Davis stock in 1980 and produced a wine from those grapes in 1985.) And Martin & Weyrich was the first winery to produce a Super Tuscan blend, called Cabernet Etrusco, typically 85 percent Cabernet Sauvignon and 15 percent Sangiovese.

Winemaking is handled by the duo of Craig Reed and Alan Kinne. Craig is a native of the region and has been with the winery since 1988. He has worked just about every job possible there, ranging from lawn mower to public relations guy to winemaker. He was originally hired by then-winemaker Dominic Martin and became his apprentice. He was promoted to head winemaker in 1994 and was awarded the accolade of Paso Winemaker of the Year. Alan came to the winery in 1999 from the East Coast. A native of Michigan, he has a degree in literature and philosophy from the University of Michigan and at one time recklessly wanted to become a philosophy professor. Luckily, he got a summer job washing wine barrels and changed his career path before any damage was done. He worked in Michigan and Long Island and established a successful consulting business in Virginia before David Weyrich hired him to help make the wines. He is also one of the original members of the Hospice du Rhône, along with Mat Garretson and John Alban.

The tasting room is separate from the winery, though you might want to visit both. At the winery you will find the now-famous Villa Toscana, one of the region's finest bed-and-breakfast inns. Eight luxury suites are available, in addition to a two-bedroom, two-and-a-half bath suite with a detached two-car garage, private courtyard, and patio with a Jacuzzi. I viewed all the rooms, and this is living in high style. Craig spent his honeymoon in the suite. Book early. The tasting room is worth a visit for the wines and the extensive merchandise available for the wine consumer. It is a beautiful structure in its own right. And remember that Craig and Alan also make the wines for York Mountain.

RECOMMENDED WINES: Craig and Alan emphasize the importance of making wines that pair well with food. They prefer to make wines that are fun, not overextracted and painful to drink. Craig recommends Il Vecchio Nebbiolo, the house flagship. I tasted the 1999, a relatively light-colored, pretty cherry-red wine. There is sweet cherry in the lovely nose, some red currants, and a touch of tobacco. The wine is ready for drinking now, as the tannins have resolved to an elegant, soft finish.

Alan suggests the Paso Robles 2000 Cabernet Sauvignon, and he picked a fine one. This wine is opaque to the stem and black-purple in color. The nose has loads of ripe cherries, tobacco leaf, and a hint of cedar from the oak. The wine has an expansive mouthfeel and enough tannin and acidity to age another three to five years.

I recommend the Dante Dusi Reserve Zinfandel. The 1999 is black cherry in color and almost opaque. There is chocolate and brambles in the nose, along with cherry preserves and clove spice. The tannins are round and soft, and the fruit shows fine ripeness. This wine has both elegance and complexity as a result. Drink it now and over the next two to three years.

RATING: Two stars (consistently well-made reds and whites)

McClean Vineyards

WINERY OWNERS: Michael and Judy McClean

WINEMAKER: Michael McClean

TASTING ROOM: No

DAYS/HOURS: By appointment only

ADDRESS: 4491 S. El Pomar, Templeton, CA 93465; 805-237-2441; 805-237-2441 (fax); mccleanvineyard.com

WINE/GRAPE VARIETY: Syrah

WINE CLUB: Yes

REGION: Paso Robles AVA, Templeton area

Meridian Vineyards

WINERY OWNER: Foster's Wine Estates

WINEMAKER: Art Nathan

TASTING ROOM: Yes

DAYS/HOURS: Daily 10 A.M.–5 P.M.

ADDRESS: 7000 Hwy. 46 E., Paso Robles, CA 93446; 805-226-7133; 805-239-9624 (fax); meridianvineyards.com

WINES/GRAPE VARIETIES: Cabernet Sauvignon, Chardonnay, Gewürztraminer, Merlot, Petite Syrah, Pinot Grigio (Classic series), Pinot Gris (Limited Release series), Pinot Noir, Sauvignon Blanc, Sangiovese, Syrah, Zinfandel

WINE CLUB: Yes

TASTING ROOM AMENITIES: Picnic area, merchandise

REGION: Paso Robles AVA

Purchased in 1988, the former Estrella River Winery is now the home of Meridian Vineyards, one of the most successful commercial wineries in the Paso Robles area, selling more than 150,000 cases of wine a year. Chuck Ortman, one of the veteran winemakers in Paso Robles, founded the label in 1984 and made his first wines primarily from Napa fruit. Ortman got his start in the wine business in 1968, spending the early part of his career as a winemaker and consultant in Napa and Sonoma. When Wine World Estates (now Beringer Blass Wine Estates, a division of Foster's Group) began investing in Ortman's label, it provided the financial wherewithal for him to move his operation to San Luis Obispo County. Meridian, now under the direction of winemaker Art Nathan, makes wines from grapes grown in Paso Robles (the home vineyard) and Santa Barbara (White Hills and Cat Canyon), where Meridian buys grapes for its Chardonnay. Art is a recent arrival from Monterey County. He holds a degree from Davis in plant science and viticulture and came aboard in July 2002. As winemaker, he works collaboratively with his staff, combining his expertise in viticulture with his expertise as a winemaker. Art is responsible for grape selection and for reserve lots and some limited releases.

At Meridian, Art emphasizes, you will get excellent value for the price paid. Meridian has access to wonderful fruit, and a great team is in place to make the most of it. In fact, of the nine plants owned by Foster's Wine Estates in California, Meridian has the reputation for being the most efficient, processing half of the fruit of the North American operations (much of it for the other Foster's Wine Estates brands).

Plan to spend some time at the remodeled stone tasting room and retail shop. The grounds are beautiful, and the view of the surrounding hills and vineyards is worth the trip.

RECOMMENDED WINES: Art recommends the Limited Reserve Petite Syrah. I tasted the 2002, an inky purple-black wine opaque to the stem of the glass. The nose shows mint, spicy oak, pepper, blackberry, and loganberry fruit. The wine has wonderful tannins and will easily reward another five years of aging. It has a long, velvety finish. This is one of the better Petite Syrahs in the area.

Although Meridian makes a fine Chardonnay for the money, I was impressed with the Gewürztraminer made from Santa Barbara County grapes. I tasted the Limited Reserve 2003. The wine is pale gold in color and is finished in the dry style of an Alsace Gewürztraminer. It has a nose of grapefruit, cinnamon spice, and some lime. The wine has sufficient acidity to balance the fruit and makes for a refreshing, satisfying finish.

RATING: Two stars (some fine values in the regular lineup); three stars (Reserve program)

Midlife Crisis Winery

WINERY OWNERS: Kevin and Jill Mittan

WINEMAKERS: Kevin and Jill Mittan

TASTING ROOM: At Wines on Pine

DAYS/HOURS: Thursday–Monday
10:30 A.M.–6 P.M.

ADDRESS: Wines on Pine, 1244 Pine St., Ste. A, Paso Robles, CA 93446; 805-237-8730; 805-237-8904 (fax); midlifecrisiswinery.com

WINES/GRAPE VARIETIES: Barbera, Chardonnay, Maggie's Magic (sparkling wine), Merlot, Pinot Grigio, Roo Berry Red (blend), Sangiovese, Sydney's Surprise (Maggie's Magic with raspberry), Syrah, Syrah rosé, Zinfandel

WINE CLUB: Yes

REGION: Paso Robles AVA

Midnight Cellars

WINERY OWNERS: Hartenberger family

WINEMAKER: Rich Hartenberger

TASTING ROOM: Yes

DAYS/HOURS: Daily 10 A.M.–5:30 P.M.

ADDRESS: 2925 Anderson Rd., Paso Robles, CA 93446; 805-239-8904; 805-239-3289 (fax); midnightcellars.com

WINES/GRAPE VARIETIES: Cabernet Franc, Cabernet Sauvignon, Chardonnay, late-harvest Zinfandel, Merlot, Petite Sirah, Pinot Noir, port, red Bordeaux, Rhône, and Italian blends, Syrah, Zinfandel

WINE CLUB: Yes

TASTING ROOM AMENITIES: Merchandise

REGION: Paso Robles AVA

Rich Hartenberger is willing to take the blame for getting his family involved in wine. But it's really not all his fault. As a child, he had some help when his family escaped from the fast pace of big-city Chicago to the more gentrified rural confines of Paso Robles. Rich's parents took him along for tasting tours in Napa and Sonoma before they made the move, and he gained some early experience with wine by working in a wine shop while still in college. One day Rich got a crazy idea and suggested to his father, Bob, that he buy a winery for Rich and his wife, Michelle, to run, and his father agreed. Rich's brother, Mike, wanted in on it as well. Sometimes you have to be careful or you might get what you ask for.

After looking at properties the width and breadth of California, Bob settled on land in San Luis Obispo County capable of producing big, rich, premium reds. Once they bought the property on the west side of Paso Robles, it was time to plant grapes and make wine. Midnight Cellars was established in 1995. The wine community there was extremely helpful and assisted the family wherever possible. Tobin James (Shumrick), in particular, was a big help and got them started as successful producers of Zinfandel. Great ratings in the *Wine Spectator* firmly established the name.

This is still very much a family-owned and -run operation. Parents Bob and Mary Jane are the major stockholders. Mike handles sales, marketing, and distribution. Rich makes the wines for Michelle's tasting room inside a renovated farmhouse next to the building that contains the winery.

RECOMMENDED WINES: If you go to taste, you'll be in the capable hands of tasting-room manager Wayne Lawrence, an indispensable part of the operation. He knows his wines, and he enjoys helping everyone through the tasting process. He recommends the Fralich Vineyards Syrah, a wonderful glass of young blackberry fruit, briars, spice, and earthiness. The wine is reminiscent of a fine Rhône, with great body in the mouth and a long, smooth finish. It should age at least another three to five years.

Rich also recommends the 2000 Mare Nectaris, which may be better than the sensational 1999. It is already showing excellent fruit and is huge in the mouth. This black-purple wine has an incredible finish that will stay with you while you go out to the car and make a call to tell your friends about the wine, and will follow you back to the tasting room, where you beg Wayne for just one more little sip. The wine has concentration, depth, and ultimately finesse, if you give it time. It's showing very well now, but please buy enough to drink over the next ten years.

I have been a great fan of Rich's Zinfandels, and the new releases confirm my ongoing interest in these wines. The 2002 is an inky-black dynamo with tons of berries and vanilla on the nose. Its breadth is impressive in the mouth, and there is a touch of sweetness in the wine. Rich thinks he might have let the wine finish too sweet, but I am convinced that it carries enough fruit, tannins, and acidity that the sweetness will only add to the wine's complexity. The French would kill if they could get this level of ripeness in their grapes year in and year out. In six months, as the wine comes together firmly in the bottle, this should be a wonderful example. My barrel tastings of the 2003 vintage suggest that there are even better things to come.

RATING: Three → four stars (this winery keeps getting better and better across the line)

Minassian-Young Vineyards

WINERY OWNER: David Young

WINEMAKER: David Young

TASTING ROOM: Yes

DAYS/HOURS: Saturday–Sunday 11 A.M.–5 P.M.

ADDRESS: 4045 Peachy Canyon Rd., Paso Robles, CA 93446; 805-238-7571; no fax; no Web site

WINES/GRAPE VARIETIES: Bordeaux blends, Rhône blends, Zinfandel

WINE CLUB: Yes

TASTING ROOM AMENITIES: Picnic area

REGION: Paso Robles AVA, west side

Nadeau Family Vintners

WINERY OWNERS: Robert and Patrice Nadeau

WINEMAKER: Robert Nadeau

TASTING ROOM: Yes

DAYS/HOURS: Saturday–Sunday 12–5 P.M.

ADDRESS: 3860 Peachy Canyon Rd., Paso Robles, CA 93446; 805-239-3574; 805-239-2314 (fax); nadeaufamilyvintners .com

WINES/GRAPE VARIETIES: Barbera, late-harvest Zinfandel, Mourvèdre, Rhône Varietal Red (blend), Roussanne, Syrah, Viognier, Zinfandel

WINE CLUB: Yes

TASTING ROOM AMENITIES: Picnic area

REGION: Paso Robles AVA

Robert and Patrice Nadeau are representative of the many couples who have dedicated their lives and passions to growing and making wine. Robert grew up in Paso Robles and served as an avionics technician in the military. And therein lies a tale. With exceptional test scores and technical aptitude, Robert was assigned to unique and challenging projects while in the Air Force. After rotating out, he was tapped for a special government service job but, given the bureaucratic regulations of the time, was required to first wait six months. While waiting, he returned to Paso Robles and ran into Gary Eberle's daughter, a friend from high school. When Gary found out through his daughter that Robert had six months of free time, he offered Robert a position in the tasting room, and his life's direction changed.

From the tasting room he dropped down into the cellar, where the action is anyway, and eventually became assistant winemaker, learning from and working with both Gary Eberle and Tobin Shumrick (of Tobin James Cellars). Before he took on the responsibilities of assistant winemaker for Eberle, he worked a stint at Martin Brothers (now Martin & Weyrich) for Nick Martin. In the mid-1990s Doug Beckett at Peachy Canyon offered him the job that Tobin James had initially held when Tobin left to start Tobin James Winery. Robert also worked with Art Norman of Norman Vineyards for ten years. He next met Dave Nichols and Rich Quinn, who were buying ground to start Opolo, and struck a deal to consult with them. And that's how the United States government lost a highly qualified employee and Paso Robles gained an outstanding winemaker.

Robert and Patrice (currently an engineer, at one time she designed golf courses) started Nadeau Family Vintners in 1997. Robert developed into one of the premier talents in Paso Robles, and you can see his hand in the myriad successes of Eberle, Peachy Canyon, Norman, Opolo, and now his eponymous winery. He has the justly deserved reputation of making some of the finest Zinfandels in the region. In 2004 he was honored for his work in the Paso Robles AVA by being named Winemaker of the Year. An extremely articulate man capable of discoursing on a variety of subjects, Robert knows what he wants to do with wine. From his perspective, winemaking is more a craft than an art. The analogy he offers is that of a furniture maker crafting great pieces—that is, art with function. The wine is made first in the vineyard, where a Zin has to be a Zin and not a Pinot Noir in style, for example, and is finished in the winery. Therefore, site selection and farming become crucial elements in obtaining the best possible fruit for crafting into great wine. In this sense his scientific training, giving him the ability to troubleshoot and solve the problems that emerge during the winemaking process, is crucial. These skills, along with the tools of the trade, the machinery, the analyzers, the pipettes, and other technologies now available, are all necessary for a winemaker to hone his craft as he produces the best possible wines. And through it all, Robert wants first and foremost to stay a Paso Robles winemaker. That means offering you a bite of his sandwich if he thinks you are hungry.

RECOMMENDED WINES: I'm convinced that in addition to his excellent Rhône program, Robert Nadeau is making some of the finest Zinfandels in all of Paso Robles. He did it while at Peachy Canyon, at Norman, while consulting at Opolo, and now under his own label. The 2003 Critical Mass Zinfandel, Robert's recommendation, is an opaque black-purple wine whose nose is an intriguing mélange of crème brûlée from the oak, blackberries, black currants, plums, cedar, earth, and sage spice. The tannins are round and soft, and the wine is outstanding in the mid-palate. The Critical Mass shows excellent integration and a long, satisfying finish that recalls the ripe lush fruit. Drinking very nicely now, this wine will reward another three to five years of maturation.

My recommendation is the Mourvèdre. The Mourvèdre grape is originally from Spain but also grows in the south of France. To ripen properly it requires warm south-facing slopes, and the French climate is often insufficient for its needs. This leads to fairly rough, herbaceous wines, often with a touch of farmyard in the nose. For this reason it is frequently used as a blending grape. On the other hand, the climate in Paso Robles seems to provide the combination of heat and evening coolness the grape needs to flourish. Nadeau may be on to something with the 2003, which is red-purple in the glass and nearly opaque to light. The nose here is red currants, raspberries, blackberries, boysenberries, and crème fraîche. The fruit is wonderfully ripe and provides a sensation of sweetness in the mouth. There is not so much as a hint of herbaceousness or barnyard flavors in the wine, thank goodness. The excellent tannin and acidity balance the fruit beautifully, making for a finely structured and well-integrated wine. The finish is nearly a minute, and I expect that this wine will improve in the bottle over the next four to six years. This is clearly one of the best examples I have tasted, and a wonderful surprise.

RATING: Four → five stars (potentially the next five-star winery in San Luis Obispo County)

Nichols Winery & Cellars

WINERY OWNER: Keith Nichols

WINEMAKER: Keith Nichols

TASTING ROOM: No

DAYS/HOURS: By appointment only

ADDRESS: 5115 Buena Vista Dr., Paso Robles, CA 93446; 310-305-0397; 310-305-0397 (fax); nicholswinery.com

WINES/GRAPE VARIETIES: Chardonnay, Cabernet Franc, Cabernet Sauvignon, Meritage (blend), Merlot, Pinot Blanc, Pinot Noir, Zinfandel

WINE CLUB: Yes

REGION: Paso Robles AVA, west side

Niner Wine Estates

WINERY OWNERS: Pam and Dick Niner

WINEMAKER: Amanda Cramer

TASTING ROOM: Due to open in summer 2008

DAYS/HOURS: Call for details

ADDRESS: Call for details; 805-239-2233; 805-239-0033 (fax); ninerwine.com

WINES/GRAPE VARIETIES: Barbera, Barbera Rosato, Cabernet Franc, Cabernet Sauvignon, Merlot, Sangiovese, Sauvignon Blanc, Syrah

WINE CLUB: Yes

REGION: Paso Robles AVA, west side

Norman Vineyards

WINERY OWNERS: Art and Lei Norman

WINEMAKER: Steve Felten

TASTING ROOM: Yes

DAYS/HOURS: Daily 11 A.M.–5 P.M.

ADDRESS: 7450 Vineyard Dr., Paso Robles, CA 93446; 805-237-0138; 805-227-6733 (fax); normanvineyards.com

WINES/GRAPE VARIETIES: Barbera, Cabernet Sauvignon, Cabernet Franc,

Chardonnay, Grenache-Syrah rosé, late-harvest Zinfandel, Nebbiolo, Meritage (blend), Merlot, Pinot Grigio, red Rhône blend, Sangiovese, Syrah, White Zinfandel, Zinfandel, Zinfandel port

WINE CLUB: Yes

TASTING ROOM AMENITIES: Picnic area, merchandise

REGION: San Luis Obispo County: Paso Robles AVA

Art Norman was formally trained as an engineer and worked in the aerospace industry in Southern California before he and his wife, Lei, came north to Paso Robles and bought land in the hills of Adelaida about 1971. The arrival of the Normans places them firmly in the forefront of modern Paso Robles wine history. Originally intended as a getaway place (Art had a boat and Lake Nacimiento wasn't that far away), the property was early on planted to hay and safflower. However, as is often the case in these situations, Art comes from a family with a history of winemaking through his father and grandfather that extends back to the nineteenth century. In 1968 Bank of America released a study on winegrowing regions, which concluded that Paso Robles was an area of prime interest. It wasn't long before the hay was gone and a vineyard was planted. Shortly thereafter, the Normans decided to build a facility to take care of the grapes. The Normans sold their house in Northridge to fund the new facility, but about the time of their first crush, Art had the misfortune of needing bypass surgery. Art recovered his health and, convinced of the great possibilities for his property and for the region in general, decided to make a go of it. Having used the ski boat only three times, he sold it.

The winemaker in the early years was an up-and-comer by the name of Robert Nadeau, who helped establish the winery's reputation. As Nadeau developed his expertise and standing within the wine community, an assistant winemaker by the name of Joe Kidd was brought on board. When Nadeau left to pursue other opportunities, Kidd was appointed head winemaker. More recently, Steve Felten, formerly of Eos Estate Winery, has become the new winemaker and general manager. Art intended to step back and enjoy the remaining years of his life, convinced that Felten would not only raise the quality of the wines at Norman to a higher level but also pass on his passion and creative sensitivity to the entire team. After all, he would not trust just anyone to manage the business and make wine from his vines now more than thirty years old.

Art Norman, an important leader in the growth and reputation of San Luis Obispo County wines, put together a state-of-the-art facility with a staff that provides excellent hospitality for guests. They put the emphasis on fun in a tasting room that is pleasant and accommodating. The vineyards are in very good hands, and the wines are currently distributed in more than forty states, thanks to Art and Lei's hard work. As Art looked back over the past thirty years, he had both the context and the history to assert that Paso Robles has a great and shining future. He told me that without doubt here was the next Napa Valley, without the crowds and high prices, and to this I can add: thanks to vintners like the Normans.

(Author's note: During the time I was editing this profile, I learned of Art Norman's untimely passing at age seventy-two. He will be sorely missed, but remembered as one of Paso Robles's authentic and important wine pioneers. Drink a glass in memory of a fine and gracious man.)

RECOMMENDED WINES: I was taken by the quality of the Zinfandels that Norman offers. Art recommended the 2001 Cucamonga Zinfandel. Made from vines more than a hundred years old, this is a dark cherry wine, almost opaque to the stem, with lovely aromatics of earth, sage, and very ripe fruit of plum and cassis. On the mid-palate the wine opens up to reveal chocolate and a touch of pepper. The finish is long and clean, and the excellent balance of this wine will allow it to age another five years.

The 2000 Zinfandel Port from Cucamonga old vines is better than some tawny ports I have tasted. The wine carries about 13 percent residual sugar but is beautifully balanced by the generous acidity. This is a red cherry wine, somewhat lighter than the 2001 Zinfandel, and possesses lovely sweet aromas of caramel, apricots, and plums. The finish on this wine will stay with you even as you drive out of the parking lot. The wine will age ten to twelve years.

RATING: Two stars (look for winemaker Steve Felten to improve and revitalize the line)

Opolo Vineyards

WINERY OWNERS: Rick Quinn and Dave Nichols

WINEMAKERS: Rick Quinn and Dave Nichols

TASTING ROOM: Yes

DAYS/HOURS: Daily 10 A.M.–5 P.M.

ADDRESS: 7110 Vineyard Dr., Paso Robles, CA 93446; 805-238-9593; 805-238-9594 (fax); opolo.com

WINES/GRAPE VARIETIES: Grenache, Montagne-Mare (red blend), Muscat Canelli, Pinot Grigio, Rhapsody (red blend), Roussanne, Sangiovese, Syrah, Viognier, Zinfandel

WINE CLUB: Yes

TASTING ROOM AMENITIES: Merchandise

REGION: Paso Robles AVA

Rick Quinn originally hails from Duluth, Minnesota. The families in the neighborhood—of Italian, Serbian, and Croatian origins—made wine from grapes shipped by boxcar to Minnesota from California. When he moved closer to the source in 1979, Rick bought his fruit from Fratelli Perata, but by 1995 the Peratas had decided to put all their fruit into their own program, so Rick was forced to find other sources. A property near Paso Robles had fallen out of escrow, and he bought it sight unseen. The next year he planted grapes to ensure a steady supply for his home winemaking hobby. In the meantime, he developed one of the largest Century 21 real estate brokerages in the country.

Dave Nichols owns a wireless electronics company and is known to make a pretty good batch of backyard wine himself. As circumstance would have it, his next-door neighbor in Camarillo, California, in 1996 was Rick Quinn. In casual conversation Rick mentioned that he had recently planted ten thousand grapevines up north. Dave, at the time looking to do something in agriculture, was researching properties in the Santa Ynez area. Not satisfied with the prospects there, he turned to Paso Robles and bought a vineyard next to Rick's, helping to maintain balance in the neighborly relationship. Over the course of the next few years, both men sold their grapes to other wineries, although Rick held back some fruit for his hobby.

In 1999 the two solidified their relationship as partners in a new venture called Opolo, named in homage to Rick's Yugoslavian heritage. Opolo is derived from the name of a Dalmatian wine called *opol*. *Opol* is produced in northern Dalmatia in the vineyards near a coastal town called Sibenik, the oldest Croatian town on the Adriatic, located at the mouth of the River Krka. The tradition in Sibenik taverns even today is to signify the types of wines being sold in the establishments: the branch of a juniper tree on the sign indicates red wine on the premises, olive branches indicate white, and pine branches indicate *opol* (rosé). On the nearby island of Vis, famous for its vineyards and orchards, *opol* is considered an outstanding light red wine. In Paso Robles, the first commercial crush of Opolo wines took place in 1999. The winery is located in the estate vineyards west of Paso Robles in the Santa Lucia Mountains.

RECOMMENDED WINES: Rick recommends the Pinot Noir. I sampled the 2001, a translucent wine of blood rubies and garnets. The nose is a mélange of cherries, jam, and spice. This is a soft Pinot ready for drinking now.

Dave suggests the Sangiovese, an inky-black wine opaque in the glass. This wine fills the mouth with wonderfully ripe tannins that give a sense of elegance. The nose is raspberries, cherries, and vanilla cream. The finish goes on long after the last swallow. In two years this will be a fine example of what Opolo can do with this variety.

My personal favorites over the years have been the great Zinfandels vinified by Robert Nadeau in his role as consultant. The 2002 Reserve Bin Zinfandel is a lovely glass of perfume, raspberry fruit, and spice. This is a highly concentrated wine of excellent balance and long, pleasing finish. Give it another three to five years and it will reward you with an outstanding bottle.

RATING: Three stars (consistently very good to excellent reds)

Orchid Hill Vineyard and Winery

WINERY OWNER: Mike Schenkhuizen

WINEMAKER: Dan Kleck

TASTING ROOM: Yes

DAYS/HOURS: Thursday–Monday 11 A.M.–
5 P.M.

ADDRESS: 1140 Pine Street, Paso Robles, CA 93446; 805-237-7525, 510-783-3831 (sales

office); 510-783-7252 (fax);
orchidhillwine.com

WINES/GRAPE VARIETIES: Pinot Noir,
Syrah, Viognier, Zinfandel

WINE CLUB: Yes

TASTING ROOM AMENITIES: Merchandise,
art gallery

REGION: Paso Robles AVA

Mike Schenkhuizen ("shenk-high-zen") is the owner of Orchid Hill, and his road to Paso Robles may be one of the longest I've encountered. Mike was born in Indonesia; his grandparents on one side of the family were Dutch, and he immigrated to the Netherlands when the political climate no longer favored the Dutch in Indonesia. He was educated in Holland in technical and mechanical fields and in 1959 made the move across the big water to the United States. For ten years he worked as a machinist until he started his own tool-and-die business in 1969. He sold to his brother, relocated to Hayward, and, with his interest in quality manufacturing, entered the medical field.

Both Mike and his wife, Estrella, have been long-time lovers of wine, and in 1998 they discovered Paso Robles. By that time, tired of the cutthroat climate in the high-tech medical manufacturing business and seeing the writing on the wall regarding outsourcing to other countries, the Schenkhuizens had decided to broaden their horizons again with real-estate investments. An enterprising agent talked them into buying a larger parcel of land than they had in mind, even though they had the expectation of planting it as a vineyard. Luckily, they found the services of viticulturist Jim Smoot, who shared their passion for quality. Although Mike is not formally trained in the wine industry, he has the specialized knowledge necessary to buy the right equipment and hire the right people for the job. The early results in the vineyard were good enough to attract the likes of Kendall-Jackson and other buyers. It was at K-J that Mike met Dan Kleck, then winemaker for K-J. Always on the lookout for talent, he knew what he had in Kleck and enlisted him to make the wines for Orchid Hill. The first production was released in 2002.

One of the things that attracted Mike to Paso Robles was the spirit of cooperation among the wine professionals here. It's not unusual to find other more established winemakers giving the newbies a helping hand. This generosity of sharing experience, and, sometimes more vitally, equipment and facilities, convinced Mike to open a co-op with Augie Hug, Dan Kleck, Craig Shannon, and Marco Rizzo. Now that their wineries are all well established, Kleck, Shannon, and Rizzo have moved to other locations. In the meantime, almost half of the original acreage has been planted. Zinfandel and Syrah were already on the property, and Mike has added Pinot Noir to the portfolio on the advice of Jim Smoot, who believes that the *terroir* at the vineyard, with its shale and rocky soils, is well suited to that grape. Mike's land is adjacent to Stephan Asseo's property, L'Aventure. In the future, the vineyard will see more grafting of both Viognier and Syrah, and some Grenache. Through it all, in his travels down a very long road indeed, Mike has made quality his primary concern, and that will continue to be his emphasis. A new tasting room recently opened in Paso Robles, and Mike and Estrella look forward to welcoming their customers.

RECOMMENDED WINES: Mike currently offers three wines, all made by Dan Kleck. I particularly liked the 2002 Pinot Noir, a red-garnet wine opaque in the glass. The nose displays roast meats, cherry cough drops, earth, some bacon fat, red currants, and anise. The wine shows excellent balance, is soft and round in the mouth, and has a long and satisfying finish. It is ready for drinking now but will improve over three years.

Mike called me back to taste the newly released Zin, which was excellent, and the 2003 Pinot Noir, of which he is justifiably proud. Where the 2002 used grapes from Dijon clone 115, the 2003 uses the 667 clone. The wine is nearly opaque in the glass but a hint lighter in color, more ruby now than garnet. The 2003 has more of a floral nose with cranberries, black cherries, and spice coming through. The tannins seem riper and rounder than the 2002, contributing to a better structure and mouthfeel for this wine. The 2002 does not show quite the same levels of ripe fruit and is vinified more in the old-world style; the 2003 will appeal more to an American palate. The 2003 has a better potential for aging, given its structure and fine tannins.

Mike recommends the 2002 Syrah, also opaque in the glass and a pretty purple-colored wine. It shows lovely ripe fruit in the nose, blackberries and boysenberries, and vanilla spice from the oak. I was impressed by the rich aromatics, and the flavor follows through wonderfully on the mid-palate, where a hint of white pepper and licorice emerges. The tannins are ripe and rounded and will contribute to another five years of life for this wine before it reaches its peak drinking years.

RATING: Three stars (very good to excellent across the line)

Ortman Family Vineyards

WINERY OWNER: Chuck Ortman

WINEMAKERS: Chuck and Matt Ortman

TASTING ROOM: Yes

DAYS/HOURS: Daily 10 A.M.–5 P.M.

ADDRESS: 3080 Biddle Ranch Rd., San Luis Obispo, CA 93401; 805-473-9463; 206-984-3882 (fax); ortmanvineyards.com

WINES/GRAPE VARIETIES: Chardonnay, Pinot Noir, Sangiovese, Syrah, Syrah rosé

WINE CLUB: Yes

TASTING ROOM AMENITIES: Merchandise

REGION: Edna Valley AVA

When a close personal friend dies, it can change your life in unexpected ways. Dave Bertoli, Chuck Ortman's longtime friend and classmate through grammar school and high school, used to make wine in his mother's basement at Berkeley. When Dave moved to Napa to work at Souverain, Chuck was often invited to barbecues there. As soon as he got a taste of the lifestyle, he was attracted to the wine industry. But, tragically, as Dave was going about the routine of taking out the garbage, he suffered a heart attack and died. Chuck Ortman, despite his degree in graphic arts, decided to take the chance and pursue his first love, wine.

He applied to Souverain for a job but didn't get hired, so he looked for other opportunities. In 1967 he was sent to Joe Heitz, who had an opening for a cellar rat. He worked under Heitz's tutelage for two years before he left to work with Mike Robbins at Spring Mountain Vineyard, where he eventually became winemaker. As he developed his expertise and winemaking skills, he branched out to become a consulting winemaker for some of Napa's finest wineries, among them Far Niente, Shafer, and St. Clement. Chuck's growing reputation was due in part to his experiments with the benefits of barrel-fermenting the Chardonnay grape. This process, which he embraced in the early 1970s, eventually swept across the California winemaking community and put the Chardonnay grape squarely in front of the American consumer. His reputation as Mr. Chardonnay firmly established, Chuck decided to make wines under his own label in 1979.

His duties as winemaker and consultant frequently brought him to the Edna Valley, where he met Jim Efrid (now co-owner at Tolosa) at Paragon vineyard. Chuck tasted Paragon's Chardonnay grapes and made a deal to bring them north to Napa for the Ortman label. In 1984 Chuck's wife, Sue, renamed the label Meridian as a salute to Chuck's love of sailing and for its meaning of the "point or period of highest development" in a person's life. In 1988 Napa Valley's Beringer Vineyards offered to acquire Meridian, with the added incentive that the label would move to the Central Coast and retain Ortman as winemaker. Over time, under Chuck's stewardship, Meridian Vineyards played a pivotal role in establishing not only Paso Robles but also the entire Central Coast as a premier wine region.

After fifteen years at Meridian and watching it grow to more than 1 million cases a year, Chuck again decided to take his life in a new direction. By then Meridian had gone through a series of ownership changes, including the sale to Nestlé, Texas Pacific, and Beringer Blass, and Chuck was ready to get back to the dirt and reinvigorate his family roots in farming. Meanwhile, his son Matt graduated from Cal Poly San Luis Obispo, which Dad had previously attended (he had finished his degree at Berkeley). Initially, Matt was not interested in following his father into the wine industry; instead, he found a job in construction management in the Bay Area. He also liked making beer, and at one point intended to use his completed apprenticeship through the American Brewer's Guild to establish a brewpub. Over time, he warmed to the idea of winemaking, and wanted to help fulfill his father's dream of establishing a family winemaking legacy. Having worked in the cellars of Napa since the age of twelve, Matt took a honeymoon in Tuscany with his wife, Lisa, and thereafter worked at Italy's Castello di Gabbiano winery, where he learned that tradition and experience can play as important a role in winemaking as technology and intensive laboratory analysis.

Now that Ortman Family Vineyards is established, Matt is the winemaker, working side by side with his father. The Ortmans currently own vineyard property near the Chamisal vineyard of Domaine Alfred, where they may eventually locate their winery. In the meantime, you can find the wines in the tasting room at Saucelito Canyon, where Bill Greenough shares space with the Ortmans. There you can find an outstanding example of Chuck and Matt's craft with Chardonnay.

RECOMMENDED WINES: I tasted the 2002 Chardonnay from the Edna Valley. This is a green-gold wine of apples, butterscotch, lemon, and pineapple. The wine is both elegant and beautifully balanced with a crisp acidity underlying the fruit. The wine is ready now but will reward another five years in the bottle. The 2003 has been selected by the Dallas Cowboys organization as one of the wines offered to patrons in the luxury suites at Texas Stadium.

I suggest the Santa Rita Hills Pinot Noir from the 2003 vintage. This is an opaque wine, black cherry in color, with a wonderful floral nose; the fruit lies beneath the flowers and shows plums, black currants, and black cherries. The finish is fine and long, showcasing the excellent fruit and the wine's lovely, elegant structure. Again, this is a beautifully balanced wine with a sufficient tannic grip to last another six to seven years in the bottle.

RATING: Three stars (look for Ortman to move up fast)

Peachy Canyon Winery

WINERY OWNERS: Doug and Nancy Beckett

WINEMAKER: Josh Beckett

TASTING ROOM: Yes

DAYS/HOURS: Daily 11 A.M.–5 P.M.

ADDRESS: 1480 N. Bethel Rd., Templeton, CA
93465; 805-239-1918; 805-237-2248 (fax);
peachycanyon.com

WINES/GRAPE VARIETIES: Cabernet Franc,
Cabernet Sauvignon, Chardonnay, Merlot,
Para Siempre (blend), Petite Sirah, port,
Syrah, Zinfandel

WINE CLUB: Yes

TASTING ROOM AMENITIES: Picnic area,
merchandise

REGION: Paso Robles AVA

Doug Beckett considers his winery to be first and foremost a family affair, and he and his wife, Nancy, a former dancer, are thankful that the winery allows them to keep their family together. Their son Josh recently took over as winemaker, and his brother, Jake, serves as vineyard manager of approximately 100 acres across five estate vineyards. Nancy and Doug both started as teachers in San Diego. Doug has a degree in business administration, but a friend and professor encouraged him to get a lifetime teaching credential. While he taught courses in family life and education and wrote drug and human sexuality programs, Nancy taught dance and phys ed classes. He finished a master's degree in psychology, and after teaching and doing workshops for ten years or so, decided to leave education and open a chain of five convenience stores. As their family grew, they sold the business and looked for a place to relocate and raise their children. They moved to Paso Robles and started over.

He worked as a carpenter and sold walnuts out of the back of his truck at the local farmers' market while Nancy taught dance. Then he met Pat Wheeler, a largely self-taught winemaker with expertise in the Zinfandel grape. They formed a partnership and became hands-on "guerilla winemakers." Their first hundred cases made from grapes grown on the famous Benito Dusi property sold out, and they were on their way. Completed in 1987, Peachy Canyon Winery opened the next year. Wheeler pursued other interests while Doug kept his day job and made wine at night, and by 1992 Peachy Canyon had the honor of being rated the top Zin for two years running in the *Wine Spectator*.

Doug sees wine as a universal art form: it is his art in the same sense that Nancy expresses herself through dance. Just as Doug has changed his career path from educator to businessman to winemaker, so too has his winemaking style changed over the years. Where previously a French winemaker produced elegant wines for him in the

Bordeaux style, Doug has recently made a concentrated effort to return the wines to the more robust style in keeping with the great wines of the early 1990s. If the 2001 Zins are indicative, I expect that Peachy Canyon is once again on the path that will allow them to achieve the greatness of its early years.

RECOMMENDED WINES: Doug recommends the Old Schoolhouse Zinfandel. The 2001 is a pretty ruby-garnet wine with black pepper and strawberry fruit in the nose ahead of raspberries and figs. The tannins are ripe but with enough presence to make for a chewy mouthful of wine. Drinking nicely now, the wine has three to five years before it will peak.

I recommend the Snow Vineyard Zinfandel. The color of the 2001 is a touch lighter than the Schoolhouse, more a pale ruby in the glass. Plums and cherries jump to the nose, with a hint of vanilla from the oak that adds structure. I like the ripeness in the fruit and the finish that stays with you. Ready for drinking now, this wine too will benefit from another three to five years of age in the bottle.

RATING: Two → three stars (quality is rapidly improving across the line)

Penman Springs Vineyard

WINERY OWNERS: Carl and Beth McCasland

WINEMAKER: Larry Roberts

TASTING ROOM: Yes

DAYS/HOURS: Friday–Sunday 11 A.M.–5 P.M.

ADDRESS: 1985 Penman Springs Rd., Paso Robles, CA 93446; 805-237-8960; 805-237-8778 (fax); penmansprings.com

WINES/GRAPE VARIETIES: Cabernet Sauvignon, Chardonnay, Meritage (blend), Merlot, Muscat Blanc, Petite Sirah, Syrah, Trembler (red blend)

WINE CLUB: Yes

TASTING ROOM AMENITIES: Picnic area, merchandise

REGION: Paso Robles AVA

Situated on a hillside overlooking Paso's east side, the vineyards at Penman Springs first put down roots in 1981. Toni and Sharon Baron planted the first grapes and established Baron Vineyards in a joint venture with Kolb Vineyards at Union Road. Joseph and Shirlene Barton, with partners Gary and Becky Porter, took control of the vineyard in the early 1990s and renamed the place Grey Wolf Cellars. Gary Porter took the existing Sauvignon Blanc vines and grafted them over to Merlot, Zinfandel, and Cabernet Sauvignon. Later, Grey Wolf Cellars relocated to its current location off Highway 46 West.

The current iteration is called Penman Springs, named after the road that fronts the property, and is the result of Carl and Beth McCasland making some life-changing decisions. In 1995 they sold their business and moved from El Paso, Texas, to El Paso de Robles, California. Carl grew up in the Central Valley and often came to visit the Central Coast. As a teenager, he gained experience by working in the vineyards. When he and wife Beth found the Grey Wolf property, they bought it. Both had an appreciation for wine and decided it would be fun and exciting to try their hand. Trained as an accountant, Carl could handle the financial side of the business, but he knew there was work to be done in order to become proficient in all the other areas required to manage a winery. He immersed himself in the study of viticulture and refurbished the vineyard, added new wells, trellised where needed, and, most important, reinvigorated the soils. Syrah was planted, Petite Sirah was replanted, and winemaker Larry Roberts was hired. The year 1998 saw the first crush, and wines from Penman Springs can now be enjoyed in the tasting room, built in 2000.

Carl believes that great wines are made in the vineyards, and he truly enjoys growing the grapes. He and Larry are interested in maintaining a consistent style for the wines they produce, with the ultimate goal of giving the consumer a great value in the bottle. Carl says, and this is probably the accountant in him speaking, "A person should be able to get a good bottle of wine for about fifteen bucks." Currently producing about 1,000 cases, Carl doesn't see production getting much above 2,500 in the near term.

RECOMMENDED WINES: Carl suggests the Cabernet Sauvignon. I tasted the 2001 and found it to be a good value, listed under 15 dollars. This is a purple and black wine, almost opaque, with a nose of black cherry, mocha, and a touch of olive. The wine shows excellent balance between the acidity and the tannic structure, making for a pleasant mouthfeel. There is good ripeness in the fruit, and although the wine is drinking very nicely now, it should hold for another three years.

I enjoyed the 2001 Syrah. This is a darker wine than the Cabernet with more black under the purple, making it opaque in the glass. In the nose I found blackberries, a hint of olive again, and a sprinkle of white pepper. The wine is excellent in the mouth thanks to its lovely balance and the ripeness of the fruit. The finish is long and smooth. The wine will easily give another five years of enjoyment.

And if you enjoy sweet dessert wines, ask if Carl has any of the 1999 Muscat Fantasque Fortifié left (he might have a bottle hidden under the counter). This was a beautiful yellow-gold wine of orange peel, ripe figs, yellow raisins, and ripe cling peaches. The wine has about 17 percent residual sugar, but the acidity keeps it balanced. The true surprise for me was the finish, which lasted almost two minutes and displayed hazelnuts and soft butterscotch at the end. Not surprisingly, this wine won a silver medal at the *San Francisco Chronicle* Wine Competition in 2004.

RATING: One → two stars (good, competently made wines with improvements in the offing)

Per Bacco Cellars

WINERY OWNERS: Craig Shannon and Marco Rizzo

WINEMAKER: Craig Shannon

TASTING ROOM: Yes

DAYS/HOURS: Thursday–Monday 11 A.M.– 5 P.M.

ADDRESS: 1850 Calle Joaquin, San Luis Obispo, CA 93405; 805-787-0485; 805-787-0486 (fax); perbaccocellars.com

WINES/GRAPE VARIETIES: Bacchus (blend), Chardonnay, Petite Sirah, Pinot Grigio, Pinot Noir, rosé, Zinfandel

WINE CLUB: Yes

TASTING ROOM AMENITIES: Merchandise

REGION: Edna Valley AVA

Craig Shannon and partner Marco Rizzo are the owners of Per Bacco Cellars, one of the four wineries that formed the Coastal Vintner's Co-op, which also included Augie Hug's Hug Cellars, Mike Schenkhuizen's Orchid Hill Vineyards and Winery, and Dan Kleck's Silver Stone Wines. Orchid Hill, Silver Stone Wines, and Per Bacco have since moved to new locations. Craig is a third-generation farmer whose family grows grapes, cotton, and other crops in the San Joaquin Valley, selling grapes to Napa vintners and Gallo, among others. At Cal Poly, Craig took a degree in agricultural business, economics, and marketing. After graduation he returned to the family ranch near Fresno and managed that operation. In 1994 his business interests took him south into Mexico to research the feasibility of growing and marketing table grapes there. The Shannons now have 350 acres planted in Sonora, Mexico.

Partner and friend Marco Rizzo owns Café Roma in San Luis Obispo. When the two heard about a vineyard for sale near San Luis Obispo, they made a call and before they knew it owned an abandoned four-year-old vineyard near Cold Canyon. Craig put his viticulture know-how to good use, and Chardonnay is again growing vigorously on the property, with its unusual admixture of talcum-powder sand and nutrient-deficient soils that stress the vines. The coldness comes from the fog that crawls in off the ocean and snakes its way up the valleys and onto the hillsides. The first vintage was crushed in 1997–98 at John Alban's winery. Currently, in addition to the Cold Canyon vineyard, Shannon is sourcing grapes from the Niven Home Ranch, some Petite Sirah from the Steinbach family in Paso, and some Pinot Noir that is grown to specifications. The name Per Bacco has an interesting derivation, being an old Italian expression of wonder and delight, literally, *per* (for) *Bacco* (Bacchus, the god of wine). For this reason you will find Greek and Roman gods on the labels.

Whereas Craig is the grower and winemaker, Marco brings a palate educated by years working in the restaurant business. In addition, the two have forged friendships with outstanding winemakers in the area. Craig and Marco are interested in making world-class wines from cold-climate grapes, with the exception of the Petite Sirah, which needs heat. Following Alban's model and under his tutelage, they are interested in producing small-lot, handcrafted premium wines. And since they are interested in aging their wines, they are not afraid to give them time in the barrel before release.

RECOMMENDED WINES: Craig likes the Chardonnay, and we tasted the 2000. The wine is a pretty lemon-gold color and has a nose of buttered toast, apples, quince, and mangoes. The wine has excellent acidity to balance the fruit and lends itself to a soft and rounded mouthfeel. The finish is long and ends with a refreshing tartness.

I found the Dionysus to be a wonderful bottle of Pinot Noir. I tasted the 2002, a barrel selection of black-purple color that is opaque in the glass. The nose is black cherries, cassis, smoke, and spice. The wine fills the mouth with its excellent texture and structure. It is drinkable now but has sufficient complexity to reward another six to eight years in the bottle.

Per Bacco also has a value-priced second label called Mani ("hands"). Craig and Marco each have three daughters, and their hands are represented on the label.

RATING: One star (Mani line); three stars (Per Bacco)

Piedra Creek Winery

WINERY OWNER: Romeo Zuech

WINEMAKER: Romeo Zuech

TASTING ROOM: No

DAYS/HOURS: By appointment only

ADDRESS: 6425 Mira Cielo Dr., San Luis Obispo, CA 93401; 805-541-1281; 805-782-0648 (fax); no Web site

WINES/GRAPE VARIETIES: Pinot Noir, San Floriano (blend), Zinfandel

WINE CLUB: Yes

REGION: San Luis Obispo County

Pipestone Vineyards

WINERY OWNERS: Jeff Pipes and Florence Wong

WINEMAKER: Jeff Pipes

TASTING ROOM: Yes

DAYS/HOURS: Thursday–Monday 11 A.M.– 5 P.M.

ADDRESS: 2040 Niderer Rd., Paso Robles, CA 93446; 805-227-6385; call for fax; pipestonevineyards.com

WINES/GRAPE VARIETIES: Grenache, Grenache rosé, Mélange (blend), Mourvèdre, Syrah, Syrah-Cabernet Sauvignon, Viognier, Zinfandel

WINE CLUB: Yes

TASTING ROOM AMENITIES: Picnic area

REGION: Paso Robles AVA

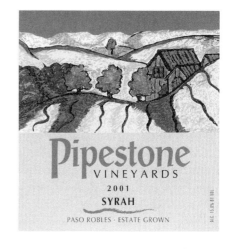

Vintners often travel intriguing career paths before they arrive in the vineyards. Some are graduates of respected enology and viticulture programs; others take a more indirect route to their calling. Jeff Pipes exemplifies the latter. Granted, his grandfather, a farmer in Ohio, made wine at home, which can have both a direct and an indirect influence on a young man. For Jeff, the impact was profound: the idea of farming grapes and making them into wine stayed with him from the second grade on. But seeds sown early sometimes flower late.

Jeff's formal education was first as an environmental engineer. In this capacity, he visited toxic and hazardous waste sites, and then analyzed and designed engineering projects for their remediation and cleanup. After the horrors that he saw, he returned to school and graduated with a degree in environmental law, better enabling him to deal with the worst offenders. After more than twenty-two years of schooling and three degrees, he and Florence Wong, who had been a fellow undergraduate at Minnesota's Carleton College, left behind a life of sludge and drudge and pursued their crazy dream of buying a small farm someplace where they could grow environmentally friendly grapes.

After first visiting Oregon for its Pinot Noir, Jeff and Florence settled in Paso Robles and bought 30 acres on Niderer Road west of Paso in 1997. They found the healthy soils and Mediterranean climate to their liking and suitable for Rhône-style wines. Florence and Jeff made a firm commitment to growing and farming their fruit as organically as possible. Their goal is to make a living while being responsible stewards of the land, instead of developing a huge agribusiness on the property. Jeff does the farming and winemaking, but not without Flo's input. A native of Hong Kong and a student of feng shui (literally, "wind and water," a discipline aimed at organizing space to harmonize with the spiritual forces that inhabit it), Florence took the layout plans for the vineyard to her feng shui master. With his input they decided on the orientation that best permits positive energy *(chi)* to flow into the vineyards while negative energy is deflected up to Napa. Jeff likens this process to his grandfather consulting the phases of the moon in his *Farmer's Almanac* before making important planting and farming decisions— even his highly trained scientific and legal mind didn't find feng shui all that strange.

RECOMMENDED WINES: Jeff recommends the Mélange, a blend of red grape varieties such as Grenache, Syrah, and Mourvèdre. The 2000 has 70 percent Grenache, making for a cherry-red wine light to the stem of the glass. The nose is cherries and black currants above grilled meat and *herbes de Provence*. This is an easy wine to drink now and ready for the table, as the tannins are mostly resolved, allowing the fruit to express itself fully.

I particularly enjoyed the 2001 Zinfandel, made from 50 percent forty-year-old vines. This reddish-purple wine is also light in the glass and has plenty of strawberry fruit lying next to peppery spice. The excellent ripeness of the grapes presents a hint of sweetness to the tongue. The finish is long and satisfying, and the wine still has five years ahead of it.

RATING: Two stars (very good wines across the line)

Poalillo Vineyards

WINERY OWNERS: Charles and Joyce Poalillo

WINEMAKER: Charles Poalillo

TASTING ROOM: Yes

DAYS/HOURS: By appointment only

ADDRESS: 1888 Willow Creek Rd., Paso Robles, CA 93446; 805-238-0600; 805-227-6689 (fax); faroutwineries.com/poalillo

WINES/GRAPE VARIETIES: Cabernet Sauvignon, Chardonnay, Sauvignon Blanc, Syrah, Zinfandel

WINE CLUB: No

REGION: Paso Robles AVA

Charles Poalillo, who has a passion for photography, worked for many years as a professional. He started as a newspaper photographer and then moved into the commercial-photography business. Through his clients and contacts, he was offered an opportunity to shoot the Academy Awards. In 1955, with Bob Hope as the host, Charles shot the first of twenty-four Academy Awards, taking pictures of the stars, the winners, and the parties afterward. In addition, he memorialized no fewer than seven presidents and stars as famous as Marilyn Monroe.

In 1969 Charles squashed his first grape. With his wife, Joyce, and some friends who were interested in full-body grape stomps, clothing optional, it was time to make wine at home. This faction of amateur winemakers would come north to Paso Robles and buy grapes from Mel Casteel until Mel decided it was time to sell his vineyard. One night when Charles was in bed at the Eden Rock Hotel in Miami reading a magazine about the romance of grape growing, a flash bulb went off in his head, and a new picture began to resolve. He sold his photography business in 1973 and bought Mel Casteel's vineyard in Paso Robles. However, he continued to commute to Los Angeles for another seven years before leaving photography behind and getting his real-estate license. Charles gives credit to Joyce for discovering the vineyard where their grapes are now grown. At the time, there were only three wineries on Paso's west side: Rotta, Pesenti, and York.

In 1992 they offered fruit from their vineyard to Tobin James. He said they were crazy to sell the fruit to others and told them to make their own wine under their own label. They sought out Art Norman, who did a custom crush for them. The wine, a Zinfandel, was released in 1995 and won a gold medal at the Orange County Fair. The next year's entry took the silver, and Charles got out of the wine competition business while still ahead.

Charles emphasizes that Poalillo is truly a family-run business. Daughter Susan and her husband, David, along with son Andrew and his wife, Val, all help tend the vineyards and lend their support and efforts during the fall harvest and crush season, as well as during the bottling process, in preparation for marketing the wine.

RECOMMENDED WINES: Charles recommends the Extreme Reserve Zinfandel II made from his home vineyard grapes. The 2003 is nearly opaque in the glass and black cherry in color. A touch of port lies atop the sweet nose; below are figs, some chocolate, and black pepper spice. The wine is huge in the mouth but finely balanced. The finish pushes beyond a minute. The wine is coming into its own but will drink beautifully for another five years. This wine definitely has the wow factor.

The Chardonnay was a real surprise, made from San Miguel grapes. I suggest the 2005, a light lemon- and butterscotch-colored wine. This is a fruity Chardonnay of apples, citrus, and pineapples in the nose. It presents an excellent balance between the acidity and the fruit and has a lovely finish in which a touch of vanilla remains after the fruit has disappeared. Drink now and over the next three years.

RATING: Three stars (very good to excellent wines)

Pretty-Smith Vineyards & Winery

WINERY OWNERS: Lisa Pretty and Victor Smith

WINEMAKER: Lisa Pretty

TASTING ROOM: Yes

DAYS/HOURS: Friday–Sunday 10 A.M.–5 P.M.

ADDRESS: 13350 River Rd., San Miguel, CA 93451; 805-467-3104; no fax; prettysmith .com

WINES/GRAPE VARIETIES: Cabernet Franc, Cabernet Sauvignon, late-harvest Zinfandel, Merlot, Palette de Rouge (red blend), Sauvignon Blanc, Zinfandel port

WINE CLUB: Yes

TASTING ROOM AMENITIES: Picnic area, merchandise

REGION: Paso Robles AVA

Some years ago, a very bright Canadian woman took a technology degree at the University of Guelph in Ontario, reputed to be Canada's top comprehensive university, and secured a high-tech job in Silicon Valley. She prospered and the business grew, and with it the requirement for more and more travel; all led to burnout. Lisa Pretty decided it was time for a lifestyle change and time to pursue her dream.

In Canada, she grew up with a love and appreciation for wine. So with Victor Smith, she looked for properties and in Paso Robles discovered that the Mission View winery, with its more than twenty-year-old vines, was for sale. They bought it in September 2000. After purchasing the property and helping to establish the new winery, Smith returned to Silicon Valley but maintained a minority partnership in the venture. Lisa Pretty is now very much on her own.

There was a certain amount of anxiety in taking on such a venture, but she has an MBA in business to fall back on for the marketing and selling of the wines. Yet everything else was new to her. She bought every book she could find from UC Davis on enology and read herself into competence. She schooled herself to become a winemaker. She still does all the work but relies heavily on the kindness of friends and the excellence of professional consultants. She keeps the Mission View line as her second label because there is still demand for the product. The Pretty-Smith line, the realization of her dream, will eventually be given over to 100 percent Bordeaux varieties.

As an example of doing it herself, she designs the labels for the Pretty-Smith line. Kokopelli, the mythical spirit of the Southwest, calls the sun to rise each morning as he plays his flute and watches over the winery. Each label is a work of art produced by Lisa, and the originals line the wall in the lab adjoining the tasting room. She chose the figure of Kokopelli because it suits her worldview. She researched Native American petroglyphs for use on her labels; then she bought herself a book and learned how to paint. She has already won a double gold medal for her original labels in a major competition.

The tasting room is newly remodeled, and there is some merchandise for sale. The orange walls might shock at first, but Lisa is not afraid to be creative and take chances. Outside the tasting room is a large rounded concrete pad for picnic tables and a wonderful view of the hills to the west of San Miguel. The facility is a great place for events including parties, receptions, and barbecues.

RECOMMENDED WINES: Given her personal taste for Bordeaux-style wines, Lisa prefers wines of elegance designed to express the character of the grape. She avoids the big, fat, jammy wines often featured in California and appreciates the artistry required to blend her Bordeaux grapes. Her personal recommendation is the Palette de Rouge, a Cal-Bordeaux–style blended wine. The 2000 is cough-drop cherry in color with a bright nose of cherries and some chocolate. The tannins are soft and rounded in the mouth, with good acidity for balance. The finish is long and pleasant, with the fruit showing through. It is ready for drinking now but will age another three to five years in the bottle if you put it down.

The 2000 Late Harvest Zinfandel is one of the best I've tasted in Paso Robles. The color is red cherry and the nose is blackberries, blueberries, and red currants. The 4.8 percent residual sugar is nicely balanced by enough acidity to keep the sweetness from tiring the palate. The wine is ready for drinking now but will certainly age another five to eight years. This wine is also an excellent value.

RATING: One → two stars (steady improvement across the line)

Rabbit Ridge Winery

WINERY OWNER: Erich Russell

WINEMAKER: Erich Russell

TASTING ROOM: Yes

DAYS/HOURS: Wednesday–Sunday 11 A.M.–5 P.M.

ADDRESS: 1172 San Marcos Rd., Paso Robles, CA 93446; 805-467-3331; 805-467-3339 (fax); rabbitridgewinery.com

WINES/GRAPE VARIETIES: Barbera, Cabernet Franc, Cabernet Sauvignon, Chardonnay, Dolcetto, Grenache, Merlot, Mourvèdre, Petite Sirah, Petit Verdot, Pinot Noir, Primitivo, Refosco, Sangiovese, Syrah, Viognier, Vortex (blend), Zinfandel

WINE CLUB: Yes

TASTING ROOM AMENITIES: Picnic area, merchandise

REGION: Paso Robles AVA

Those who follow track and field know that in major distance races one runner is often designated as the pacesetter so that other runners in the pack do not have to waste energy taking the lead too early. This runner is designated as the "rabbit." During his athletic career at San Jose State, Erich Russell often set the pace; hence the name he gave his winery. In addition to being an outstanding athlete (he still puts in the miles today, but the knees are not what they once were), Erich was a teacher for a time. He was making wine at home and during one summer vacation entered his wine in an amateur winemaking contest where the judge just happened to be the winemaker at Chateau St. Jean. The judge offered him a job.

He worked at Chateau St. Jean for two years before moving on to Simi Winery for the next nine. In 1990 he was the head winemaker at Belvedere in Sonoma. In the meantime, he opened Rabbit Ridge Winery in Healdsburg. In the 1990s Rabbit Ridge was identified by wine critic Robert M. Parker Jr. as one of ten wineries to watch. Erich read an article about Paso Robles wines in 1996 and came south to taste for himself and do research. What he found convinced him that in time Paso Robles could become greater even than Sonoma. He found an excellent climate and soil features that Sonoma did not have. In 1997 he purchased properties including the current winery location, acreage around Adelaida, and off Highway 46 West. In sum, he purchased 700 acres, of which approximately 400 are now planted to grapes. He and wife Joanne drew up the plans for the winery and tasting room.

Erich believes his wines will always deliver value for the consumer. He lets the wine speak for itself but offers tasty wines at an affordable price. Although the winery is now producing upwards of 200,000 cases yearly, his intention is to keep it very much a family-oriented business; Joanne makes a contribution in marketing while Erich sees to the winemaking.

RECOMMENDED WINES: Erich recommends the Primitivo, a black cherry–colored wine of blackberry fruit, a taste of loganberry, raspberry, and soft vanilla undertones in the nose. This is a soft, well-balanced wine with lots of fruit and a satisfying finish. I tasted the 2003 blend. The Primitivo grape, thought to be genetically similar to Zinfandel, is grown in southern Italy and has experienced something of a renaissance thanks to the success of Zinfandel in the United States. Here is an opportunity to compare.

I suggest the excellent Vortex, a Bordeaux blend of Cabernet Sauvignon, Cabernet Franc, Petit Verdot, and a bit of Syrah. Tasted in the barrel, the 2003 will surpass the fine 2002 in quality. The perfumed nose shows flowers, black currants, and baked cherry pie. The wine fills the mouth and has a long, lingering finish. The ripe, rounded tannins bode well for a long life in the bottle.

RATING: Two stars (three stars for the Reserves)

Rainbows End Vineyard

WINERY OWNERS: Jim and Shirley Gibbons

WINEMAKER: Jim Gibbons

TASTING ROOM: Yes

DAYS/HOURS: Friday–Sunday 11 A.M.–4 P.M. or by appointment

ADDRESS: 8535 Mission Ln., San Miguel, CA 93451; 805-467-0044, 866-999-9463; 805-467-2304 (fax); rainbowsendvineyard .com

WINES/GRAPE VARIETIES: Barbera, Cabernet Sauvignon, Merlot, Nebbiolo, Prism (red blend), Syrah, Tempranillo, Zinfandel

WINE CLUB: Yes

TASTING ROOM AMENITIES: Picnic area, merchandise

REGION: Paso Robles AVA

When I started this project I decided that the first winery I would visit would be Rainbows End. What better place to start a search for wine treasures? This boutique winery, located south of San Miguel and northeast of Paso Robles, affords spectacular views of the surrounding hills. In the rustic building where the wine is made, a small tasting room pours the wines of Jim and Shirley Gibbons. You cannot help but notice that the word *Love* is written in lights across the header above the tasting bar. If you have given up on gold, you can at least find love at Rainbows End.

Jim and Shirley got their start in the water pipeline business in Los Angeles. Once established in life, they were interested in purchasing a property that afforded them pasture and room for horses. Ironically, the 10 acres they purchased in 1990 lacked water. They decided to plant grapes and in one year lost 90 percent of the crop to a freeze. In those early years Jim tried to grow Chardonnay but discovered the area was too hot for that variety, so he grafted the vines over to Merlot. In the meantime, Cabernet Sauvignon was planted, and he now has an eye toward trying some Pinot Noir. After an early start as an amateur winemaker, Jim took classes at UC Davis, but he emphasizes that he learned his winemaking skills from the generous tutelage of other winemakers in the area. In 1999 the winery was up and running, and Jim says the Gibbons family has successfully made the transition from water to wine.

Jim and Shirley have traveled and tasted wines for more than fifteen years, and during those explorations Jim has sampled some fine ones. His motivation is to recapture in his bottles the greatness of the best wine he has ever tasted. Rainbows End is truly a family-run business from the vineyard to the winery; Shirley will regale you with stories in the tasting room while Jim sees to the wines. Eventually, they hope to pass the operation along to their son.

RECOMMENDED WINES: Jim recommends the Prism, a Bordeaux-style blend of mostly Merlot and Cabernet Sauvignon that has a dark cherry color with good depth. The nose is sweet vanilla oak with jammy cherry fruit, plum, and a hint of strawberries. The wine is drinking very well now but will reward an additional few years in the bottle.

I suggest the Syrah. I tasted the 2001 from Cagliero Vineyards, a purple- and cherry-colored wine with blackberries, currants, and a whiff of violets on the nose. A touch of spice lingers on the tongue for an enjoyable, drinkable Syrah. Enjoy it now and over the next two years.

RATING: One star (drinkable, well-made wines)

Rancho Arroyo Grande Winery & Vineyards

WINERY OWNER: Christopher J. Conway

WINEMAKER: Clarissa Nagy

TASTING ROOM: No

DAYS/HOURS: By appointment only

ADDRESS: 591 High Mountain Rd., Arroyo Grande, CA 93420; 805-474-0220;

805-474-0330 (fax); ranchoarroyograndewines.com

WINES/GRAPE VARIETIES: Chardonnay, Syrah, Thereza Cuvée (blend), Zinfandel

WINE CLUB: Yes

REGION: Arroyo Grande Valley AVA

Rio Seco Vineyard & Winery

WINERY OWNERS: Tom and Carol Hinkle

WINEMAKER: Tom Hinkle

TASTING ROOM: Yes

DAYS/HOURS: Thursday–Monday 11 A.M.–
5:30 P.M.

ADDRESS: 4295 Union Rd., Paso Robles, CA
93446; 805-237-8884; 805-237-8884 (fax);
riosecowine.com

WINES/GRAPE VARIETIES: Cabernet Franc,
Cabernet Sauvignon, late-harvest
Zinfandel, Roussanne, Syrah, Viognier,
Zinfandel, Zinfandel port

WINE CLUB: Yes

TASTING ROOM AMENITIES: Picnic area,
merchandise

REGION: Paso Robles AVA

Notice that the footrest below the eucalyptus wood that tops the bar in the Rio Seco tasting room is taken from a set of uneven parallel bars, an apparatus used by female gymnasts. How it got there involves the story of two athletes, Tom and Carol Hinkle, who came home after their athletic adventures had taken them far afield. Tom played baseball well enough to be named a second-team all-American and then signed with the Detroit Tigers in 1963. After his professional baseball career ended, he took a teaching degree and coached at both the high school and collegiate levels. During his time at Cal Poly State University he recruited such stars as Mike Krukow and Ozzie Smith. Tom has been a professional scout since 1982 in the Milwaukee Brewers organization and was the scout who signed Randy Johnson, among other prominent major leaguers.

Carol was a national-caliber gymnast and a member of a squad that placed fifth in the 1971 nationals. She too has been both a coach and an educator, with more than twenty years' experience in dance, swimming, cheerleading, and, of course, gymnastics. Before she and Tom took the plunge into wine, she was the co-owner of a renowned local dance studio.

Because of their long (more than thirty years') association with San Luis Obispo County and Paso Robles, the Hinkles saw the potential of the area to produce world-class wines. Since they both loved the community, in April 1996 they bought property and planted a vineyard. Therein lies a second story.

After looking at more than two hundred potential parcels, the Hinkles settled on the current property of 63 acres along Huer Huero Creek. A Hollywood producer originally owned the ranch, and a movie was shot on the grounds in the 1980s. After his unfortunate demise, his family leased the property, but it fell into disrepair and misuse. At one low point there was even a shoot-out between local law enforcement and the residents. Carol will show you the bullet holes by the door. (Coincidentally, on the day of my tasting and interview a gentleman came in to taste who was one of the arresting officers who had "visited" the property the night of the drug bust and its subsequent gunplay. He was not armed during the tasting.)

Tom and Carol consider their small boutique winery very much a mom-and-pop operation. They start with the farming of good grapes and let Mother Nature do her work, instead of relying on a swimming pool of chemicals. The artistry for the Hinkles is in the blending of the wines. They make no apologies for not having enology degrees, preferring instead their hard-won "people degrees." However, John Munch, the owner and winemaker at Le Cuvier and before that, Adelaida, has served as a consultant winemaker. Tom grows the grapes on the property and makes the wine in the building that used to be the old marijuana barn during the property's infamous days.

RECOMMENDED WINES: The Hinkles recommend the late-harvest Zinfandel. The 2001 was a dark cherry color and thus nearly opaque in the glass. The sweet nose is blackberries, black cherry, wild strawberries, and vanilla cream. The wine is finished to leave a touch of sugar (2 percent), but the excellent acidity provides the needed balance to keep it from being cloying on the tongue. This is a fruity late-harvest ready for drinking now and over the next three to five years.

I recommend the estate-grown Syrah. The 2001 is a nearly opaque black-cherry color with a purple base. The nose delivers stewed plums, blackberries, and a touch of ripe black olives ahead of pepper spice. The wine is well balanced and has enough tannic grip for some aging, though it is showing very nicely now. This is a fine example of a fruit-forward Syrah.

RATING: One star (competently made, drinkable wines across the line)

River Wild Winery

WINERY OWNERS: Thereza and Gary Verboon

WINEMAKER: Eric Hickey

TASTING ROOM: No

DAYS/HOURS: By appointment only

ADDRESS: 591 High Mountain Rd., Arroyo Grande, CA 93420; 805-474-0220; 805-474-0330 (fax); no Web site

WINES/GRAPE VARIETIES: Wild Game blends for trout, turkey, venison, waterfowl

WINE CLUB: Yes

REGION: San Luis Obispo County

RiverStar Vineyards & Cellars

WINERY OWNERS: Ed and Muriel Dutton

WINEMAKER: Michael Coyne

TASTING ROOM: Yes

DAYS/HOURS: Friday–Sunday 12–5 P.M.

ADDRESS: 36 N. Ocean Ave., Cayucos, CA 93430; 805-995-3741, 805-467-0086; 805-467-2846 (fax); riverstarvineyards.com

WINES/GRAPE VARIETIES: Cabernet Sauvignon, Merlot, Sauvignon Blanc, Syrah

WINE CLUB: Yes

TASTING ROOM AMENITIES: Picnic area

REGION: Paso Robles AVA, San Miguel area

RN Estate Vineyard & Winery

WINERY OWNER: Roger Nicolas

WINEMAKER: Roger Nicolas

TASTING ROOM: No

DAYS/HOURS: By appointment only

ADDRESS: 7986 N. River Rd., Paso Robles, CA 93446; 805-610-9802; rnestate.com

WINES/GRAPE VARIETIES: Cuvée des Artistes (blend), Cuveé des Trois Cépages, Pinot Noir, Syrah-Mourvèdre, Westside Cuveé, Young Vine Mourvèdre

WINE CLUB: No

REGION: Paso Robles AVA, east side

Robert Hall Winery

WINERY OWNERS: Robert Hall and
Margaret Burrell

WINEMAKER: Don Brady

TASTING ROOM: Yes

DAYS/HOURS: Daily 10 A.M.–6 P.M.

ADDRESS: 3443 Mill Rd., Paso Robles, CA
93446; 805-239-1616; 805-239-2464
(fax); roberthallwinery.com

WINES/GRAPE VARIETIES: Cabernet
Sauvignon, Chardonnay, Meritage (blend),
Merlot, Orange Muscat, Rhône de Robles
(blend), Rosé de Robles, Sauvignon
Blanc, Syrah, vintage port, Zinfandel

WINE CLUB: Yes

TASTING ROOM AMENITIES: Picnic area,
merchandise, cave tours, boccie court

REGION: Paso Robles AVA

Robert Hall spent the first thirty-five years of his life in White Bear Lake, Minnesota, where he developed a variety of businesses, including shopping centers and travel agencies, and pursued a great passion in his life, champion horses. Having established his fortune and taking advantage of his connections in the travel industry, he spent time in France and visited the Rhône valley, where he tasted the wines and discovered a second great passion: Rhône wines. He expanded his business interests into the wine industry and searched for suitable places similar to the Rhône. Consultants at UC Davis confirmed his intuition that Paso Robles exhibited geographical similarities to the Rhône. Robert is not the sort of man to chase dreams half-heartedly. When you see the winery and the new hospitality center, you will understand his level of commitment to realizing his new dream to plant vineyards, grow grapes, and make wine.

Robert's early purchases, acquired with the help of Howie Steinbeck (one of the preeminent growers in Paso Robles) in 1995, now comprise the Hall Ranch and contain the "home vineyard." Located just above the Estrella Plain, this 140-acre vineyard serves as the primary source of his Cabernet, Merlot, Zinfandel, Chardonnay, Sauvignon Blanc, and Syrah grapes. In the past the fruit was sold to major wineries such as Beringer and Fetzer up north. When the wineries kept raving over the quality of the fruit Robert sent them, he decided there was no reason to let them have all the credit and set in motion the process for planning and constructing his winery. In the meantime, he added to the ranch and bought additional vineyards. With all but one of the pieces in place, he hired the best winemaker available. Enter Don Brady.

Don's family ranched in Texas, near vineyards owned by the University of Texas. After the oil money dried up in the county, the Bradys, taking the lead from UT, planted grapes on Don's cousin's place, giving him his first exposure to viticulture. He received a degree in horticulture from Texas Tech in 1984 and after graduation went to work as a winemaker in Texas. His career took him to a French company at Fort Stockton, which he grew from 100,000 cases to 700,000, almost all of which was sold in Texas. Don put Texas winemaking on the map during his tenure at Llano Estacado, and his wines were served to such notables as presidents Reagan and Bush, Queen Elizabeth, and Prince Charles. He came to California to work for Delicato Family Vineyards and then moved to Modesto. His job entailed traveling to King City and allowed him to discover Paso Robles, which, not surprisingly, with its vineyards, horse ranches, golden hills, and red oaks, felt much like home. He had a friend who knew Robert Hall, and he saw what Robert was creating in Paso. By that time, Don had built a reputation on twenty years in the business, with numerous accolades for his work at Delicato. At one point he won international acclaim as the recipient of the prestigious International Wine and Spirits "Wine of America" award. When Robert asked him what was the first thing he would do as winemaker, Don told him, quit spending money! He was hired in 2001.

Given his experience in the vineyards first and in the facility as winemaker second, Don is convinced that you make the wine in the vineyard and fix it, if needed, in the winery. His goal is to overdeliver in terms of value for the consumer dollar. When you taste the recommended wines, you will be convinced that Robert and Don are succeeding.

The tasting and hospitality facility is now finished, and the building is a remarkable sight. It is a monumental edifice that stands as a testament to Robert's dream and vision for Paso Robles wines. The completed structure serves as a landmark destination for wine consumers visiting the area. After you taste the wines, be sure to take the tour of the underground caves. Robert is likely to be there on the weekends, giving the tours himself, unless he's grooming the boccie ball grounds for a game during lunch.

RECOMMENDED WINES: Don recommends the Syrah. I tasted the 2001, a ruby and purple opaque wine of ripe blackberries, black cherries, and sweet tobacco in the nose. The tannins are soft and rounded, and a taste of crème brûlée appears on the mid-palate. The wine exhibits a silky-smooth, long finish and is ready for drinking now.

Robert suggests the Rhône de Robles. The 2002 is opaque and purple-red, a blend of Grenache, Syrah, and Cinsaut. The wonderful nose presents blueberries, cherries, and then crushed peppercorn spice. The wine shows finesse and a well-integrated structure and is ready for drinking now. It has won numerous prizes already, including Best of Class in the *San Francisco Chronicle* Wine Competition of 2004.

I was impressed with Don's Sauvignon Blanc. I tasted the 2003, a clear, golden-green wine of pears, grapefruit, and apples, with a slight nuttiness. The wine has a wonderful minerality on the tongue, with excellent acidity to provide a crisp, tart finish. It is an excellent example of what Sauvignon Blanc can be in Paso Robles, and I consider it one of the best in the area.

RATING: Three stars (wines are excellent and continue to improve year after year)

Rotta Winery

WINERY OWNER: Michael Giubbini

WINEMAKERS: Steve Pesenti and Mark Caporale

TASTING ROOM: Yes

DAYS/HOURS: Daily 11 A.M.–5 P.M.

ADDRESS: 250 Winery Rd., Templeton, CA 93465; 805-237-0510; 805-434-9623 (fax); rottawinery.com

WINES/GRAPE VARIETIES: Black Monukka (dessert wine), Cabernet Franc, Cabernet Sauvignon, Chardonnay, cream sherry, Merlot, Muscat Canelli, Zinfandel, Zinfandel port, Zinfandel rosé

WINE CLUB: Yes

TASTING ROOM AMENITIES: Picnic area, food items, merchandise

REGION: Paso Robles AVA, west side

One of the oldest original wineries in Paso Robles is once again in production. Readers of the "Wine History" section of this chapter might recall that Adolphe Siot established a winery on what is now Rotta's property in 1856, one of the first three in the area, with York and Pesenti. In 1908 Joe Rotta bought the winery and vineyard from Siot and sold it to his brother Clement and his sister-in-law Romilda Rotta in the '20s. After Clement's death in 1962, Mamma Romilda Rotta, a native of Locarno, Switzerland, ran the winery with her son Mervin and her grandsons by her side. Even in those early days Mamma Rotta, using recipes for winemaking brought from the Old World to the New, made pure, delicious table wines with no preservatives or sugar added. In the '70s the Rottas, also into trucking and farming at the time, made a decision to sell the winery.

After the property had been sold, the family received information that the land was not getting the care and attention it deserved, so they decided to reacquire the land and reestablish the winery. After some twelve years of dogged determination, passionate persistence, and not a little litigation for leverage, grandson Michael—the son of Romilda's daughter, Irene Giubbini—recovered most of the property. But it wasn't easy. A Cal Poly graduate, Michael is now a captain in CAL FIRE (the California Department of Forestry & Fire Protection), and during the struggle to regain control of his family's heritage he was busy growing his own family and attending to his career. The good news is that the suit has been settled, and most of the property is once more in the possession of the Giubbini family. Longtime friend and neighbor Steve Pesenti, a grandson of the founder of the original Pesenti winery, is on board as partner and cowinemaker. Mark Caporale is also a partner in the winery. Given the winery's history with Zinfandel, the partners will emphasize that grape in addition to Cabernet Sauvignon, Cabernet Franc, and Merlot. It is indeed good to see a family-owned and -run winery back in the hands of the family.

RECOMMENDED WINES: Mike recommends the Estate Zinfandel, and I tasted the 2002, a brick-red wine nearly opaque in the glass. The wine shows raspberry and black cherry fruit in the nose alongside a hint of vanilla and spice. The soft, rounded tannins provide for an excellent mouthfeel, and the wine has a ripe and satisfying finish.

I suggest the Cabernet Sauvignon. I tasted the 2002 and came away thoroughly impressed. The wine is opaque to the stem and almost black ink in the glass. The nose is black cherries and black currants with a touch of cedar spice. This wine shows excellent balance and has enough tannins left to age another eight years. The wine has outstanding ripeness, which contributes to the lingering finish. When I tasted it again at the table, it had developed further complexity and interest.

Much as I like this wine, I would be remiss if I did not mention the Giubbini Vineyards Estate Zin port. It is one of the best ruby ports made from Zinfandel grapes in this region. If the excellent quality of the wines again being produced at Rotta maintains or even improves, its future reputation will surpass the past.

RATING: Three stars (reds are somewhat ahead of whites)

Salisbury Vineyards

WINERY OWNER: John Salisbury

WINEMAKER: John Salisbury

TASTING ROOM: Yes

DAYS/HOURS: Daily 11 A.M.–6 P.M.

ADDRESS: 6985 Ontario Rd., Avila Valley, CA 93405; 805-595-9463; 805-595-2104 (fax); salisburyvineyards.com

WINES/GRAPE VARIETIES: Cabernet Sauvignon, Chardonnay, Pinot Noir, Pinot Grigio, Zinfandel

WINE CLUB: Yes

TASTING ROOM AMENITIES: Picnic area, merchandise

REGION: San Luis Obispo County

San Marcos Creek Vineyard

WINERY OWNERS: Fling and Annette Traylor, Cathy and Brady Winter

WINEMAKERS: Paul Ayers and Brady Winter

TASTING ROOM: Yes

DAYS/HOURS: Daily 11 A.M.–6 P.M.

ADDRESS: 7750 N. Hwy. 101, Paso Robles, CA 93446; 805-467-2760; 805-467-0160 (fax); sanmarcoscreek.com

WINES/GRAPE VARIETIES: Cabernet Sauvignon, Chardonnay, late-harvest Zinfandel, Merlot, Nebbiolo, Petite Sirah, Syrah, Viognier, White Merlot, Zinfandel

WINE CLUB: Yes

REGION: Paso Robles AVA

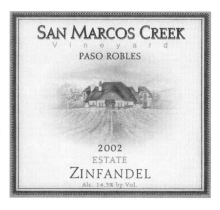

TASTING ROOM AMENITIES: Picnic area, merchandise, bed-and-breakfast

The San Marcos Creek Vineyard label was established in July 2002. The winery (formerly a charming horse barn), the new tasting room, and a bed-and-breakfast on the property are now open for business. Fling and Annette Traylor are co-owners of the venture with their daughter Cathy Winter and her husband, Brady Winter. When Fling and Annette were scouting retirement properties in 1981, they found 100 acres north of Paso Robles, a suitable distance from Los Angeles. What had once been a sheep ranch was converted to a horse property from 1985 to 1990. The Traylors, in establishing their ranch, noticed that others in the vicinity were planting grapes. With a desire to make the Paso Robles area their new home, they established a vineyard in 1992 with 40 acres planted to Merlot, Zinfandel, Syrah, Petite Sirah, Nebbiolo, Cabernet Sauvignon, and some Cabernet Franc. For years, Fling operated as a grower supplying grapes to the premium wineries in the area before he decided to make wine under his own label.

The Traylors eventually brought Cathy into the family business as manager, with son-in-law Brady assisting senior winemaker Paul Ayers. Brady had nurtured an interest in wine during his years in the restaurant business; his establishment was one of the first in the Los Angeles area to offer wine by the glass. There he met his future wife, Cathy. Eventually he moved on and became the finance manager at a major Honda dealership in

Southern California while Fling and Annette were establishing themselves in Paso Robles. When Cathy and Brady were invited to join the business partnership, Brady educated himself by reading enology texts, taking courses at Davis, and learning by doing under Paul's tutelage. Brady emphasizes that San Marcos will produce estate-grown, single-vineyard, and estate-bottled wines with control over each step of the process.

RECOMMENDED WINES: Brady recommends the Syrah, their first gold-medal wine. I tasted the 2001, a black-purple, opaque wine. The aromatics were wonderful: wild plums, candied cherries, and red currants, with a hint of chocolate truffles. The lovely nose is enhanced by the excellent ripeness of the grapes and the lingering finish. This is a delightful example of an older-vineyard Syrah.

I recommend the Zinfandel. I tasted the 2000, a translucent, cherry-red wine. The nose is redolent of blueberries, raspberries, and currants. This is a well-balanced wine that spent twenty-seven months in the barrel. It is ready for drinking. Do try the late-harvest Zinfandel as well. It is a fine example of an off-dry late-harvest Zin.

RATING: Two → three stars (reds currently ahead of whites)

Saucelito Canyon Vineyard & Winery

WINERY OWNERS: Bill and Nancy Greenough

WINEMAKER: Bill Greenough

TASTING ROOM: Yes (shared with Ortman Family Vineyards)

DAYS/HOURS: Daily 10 A.M.–5 P.M.

ADDRESS: 3080 Biddle Ranch Rd., San Luis Obispo, CA 93401; 805-543-2111; no fax; saucelitocanyon.com

WINES/GRAPE VARIETIES: Cabernet Sauvignon, Dos Ranchos Zinfandel, late-harvest Zinfandel, Zinfandel Estate, Zinfandel Reserve

WINE CLUB: Yes

TASTING ROOM AMENITIES: Merchandise

REGION: Arroyo Grande Valley AVA

The Zinfandel roots at Saucelito Canyon run long and deep, figuratively and literally, going all the way back to the 1880s, when English engineer Henry Ditmas owned the property. When Bill and Nancy Greenough bought the property in 1974, vestiges of the original Zinfandel plantation remained, though thoroughly pruned by the deer population then running the property. Bill's dream, after moving up from Santa Barbara, was to restore the vineyard to its former glory. The University of Arizona graduate did what any English major would do: he bought a book and taught himself the elements of viticulture. It also helped that one of his best friends back in Santa Barbara was none other than Michael Benedict, of the Sanford and Benedict vineyard.

This is not to say that the Greenoughs got into grape growing and winemaking as rank amateurs. To the contrary, they were part of a neighborhood group that would buy Paso Robles Zinfandel from Casteel Vineyards, designate a wine queen, and start stomping some grapes. (I have an unverified suspicion that Charles Poalillo was part of this bacchanalian group at one time, given the remarkable similarities of their stories.) As the quality of the neighborhood Zinfandel improved, Bill looked for properties to buy in order to make wine full-time. He found Saucelito Canyon quite by accident after looking extensively in Oregon and Northern California. When he saw the beauty of the setting and learned the history of the place, the romantic in him decided to put down roots. The vineyard didn't have much to offer on the face of it, but he was young and his romantic nature pushed him to go for it. When Bill took over the property, deserted since the early 1940s, only 3 acres of rootstock had survived the years of benign neglect and munching by the deer. Bill did his bookwork and reworked the vineyard, adding Cabernet Franc, Malbec, and Merlot for blending with the Cabernet Sauvignon to augment the Zinfandel plantings. After almost four years of hard work and nearly thirty-five years of quiescence, the original rootstock again produced fruit. In 1982 he bonded the winery. Bill made his wines on-site from 1982 until 1998, when he moved the winemaking to Tolosa/Courtside while he upgraded the facility. In 2001 he returned the winemaking to Saucelito Canyon. A new tasting room opened, which he shares with Chuck Ortman, formerly of Meridian.

RECOMMENDED WINES: Bill suggests the Zinfandel. We tasted the 2002, an opaque black cherry–colored wine with a classic old-vines nose of blackberries, cherries, and black currants. The wine has a lovely balance among ripe fruit, tannins, and the judicious use of oak. The finish gives up hints of spice that start on the mid-palate. Drink now and over the next three years.

I suggest the 2001 Cabernet Sauvignon, blended with Merlot and Cabernet Franc. The black-purple wine is nearly opaque in the glass and displays an aroma of cherry, blackberries, plums, and forest floor. This is a fruit-forward Cabernet with some cassis emerging on the mid-palate as it resolves into a velvety smooth finish. Drink now and over the next four to five years.

RATING: One → two stars (quality is improving)

Saxum Vineyards

WINERY OWNERS: Smith family

WINEMAKER: Justin Smith

TASTING ROOM: No

ADDRESS: 2810 Willow Creek Rd., Paso Robles, CA 93446; 805-610-0363; no fax; saxumvineyards.com

WINES/GRAPE VARIETIES: Grenache, Mourvèdre, and Syrah-based blends

WINE CLUB: Mailing list

REGION: Paso Robles AVA

Scott Aaron

WINERY OWNER: Scott Aaron

WINEMAKER: Scott Aaron

TASTING ROOM: Yes

DAYS/HOURS: Thursday–Tuesday 11 A.M.– 7 P.M.

ADDRESS: 422 S. Main St., Templeton, CA 93465; 888-611-9463; 866-799-2895 (fax); scottaaron.com

WINES/GRAPE VARIETIES: Bordeaux blend, Cabernet Franc, Nobility (red blend), Viognier

WINE CLUB: Yes

TASTING ROOM AMENITIES: Picnic area, merchandise, tours

REGION: Paso Robles AVA

Sculpterra Winery & Vineyards

WINERY OWNERS: Warren and Kathy
   Frankel

WINEMAKER: Shannon O'Neill

TASTING ROOM: Yes

ADDRESS: 5125 Linne Road, Paso Robles, CA
   93446; 888-302-8881; 805-226-8883 (fax);
   sculpterra.com

WINES/GRAPE VARIETIES: Cabernet
   Sauvignon, Chardonnay, Pinot Grigio

WINE CLUB: Yes

TASTING ROOM AMENITIES: Sculpture
   garden by John Jagger, merchandise

REGION: Paso Robles AVA

Sextant Wines

WINERY OWNERS: Stoller family

WINEMAKER: Kevin Riley

TASTING ROOM: Yes

DAYS/HOURS: Thursday–Monday, 11 A.M.–
   5 P.M.

ADDRESS: 3536 S. Higuera St., Ste. 250, San
   Luis Obispo, CA 94301; 866-833-9463;
   805-542-0133 (fax); sextantwines.com

WINES/GRAPE VARIETIES: Chardonnay,
   Pinot Noir, red blends, white blends,
   Zinfandel

WINE CLUB: Mailing list

TASTING ROOM AMENITIES: Some
   merchandise

REGION: Edna Valley AVA

Sextant Wines has opened a tasting room at the former location of Windemere and Cathy MacGregor Wines. Sextant, a winery known for its Templeton-grown Zinfandel, bought Windemere in February 2007. Area locals Craig (a Cal Poly alumnus) and Nancy Stoller are the new owners. The winemaker is Cal Poly graduate Kevin Riley, known for his Rhône-style wines. When an opportunity to buy the Windemere vineyard presented itself, the Stoller family purchased the property from Cathy MacGregor. The vineyard is the oldest in the Edna Valley AVA.

A short narrative of Cathy's contributions to the Central Coast wine scene follows. To my knowledge, Cathy MacGregor has the distinction of being the first female winemaker in San Luis Obispo County. In a sense, her reputation as a high-quality winemaker paved the trail for other women aspiring to make wine on the Central Coast. Slowly but surely, the ranks of the female winemakers in the area are increasing, to the benefit of the consumer and the industry. Signe Olson, formerly of Meridian, Denise Shurtleff at Cambria, Kathy Jacobs at Fiddlehead Cellars, Lisa Pretty of Pretty-Smith, Leslie Melendez of Eos, and Kris Curran at Sea Smoke are other notables who followed Cathy's lead.

Cathy earned a master's degree from UC Davis in 1977, but her early career was not in wine. After finishing her studies, she worked for Wrigley in Chicago, helping develop flavors for chewing gum. Hubba Bubba is one of her contributions to chewing-gum fame. She escaped the winters of Chicago and returned to Fullerton, where she had lived previously, to work at Hunt-Wesson and Orville Redenbacher, the renowned popcorn company. In Salinas she worked at Fresh Express. During the early '80s she made wine at home, starting with the Chardonnay grape for which Windemere is now recognized; later she tried her hand at Pinot Noir. In 1982 she made the transition from food scientist to enologist, working at La Crema and Grgich Hills Cellars. There she learned how to make high-quality Chardonnay at the side of Mike Grgich. Why did she leave a highly successful career in the food science industry for the trials and tribulations of a new career in wine? For the answer, we turn to her father, Andy.

Cathy's father, originally a space engineer, also came relatively late to the wine business. Andy MacGregor, preceding his daughter in radical career changes, left behind a job launching satellites and spaceships into orbit for the more earthly and mundane pursuit of vineyardist. In 1974 he purchased land in Price Canyon in Edna Valley and planted it to Pinot Noir, which he later budded over to Chardonnay. He also planted Chardonnay on the Orcutt vineyard, and 1978 marked the year of his first commercial harvest of fruit from his Edna Valley vineyard. In 1985 Andy shipped his daughter twenty tons, or one truckload, of grapes. In 1986 Windemere released its first Chardonnay wines. (The name Windemere is taken from the small town in Scotland where the MacGregor clan is based.) Cathy's dad was a true pioneer in the sense that he was among the first to plant Chardonnay and Pinot Noir in the Edna Valley, and only the third grower to plant grapes there. Andy sold a large portion of the vineyard to neighbor Jean-Pierre Wolff, who continues the legacy of the vineyard in his own wines. The Stoller family will make further contributions to that legacy.

Silver Horse Winery

WINERY OWNERS: Jim and Suzanne Kroener

WINEMAKER: Stephen Kroener

TASTING ROOM: Yes

DAYS/HOURS: Friday–Monday 10 A.M.–5 P.M.

ADDRESS: 2995 Pleasant Rd., San Miguel, CA 93451; 805-467-WINE (9463); 805-467-9414 (fax); silverhorse.com

WINES/GRAPE VARIETIES: Albariño, Bordeaux blends, Cabernet Sauvignon, Grenache, Malbec, Merlot, Petit Verdot, rosé, Syrah, Tempranillo, Zinfandel, Zinfandel port

WINE CLUB: Yes

TASTING ROOM AMENITIES: Picnic area, 6,000-square-foot special-events facility, boccie court, horseshoe pits, merchandise

REGION: Paso Robles AVA

The proud silver stallion of Silver Horse Winery is champing at the bit, ready to run again, albeit in a slightly different incarnation. The Silver Horse vineyard got its start in 1989, when most of the grapes on the property were planted. The winery was officially bonded in the early '90s and there was a tasting room at the time, though rumor has it that not all the paperwork for the permitting process arrived at the requisite offices. Despite such occasional laxity in getting all the *t*'s crossed and the *i*'s dotted, the vineyard produced some pretty good grapes—good enough to attract the interest of Mondavi, no less. About 1996 the Kroener family came on the scene. Jim and Suzanne Kroener have always loved wine; in fact, Jim's father made it back home in Los Angeles. At the time, the Kroener family and friends would take trips to Paso Robles to taste wine. One Christmas, as a present, some friends of Jim and Suzanne purchased a winemaker's dinner at Silver Horse Winery hosted by Rich and Kristin Simon, then the owners. During the evening, Jim and Suzanne's love for wine became the topic of conversation, and they learned that the Simons were in the market for a partner in the winery. After discussing the matter with their daughter Jamie and son Stephen, Jim and Suzanne entered into a partnership with the Simons. Unfortunately, the partnership failed, and the Kroeners bought out the Simons' share in 1997. Jim Kroener decided he did not want to return to Los Angeles and wanted very much to make a go of the winery, as well as the vineyard. With John Munch of Adelaida and Le Cuvier as the consultant winemaker for a time, things were starting to look up. Then Jim fell unfortunately and unexpectedly ill, and the last Silver Horse vintage was made in 1998, though the wine was sold in the tasting room until 2001 or shortly thereafter.

Stephen, Jim's son, attended Colorado State University. With a degree in construction management, Steve returned to Los Angeles to start his career in the building industry. Steve came to Paso Robles in 2000 to help his father look after things in the vineyard during his illness and to make certain their contractual obligations were fulfilled. As Jim recovered, the two decided to restore the Silver Horse brand and Jim put Steve to work designing a new winery with tasting room on-site. Steve tried his hand at making wines, following in his grandfather's footsteps. Under the friendly tutelage of winemaker Scott Hawley of Summerwood, he produced a small vintage for 2002. Mat Garretson permitted Steve to make the wines at his place in 2003 while the winery was being built at Silver Horse. This fortuitous event brought him into contact not only with Hawley, but with up-and-coming luminaries on the Paso Robles winemaking scene such as Justin Smith and Matt Trevisan, who also became fast friends. It was time to ride the silver horse again.

Forty acres of the original 80 are currently under cultivation to grapes, and Steve has permission to farm the property as he chooses. Most of the ground is planted to Cabernet Sauvignon, some to Grenache, Malbec, Petit Verdot, Syrah, Tempranillo, and Zinfandel. Both Jim and Steve prefer to make wines that pair well with food. That said, they also want to make wines that have lots of fruit but enough structure to last. Now that his father is well again, Steve is ready to offer the consumer the complete package: new wines that are handmade and handcrafted from their premium vineyards and a brand-new facility that opened in 2005, affording tasters a beautiful view of the surrounding area. These are all important reasons that folks linger and enjoy what the Kroeners have to offer and are more than willing to share. Hence the statement on the back of every bottle, "Not for Us Alone!"

RECOMMENDED WINES: Steve suggests the 2002 Carame, named after his wife (it means "precious one" in Swahili). This wine is a blend of mostly Cabernet Sauvignon with about 35 percent Petit Verdot. It blocks all light and is black-purple in the glass. In the nose I found black cherries, vanilla spice, black currants, some tobacco, and briars. The wine is wonderful in the mouth, with ample tannin still in evidence above the ripe fruit. It would be a shame to drink this wine too soon; it should be drinking at its peak around 2010.

I recommend the 2002 Syrah-Cab blend (65-35 percent), a wine of dense opaque purple and black in the glass. The dominant note in the nose is blackberries, figs, some spice, and bacon fat. The tannins are present but ripe and rounded, making this wine accessible now, but it will improve even more in three years. This is a fine blend and if it is sold out, don't worry. I tasted the 2003 in the barrel, and it will surpass the 2002.

RATING: Two stars (very good and competently made wines)

Silver Stone Wines

WINERY OWNER: Dan Kleck

WINEMAKER: Dan Kleck

TASTING ROOM: Yes

DAYS/HOURS: Thursday–Monday 11 A.M.–
5 P.M.

ADDRESS: 827 13th St., Paso Robles, CA
93446; 805-227-6434; 805-980-4386 (fax);
silverstonewines.com

WINES/GRAPE VARIETIES: Cabernet
Sauvignon, Chardonnay, Merlot,
Pinot Noir, Sauvignon Blanc, Syrah,
Zinfandel

WINE CLUB: Yes

TASTING ROOM AMENITIES: Merchandise   REGION: Paso Robles AVA

Most of the formally trained winemakers and owners profiled in this book hail from the enology or viticulture programs at UC Davis, Fresno State, or Cal Poly. Dan Kleck is an exception, having established himself back east before coming west. He sees himself as a vagabond winemaker, but it seems he has found a home at last on California's Central Coast. The journey was a long and prosperous adventure indeed. He grew up in Ohio and at age fifteen visited a winery in southwestern Michigan with his parents. Fascinated by the tour, he loved what he saw so much that he took a matchbook from the winery as a keepsake. At nineteen he went to live with his aunt and uncle in

Michigan, found the matchbook among his souvenirs, and, taking a chance, called the winery. They interviewed him, saw that he was big enough to do the manual labor required, and hired him. The job suited his personality to a T: accustomed to the hard work of farm life but also loving all things scientific, he found a perfect way to conjoin his two interests in working the vineyards and making wine. He stayed for two years before going to Hargrave Vineyards on Long Island, where he worked for four years.

Fairly well established on the East Coast by then, he took on work as a consultant to help start-ups with vineyards, wineries, and the hiring and training of vineyard crews. Over the next twenty or so years, he achieved near-legendary status as one of the great winemakers on the East Coast. The *New York Times,* for instance, referred to him as "arguably Long Island's best winemaker." This afforded him the opportunity to travel, and he worked in Chile for a time, meeting the famous wine writer Hugh Johnson, who became a partner in a venture. In 1990 he went to Palmer Vineyards, and one day in 1998, some movers and shakers from Kendall-Jackson wanted a tour; in fact, the head sales manager of K-J informed Dan that Jess Jackson, no less, wanted to come the very next day. During the tour Jackson informed Dan that he was building a new winery in Monterey and there was an opening for a winemaker. Dan took this as an item of interest. Jackson flew him back to Monterey in his private jet; they landed in Santa Rosa and he had a good look at the winery, where mostly white wines would be produced. He took the job and became a Chardonnay specialist at a winery capable of pushing up to 2.5 million cases a year out the door and onto the trucks.

During his nearly six years at Kendall-Jackson he discovered the quality of Central Coast fruit and decided to start a program of smaller lots featuring finer wines for the company. Despite his success with the new lines, he rued the fact that he was becoming slowly but surely a corporate winemaker, forced to spend most of his time in front of a computer instead of in the vineyards and barrel rooms. Because K-J acquired a substantial quantity of premium grapes from Paso Robles, he looked south for possibilities. He was able to pick up contracts from growers needing consulting advice, and in the course of making such contacts, met Bob and Steve Miller of Bien Nacido vineyard, who were then preparing to expand their cooperative winemaking facilities from Santa Maria to Paso Robles. With several clients in his back pocket eager and ready to make wine, Dan assured Bob that the new facility was not only needed but would be well received in Paso. After Bob's untimely death, his brother Steve took over operations. Dan also worked as head winemaker for Central Coast Wine Services, as the venture was named, and by 2003 there were more than twenty-three clients for the new custom-crush and winemaking establishment at Paso Robles. The facility has been so popular that they are ready to break ground for an additional building out near the airport.

In the meantime, Dan turned his attention to his own label. Silver Stone Wines was started back in New York in 1997, with 2001 his last vintage there. Although Dan uses the best possible fruit for his wines regardless of the growing region, he is now focusing on the Central Coast and has in fact started a second label, Red Horse Ranch, that will feature fruit only from this region. His time spent back east exposed him to a broad range of European wines, particularly French, with their elegance and nuance, which influences the style of his wines. Dan and his wife, Debra, originally joined Augie Hug, Mike Schenkhuizen, Craig Shannon, and Marco Rizzo to establish Coastal Vintner's Co-op. Dan's wines are now available for tasting in downtown Paso Robles.

RECOMMENDED WINES: Dan recommends the Silver Stone Syrah. I tasted the 2002 made from the east side's Hall Ranch fruit. This is a black and purple wine opaque in the glass. The nose exhibits spiced oak, blackberry fruit, toffee, crème brûlée, and earth. The wine has a wonderful acidity to balance the tannins. In the mouth the wine is silky, well integrated, and luscious on the tongue. The finish is long and lingering and invites you back for another glass. This wine is ready now but will be at its best in three to five years.

I suggest the Chardonnay made from Bien Nacido grapes. The 2003 is a gold-colored gem of apples, pears, and mangoes, with an underlying minerality. The wine has excellent acidity to balance the luscious fruit, and the oak contributes to its complexity in the mouth. The finish is long, crisp and tart, making this a fine example of wines produced from outstanding Bien Nacido fruit. It will easily age another ten years.

The *Los Angeles Times* has featured the 2002 Red Horse Ranch Zinfandel, made of Paso Robles fruit, as its Wine of the Week. Dan and I also tasted his 2004 Sauvignon Blanc from Arroyo Seco grapes, and I mention it here because it is one of the best I have tasted. This lovely wine was light lemon with hints of gold after less than a week in the bottle. The aromatics are wonderful: a wet stone minerality sits below the lush grapefruit and lime. The acidity makes the wine and gives the lush citrus fruit a cushion of support. This wine is vinified in the style of a French Sancerre, making it a true expression of the variety. Dan made only about 150 cases, but he has promised to continue making Sauvignon Blanc for his line.

RATING: Four stars (two stars for the Red Horse Ranch line)

Skyhawk Lane

WINERY OWNERS: Charlie and Renee Jobbins

WINEMAKERS: Charlie and Renee Jobbins

TASTING ROOM: No

DAYS/HOURS: By appointment only

ADDRESS: 1605 Commerce Way, Ste. P-28, Paso Robles, CA 93446;

805-474-4277; 805-474-4277 (fax); skyhawklane.com

WINES/GRAPE VARIETIES: Chardonnay, Cabernet Sauvignon, Three Cane (blend), Red Fusion (blend)

WINE CLUB: Yes

REGION: Paso Robles AVA

Stacked Stone Cellars

WINERY OWNER: Donald Thiessen

WINEMAKER: Donald Thiessen

TASTING ROOM: Yes

DAYS/HOURS: Saturday–Sunday 11 A.M.– 5 P.M.

ADDRESS: 1525 Peachy Canyon Rd., Paso Robles, CA 93446; 805-238-7872; 805-238-7495 (fax); stackedstone.com

WINES/GRAPE VARIETIES: Bordeaux blends, Chardonnay, port, Rhône blends, Sauvignon Blanc, Zinfandel

WINE CLUB: Yes

TASTING ROOM AMENITIES: Picnic area

REGION: Paso Robles AVA, west side

Stephen Ross

WINERY OWNERS: Stephen and Paula Dooley

WINEMAKER: Stephen Dooley

TASTING ROOM: No

DAYS/HOURS: By appointment only

ADDRESS: 2717 Aviation Way, Ste. F-1, Santa Maria, CA 93455; 805-594-1318;

805-594-0178 (fax); stephenrosswine.com

WINES/GRAPE VARIETIES: Chardonnay, Petite Sirah, Pinot Noir, Zinfandel

WINE CLUB: Yes

REGION: Edna Valley AVA

Stephen's Cellar & Vineyard

WINERY OWNERS: Steve Goldman and Lori Stone-Goldman

WINEMAKER: Steve Goldman

TASTING ROOM: At Wine Pallet and Ocean Art

DAYS/HOURS: Wednesday–Sunday 11 A.M.–5 P.M.

ADDRESS: Wine Pallet and Ocean Art, 148 N. Ocean Ave., Cayucos, CA 93430;

805-238-2412; 805-238-2412 (fax); stephenscellar.com

WINES/GRAPE VARIETIES: Cabernet Sauvignon, Chardonnay, Claret (Bordeaux blend), Pinot Noir, Rocky's (red blend)

WINE CLUB: Yes

REGION: York Mountain AVA

Still Waters Vineyards

WINERY OWNERS: Paul and Patty Hoover

WINEMAKER: Paul Hoover

TASTING ROOM: Yes

DAYS/HOURS: Friday–Sunday 11 A.M.–5 P.M.

ADDRESS: 2750 Old Grove Ln., Paso Robles, CA 93446; 805-237-9231; 805-438-3197 (fax); stillwatersvineyards.com

WINES/GRAPE VARIETIES: Cabernet Sauvignon, Cabernet Franc, Chardonnay, Malbec, Merlot, Pinot Grigio, Sauvignon Blanc, Syrah, Viognier

WINE CLUB: Yes

TASTING ROOM AMENITIES: Picnic area, merchandise

REGION: Paso Robles AVA

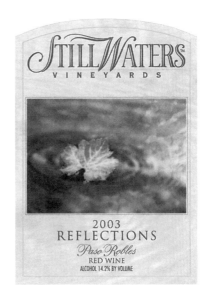

2003
REFLECTIONS
Paso Robles
RED WINE
ALCOHOL 14.2% BY VOLUME

Once upon a time, all Patty and Paul Hoover wanted was a one-acre vineyard to fulfill a lifelong dream. Nothing fancy, just an acre of ground to grow a few grapes and try their hand at making wine. That dream went horribly wrong, and they wound up with sixty times the acreage they had envisioned. Luckily, Paul is an agricultural engineering graduate of Cal Poly and was more than able to handle the additional largesse.

After graduation, Paul started a career in the food and restaurant business. His next career move was into insurance, and he is currently the CEO of an insurance company. Those early years in hospitality made an impression, however, leaving him determined to dabble in home winemaking. Winning awards for his early attempts, he realized that his wines were winning competitions because of the quality of the fruit. Then serendipity sprinkled a bit of good luck in his path. Driving home to Atascadero one day, he noticed a crew on the east side of Paso Robles planting a new vineyard. He stopped, introduced himself to the supervisor, and made the acquaintance of wine-growing consultant Lee Alegre. After a pleasant conversation, Lee agreed to help the Hoovers get started on their one acre, moving the Hoover family closer to the realization of their dream.

Serendipity fluttered by again. Looking to expand their little acre, given Paul's success with the home winemaking project, the Hoovers found a 14-acre plot in the Templeton Gap. A neighboring property, planted in 1995 to Cabernet Sauvignon and Merlot, was in escrow. Those two varieties were contributing to a glut of wine, prices were dropping for the grapes, and the owner was highly motivated to sell. When the property fell out of escrow, the Hoovers were there to jump in with an offer, having had the time to research the *terroir* of the 58-acre property. Hoover was certain the place had the potential to become a premium vineyard, and with Lee Alegre's help they grafted other varieties onto 6 acres of the original plantings. The 14 acres they were originally considering? They manage those too.

Despite the glut of grapes at the time, Paul is certain he paid a premium price for the property, but it contained a few added bonuses: next to a 1,200-square-foot house—which Paul and family remodeled into a tasting room with tiled floors, oak furniture, and a fireplace—sits an eighty-year-old olive orchard, now revitalized. A relaxing visit under the olive trees affords one a tranquil view across the vineyards and over to the hills in the distance.

Drawing on his background in agricultural engineering and business, Paul thought through the economics of the operation. For the time being, some 80 percent of the fruit will be sold to other wineries. The remainder will go into Still Waters bottles, with the winery set to fill about 1,500 cases annually. Paul emphasizes that the winery is very much a small, family-run operation. While he oversees the growing and the winemaking, he also does the marketing to restaurants. Patty keeps the books, children Stephanie and Ben help with operations, and even brother-in-law Bill Elrod and his son, Chris (a former student of mine, I'm proud to say), all make important contributions in the establishment of Still Waters Winery. The tasting room opened for business in May 2004.

RECOMMENDED WINES: Paul recommends his Bordeaux blend called Reflections. I tasted the 2003, which was Cabernet Sauvignon, Merlot, Cabernet Franc, and some Malbec. Reflections is a dark purple wine almost opaque to the stem of the glass. The nose suggests red currants and red cherries, with soft and rounded tannins contributing to a luscious mouthfeel. The wine displays fine balance, great fruit, and a long, persistent finish. It is drinkable now but five years will allow it to achieve full integration.

I recommend the 2001 Syrah, with its blackberry fruit, smoke, bacon, and a hint of coconut in the nose. This is an opaque purple-black wine that offers crème brûlée on the mid-palate. Although it is drinking wonderfully now, the excellent ripeness of the grapes contributes to a long, silky finish and will reward those patient enough to let it age another three to five years.

RATING: Two stars (very good whites and reds)

Summerwood Winery

WINERY OWNER: Summerwood Winery & Inn, Inc.

WINEMAKER: Chris Cameron

TASTING ROOM: Yes

DAYS/HOURS: Daily 10 A.M.–6 P.M. (winter 5:30 P.M.)

ADDRESS: 2175 Arbor Rd., Paso Robles, CA 93446; 805-227-1365; 805-227-1366 (fax); summerwoodwine.com

WINES/GRAPE VARIETIES: Cabernet Sauvignon, Cab-Syrah (blend), Diosa (blend), Diosa Blanc, GSM (blend), Merlot, port, rosé, Sentio (blend), Syrah, Vin Rouge (blend), Viognier

WINE CLUB: Yes

TASTING ROOM AMENITIES: Inn, picnic area, merchandise

REGION: Paso Robles AVA

Some of the greatest wines in the world are blends, and more and more top *vignerons* on the Central Coast are taking this direction. Summerwood has recently won top accolades for both its Rhône-style and its Bordeaux-style blends. For example, the 2001 Sentio III won the top award at the Critics Challenge International Wine Competition in San Diego. The Diosa wines also won awards at that competition. The wines were made under the direction of Scott Hawley, who has left for another position. The Summerwood team conducted a national search for a winemaker who embodies the philosophy and vision that Summerwood has set forth for its mission to become a top producer of premium-quality wines. Veteran Australian winemaker and educator Chris Cameron is now in position to help the winery achieve those lofty goals.

At Summerwood the intent is to be consumer-friendly, and once you sink into the plush leather chairs in the tasting room, this becomes self-evident. In keeping with that approach, the tasting room affords views into the wine processing facility itself. Tasters searching for the authentic wine-country experience can stay at the well-appointed bed-and-breakfast a short stagger across the street from the tasting room, where nine rooms are available. In the winery, members of the Summerwood team concentrate on producing wines of power and elegance. The key is to start with the best possible fruit, blending to add complexity to the wines. Not interested in one-note wines, they see their barrels, bought from as many as twelve different coopers, as a spice rack for adding additional flavor elements to the fruit.

RECOMMENDED WINES: Summerwood recommends the Sentio IV, a Bordeaux blend of Cabernet Sauvignon and Merlot and paean to the sensory experience of wine. I first tasted the 2001, a nearly opaque wine of black cherry color with black currants, cherry, and a hint of plum in the nose. I found cedar, smoke, and a touch of dark chocolate beneath the ample fruit. The wine is beautifully balanced and well integrated, and it has a long, silky finish thanks to the ripe tannins. This wine will easily last another three to five years. It is truly a wonderful blend. I also tried the 2002, a black cherry–colored wine also opaque to light. The nose has intense flavors of boysenberry, loganberry, and sweet red cherries, with a touch of chocolate powder. Dusty tannins support and give structure to the wine. Showing excellent integration of all of its components, the wine is soft and round in the mouth. This splendid wine is ready for drinking now but will hold another four to six years.

The 2003 Diosa ("goddess") is my recommendation. I first tasted the 2001, a blend of Syrah, Mourvèdre, and Grenache, which represents Summerwood's interest in the wines of the Rhône. The 2001 is an opaque reddish-black color and presents blackberries, plum, and a hint of blueberries to the nose. I also found brown sugar, honey, and pepper under the fruit. The wine is huge in the mouth with a lasting, chewy finish. I would open this excellent blend an hour before drinking. It will last another eight years in the bottle. The 2003 Diosa is a blend of 82 percent Syrah, 10 percent Grenache, 7 percent Mourvèdre, and 1 percent Roussanne. This is a black wine so dark that it blocks the light. The nose is redolent of chocolate-covered cherries, bacon fat, sweet blackberry jam, black currants, and freshly turned earth. This well-structured wine has a mouth-filling body with ripe, rounded tannins supporting the lush fruit. The finish lasted more than a minute. Drink now and over the next three to five years.

RATING: Three stars (four stars Sentio and Diosa blends)

Sylvester Vineyards & Winery

WINERY OWNER: Sylvester Feichtinger

WINEMAKER: Jac Jacobs

TASTING ROOM: Yes

DAYS/HOURS: Daily 10 A.M.–5 P.M.

ADDRESS: 5115 Buena Vista Dr., Paso Robles, CA 93446; 805-227-4000; 805-227-6128 (fax); sylvesterwinery.com

WINES/GRAPE VARIETIES: Cabernet Sauvignon, Chardonnay, Cabernet Franc, Merlot, Sangiovese, Syrah, Zinfandel

WINE CLUB: Yes

TASTING ROOM AMENITIES: Merchandise, gourmet foods shop, antique train cars

REGION: Paso Robles AVA

SYLVESTER
VINEYARDS & WINERY

Because his first name in German refers to the New Year's Eve holiday of celebration (*der Silvester*), Sylvester Feichtinger chose it to name his winery. Given the alternative, this was probably a wise choice. Sylvester received his training in agriculture and fruit orchards at the Realschule (technical high school) in Ritzlhof, Austria. Once in the United States, he developed a variety of business interests including cattle, orchards, and vineyards. In the early 1960s he bought an alfalfa ranch called Rancho Robles, a property of some 430 acres. At one time a maker of fruit wines in the Austrian tradition, Sylvester planted vineyards on the property in 1982. Thirteen years later the winery and tasting room was constructed. The combined building, where one can see into the winemaking operation while sampling the wines, resulted in a beautiful complex fronted by a patio and an old wine tank. Farther over is a fountain in which a marble globe reposes, the creation of Sandri Oscar. The purpose of the facility was to get it right the first time, so Nick Martin of Martin & Weyrich fame was consulted to help build the place; they did indeed get it right.

They also got it right in hiring Jac Jacobs, the new winemaker, who is ringing in a new era at Sylvester in terms of viticultural practices, winemaking, and marketing. In a sense, his leadership at the winery parallels the growth and change he experienced throughout his career. Jac was originally with the phone company in Los Angeles (where his wife worked as a dental assistant), but the family moved to Sonoma County and bought a home in Santa Rosa. Their new location afforded them the opportunity to taste wine as Jac toyed with the idea of changing careers. When a friend took him aside and told him a degree in enology was not required to get started in the industry, he went out and got a full-time job working at a winery. For a short time he tried his luck in the bottling business, but it wasn't long before he was back working in the cellars. By 1987 he had worked his way up to head winemaker at Konocti Winery in Lake County. After six years there he was hired at Topolos Winery, where he served as winemaker for twelve years before Feichtinger hired him away.

Jac's winemaking style results in fruit-driven wines, and to get those he has completely revamped the vineyards. A new vineyard crew was hired and follows his directions to the letter. Sylvester gives him the freedom to do what he feels is required to produce high-quality wines for the winery. Once the new viticultural practices have been established, the key, according to Jac, is attention to detail. For instance, he began a program for the purchase and replacement of up to five hundred wine barrels. A high-quality French oak barrel can cost as much as 900 euros, so this is a costly but necessary endeavor. It speaks to the new level of commitment in evidence at the winery. Some of these new barrels are now being used for a reserve program.

RECOMMENDED WINES: Jac and I tasted his wines directly from the barrel. He recommends what will be the 2003 Merlot. This wine shows an opaque black cherry color and already has a wonderful nose of cassis, cherries, and mint above a subtle touch of vanillin oak. It is indeed a fruit-forward wine, but the oak gives it enough structure for complexity and five years of aging. The ripe tannins provide for an elegance that shows through on the long, satiny finish.

I recommend the 2003 Sangiovese port, also tasted from the barrel. The red and purple colors are slightly opaque in the glass, and the wine has a bright nose of sweet plums, raspberry jam, and vanilla cream. The wine fills the mouth and is backed by sufficient acidity to balance the ripe, sweet fruit. The finish is more than a minute in length. Done in a ruby port style, this wine is enjoyable now but in five years should be even better. As you sip a glass, take the time to admire the antique train cars displayed behind the winery.

RATING: One → two stars (look for Jac Jacobs to raise quality level across the line)

Tablas Creek Vineyard

WINERY OWNERS: Robert Haas, Jean-Pierre Perrin, and François Perrin

WINEMAKER: Neil Collins

TASTING ROOM: Yes

DAYS/HOURS: Daily 10 A.M.–5 P.M.

ADDRESS: 9339 Adelaida Rd., Paso Robles, CA 93446; 805-237-1231; 805-237-1314 (fax); tablascreek.com

WINES/GRAPE VARIETIES: Chardonnay, Côtes de Tablas (red blend), Côtes de Tablas Blanc (blend), Counoise, Esprit de Beaucastel (red blend), Esprit de Beaucastel Blanc (blend), Grenache Blanc, Mourvèdre, Panoplie (red blend), Picpoul Blanc, rosé, Roussanne, Syrah, Tannat, Vermentino, Vin de Paille (dessert wine), Viognier

WINE CLUB: Yes

TASTING ROOM AMENITIES: Merchandise, nursery tours

REGION: Paso Robles AVA

There is a powerful French presence in Paso Robles, and that presence is evident at Tablas Creek Vineyard. Although the winery was established in 1989, its pedigree can be traced back to the mid-sixteenth century in the southern Rhône region of France. The winery is the result of a friendship between Robert Haas on the American side and the Perrin brothers, Jean-Pierre and François, of Château de Beaucastel, one of Châteauneuf-du-Pape's finest properties. The 1989 Hommage à Jacques Perrin from this estate received a rare 100-point rating from wine critic Robert M. Parker Jr. Robert Haas, a Yale graduate, has been in the wine industry for more than fifty years in his capacity as a retailer, wine taster, and importer of fine wines from France. He is one of only four American members of the prestigious Académie Internationale du Vin. In the 1970s, Robert was convinced that certain regions of California were perfect for Rhône varietal grapes. His arguments persuaded the Perrin brothers, a partnership was born, and the search was on.

Using the region surrounding Château de Beaucastel as a model for desirable soils and climate, the three searched California for a location that could provide the high-pH soil and Mediterranean climate for which the Rhône region is famous. After noticing the chalk cuts along the road in their drives through the hills of Paso's west side, they brought in a French expert to analyze the soils. Their intuition was correct. The shallow, rocky limestone gave them the high pH they were looking for. The climate matched; hot, sunny days were cooled by the influence of the nearby Pacific. In a scientific paper, Robert discovered confirmation that the soils on the Adelaida property they were interested in were of the same geologic origin as those in Beaucastel. They built a winery that sits on 120 acres 12 miles from the Pacific Ocean on Adelaida Road, just west of Paso Robles. The small creek running through the property gave them the name.

In order to maintain their vision of a new winery based on their French model, Robert and the Perrin brothers decided to import Rhône-variety cuttings from Beaucastel grapevines. The first cuttings arrived in 1990 and were released to Tablas Creek after three years in a quarantine mandated by the government to assure that they were free from any viruses or infection. When the partners learned that about 20 percent of stock coming from nurseries was contaminated with viruses, they decided not to farm out the propagation of their vines and elected instead to develop their own high-tech nursery. Their nursery business grew the stock for the vineyard and supplied high-quality rootstocks to other vineyards. As a result, a good number of vines currently planted in the Paso region came directly from the French-origin clones propagated at Tablas Creek.

Robert is a firm believer in organic farming. Staying true to the model (Beaucastel has been fully organic since 1964), Tablas Creek follows the principles and practices of organic farming "right down to allowing chickens to graze in between the rows to keep weeds down," he says. Labor-intensive hand hoeing controls weeds, and where possible the vineyard is dry-farmed. As a result, Tablas Creek is a certified organic winery. In addition, the wines of Tablas Creek use only native yeasts in order to allow for the full expression of the *terroir*. In the same vein, the wines rest in fairly neutral oak. As Robert explains, "We want to taste the *terroir,* not the barrel." All the grapes for Tablas Creek wines are grown on the property.

Winemaker Neil Collins has been with the winery since its first vintage in 1998. Collins was formerly assistant winemaker at Wild Horse and Adelaida Cellars and brought with him an extensive knowledge of the region. Neil, Robert, Robert's son Jason, assistant winemaker Ryan Hebert, and the Perrin brothers serve as the winemaking committee. Each committee member contributes a unique personal viewpoint on the wines being blended. About two-thirds of the vineyard's wines are reds, and the committee tastes and blends from the vineyard's production of Mourvèdre, Grenache Noir, Syrah, and Counoise. The white wines are blends of Roussanne, Viognier, Marsanne, and Grenache Blanc. Vermentino, a grape traditional to the islands of Sardinia and Corsica, is a recent addition to the line; in Provence, the grape is known as Rolle.

The winery has a tasting room with an outdoor patio and tables, affording spectacular views of the rolling hills and oak forests. Tablas Creek is a first-class organization, and attention to detail and quality is evident in its brochures, marketing, staff, and wines. The flagship wine is the Panoplie, made only during the greatest vintages. This is Tablas Creek's version of Château de Beaucastel's Hommage à Jacques Perrin. The Esprit de Beaucastel, both red and white, is made in the spirit of great Châteauneuf-du-Pape wines. Côtes de Tablas, in both red and white, is a less-expensive version of the Esprit wines. The Antithesis is made from 100 percent Chardonnay. A Roussanne, a Grenache Blanc, and a Vermentino are also produced. Additionally, Tablas Creek has the distinction of producing a rosé considered by Parker to be "one of the finest dry California rosés" he has tasted. Will one of Tablas Creek's wines be good enough to merit a perfect score? Given the overall excellence of the winery, the partnership with the Perrin brothers at Château de Beaucastel, the climate, and the *terroir,* the possibility is very good indeed.

RECOMMENDED WINES: Jason Haas recommends the red Esprit de Beaucastel. The 2003 is a blend of 50 percent Mourvèdre, 27 percent Syrah, 16 percent Grenache, and 7 percent Counoise. This beautiful black and purple wine is opaque to light in the glass. The nose is classic Mourvèdre with blackberries, purple plums, leather, and earth. The fruit has achieved fine physiological ripeness, leading to a wonderful sense of sweetness on the mid-palate. The wine shows a fine tannic grip that is well integrated with the fruit. The wine has both complexity and multiple layers of interest, along with a finish that lasted more than a minute. This wine is ready now but will reward another four to six years in the bottle.

I recommend the Esprit de Beaucastel Blanc. The 2004 is a blend of 65 percent Roussanne, 30 percent Grenache Blanc, and 5 percent Picpoul (noted for its high acidity). The wine is a steely gold color in the glass. The outstanding aromatics feature honeysuckle, lemon rind, caramel apples, brandied pears, and apricots. The crisp acidity combines with excellent minerality to give the wine a superb mouthfeel. The finish is crisp, clean, and tart, and lasted nearly a minute. Beautifully integrated and showing both elegance and finesse, this wine should give another three to six years of peak drinking.

RATING: Four stars (outstanding reds ahead of excellent whites, but whites improving every year)

Talley Vineyards

WINERY OWNERS: Talley family

WINEMAKER: Leslie Mead

TASTING ROOM: Yes

DAYS/HOURS: Daily 10:30 A.M.–4:30 P.M.

ADDRESS: 3031 Lopez Dr., Arroyo Grande, CA 93420; 805-489-0446; 805-489-0996 (fax); talleyvineyards.com

WINES/GRAPE VARIETIES: Chardonnay, Pinot Noir, Sauvignon Blanc; Bishop's Peak varieties: Cabernet Franc, Cabernet Sauvignon, Chardonnay, Pinot Noir, red blend, rosé, Syrah

WINE CLUB: Yes

TASTING ROOM AMENITIES: Picnic area, flower garden, merchandise

REGION: Arroyo Grande Valley AVA

Brian Talley shares an educational connection with neighbor to the north Robert Schiebelhut of Tolosa. Both are graduates of UC Berkeley with degrees in history. Brian is, in fact, a third-generation graduate, following in his grandfather's and father's footsteps in education and business. In 1948 his grandfather Oliver was already growing vegetables in Arroyo Grande. He bought out his partner at that time and founded Talley Farms. After his graduation in 1962, Brian's father, Don, entered the business. He encouraged Oliver to buy additional land, and in 1974 they acquired Adobe Ranch. By 1981 this area had become the center of their grape-growing enterprise. The hillsides surrounding the ranch, once planted to avocados, were replanted to grapes, and by 1985 the vineyards were firmly established, the result of analyzing the best possible use for the land in an effort to diversify their agricultural holdings. Up to that point Don had envisioned the business as primarily a grape-growing enterprise, but that changed when they made wine from their grapes. They hired Steve Rasmussen in 1986 from Corbett Canyon as winemaker for their new enterprise. The first wines produced at Talley were made in a building serving as a vegetable cooler, until the current facility for winemaking was built in 1991.

After his graduation in 1988, Brian worked primarily on the vegetable side of the family business until he talked his father into letting him take over the winery operations. His first job in 1991 was selling the wines. In the mid-'90s, he turned his talents to winemaking with the help of UC Davis graduate Rasmussen. Steve's technical training and outstanding skills complemented Brian's old-world, minimalist style. With the winemaking in Steve's able hands, Brian focused again on viticulture, and he is pleased to say that he now spends most of his time farming and growing grapes.

The success of Talley wines resulted in a larger barrel and case-goods facility, designed by Steve and built adjacent to the winery in 2000. The beautiful tasting room was completed in 2002. Brian now has the control he needs in the vineyard, producing estate-grown and -bottled wines that showcase the excellent fruit of the Arroyo Grande Valley, an AVA his father helped set up. The house specialties at Talley are Pinot Noir and Chardonnay, and there is a second line called Bishop's Peak. The new winemaker is Leslie Mead.

RECOMMENDED WINES: Brian recommends the Estate Chardonnay, one of the *Wine Spectator*'s top 100 wines two years in a row (2002 and 2003). The 2002 is a fine example of Chardonnay in the Burgundian style. There is lovely fruit—a mélange of ripe figs, lemon zest, and pineapple chunks—in the pale gold wine, behind a soft oak nuttiness that resolves to buttered toast. Well balanced, the wine has a lively, refreshing finish. If the 2002 is sold out, the 2003 is also wonderful.

The Estate Pinot Noir is my selection. I tasted the 2002, a bright red cherry color, light to the stem, reminiscent of a true Burgundy. The nose is wonderfully ripe, sweet cherries and red currants above a taste of roasted lamb. The tannins lead to a soft, luscious middle of elegant and concentrated flavors. The finish lasted nearly a minute, making this an altogether exceptional bottle of Pinot Noir. Among the Bishop's Peak line, the Syrah and the Cabernet Sauvignon are standouts.

RATING: Four stars (Estate line); two stars (Bishop's Peak)

Tangent Winery

WINERY OWNERS: John Niven and Michael Blaney

WINEMAKER: Christian Roguenant

TASTING ROOM: Yes

DAYS/HOURS: Daily 10 A.M.–5 P.M.

ADDRESS: 5828 Orcutt Rd., San Luis Obispo, CA 93401; 805-269-8200; 805-269-8201 (fax); tangentwines.com

WINES/GRAPE VARIETIES: Albariño, Ecclestone (white blend), Pinot Blanc, Pinot Gris, Sauvignon Blanc, Viognier

WINE CLUB: Yes

TASTING ROOM AMENITIES: Gourmet foods, lounge, terraces

REGION: Edna Valley AVA

Terry Hoage Vineyards

WINERY OWNERS: Terry and Jennifer Hoage

WINEMAKERS: Terry and Jennifer Hoage

TASTING ROOM: Yes

DAYS/HOURS: By appointment only

ADDRESS: 870 Arbor Rd., Paso Robles, CA 93446; 805-238-2083; 805-238-2091 (fax); terryhoagevineyards.com

WINES/GRAPE VARIETIES: Grenache, Grenache Blanc, Picpoul, red Rhône blend, Syrah, white Rhône blend

WINE CLUB: Yes

REGION: Paso Robles AVA

Thacher Winery

WINERY OWNERS: Sherman and Michelle Thacher

WINEMAKER: Sherman Thacher

TASTING ROOM: Yes

DAYS/HOURS: By appointment only

ADDRESS: 8355 Vineyard Dr., Paso Robles, CA 93446; 805-237-0087; 805-237-0087 (fax); thacherwinery.com

WINES/GRAPE VARIETIES: Syrah, Zinfandel

WINE CLUB: Yes

REGION: Paso Robles AVA

Thunderbolt Junction Winery

WINERY OWNERS: Richard and Aurora Gumerman

WINEMAKER: Fintan DuFresne

TASTING ROOM: Yes

DAYS/HOURS: Daily 11 A.M.–5 P.M.

ADDRESS: 2740 Hidden Mountain Rd., Paso Robles, CA 93446; 805-226-9907; 805-226-9903 (fax); thunderboltjunction.com

WINES/GRAPE VARIETIES: Cabernet Sauvignon, Chardonnay, Grenache, Merlot, Mourvèdre, Muscat Canelli, port, Rhône blend, Syrah, Zinfandel

WINE CLUB: Yes

TASTING ROOM AMENITIES: Picnic area, merchandise

REGION: Paso Robles AVA, west side

Tobin James Cellars

WINERY OWNERS: Tobin James, Lance and Claire Silver

WINEMAKERS: Tobin James, Lance Silver, and Jeff Poe

TASTING ROOM: Yes

DAYS/HOURS: Daily 10 A.M.–6 P.M.

ADDRESS: 8950 Union Rd., Paso Robles, CA 93446; 805-239-2204; 805-239-4471 (fax); tobinjames.com

WINES/GRAPE VARIETIES: Barbera, Cabernet Franc, Cabernet Sauvignon, Chardonnay, Dolcetto, Johannisberg Riesling, late-harvest Muscat, late-harvest Zinfandel, Merlot, Muscat Canelli, Petite Sirah, Pinot Noir, Primitivo, Refosco, Sangiovese, Sauvignon Blanc, sparkling wine, Syrah, Viognier, Zinfandel

WINE CLUB: Yes

TASTING ROOM AMENITIES: Old West memorabilia, picnic area

REGION: Paso Robles AVA

At Tobin James, expect to be transported nostalgically to the yesteryear of the nineteenth-century Wild West. Instead of throat-searing rye whiskey or a watered-down near-beer, cut the dust of a long day on the wine trail with a Zinfandel or a Cabernet Sauvignon. After a session of tasting down the line, don't be surprised if you turn from the bar and see the ghosts of the James brothers enter the western-style saloon. When Toby Shumrick (a.k.a. Tobin James) built his facility on what was once known as the Ten Mile Stagecoach Stop at the end of Union Road, he wanted the place to reflect the history of Paso Robles, a place where a cowboy might feel comfortable after a hard day in the saddle. So sidle up to the antique Brunswick mahogany bar, built in 1860 and brought out west from Blue Eye, Missouri; let the kids play in the jail; and enjoy the western theme that wraps around you like a well-oiled wet-weather slicker.

The impressive reach of Gary Eberle pulled Tobin James west from Cincinnati, where Toby was working in his brother's wine store. A fairly persuasive talker, Toby roped Eberle into giving him an apprenticeship at Eberle's Estrella River Winery. When Eberle sold Estrella to start Eberle Winery, he took the young man along as assistant winemaker. In 1987 Toby made his first vintage from Zinfandel grapes. Positive feedback convinced him to start Tobin James Cellars. Two years later, he worked out a deal with Doug Beckett to make Peachy Canyon's wines, in the role of that winery's founding winemaker, in exchange for space to make his own label's wine. Continued success with his label led him to secure the 41 acres where Tobin James Cellars now stands, the culmination of his longtime dream to own his own winery and maybe, just maybe, give the spirits of the James boys a place to rest before the long arm of John Law wraps itself again around their shoulders.

One of the harsh realities of the wine world is that wine doesn't sell itself, despite the hard work of the winemaker in producing the best-quality wines possible. In 1997 Tobin James invited Lance and Claire Silver to join the winery as co-owners after he heard that they were looking to buy a winery of their own. Lance and Claire brought their degrees in hotel administration from the University of Nevada–Las Vegas to the operation. Lance and Claire believe that in addition to producing good wines, the winery business is also about entertainment, and this perspective is fully reflected in the contributions they have made to the vision established by Toby. They want personality behind the bottle. They want a tasting room that provides an enjoyable experience for the wine consumer, as opposed to a library or museum atmosphere where people go to revere the wines in quiet, studied solitude. If that's what you expect, the western and rock music coming across the speakers will quickly set you straight.

The Silvers believe strongly that Paso Robles fruit might be one of the wine world's best-kept secrets, but not for much longer. Toby is gradually backing away from the everyday duties of winemaking to take his Wild West wine show on the road. Lance, having learned from Toby, works side by side with winemaker Jeff Poe, formerly of Simi Winery and Clos du Val. Jeff brings along the necessary technical expertise with his enology degree from Fresno State, in addition to a fastidious attention to detail and a strong work ethic. Claire Silver, who met Lance at UNLV, handles daily business operations, hospitality in the tasting room, and final wine blends. Together, the team at Tobin James works to produce wines that are drinkable now but capable of improving with age. The overarching goal is to get better with every successive year.

RECOMMENDED WINES: Lance recommends the Zinfandel, for him the embodiment of Paso Robles in the glass. The black cherry–colored James Gang Reserve Zinfandel is a touch lighter in hue than some Paso Robles Zins. The 2001 has an agreeable touch of sweetness in the nose owing to the fully ripened fruit above a layer of raspberries and spice. This is a big wine in the mouth but shows well-balanced acidity and tannin. The finish is long and satisfying. Drink this excellent Zinfandel now and over the next three years.

I enjoyed the 2000 James Gang Reserve Cabernet Sauvignon. The wine is purple and red, almost opaque in the glass. The bouquet leaps from the glass to the nose, where it displays ripe berries, cherries, some cassis, and soft vanilla from the oak. This well-balanced wine is lovely in the mouth, with a fine finish that lasted nearly a minute. It is ready to drink now but will reward another three to five years in the bottle. In a blind tasting for winemakers and owners in Paso Robles, the James Gang Reserve was selected the top Cabernet out of twenty-eight entries.

RATING: Two stars (regular line); three stars (Reserve line, very good to excellent reds)

Tolo Cellars

WINERY OWNER: Josh Gibson

WINEMAKER: Josh Gibson

TASTING ROOM: Yes

DAYS/HOURS: Friday–Monday 11 A.M.–5 P.M.

ADDRESS: 9750 Adelaida Rd., Paso Robles, CA 93446; 805-226-2292; 805-226-2282 (fax); tolocellars.com

WINES/GRAPE VARIETIES: Cabernet Sauvignon, Rhône blends, Sangiovese-Zinfandel, Syrah, Viognier

WINE CLUB: No

TASTING ROOM AMENITIES: Merchandise

REGION: Paso Robles AVA, west side

Tolosa Winery

WINERY OWNERS: Robert Schiebelhut, Robin Baggett, Jim Efird

WINEMAKER: Larry Brooks

TASTING ROOM: Yes

DAYS/HOURS: Daily 11 A.M.–6 P.M.

ADDRESS: 4910 Edna Rd., San Luis Obispo, CA 93401; 805-782-0500; 805-782-0301 (fax); tolosawinery.com

WINES/GRAPE VARIETIES: Chardonnay, Pinot Noir, Syrah

WINE CLUB: Yes

TASTING ROOM AMENITIES: Picnic area, merchandise

REGION: Edna Valley AVA

One of the pleasures of researching and writing this book was telling the tale of the region's rich history going all the way back to the 1700s, when the Spanish missionaries mounted their excursions north from Mexico. Tolosa Winery is a part of that history. I spoke in 2004 with Berkeley grad and co-owner Robert Schiebelhut and Ed Filice, who was then the winemaker. Robert's family had vineyards in Fresno Valley, but he did not want to become a farmer. Making wine, however, was another issue entirely, and he tried his hand at home winemaking. He started with one barrel of Pinot Noir; moved on to a Zinfandel, made from Benito Dusi's grapes in Paso Robles; and then branched out into Chardonnay. To his surprise, he began to win awards for his efforts. In 1998, in an effort to get more serious about winemaking, he became financially involved with vineyards at Edna Ranch. Robert believed that the Edna Valley, its reputation already established for fine Chardonnay, was a diamond in the rough for Pinot Noir.

Although he is now a law partner with Robin Baggett, another Tolosa co-owner, Robert's first degree is in history. That degree led him to appreciate the early wine history of San Luis Obispo. The mission there had a reputation for producing the best-tasting wines of all the missions stretching the length of California. The name Tolosa (the Spanish spelling for the French city of Toulouse) is taken from the full name of the city, San Luis Obispo de Tolosa (St. Louis Bishop of Toulouse).

Ed Filice, former winemaker at Tolosa, has taken over another division of Tolosa's affiliate company, Courtside Cellars. The senior winemaker at Tolosa is now Larry Brooks. Of the 180 acres available to Larry, he selects about 5 percent of the grapes for Tolosa wines. The flagship wine is Pinot Noir, with Syrah a close second.

RECOMMENDED WINES: Robert suggests the 1772 Pinot Noir, the date taken from the founding year of Mission San Miguel Arcángel. We tasted the 2002, a medium garnet color, almost opaque, with a wonderful nose of rose petals, ripe cherries, smoke, earth, and a touch of raspberry jam. The tannins are soft and smooth, leaving the fruit ahead of the sweet vanilla. This is an excellent Edna Valley Pinot Noir and will reward five more years of bottle time.

I was impressed with the Syrah. The 2001, a nearly opaque dark cherry–colored wine, has a nose of bay leaf, black pepper, black cherries, smoke, and ripe plums. The wine is well integrated and has multiple layers of interest. The finish is long and satisfying and equal to the ripe fruit and wonderful mouthfeel. Ready for drinking now, it will improve even more over the next five years.

RATING: Two → three stars (both reds and whites very good across the line)

Treana Winery

WINERY OWNERS: Hope family

WINEMAKER: Austin Hope

TASTING ROOM: No

ADDRESS: P.O. Box 3260, Paso Robles, CA 93447; 805-238-6979; 805-238-4063 (fax); treana.com

WINES/GRAPE VARIETIES: Cabernet Sauvignon, Chardonnay, Marsanne-Viognier, red table wine, Syrah

WINE CLUB: Yes

REGION: Paso Robles AVA

Turley Wine Cellars

WINERY OWNER: Larry Turley

WINEMAKER: Ehren Jordan

TASTING ROOM: Yes

DAYS/HOURS: Daily 9 A.M.–5 P.M.

ADDRESS: 2900 Vineyard Dr., Templeton, CA 93465; 805-434-1030; 805-434-4279 (fax); turleywinecellars.com

WINES/GRAPE VARIETIES: White Coat (Rhône blend), Zinfandel

WINE CLUB: Mailing list

TASTING ROOM AMENITIES: Merchandise

REGION: Paso Robles AVA

Larry Turley's mother first introduced him to Bordeaux wines by giving him a sip of the St.-Émilion in her glass. Unorthodox even in his youth, Turley went to Europe and learned to make beer. Along the way he had the discipline to become an emergency-room physician, and later dabbled in making wine. This pursuit resulted in a little venture called Frog's Leap in 1981. After shepherding that enterprise to great success, he sold the label in 1993. His sister, the famous winemaker and proprietor of Marcassin, Helen Turley, noted for Chardonnay, joined her brother in establishing the Turley brand in Saint Helena. Always fans of big reds, the Turley family bought old-vine Zinfandel grapes. After buying all they could up north, they directed their attention to the hotbed of Zinfandel in California, Paso Robles and the Central Coast. At this point, Ehren Jordan entered the picture.

During college Ehren worked in a wine shop, and on summer vacation one year he visited Napa. He liked what he saw and got work in a wine cellar before working in the Rhône region of France for two years in an effort to establish his winemaking credentials. He returned to work for Helen Turley, who introduced him to Larry, the start of a long relationship. Originally trained as an archaeologist, Ehren knows good soil when he sees it. While seeking new growers and grape contracts for Turley wine, Ehren spoke with Mat Garretson, who pointed him to the old Pesenti vineyard property. He discovered that the ground there had limestone and pH levels resembling those found in parts of Burgundy. After tasting wine made from the fruit of the Pesenti and Nerelli vineyards in Paso, Ehren convinced Larry that they should buy the grapes. Unfortunately, they weren't for sale, as the Pesentis and Nerellis were interested at the time in selling the property. The vineyard, one of the three oldest in the Paso Robles–Templeton area, had originally been planted in 1923, but family complications made it difficult to pass the property on, so they decided to sell instead. Ehren sat down and talked with the owners, a deal was struck, and he presented it to Larry, arguing that they should forget about buying the grapes and buy the property instead. In the spring of 2000, they became owners of the old-school, Italian-style winery and the property, including eighty-year-old Zinfandel vines.

Ehren and Larry have since grafted over some of the vines to Petite Syrah and planted some Grenache. The winery has been redone: a new well was dug, new drains were emplaced, and modern power was installed. They put the right people in the right jobs and made a commitment to farming the property organically, right down to the Belgian workhorses used for plowing and generating manure and compost. A diamond in the rough has now undergone a polishing, and the brilliant wines from the new Turley Wine Cellars, made by Ehren Jordan, are ready to compete with the best in the world. They found a great old vineyard, lovingly farm it, love what they do, and are enthusiastic about the potential of their wines.

RECOMMENDED WINES: Ehren recommends the Pesenti Vineyards Zinfandel. I tasted the superb 2002, black and purple married in the glass with a sweet nose of sun-ripened blackberries, violet perfume, and a touch of dark chocolate. The wine shows a fine blend of acidity and tannins and, though showing nicely now, will reward another two to four years of aging.

I suggest the Zinfandel from the Ueberroth vineyard. The 2002 was almost pure dark black to the stem and gave up blueberries, white pepper spice, and a touch of sweetness in the sensational nose. The tannins are still huge in this wine, and I have no doubt it will live another five to eight years in the bottle. The finish, given the great ripeness in the fruit, wanted to live on and on in the mouth. These two wines are stellar examples of what Paso Robles Zinfandel can be.

RATING: Four stars (Zinfandel is excellent to outstanding)

Venteux Vineyards

WINERY OWNERS: Scott and Bobbi Stelzle

WINEMAKER: Scott Stelzle

TASTING ROOM: Yes

DAYS/HOURS: Friday–Sunday 10 A.M.–5 P.M.

ADDRESS: 1795 Las Tablas Rd., Templeton, CA 93465; 805-369-0127; 805-434-9739 (fax); venteuxvineyards.com

WINES/GRAPE VARIETIES: Cabernet Sauvignon, Petite Sirah, Syrah

WINE CLUB: Yes

TASTING ROOM AMENITIES: Bed-and-breakfast

REGION: Paso Robles AVA

Victor Hugo Vineyards and Winery

WINERY OWNERS: Victor and Leslie Roberts

WINEMAKER: Victor Hugo Roberts

TASTING ROOM: Yes

DAYS/HOURS: By appointment and special-event weekends

ADDRESS: 2850 El Pomar, Templeton, CA 93465; 805-434-1128; 805-434-1124 (fax); victorhugowinery.com

WINES/GRAPE VARIETIES: Cabernet Sauvignon, Chardonnay, Merlot, Opulence (blend), Petite Sirah, Syrah, Viognier, Zinfandel

WINE CLUB: Yes

TASTING ROOM AMENITIES: Picnic area, merchandise

REGION: Paso Robles AVA

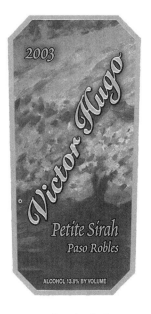

Victor Hugo Roberts and his wife, Leslie, invite you to taste wines in their renovated hundred-year-old redwood barn outside Templeton. The tasting room is situated inside among the oak barrels, and there is just enough space to accommodate four or five tasters at one time. Vic suggests calling for an appointment so that he can set things up and give you the personal time you might need to taste through the wines of this family-owned and -operated winery. In fact, Vic counts this as one of the strengths of the winery: the operation is small enough to be run entirely by him and his wife. Leslie, a part-time emergency-room nurse in San Luis Obispo, handles the administrative side of the business, and Vic, a graduate of UC Davis in 1979, is a professional enologist.

After working for other wineries through the '80s, Vic and Leslie realized a dream of owning their own winery in 1985 when they purchased 15 acres near Templeton. Over the years, additional acreage was bought (almost 80 acres), and the first wines made under the Victor Hugo label were released in 1999. Established in 1997, the winery currently has a case production of about 3,500, with a gradual expansion to 5,000 planned. Vic's philosophy is to spend his money on the grapes and the barrels and not worry so much about building monumental tasting rooms. Vic is also one of the founding board members of the Paso Robles Vintners and Growers Association, now the Paso Robles Wine Country Alliance. Vic is convinced that great wine starts in the vineyard, and he takes pains to thin shoots and clusters. He looks for good ripeness in his grapes and thus pays attention to canopy management, to the point of pulling leaves on the shady side of the vines. He looks for relatively soft tannins but seeks enough to encourage aging potential. He rarely filters his intense, clean fruit and keeps the wine in about one-half new oak, up to twenty-seven months for the Cabs.

RECOMMENDED WINES: Vic recommends the Opulence, a blend of five grapes: Merlot, Cabernet Franc, Cabernet Sauvignon, Petit Verdot, and Malbec. I tasted the 2000, an opaque black-purple wine that showed cherries, red currants, and a touch of sage in the nose. This is a well-balanced wine with lovely aromatics and a smooth, long finish. It is accessible now but will reward another five years of age.

I also enjoyed Vic's Zinfandel, a red and purple wine almost opaque to the stem. I loved the cranberries in the nose of the 2001, with its blackberry fruit and the hint of plum next to a touch of spice. Although the wine is vinified dry, the ripe grapes intimate sweetness, and the balance is just right between the acidity and the tannins. Drink this lush wine now but save a few bottles for the next three years.

RATING: Three stars (excellent quality across the line)

Vihuela Winery

WINERY OWNER: Matt Mikulics

WINEMAKER: Matt Mikulics

TASTING ROOM: Yes

DAYS/HOURS: Saturday–Sunday 11 A.M.–5 P.M.

ADDRESS: 995 El Pomar, Templeton, CA 93465; 805-423-8423; no fax; vihuelawinery.com

WINES/GRAPE VARIETIES: Cabernet Sauvignon, Chardonnay, Syrah, Zinfandel

WINE CLUB: Yes

REGION: Paso Robles AVA, Templeton area

Villa Creek Cellars

WINERY OWNERS: Cris and JoAnn Cherry

WINEMAKER: Cris Cherry

TASTING ROOM: Yes

DAYS/HOURS: Saturday–Sunday 10 A.M.–
3 P.M.

ADDRESS: 1144 Pine St., Paso Robles, CA
93446; 805-238-3000; 805-238-7145 (fax);
villacreek.com

WINES/GRAPE VARIETIES: Grenache,
Mourvèdre, red blend, rosé, Syrah,
Tempranillo, white blend

WINE CLUB: No

TASTING ROOM AMENITIES: Restaurant

REGION: Paso Robles AVA

Villicana Winery

WINERY OWNERS: Alex and Monica
Villicana

WINEMAKER: Alex Villicana

TASTING ROOM: Yes

DAYS/HOURS: Friday–Sunday 11 A.M.–5 P.M.

ADDRESS: 2725 Adelaida Rd., Paso Robles,
CA 93446; 805-239-9456; 805-239-0115
(fax); villicanawinery.com

WINES/GRAPE VARIETIES: Cabernet
Sauvignon, dry rosé, proprietary blends,
Syrah, Viognier, Zinfandel

WINE CLUB: Yes

TASTING ROOM AMENITIES: Picnic area,
merchandise

REGION: Paso Robles AVA

When life threw Alex Villicana (a name of Basque origin) grapes, he did what any sensible person would do: he made wine. His first love, however, was making food, not wine: Alex was intent on becoming a chef and restaurateur. Granted, wine was already an integral part of his life post-college because it is, after all, food. Unfortunately, he had to find another career path when the Los Angeles–based cooking school in which he was enrolled never opened its doors. In 1991 he found a job at the old Creston Vineyards and had the good fortune to work under the tutelage of winemaker Victor Roberts (now of Victor Hugo winery). In the meantime he took enology and viticulture classes at UC Davis. In 1992 he got his chance. Offered grapes missed by the mechanical harvester free of charge, he made his first barrel of wine. A year later, fortune favored him again when he was offered three tons of Cabernet Sauvignon fruit from the HMR vineyard originally planted by André Tchelistcheff in the Adelaida hills. His experience with those grapes convinced him to start his own winery in Paso Robles.

With much of the groundwork in place for starting his new venture, Alex married Monica in 1995. The couple took on the hard work of transforming their 72 acres of west-side Paso Robles ground into vineyard and winery. Good luck is one thing, but a vineyard requires hard labor, and they did most of it themselves, turning the business venture into a family endeavor. Alex saw to the planting and farming of the soils, a tasting room and winery were established on the property, and in 1996 the Villicana label was bonded. What was once a hobby run amok is now a lifestyle. In 1999 all their hard work and sweat equity paid off with the production of their first estate-grown wines. Through it all Alex has not forgotten the siren lure of that first calling. He expresses his love of food now through the production of wines specifically vinified to pair with the food brought to the table.

RECOMMENDED WINES: Gold medals won by the winery include Alex's recommendation: the 2000 Estate Cabernet Sauvignon. This is an opaque black cherry–colored wine with raspberries, vanilla spice, and cherries in the fruity nose. The wine grows and expands in the mouth thanks to the ripe, rounded tannins. The wine is a deserved winner of its medals and is ready for drinking now, though it will give another two or three years of pleasure.

Despite certain cinematic pressures to the contrary, I suggest you try the Villicana Merlot. The 2001 is a fine example of an opaque, black-garnet-colored wine with strawberry jam and mocha in the nose. Soft tannins give the wine a velvet mouthfeel and a long, satisfying finish. This wine will easily last another three to five years.

RATING: One → two stars (competently made and very good red and white wines)

Vina Robles

WINERY OWNERS: Hans Nef and Hans Michel

WINEMAKER: Matthias Gubler

TASTING ROOM: Yes

DAYS/HOURS: Sunday–Thursday 10 A.M.– 5 P.M., Friday–Saturday 10 A.M.–6 P.M.

ADDRESS: 3700 Mill Rd. (Hwy. 46 E.), Paso Robles, CA 93446; 805-227-4812; 805-227-4816 (fax); vinarobles.com

WINES/GRAPE VARIETIES: Cabernet Sauvignon, Chardonnay, Petite Sirah, red blends, rosé, Sauvignon Blanc, Syrah

WINE CLUB: Yes

TASTING ROOM AMENITIES: Merchandise, banquet room, picnic area, restaurant

REGION: Paso Robles AVA

Switzerland's traditional wine industry is influenced by her neighbors, the Germans, French, and Italians. The Swiss made their presence known in Paso Robles with the arrival of Hans Nef and Hans Michel, longtime business partners and friends in Switzerland, now owners of Vina Robles. With the addition of young star winemaker Matthias Gubler, the Swiss are now here in force. Given their cultural heritage, both Nef and Michel have a long-standing interest in agricultural production and fine wines (particularly those of the Bordeaux and Rhône varieties), and this passion, in part, brought them together across an ocean and a continent.

Michel, an agricultural economist by training, first came to California in 1983 and became involved in farm management and agricultural consulting in Fresno, managing vineyards, almond orchards, and other permanent crops. Interestingly, one of his first early projects was a vineyard on Paso's west side today known as JanKris. His business interests there gave him an opportunity to learn the area's potential. One of his other clients at the time was Hans Nef. Nef, a civil engineer by training, was looking for land to plant a vineyard even as Michel was looking at land in terms of its investment and business value. Both men realized the enormous potential for growth in Paso despite their differing perspectives. In 1995 those perspectives merged when they paired up and bought land near the airport on the east side, planted it to grapes, and sold them to Meridian. Their next property was a sheep ranch on Pleasant Road near Silver Horse Winery. Eventually they purchased more land near Creston (formerly owned by Alex Trebek of *Jeopardy* fame), and part of the Chandler Ranch bordering the city of Paso Robles. The latter property, now called the Huer Huero vineyard, is planted with fifteen different varieties, some on narrow 6-by-4-foot spacing, and is the key vineyard for Vina Robles and the location of the new winery.

With the right properties in the portfolio, the land planted to the right grapes, and the winery in the works, it was time to emplace the right winemaker for their enterprise. They selected fellow countryman Matthias Gubler in 1999. His family grew Pinot Noir, known as Blauburgunder in Switzerland, and by age fourteen he was buying and reading books about wine. At twenty-one he came to Mendocino to work the harvest and was permitted to help make wine. He returned to Switzerland and worked in the wine industry before quitting his job and starting his formal education in viticulture and enology. To round out his formal training and hone his craft, he traveled and worked in Italy and France. When Nef and Michel contacted him about coming back to the States to work for them, he quit his job near Basel and came to Paso Robles to make wine for Vina Robles.

One of the benefits of working in the States, according to Matthias, is the freedom to do and try new things without worrying about onerous governmental or traditional restrictions. Under his direction, the focus at the winery is on red varieties that excel in Paso Robles, including Petite Sirah, Cabernet Sauvignon, and Zinfandel. In an effort to establish their own unique identity for their winery, Michel and Nef give him full control over the wines, and his blending talents are already in evidence. For example, Vina Robles produces an ultrapremium red wine called Signature, a distinctive blend of Petit Verdot, Syrah, and Petite Sirah. Also, Matthias has crafted small specialty bottlings from the famous Portuguese grape Touriga Nacional and the great Spanish grape Tempranillo, both well suited to the growing conditions in the Vina Robles vineyards. Stylistically, Vina Robles wines offer the bright intense fruit of Paso Robles combined with a European emphasis on balance and structure. If the professionalism demonstrated by the team at Vina Robles is any indication of future success, this winery has outstanding prospects. I am certain it will become one of Paso's outstanding producers. The new tasting room and hospitality facility on Highway 46 is now open and is a remarkable addition to the Paso Robles wine scene.

RECOMMENDED WINES: Matthias suggests the Petite Sirah, to my palate one of the best being made in the area. The 2003 is a black-purple wine completely opaque in the glass. It has a wonderful nose of currants, peaches, vanilla, and spice. The wine has lush, ripe fruit first but enough tannin underneath to carry it forward another eight to ten years.

I loved the Viognier. The 2003 is pale gold and shows pineapple, ginger, and orange zest in the nose. The wine is wonderful in the mouth and has plenty of acidity to balance the ripe fruit. A touch of Sauvignon Blanc gives it an additional dimension.

RATING: Four stars (excellent to outstanding wines)

Vista Creek Cellars

WINERY OWNERS: Charles and Patti Youngclaus

TASTING ROOM: Yes

DAYS/HOURS: Thursday–Monday 11 A.M.– 6 P.M.

ADDRESS: 729 13th St., Paso Robles, CA 93446; 805-610-1741; 805-226-2048 (fax); vistacreekcellars.com

WINES/GRAPE VARIETIES: Cabernet Franc, Cabernet Sauvignon, Chardonnay, red blend, rosé, Syrah, Tempranillo (dessert wine)

WINE CLUB: Yes

TASTING ROOM AMENITIES: Merchandise

REGION: Paso Robles AVA

Vista Del Rey Vineyards

WINERY OWNERS: Dave King and Carol DeHart-King

WINEMAKER: Dave King

TASTING ROOM: Yes

DAYS/HOURS: Sundays 11 A.M.–5 P.M. or by appointment

ADDRESS: 7340 Drake Rd., Paso Robles, CA 93446; 805-467-2138; 805-467-2765 (fax); no Web site

WINES/GRAPE VARIETIES: Barbera, Pinot Blanc, Zinfandel

WINE CLUB: Yes

TASTING ROOM AMENITIES: Merchandise

REGION: Paso Robles AVA

Naval Commander David King (ret.) is in the third phase of a very productive life. At Oregon State University he earned a degree in agricultural engineering, a degree that twice became useful. He then joined the Navy and made it his career, shipping out for five tours at sea, with an additional two tours working in high-tech naval labs, where he specialized in state-of-the-art undersea warfare systems. He put his experience to work while teaching at the United States Naval Academy, where he taught courses in geology, chemistry, and oceanography. After his distinguished career in the Navy, he worked for eight years as a systems engineer for Science Applications International Corporation.

Retirement brought him to Paso Robles, where his degree once again paid dividends. In 1993 he worked the crush at Wild Horse and got to know the owner and winemaker, Ken Volk. He bought a dry-farmed Zinfandel vineyard in 1994 and planted more Zinfandel and Barbera in 1996 and 1997. Although he considered himself primarily a grower, with Volk's assistance and encouragement he decided to produce his own wines. Vista Del Rey ("King's View") was established in 1996, and when you visit the winery and enjoy the views of the surrounding hills and vineyards from the 900-foot elevation, you will discover how aptly he named the winery. You can see Black Mountain 35 miles away, east of Pozo.

Dave does all the farming on the property and makes the wines. His wife, Carol, who has a degree in conservation of natural resources from UC Berkeley, is co-owner and ambassador. Dave practices dry farming and treats the vines like small trees; thus no trellising, as you might expect in other vineyards, so don't be alarmed when you see them for the first time; they have not been neglected. In fact, Frank Nerelli of Zin Alley Winery farms much the same way. Dave knows what he is doing. His wines are vinified to be user- and food-friendly. At fewer than 1,000 cases a year, this is a small family operation, giving Dave control from the vineyard to the bottle. And if that and the wines and the view are not enough to impress you, Dave is also a noted local wine writer. Give Dave and Carol a call and they will treat you like a king.

RECOMMENDED WINES: Dave's Zinfandels reflect the differences exhibited by each growing season. I tasted the 2001, a dark wine of black cherry color. The nose is white pepper, red currants, and wild strawberries. The wine has a fine tannic grip, and the acidity is perfectly balanced by the fruit. There is elegance and finesse in the mouth, with a lingering finish that invites you for another glassful. The Zinfandels are a pleasure to drink now but will continue to improve in the bottle.

The 2001 Toro Negro Barbera (named after the black bull that once patrolled the area) is my recommendation. This is a dark purple, opaque wine of wonderful complexity. The nose is redolent of black currants, passion fruit, roasted game, and intimations of sweetness from the ripeness of the grapes at harvest. There is enough structure to age this wine an additional five to six years; it has ample fruit but enough tannin and acidity to maintain its balance. I later drank it with roast duck, and the pairing was inspired. That said, if you are interested in the late-harvest or port versions of this wine, ask Dave if there is any left. The late-harvest Barbera is simply one of the best I have tasted, and the price makes it an extraordinary value.

RATING: Three stars (excellent wines showing yearly improvements)

Wedell Cellars

WINERY OWNERS: Maurice and Susie Wedell

WINEMAKER: Maurice Wedell

TASTING ROOM: No

DAYS/HOURS: By appointment only

ADDRESS: Call for details; 805-489-0596; 805-481-9708 (fax); wedellcellars.com

WINES/GRAPE VARIETIES: Chardonnay, Pinot Noir

WINE CLUB: Yes

REGION: Edna Valley AVA

Whalebone Winery

WINERY OWNERS: Bob and Janalyn Simpson

WINEMAKER: Jeff Branco (consultant)

TASTING ROOM: No

DAYS/HOURS: By appointment only

ADDRESS: 8325 Vineyard Drive, Paso Robles, CA 93446; 805-239-8590; 805-237-1684 (fax); whalebonevineyard.com

WINES/GRAPE VARIETIES: Cabernet Sauvignon, red table wine

WINE CLUB: Yes

REGION: Paso Robles AVA

Wild Coyote Winery

WINERY OWNER: Gianni Manucci

WINEMAKER: Gianni Manucci

TASTING ROOM: Yes

DAYS/HOURS: Daily 11 A.M.–5 P.M.

ADDRESS: 3775 Adelaida Rd., Paso Robles, CA 93446; 805-610-1311; 805-239-4770 (fax); wildcoyote.biz

WINES/GRAPE VARIETIES: Merlot, Syrah, Zinfandel

WINE CLUB: Yes

TASTING ROOM AMENITIES: Bed-and-breakfast, picnic area, merchandise

REGION: Paso Robles AVA

Gianni Manucci of Wild Coyote has returned to the earth after a long walk down many trails. His grandparents were farmers and grape growers, and he fondly remembers the times when as a young boy he played in the vineyards until dusk. This proximity to the land fostered in him an early appreciation for what is important in life. As he grew older, he became a successful architect. Ultimately he decided to give up the glass and steel and return to nature, where it is possible to feel the fruits of your passion and labor, literally hold them in your hands, before you share their beauty and mystery with others. The smiles on the faces of others nurture you and become your reward for all the hard work.

In 1995, after an exhaustive search, Gianni bought 40 acres of land on Paso's west side and journeyed back to the land. His style is hands-on; he is not afraid to make mistakes and learn something in the process—that's his personality. He took winemaking classes at UC Davis and jumped into home winemaking with both feet. He is drawn to the wine in the same way he is drawn to Native American culture. Both are consistent with and have contributed to the emergence of his worldview. Growing grapes and transforming them into wine is an act of creation. It is a product of nature.

It is fruit made into art. This too coheres with his hopes for the property. A wigwam for outdoor gatherings is already on-site. A five-room adobe-style bed-and-breakfast, finished in 2005, followed the tasting room. In time, this will be a place for enjoyment and reflection and art, as Gianni hopes to transform the place into a small art colony. He is a sculptor of stone in addition to being a designer of buildings. You will see evidence of his work at the tasting room, where he wraps art around wine. In this way he can share the best parts of three cultures: Native American, art, and wine—an appealing confluence indeed. In keeping with his philosophy, Gianni intends to stay relatively small in order to maintain the quality of his wine and, as important, to maintain the balance in the vineyard and in his life.

RECOMMENDED WINES: Gianni suggests the Syrah: the 2001 is opaque in the glass with black cherry and garnet colors. I detected blackberries, earth, and spice in the lovely nose. The tannins, though huge now, are wonderfully ripe and will add three to five years of life to the wine. As those tannins drop over time the fruit will emerge even more, and the wine will further integrate to become an excellent Syrah.

I suggest the Zinfandel. I tasted the 1998 and the 2001. The 1998 is a dark, black cherry, while the 2001 shows a lighter red color. Plums and raspberries enliven the nose of the 2001. The 1998 presents blackberries, spice, pepper, and dark chocolate to the nose and is ready for the table now. Compare the two wines side by side and choose your favorite as you revel in the spirit of the wild coyotes that still run the hills surrounding the winery.

RATING: One → two stars (good to very good wines showing steady improvement in quality)

Wild Horse Winery & Vineyards

WINERY OWNER: Constellation Brands

WINEMAKER: Mark Cummins

TASTING ROOM: Yes

DAYS/HOURS: Daily 11 A.M.–5 P.M.

ADDRESS: 1437 Wild Horse Winery Court, Templeton, CA 93465; 805-434-2541; 805-434-3516 (fax); wildhorsewinery.com

WINES/GRAPE VARIETIES: Cabernet Sauvignon, Chardonnay, Malvasia Bianca, Merlot, Roussanne, Négrette, Mourvèdre, Pinot Noir, Syrah, Verdelho, Viognier, Zinfandel

WINE CLUB: Yes

TASTING ROOM AMENITIES: Picnic area, merchandise

REGION: Paso Robles AVA

Any discussion of Wild Horse needs to start with Kenneth Q. Volk, the founder and longtime winemaker. Volk—with Gary Eberle, Justin Baldwin, John Munch, and Chuck Ortman, to mention a few others—has had an extraordinary impact on winemaking in the Paso Robles–Templeton area. Time and again others with whom I spoke told me how generous a man he is with his time, tutelage, and talent, to say nothing of the loan of his facilities to neophyte winemakers in need. There are at least seven winemakers in this area alone who owe their start to the graciousness of Ken Volk.

The Wild Horse legacy started in 1981 out of an old barn that still sits on the property. The first crush reached the pad in 1983. Over the years, in addition to the estate-grown grapes, Wild Horse cemented relationships with as many as forty-five select growers. Even after selling in 2003 to Peak Wines International (subsequently named Beam Wine Estates), the fine-wines division of Beam Global Spirits & Wine, a Fortune Brands company, Volk left his stamp on the winery. When Volk ran the operation, Wild Horse was renowned for its community outreach, its work with the wine program at Cal Poly, and a fearless attitude that led the producer to take chances and try new varieties most people could hardly pronounce. That continuity is manifest in people such as winemaker Mark Cummins and his excellent team.

Although Wild Horse once featured upwards of thirty-one wines, the intent is to scale back to fifteen or so under Cummins's direction. Three distinct labels will be used: Wild Horse, the flagship brand; the Unbridled label, for small-production vineyard-designated reserve wines; and Cheval Sauvage (French for "wild horse"), the winery's ultimate expression of Pinot Noir. Mark grew up in Saratoga and worked summer jobs there at a small winery to get his start in the business. He later did internships in Napa and the foothills of the Sierra Nevada, learning to appreciate both the art and the science of wine. He came to the Central Coast in 1985, working for Byron Winery in Santa Barbara County. One day he gave Volk a call and was invited to join the team at Wild Horse, where he served as associate winemaker for three years. After Volk was bought out, Mark became the winemaker through a vote by his peers at the winery, a testament to his skills and abilities.

RECOMMENDED WINES: Honoring Ken Volk's legacy, the focus during Mark's tenure will continue to be on Pinot Noir. The 2001 is light to the stem and cherry in color. There are blackberries, some kola nut, black cherries, and cinnamon and clove spice in the nose. The wine is well balanced and ends with a satisfying, creamy finish.

I recommend the Merlot. The 2001 is black cherry and almost opaque in the glass. Black cherries, plums, and cedar mix in the nose with an intriguing hint of green chile on the palate. The wine shows a sophisticated structure of lush fruit, spicy oak, and enough tannin to age the wine another three to five years. This is a fine example of Merlot.

RATING: Two stars (an eclectic, competently made lineup); four stars (Reserve line)

Wild Wood Vineyard & Winery

WINERY OWNERS: Wood family

WINEMAKER: Craig Wood

TASTING ROOM: Yes

DAYS/HOURS: By appointment only

ADDRESS: 555 El Camino Real, San Luis Obispo, CA 93401; 805-546-1088; 805-546-1088 (fax); wildwoodwine.com

WINES/GRAPE VARIETIES: Cabernet Sauvignon, Pinot Noir, Syrah

WINE CLUB: Yes

TASTING ROOM AMENITIES: Picnic area

REGION: San Luis Obispo County

Windward Vineyard

WINERY OWNERS: Marc Goldberg and
Maggie D'Ambrosia

WINEMAKER: Marc Goldberg

TASTING ROOM: Yes

DAYS/HOURS: Daily 11 A.M.–5 P.M.

ADDRESS: 1380 Live Oak Rd., Paso Robles,
CA 93446; 805-239-2565; 805-239-4005
(fax); windwardvineyard.com

WINE/GRAPE VARIETY: Pinot Noir

WINE CLUB: Yes

TASTING ROOM AMENITIES: Picnic area,
merchandise

REGION: Paso Robles AVA

Marc Goldberg and Maggie D'Ambrosia, both former hospital administrators, focused their considerable passion, knowledge, and experience on one grape variety: the noble but excruciatingly fickle Pinot Noir of Burgundian fame. As a young man growing up in Pittsburgh, Marc often worked after hours in restaurant kitchens, where he gained access to and learned about wines from California and France. What struck him most about wines made from the Pinot Noir grape was how beautifully they paired with food. Two wines in particular tickled his fancy: the 1975 and 1976 Hoffman Mountain Ranch (HMR) Pinot Noirs from Paso Robles on California's Central Coast. As he pursued his career in hospital administration, he never forgot the lure of great California Pinot Noir and French Burgundies.

Marc moved to San Luis Obispo County to become San Luis Obispo General Hospital's administrator, and he found himself at the confluence of two historic events in the Paso Robles region. Dr. Stanley Hoffman once made great Pinot Noir there under the direction and guidance of André Tchelistcheff, and Ken Volk of Wild Horse Winery was currently producing and promoting excellent Pinot Noir at his place. Marc began to ask questions of winemakers in an effort to understand the grape. There were certainly enough doctors walking around the hospital who had turned to winemaking as a hobby or second vocation.

Stanley Hoffman, at HMR, unfortunately went bankrupt, and not much Pinot Noir was grown in the region thereafter; what little there was got sent north, as usual. After studying the vicissitudes of the grape and questioning every producer he could find on the Central Coast, Marc was convinced that Tchelistcheff had it right all along. The soils and climate, in addition to the cooling maritime influence on Paso's west side, were a wonderful fit for the fitful grape. What needed to be changed was the way the farmers in the vineyard handled the crop. At the time, not surprisingly, farmers thought and farmed the grape like farmers, not vintners. Practices that contributed to making an already difficult grape even more problematic needed to be changed. When he met Ken Volk in the 1980s, Marc knew he had found a kindred spirit, one who would become his teacher, mentor, and friend. Marc, in his effort to replicate a fine Burgundy, put a great amount of time into figuring out which clones were best suited to Paso *terroir*. As it turned out, the Pinot Noir he identified was being grown at the same four vineyards that Volk was considering for his property: HMR (Paso Robles),

Adelsheimer (Oregon), and Bien Nacido and Sanford and Benedict vineyards of Santa Barbara, the latter being reputedly sourced from Domaine de la Romanée-Conti in Burgundy. Once Marc and Maggie found the property that best suited their vision for a great American Pinot Noir, they planted a vineyard in 1989 from field selection cuttings Volk took from those four vineyards. The first wines, produced in 1993, were released in 1995. In the Burgundian fashion, the wines are denoted "Monopole," which signifies that one proprietor owns the entire vineyard.

As the Windward vineyard matures, the wines will take on the classic characteristics of great Burgundy: elegance and finesse, a balance between the oak and the fruit, soft tannins for food pairing, and a lovely nose of strawberries and bing cherries. To add another dollop on interest to the story, Marc's great friend Stephan Asseo, of L'Aventure fame, was consulting winemaker on the 1998, 1999, and 2000 vintages.

RECOMMENDED WINES: In the vertical tasting I did, it was a pleasure to see Marc and Maggie's shared passion and romance come to fruition as each vintage year brings them closer and closer to their goal. The 2003 vintage was outstanding. The Sanford clone Pinot Noir is more red than purple and rests lightly in the glass. Cherries and strawberries insinuate themselves among the soft vanilla and crème brûlée. This is a luscious wine with plenty of soft, ripe tannins to support the layers of fruit. The finish lasts well over a minute. This wine will easily last another eight to ten years. André Tchelistcheff, after a sniff and a whistle of this wine, no doubt would be nodding his head knowingly and smiling.

RATING: Three stars → four stars (Pinots have shown steady improvement in quality year after year)

Wolff Vineyards

WINERY OWNERS: Jean-Pierre and Elke Wolff

WINEMAKER: Jean-Pierre Wolff

TASTING ROOM: Yes

DAYS/HOURS: Daily 11 A.M.–5 P.M.

ADDRESS: 6238 Orcutt Rd., San Luis Obispo, CA 93401; 805-781-0448; 805-781-0428 (fax); wolffvineyards.com

WINES/GRAPE VARIETIES: Old-vines Chardonnay, Petite Sirah, Pinot Noir, Riesling, Syrah, Teroldego

WINE CLUB: Yes

TASTING ROOM AMENITIES: Patio picnic area

REGION: Edna Valley AVA

Jean-Pierre Wolff, a native of Belgium, was educated as an electrical engineer. In the United States he received an MBA at Pepperdine and a Ph.D. from Indiana University. While at Westinghouse and Stanford, he worked as a research scientist. Over time he developed a consulting business in San Francisco and taught as an adjunct professor at San Francisco State. In addition to his success as a businessman and a scientist, Jean-Pierre maintained a dream from the age of fourteen to become involved with nature as an agronomist; in his bedroom in Brussels, he grew a pineapple tree. The chance of owning his own winery as an adult allowed him to reconnect with his childhood dream.

The Wolff winery is now the home where he lives with his wife, Elke; his son works in the tasting room, and his sister Martine, an artist in Paris, designs the labels. His choice for the vineyard location was not the result of whim or fancy or even a dream. He used both critical and matrix analyses to find the right combination of factors such as soil, climate, and geology, all in a place where art and culture also flourish. Having done his research and due diligence, he purchased 125 acres that included a vineyard planted more than thirty years ago by Andy MacGregor, father of winemaker Cathy MacGregor of Windemere. Over the years that vineyard produced award-winning Chardonnays. The vineyard was renamed Wolff Vineyards when Jean-Pierre expanded it to include Pinot Noir, Teroldego (an Italian-Tyrolean grape grown primarily near Bolzano, Italy), Syrah, and Petite Syrah.

Jean-Pierre has been a winemaker now since the late 1990s, bringing his formidable training and experience as a scientist to bear in the vineyard. Dr. Wolff calls his craft "l'élevage du vin," or winegrowing. He was one of the first to plant Petite Sirah in the Edna Valley when others assured him it would not grow. Now they are coming to him for grapes. And in keeping with his love for giving back what he has learned, Jean-Pierre teaches classes at Cal Poly in the wine certificate program. Interestingly, much of the Petite Syrah in California, owing to identification problems going back years, is actually Syrah. True Petite Sirah as grown by Wolff is a cross between the two grapes, Syrah and Durif.

In time, Jean-Pierre will offer the wine consumer a retreat for the enjoyment of wine that also includes the pleasures of hiking and fishing. He practices sustainable organic agriculture in the vineyard, including the use of falcons for pest management. In his ongoing research and experimentation into the practices that will best benefit his land, his grapes, and the people who live nearby, he uses stingless wasps to fend off the mealybug instead of using pesticides. He works with both state and federal agencies to restore habitat for steelhead trout in the West Corral de Piedra Creek, which runs through his property. His work has resulted in a pristine riparian habitat upstream. Jean-Pierre has also initiated an estate-grown Riesling program and released a dry Alsace-style wine in 2006. The tasting room was recently remodeled and is now open seven days a week.

RECOMMENDED WINES: Jean-Pierre recommends the Old Vine Chardonnay made from thirty-year-old vines. We tasted the 2002, a bright, lemon-colored wine that tastes of Fuji apples, Anjou pears, and soft butter, with vanilla accents below guava and pineapple. The wine is lush in the mouth, with the fruit wonderfully balanced between the acidity and the oak. The finish is smooth and long, lasting nearly a minute. Enjoy this wine now and over the next three to five years.

I recommend the Petite Sirah, first tasted from the barrel; even then the wine showed extraordinary potential. Tasted again in the bottle, the 2003 is realizing its potential, and has won a double gold medal in competition. It is opaque to the stem and a pretty black-purple color. The wonderful nose shows the sweet fruit of grape jelly, blackberries, damson plums, and vanilla cream. The wine is lush and full in the mouth with a fine tannic grip. It is complex and shows layers of interest before its long, satisfying finish. I would drink this beauty now and over the next six to nine years. No doubt there are more gold medals on the way for this wine.

RATING: Three → four stars (consistently excellent to outstanding wines)

York Mountain Winery

WINERY OWNERS: David and Mary Weyrich

WINEMAKERS: Craig Reed and Alan Kinne

TASTING ROOM: Yes

DAYS/HOURS: Daily 11 A.M.–4 P.M.

ADDRESS: 7505 York Mountain Rd.,
Templeton, CA 93465; 805-238-3925;
805-238-0428 (fax); yorkmountainwinery
.com

WINES/GRAPE VARIETIES: Black Muscat,
Cabernet Sauvignon, Chardonnay, Pinot
Noir, Merlot, Roussanne, Syrah, Viognier,
Zinfandel, Zinfandel port

WINE CLUB: Yes

TASTING ROOM AMENITIES: Merchandise

REGION: York AVA

There is something inherently appealing about visiting a place of origin. It is so much the better if that place has the added benefit of being located in one of the prettiest areas in California. In 1882 Andrew York drove a team of oxen from Indiana to Paso Robles and bought the Grandstaff Ranch, land deeded to Jacob B. Grandstaff seven years prior by President Ulysses S. Grant. York built a winery on the grounds with local fieldstone and timbers taken from a dismantled Cayucos pier. He called it Ascension Winery, and to get there does require a modest ascent through the oaks and madrones that line York Mountain Road. With the help of his three sons, the operation at one time produced upwards of 80,000 gallons of wine. The wine was shipped in barrels north to San Francisco by steamer and by horse-drawn wagon to the San Joaquin Valley. In 1913, after Andrew's death, his sons Walter and Silas took over operations and renamed it York Brothers Winery. At one point they made the acquaintance of Ignacy Jan Paderewski, the great Polish pianist and statesman who gave more than fifteen hundred concerts during his time in the United States, which he considered "the country of my heart, my second home." In 1913 Paderewski bought 2,800 acres of land in the Adelaida hills and called his property Rancho San Ignacio. There he grew plums, walnuts, and almonds and, in 1923, planted 200 acres to Zinfandel and Petite Syrah grapes. He brought the Zinfandel to the York brothers for vinification and won a gold medal for it at the California State Fair in 1933. A third generation of the York family, Wilfrid and Howard, ran the winery from 1944 to 1970 before selling to Max Goldman, an experienced winemaker. His son Steve eventually took over as winemaker and general manager. In 1983 the Goldman family was instrumental in gaining a viticulture appellation (AVA) for York Mountain Winery, one of the smallest AVAs in the United States. In 2001 David and Mary Weyrich bought the winery from the Goldman family.

David and Mary, owners of the Martin & Weyrich Winery in Paso Robles, are firmly committed to continuing York Mountain Winery, given its historical significance to the region. New vineyards have been established, old ones remade and replanted. There are plans to refurbish the old farmhouse on the property as a bed-and-breakfast and, ultimately, to build a wine museum. The winemakers are Craig Reed and Alan Kinne of Martin & Weyrich.

RECOMMENDED WINES: Two wines stood out in the tasting. The nonvintage red table wine, a blend of Zinfandel, Cabernet Sauvignon, and Pinot Noir, is a fine value. The color is ruby-red and the wine is transparent to the stem. The nose is bing cherries, some raspberry, and a touch of mocha. The tannin keeps the wine structured and will permit another three years of aging, but at the price listed for this wine, take it right to the table and drink it all.

The Syrah shows promise. I tasted the 1999, fairly light for a Syrah but bright cherry in color. This is a spicy, peppery Syrah with blackberries, plums, and a touch of port in the nose. The wine is ready for drinking now. Take a bottle, sit out under the ancient oaks, and know that you are in the place where it all began for the wines of the Paso Robles and Templeton region. That alone makes the visit worthwhile.

RATING: One star (some good wines, but winemakers Reed and Kinne will revitalize this line)

Zenaida Cellars

WINERY OWNER: Eric Ogorsolka

WINEMAKER: Eric Ogorsolka

TASTING ROOM: Yes

DAYS/HOURS: Daily 11 A.M.–5 P.M.

ADDRESS: 1550 Hwy. 46 W., Paso Robles, CA 93446; 805-227-0382; 805-227-0349 (fax); zenaidacellars.com

WINES/GRAPE VARIETIES: Cabernet Sauvignon, Chardonnay, Merlot, Sangiovese, Syrah, Viognier, Zinfandel

WINE CLUB: Yes

TASTING ROOM AMENITIES: Picnic area, merchandise, guest rooms

REGION: Paso Robles AVA

Any hunter will tell you that to find birds you often have to hop a few fences, and that is exactly how Eric Ogorsolka's father got started in the wine business. Originally from Nebraska, where his family farmed, Ennis Ogorsolka moved the family from Seattle to the Central Coast in 1978 to develop his veterinary practice in Atascadero. One day he and Eric's mom were driving past the property where the winery now sits and saw the farmer working the land from atop his tractor. Eric's dad hopped the fence, chatted with the farmer about the possibility of acquiring the land, made the deal, and shook hands. In 1987 the Ogorsolka family was back in farming, planting vines and growing grapes.

With his father once again comfortably settled on the tractor seat, back in the barn Eric made some of the property's grapes into wine. He carved out a space for the twenty barrels or so needed for his new enterprise, and the winemaking experiments went so well that his family decided to build a winery in 1999. Eric is a Cal Poly graduate in biology, but he worked originally as a fisheries biologist after graduating in 1992. In 1996 he left his career as a marine biologist for the state of California and moved full-time into winemaking. He worked for a time at Wild Horse, and since most of his friends already were in the wine business, he decided to put his degree to work first in the vineyard and then in the winery. The Zenaida brand was launched in 1998. Eric named the winery after the genus of birds that includes the mourning dove, *Zenaida.*

All Zenaida's grapes are estate-grown in the clay, limestone, and chalky soils of the Ogorsolkas' property. High-quality grapes require knowing the site and farming it correctly. Eric emphasizes the need to use sustainable agricultural practices, and this means beneficial insects, no-till farming, anti–soil erosion programs, and mulching to enhance the soil's biodiversity. Currently, most production goes to other wineries, but the best 10 percent or so is reserved for Zenaida wines. Eric plans to keep production at about 10,000 cases in an effort to sustain the quality and keep his hands on the wines from farming to finishing. The winery and tasting room building on the property also features a 1,500-square-foot two-bedroom suite in the loft that includes a fully equipped kitchen and laundry facilities, available for rent. The rooms open onto a veranda that overlooks the winery and the shade of hundred-year-old oak trees.

RECOMMENDED WINES: As you relax in the tranquillity of the vineyard, you might hear the cooing of the doves while you sample Eric's recommendation, the Estate Syrah. The 2001 was opaque as a blackbird, with a hint of iridescent purple showing through the ink. This is a meaty wine of pomegranates, blueberries, and spice. The ripeness of the grapes adds to lusciousness in the mouth. The tannin supports the fine fruit and will add another three to five years of life to the wine.

I enjoyed the Cabernet Sauvignon but was drawn back to the Zinfandel. The 2001 is also opaque to the stem, but red underlies the purple this time. The nose is sweet ripe raspberries, black pepper spice, and black cherry for added interest. This is a well-balanced and well-integrated wine ready for drinking now but capable of living another five years.

RATING: One → two stars (quality is coming up across the line)

Zin Alley Winery

WINERY OWNERS: Frank and Connie
Nerelli

WINEMAKER: Frank Nerelli

TASTING ROOM: Yes

DAYS/HOURS: By appointment only

ADDRESS: 3730 Hwy. 46 W., Templeton,
CA 93465; 805-238-0959; 805-237-9097
(fax); zinalley.com

WINES/GRAPE VARIETIES: Zinfandel,
Zinfandel port

WINE CLUB: Mailing list

TASTING ROOM AMENITIES: Pottery and
photographs

REGION: Paso Robles AVA

The smallest of things can sometimes serve as motivation: a word, a glance, an idea, a slight. Imagine working all your life to produce the best product possible, and just because you sell your wines in a screw-cap bottle, others summarily dismiss your work. You know the quality of your wines; after all, many of the same producers who sniff and turn up their noses at your wines are using the grapes you sold to them, that is, the very same grapes that go into your wine, screw top or no. When Frank Nerelli finally sold the old Pesenti winery to Turley, he was both liberated from his screw-cap legacy and highly motivated.

He took with him to Zin Alley forty years of experience and more than three generations of the Pesenti and Nerelli families working the soil and growing grapes. On his dad's side, Grandfather Lorenzo had a winery at the foot of the old York property. On his mom's side, Grandfather Pesenti came to this country in 1917, bought the old Ward ranch, and planted vineyards by 1922. With York and Rotta, the Pesenti winery was one of the original three in the Paso Robles area. Frank has the distinction of being the only one of twenty grandkids who stuck it out at Pesenti. He had the ideas, the dogged determination, and the talent. He had already produced a four-star port. He tried to persuade his father to move in new directions but was told his new ideas would take too much money and that it was too late in the game to change the winery's focus. Then the offer to buy the property came from Turley and gave Frank the financial wherewithal and the freedom to pursue his ideas.

Frank moved to his current location, a parcel of ground that was originally part of the Pesenti holdings. When he first took it over, he planted walnuts and barley, giving himself time to learn the ground and do some research. From his experience with his grandfathers, he knew Zinfandel was the way to go. To his way of thinking, the potential in that variety was not being fully exploited. In Amador County he found the clone best suited to the *terroir* of his property. He spent four years preparing the soil. He dry-farms, which means the vines get the water they need from the moisture in the ground. Frank had special equipment fabricated to fit his needs as a grower. You won't find all his techniques in a book. He relies on observation and makes changes accordingly, but his overarching philosophy is that the vine comes first—hence his meticulous detail in finding the right clone for the soils of the vineyard and his daily work with the vines. Except for the picking at harvest, he does all the work himself. This speaks to his vision for Zinfandel: he wants an elegant and refined expression for the grape, at the same time keeping all the nuances that have elevated the variety to greatness—the fruitiness, the spice, the ripeness, and ultimately the diversity of flavors.

Nerelli knows now what the vineyard can do. Though just ten years old, the root-stocks look twenty-five, thanks to his viticultural practices. This is by strict design. He wants an old-world vineyard, like the ones that used to be here at the turn of the twentieth century and up until the 1940s. Very few grape growers and winemakers still do it this way. Frank will tell you with pride that he maxed out the vineyard in each of the past three years and each of those vintages was different as the vineyard is maturing.

RECOMMENDED WINES: In the 2003 vintage Frank got the refined elegance he was shooting for. Tasted from the barrel (it was bottled in January 2005), this black-purple Zin is just a touch lighter than the inky 2002. The fruit is forward, similar to the 2002, but now there is the added dimension of mocha and chocolate in the nose to go with the black cherries and red currants. The spice is still there but not to the degree featured in the '01. All three wines have excellent ripeness in the fruit, but the '03 already presents soft and rounded tannins that add to its elegance and lovely finish. In a sense, the 2003 is the first true expression of Frank's idea for a Zinfandel that incorporates some of the lusciousness and finesse of a great Pinot Noir. It is capable of aging at least five years in the bottle, but is wonderful now. As the vineyard matures, we will see even greater expressions of Frank's unique vision and style.

Zin Alley is also true to Frank's roots and those early days of producing a four-star Zin port. Most likely he or his wife, Connie, will be in the tasting room, and he greatly enjoys sharing his wines and speaking with his customers. Take the time to linger with him as you sample the 2002 Zin port, my recommendation. It shows all the characteristics of the 2002 regular Zin but is finished with brandy distilled from the Sémillion grape. This imparts a neutrality to the port that allows the original Zin fruit to show. You don't notice the alcohol, and the wine comes across the palate as light, elegant, and invigorating. Quite simply, this is one of the finest Zinfandel ports I have tasted.

RATING: Four stars (excellent to outstanding wines)

CHAPTER 8

The South-Central Coast
(Santa Barbara County)

WINE HISTORY

The early days of Alta California's wine production were in service to the Spanish missions, pueblos, and presidios. In the spring of 1782, during his great trek through the Central Coast, Father Junípero Serra arrived in what we now call Santa Barbara County with the intent of establishing another mission for the Church. He died before his request was granted, and Father Fermín Lasuén founded Mission Santa Bárbara in 1786. Grapevine cuttings, probably taken from Mission San Gabriel Arcángel, were planted near Sycamore Creek in Santa Barbara. Between 1824 and 1834 a mission vineyard of about 8 acres was planted adjacent to San José Creek in nearby Goleta. According to Michael Redmon, director of research at the Santa Barbara Historical Society, these dates are tentative because the first documented mention of a winery and vineyard comes from a traveler's report written in 1834. The *New York Times* of August 8, 1882, called the vineyard next to San José Creek "the oldest vineyard in California." However, Dan Krieger shows that ten missions were already producing grapes by 1798, with Mission San Gabriel Arcángel growing grapes by 1779. Most likely, the San José vineyard became the earliest commercial enterprise in Santa Barbara County when James McCaffrey bought the San José facilities in 1871, offering wine and table grapes for sale. After McCaffrey's death in 1900, his widow sold the operation to Michele Cavaletto, who ran it until Prohibition. The San José adobe winery is now the oldest historical landmark in Goleta, though the vineyards have perished.

According to UC Berkeley wine historian Victor Geraci's *Salud!*—his history of the Santa Barbara wine industry—in 1789 explorer Gaspar de Portolá pushed into the Santa Ynez Valley north of Santa Barbara, and his diarist, Father Juan Crespi, made note of the "valley's fine soil, rolling grassy hills, and abundance of water." Juan Bautista de Anza followed five years later and also left behind his praises for the region's agricultural potential. These glowing reports led to the introduction of grapevine cuttings into the region to support the area's three missions, La Purísima Concepción, Santa Inés, and Santa Bárbara, assuring a steady supply of sacramental wine for the mission fathers and their charges.

After the Mexican secularization laws of 1833, mission wine production ended and secular production began. By the time California became a state in 1850, there were already fifteen vineyards on the land grants in Santa Barbara County. Favorable tax laws after 1859 (vineyards were not taxed) contributed to the economic viability of the burgeoning wine industry.

More and more settlers from Europe entered the region, bringing with them their knowledge of wine culture and viticulture. Early settlers around the Guadalupe area (starting in 1870) were largely of Portuguese and Swiss origin. The Swiss established dairy farms and the Portuguese farmed sugar beets and beans, but both peoples had an appreciation for wine. For example, Dick Kelsey of See Canyon Vineyards and Winery remembers that when he first established his winery in the canyon, below San Luis Obispo, he sold wine to the Portuguese in the area, making household deliveries much like a milkman.

The Sisquoc Valley winegrowing region has an impressive history. Erlinda Ontiveros, a descendant of one of the valley's pioneers, wrote *San Ramon Chapel: Pioneers and Their California Heritage,* in which she traces the history of the region. She notes that William Benjamin Foxen, a British trader who settled in Santa Barbara County in 1829, received the land grant of Rancho Tinaquaic (Chumash for "little stream") in 1837 from Mexican governor Juan Bautista Alvarado. His son had a small vineyard of Mission grapes, from which he made wine for his family's consumption. Foxen's descendant Dick Doré now runs Foxen Winery on part of that original land grant, though the vineyards there date only to 1987. The anchor-shaped Foxen brand of the original rancho now adorns the label of Foxen Winery.

Rancho Sisquoc, which has played a pivotal historical role in the viticulture of the region, was granted by Governor Pio Pico to María Antonia Domínguez Caballero on April 17, 1845. Over time the ranch was divided and sold, but in 1891 Thomas B. Bishop, a San Francisco attorney, and John T. Parker, a Watsonville rancher, repurchased the divided properties. In 1899 the two partners formed the Sisquoc Investment Company. The corporation became the Sisquoc Ranch Company in the 1920s, and by 1930, Rancho Tinaquaic, in Foxen Canyon, had been added to the holdings. The Sisquoc ranch was now at its maximum size of 41,390 acres. The Green Cattle Company of San Luis Obispo, owned by Edwin L. Green and Claude Arnold, bought the property in 1950 and sold it in 1952 to James Flood III.

Flood, who already owned Rancho Santa Margarita, lost that property to Camp Pendleton during World War II. Rancho Sisquoc met his requirements for supporting his cattle business and was relatively close to San Francisco. Harold Pfeiffer came on as ranch manager for Flood in 1963, and he supervised the first planting of grapes there in 1968.

At about the same time that Governor Alvarado granted land to Foxen for Rancho Tinaquaic, he provided nearly 9,000 acres (2 square leagues) to Tomás Olívera. Eighteen years later, Olívera sold Rancho Tepusquet to Don Juan Pacífico Ontiveros, who built an adobe on the property and established the rancho's first vineyard in about 1856. Over time, this property, at the confluence of the Sisquoc and Cuyama rivers, became part of the famous Bien Nacido vineyards in the Santa Maria Valley.

The nineteenth century saw several successful winemaking operations in Santa Barbara County. Alfred Packard, a lawyer from Rhode Island, established La Bodega, the first successful winery in the city of Santa Barbara, in 1865. Victor Geraci writes that Packard's vineyard was likely destroyed by disease at the opening of the twentieth century, but other vineyards were unaffected. According to Geraci, about forty-five vineyards were producing grapes in the area by the 1890s.

Santa Cruz Island Winery was perhaps the most successful winery of its time. Twenty-five miles offshore from Santa Barbara Harbor, Santa Cruz Island was originally settled by the Chumash Indians, but they were gone by 1822. In 1869, according to wine historian Thomas Pinney in *The Wine of Santa Cruz Island,* the island was sold to a group of ten directors of a French savings bank in San Francisco. They called their consortium the Santa Cruz Island Company and hoped to develop the island as a working ranch. The president of the company, Justinian Caire, was a native of the French Alps.

By 1880 Caire was sole owner of the company, and his mostly Italian workers (his wife was from Genoa) prepared land for vineyards in 1884. Caire imported some vine cuttings from France in 1885, and at one point, at least ten varieties of red grapes and five of white were grown on the island. Zinfandel appeared to be the dominant red grape, although Cabernet Sauvignon and

Pinot Noir were also planted; Berger (probably Bergeron), Muscat, and Riesling were the dominant whites.

Nearly two-thirds of European vineyards were devastated by the phylloxera infestation (the attack of grapevine roots by yellow aphid-like insects that feed on and eventually kill the vines) during the late 1880s. The pest arrived in California at about the same time, but the island remained largely unaffected due to its natural water barrier. A small winery was constructed in 1890, and two substantial buildings of brick made on the island were added later. The first recorded vintage was in 1891.

Records from 1910, according to Pinney, indicate that the winery's 150 acres planted to grapes produced upwards of 83,000 gallons of wine, mostly Zinfandel. Although the winery used good varietal grapes and kept the wines in oak casks, and despite the island's temperate growing season, the wines were reputed to be best for "heavy blending." Even so, the wines seemed to be well received by wine drinkers between Los Angeles and San Francisco, according to Victor Geraci. Pre-Prohibition vintages stopped after 1918, and although vintages (again, mostly of Zinfandel) were recorded until 1936, by that time the winery was finished as a viable commercial enterprise. Edwin L. Stanton bought the island and the winery in 1937 and maintained the bond solely for selling off the remaining inventory. In fact, he grazed sheep throughout the vineyard and sold the cooperage, and in March 1939, what remained of the Zinfandel, now gone bad, was drained from the barrels under official supervision. In January 1950, the two winery buildings caught fire, although the brick walls remained standing. They have since been reroofed and are used for storage. Brett Escalera, winemaker-owner of Consilience, believes that one day wine will be made again on Santa Cruz Island, given its important role in the early history of Santa Barbara County.

Prohibition came to California in 1919 with the ratification of the Eighteenth Amendment. As a prime example of what happens when government tries to legislate and enforce morality, wine production during Prohibition actually increased by almost 25 million gallons per year, as home winemakers were permitted 200 gallons per year for personal and family use. Some of those uses involved selling wine on the black market to those who could not make their own. Although Prohibition nearly destroyed the legal commercial wine industry in California, the state nevertheless was awash in privately produced wine that flowed out the back doors of home winemakers. In 1933 the nation repealed Prohibition, though a recalcitrant Mississippi held out until 1966.

With the repeal, California and Santa Barbara winemakers went to work replanting the vineyards and rebuilding the wineries, but not without a series of false starts. Umberto Dardi got a bond in 1933 to make wine at his property in Goleta. Tragedy struck Dardi twice in 1937: he was forced to declare bankruptcy, and shortly thereafter, according to Geraci, "both he and his daughter died in [a] bizarre home winemaking accident." Supposedly, Dardi fell into a large vat of homemade wine while punching down the floating cap, and his unlucky daughter suffocated from fermentation gases in her failed attempt to save her father. Benjamin Alfonso also received his bond in 1933, and despite his subsequent failure, came to a less untimely end. After a succession of spoiled wines, Alfonso—also unable or unwilling to keep up with paperwork required by the government—closed his doors and sold out in 1940 when the Bureau of Alcohol, Tobacco, and Firearms charged him with illegal winemaking.

Geraci provides an important overview of the modern growth of the Santa Barbara County wine industry. He shows that one of the engines that drove the development of Central Coast vineyards was the success of wineries in the San Francisco area. Unfortunately, as population pressures in that area contributed to the selling of land for houses instead of vineyards, wineries were forced to look elsewhere to source high-quality grapes. Necessarily, they looked south to the Central Coast. Urban sprawl became so bad in the 1960s that the state, in an effort to protect farmlands, passed the California Land Conservation Act (Williamson Act) of 1965, which was intended to slow the sale of valuable agricultural land to housing developers. It also resulted in more land being sold for viticulture.

The early success of viticulture in Santa Barbara County prior to Prohibition, coupled with changing laws and the almost insatiable need for grapes up north in the 1960s, laid the groundwork for the Santa Barbara boom. In 1965 a report issued by the Santa Barbara County Agricultural Extension Service verified what many early pioneers had predicted: the county's Santa Ynez and Santa Maria areas had excellent soils and growing conditions for grapes. The time was ripe, so to speak, for planting grapes again.

Commercial winemaking came to the eastern Santa Maria Valley in 1963 when William DeMattei and Uriel J. Nielsen bought 100 acres of Ellis Fesler's cattle ranch. Both men were students at UC Davis in the late 1930s and had worked on a research project to map out the coastal climates best suited for growing premium grapes. World War II intruded, but ultimately they returned to their data, which suggested that the Santa Maria and Santa Ynez valleys were suitable for establishing vineyards. The next year, they engaged grape grower Bill Collins to plant Cabernet Sauvignon, Chardonnay, Riesling, Sauvignon Blanc, and Sylvaner grapes on their property. Interestingly, according to Erlinda

Ontiveros, the crew Collins used at the time consisted largely of housewives from the area.

The second important commercial vineyard was planted at the historic Sisquoc Ranch when Harold Pfeiffer, taking the lead from Nielsen, DeMattei, and Collins, decided that growing grapes on his property would not be such a bad idea. Pfeiffer's 1968 decision encouraged others in the area to follow his lead, and once the potential of the area was recognized, more and more acreage in the area was given over to grapes. These four men thus became important contributors to the establishment of the area as a center of viticulture. Nielsen's first harvest, in 1966, yielded about 8 tons, and he sold to the Christian Brothers Winery up north. At the time, Collins informed Brother Timothy, then head of Christian Brothers, that Santa Barbara County would one day rival Napa for quality wine production. He was right.

Another important pioneer was Louis Lucas. Members of the Lucas family of Delano, California, had been in agribusiness since 1943 and decided to expand their grape growing into Santa Barbara County. With Dale Hampton, a high school friend from Delano, and his brother George Lucas, Louis identified the Santa Maria Valley, at the confluence of the Cuyama and Sisquoc rivers, as ideal for grape production. After doing extensive technical research, including reading the history of the area, they consulted with friends DeMattei, who had been Louis's Little League coach, and Nielsen, a former neighbor in Delano. When Brother Timothy assured the three that he would pay Napa prices for their grapes, the Lucas brothers and Hampton put a corporation together and planned a model vineyard in the early 1970s. Their venture failed when they were unable to attract enough investors to make the deal financially viable, and they returned their investors' seed money.

One of those investors was Alfred Gagnon, a senior partner in a major consulting firm. He decided, after doing his due diligence, that the team of Lucas and Hampton was on the right track despite being underfunded. In 1969 he came on as a 50 percent partner, and the new team created the Tepusquet vineyards, named for an old land-grant rancho of the 1830s (the name is Chumash for "fishing for trout"). Their luck changed when Beringer signed a five-year contract with them the next year. Building on this success, Hampton planted the 350-acre Paragon vineyard for Jack Niven in the Edna Valley, in addition to the 190-acre Delon White vineyard near Tepusquet Ranch. With partners, Hampton then formed the Coastal Farming Company in Santa Maria, which either created or served as consultants to many additional vineyards in the area.

After William Randolph Hearst bought a large section of the central coastlands in 1921 from the Newhall family, the Newhalls purchased the 3,500-acre

Suey Ranch for cattle and orchard farming. Ed Mirassou and son Peter, looking to expand their vineyard sources, came south in the late 1960s and convinced then–ranch manager Bob Woods to plant a vineyard with sixteen grape varieties taken from the UC Davis nursery in what became the Rancho Viñedo vineyard in the Santa Maria Hills. By 1973 the plantings covered more than 1,000 acres. Harley D. Martin bought 1,000 acres of Suey Ranch and contracted with Dale Hampton to establish the Sierra Madre vineyard in 1973. Hampton took over Sierra Madre after it was placed in receivership and turned it into a viable enterprise by selling grapes to northern wineries.

The next important contributors to the Santa Barbara County wine history were the Miller brothers, Robert and Steve, from a fourth-generation California farming family. In the Santa Maria Valley in 1969, they purchased two neighboring parcels of the original 9,000-acre Ontiveros land grant called Rancho Tepusquet. The property lies between the San Rafael and Santa Ynez mountains, the only two transverse ranges on the West Coast of the Americas.

The Miller brothers, noting the success of their neighbors Pfeiffer, Nielsen, and Lucas, decided to plant grapes on the benchlands in 1972. Again, Hampton was hired to produce the best grapes possible, and as other growers began to call his work a "Cadillac vineyard," the Miller brothers named the vineyard Bien Nacido, which means "well-born" in Spanish, a fitting name for the quality of its grapes. In 1999, based on their resounding success with Bien Nacido, they planted the Solomon Hills vineyard.

The Millers also made extraordinary contributions in 1988 through the establishment of Central Coast Wine Services, a facility in Santa Maria that provides a full range of winemaking expertise and technology for wineries unable to afford expensive capital outlays for start-up. A truck scale, a crusher-destemmer, three presses, stainless steel tanks, and two bottling lines are all provided. In addition, the company offers storage room for wines in barrel and bottle, a fully equipped enology laboratory, a kitchen, and a tasting room, making the facility truly an integrated one-stop shop for winemakers. A sister facility, located near the airport in Paso Robles, has been built to assist new winemakers to the north in San Luis Obispo County. At last count, more than seventy wineries called the two facilities their home base.

Farther south, in the Santa Ynez Valley, Daniel J. Gainey, despite a false start in the mid-1960s, eventually planted some of his nearly 2,000-acre ranch with grapevines after a favorable report convinced him of the area's potential. Boyd and Claire Bettencourt, in an effort to diversify production on their dairy farm, planted 15 acres of vines in 1966 with the help of friends Nielsen and De-Mattei, using Bill as vineyard consultant. Richard Sanford and Michael Benedict planted their vineyard in 1971 at the western end of the valley. Although Sanford had no experience in enology, he had a degree in geography and geology from UC Berkeley. He used that training to locate a property he thought would provide ideal soils and growing climate for Pinot Noir and Chardonnay. He and Benedict planted the vineyards, then built a winery and tasting room once the quality of the fruit became evident, thus setting the pattern for the vertical integration of vineyard and winery that many other growers were soon to imitate. This proved to be a prudent move in that when a grape glut developed, growers who were having difficulty selling their grapes put the fruit toward creating their own line of wines.

When automobile-tire manufacturer Leonard Firestone was looking for investment opportunities, the former ambassador to Belgium bought 550 acres of the Rancho Corral de Quati. The property was a section of 2,200 acres owned by Dean Brown, a third-generation cattle rancher from Betteravia. He hired Dale Hampton to establish the vineyard for him and by 1972 was selling grapes to the Martini and Geyser Peak wineries. Firestone put his son Brooks to work, and soon the Firestones had planted 260 acres of grapes and, in time, built a winery and tasting room. The Zaca Mesa vineyard was established in 1972 when Marshall Ream, vice-chairman of ARCO, put together a consortium of seven investors, including himself, and bought 1,800 acres of land, planting 200 with wine grapes. In the same year, Montreal architect Pierre Lafond planted 72 acres of his Santa Ynez Valley ranch in order to supply his Santa Barbara Winery with fruit, naming Bill Collins the vineyard manager. In 1973 Jack McGowan hired Hampton to plant a vineyard near the town of Solvang. The Brander family came to the Santa Ynez Valley from Switzerland via Argentina in 1975 and established a vineyard that soon featured award-winning Sauvignon Blanc. Dentist Bill Mosby, encouraged by the advice of his friend Bob Gallo, purchased Rancho de la Vega in 1976, after earlier successes in establishing cuttings sent him by Gallo. Another dentist, Walter Babcock, purchased 100 acres near Lompoc and started as a lima-bean grower. In 1979, after conversations with the likes of the Firestones, the Bettencourts, and the Branders, Babcock planted 30 acres to vines, with a winery and tasting room to follow. Byron "Ken" Brown, the first winemaker at Zaca Mesa, introduced Rhône-style varieties to Santa Barbara County in the mid-1980s and also focused on Burgundian-style wines at Byron Winery. In 1990, the Mondavi family established a presence in the area with their purchase of Byron.

Over the next twenty-five years or so, building on the momentum fostered by its grape-growing and winemaking pioneers, Santa Barbara County firmly established itself as a premier winegrowing region. In the intervening years, others followed the lead set by earlier entrants into the business, and their history is mentioned in the winery profiles below.

TERROIR

As you cross the San Luis Obispo County line into Santa Barbara County, the broad, flat plain of the Santa Maria Valley opens up before you. The city of Santa Maria averages eighty-seven days of fog, mostly in the late summer. Ocean currents pull cold water into the warmer surface water in a process called upwelling, which contributes to the formation of fog. As a counterbalance, the hot southern-latitude sun burns off the fog but is in turn tempered by late-afternoon breezes that keep temperatures from rising too high and scorching the grapes. This pattern results in average temperatures of 75 degrees, and the daily high generally peaks about 2 P.M., when the cooling breeze freshens—unlike in Napa, where the daily temperature high occurs at about 4 P.M.

The Santa Maria Valley AVA (established in 1981), with its valley floor and river benchlands, has a climate that results in early budding and a long ripening season. The soils are well-drained sandy loam with some marine limestone and chalk. The average rainfall is 12 to 15 inches per year. Within this area, you will find the famous Bien Nacido, Sierra Madre, and Tepusquet vineyards. In 1969 the Miller family purchased acreage from the old Rancho Tepusquet property and planted grapes because of the excellent soils there. Fifth-generation viticulturist Nicholas Miller, second son of Steve Miller, is now in charge of the nearly 900-acre operation. The proper name of their enterprise is Bien Nacido Vineyards of Rancho Tepusquet. James Rey Ontiveros, a ninth-generation Californian and descendant of the Ontiveros family of the original Rancho Tepusquet, is director of sales and marketing for the vineyard. Bien Nacido is also one of California's major viticulture nurseries, supplying certified rootstock to the area's vineyards.

As you round out of the valley and cross the Solomon Hills, you begin a descent into the Los Alamos Valley (Los Alamos means "cottonwoods" in Spanish), which awaits status as an AVA. The valley straddles both sides of Highway 101, and Louis Lucas has had vineyards there since 1980. Soils are clay loam, and the climate is slightly warmer than in Santa Maria to the north, but cooler than in Santa Ynez to the south.

In the middle of Santa Barbara County lies the Santa Ynez Valley AVA (1983), which follows the Santa Ynez River eastward from Lompoc to Lake Cachuma. This is a long valley bordered by the Purisima Hills and the San

Rafael Mountains to the north and the Santa Ynez Mountains to the south. East of Highway 101, the soils are well-drained benchlands and the climate is warmer than on the west side. On the west side of the highway, vineyard soils are mostly diatomaceous earth, and temperatures are cooler. As you follow the Santa Ynez River eastward, the altitude rises to about 800 feet, and in the north and south the climate warms, with greater temperature fluctuation from day to night, and you see an increasing number of Syrah plantings. Colson Canyon vineyards is a prime example.

Happy Canyon (known by the locals as Happy Valley) is in the southeastern part of the Santa Ynez Valley and has applied for AVA status. The days are warm and the nights are cool due to marine influence. Vineyards are planted at varying elevations near the San Rafael Mountains in soils that range from sand and loam to clay. The hotter climate is ideal for Bordeaux varieties such as Cabernet Sauvignon, Sauvignon Blanc, and Merlot. Syrah also has been planted there. Happy Canyon is the home of Barrack, Starlane, Vogelzang, and Westerly vineyards.

Lastly, the Santa Rita Hills AVA (2001) takes its name from the hills that form its southern border. It lies entirely within Santa Barbara County and 99 percent within the Santa Ynez Valley appellation. Planted largely to Chardonnay and Pinot Noir grapes, the area is receiving accolades from wine critics for producing excellent wines from both grape varieties. The soils are shallow hardpans of Monterey shale, clay loam, and Lompoc dune sand. Located between Lompoc and Buellton, the east-west–oriented hills benefit from the ocean fog and cool breezes that make this area cooler than the eastern region of the Santa Ynez Valley.

ℐℛ WINERIES AND PROFILES

Addamo Vineyards

WINERY OWNERS: David and Liz Addamo

WINEMAKER: Russell From

TASTING ROOM: Yes

DAYS/HOURS: Tuesday–Sunday 11 A.M.–7 P.M.

ADDRESS: 400 E. Clark Ave., Ste. A, Orcutt, CA 93455; 805-937-6400; 805-937-5656 (fax); addamovineyards.com

WINES/GRAPE VARIETIES: Chardonnay, Dolcetto, Grenache, Pinot Noir, Syrah, White Riesling

WINE CLUB: Yes

REGION: Santa Barbara County

Alexander and Wayne

WINERY OWNERS: Earl W. Brockelsby and
Arthur A. White

WINEMAKER: Arthur A. White

TASTING ROOM: Yes

DAYS/HOURS: Daily 11 A.M.–6 P.M.

ADDRESS: 2923 Grand Ave., Los Olivos,
CA 93441; 805-688-9665; 805-686-1690
(fax); alexanderandwayne.com

WINES/GRAPE VARIETIES: Cabernet Franc,
Cabernet Sauvignon, Chardonnay,
Gewürztraminer, Malbec, Merlot, Petit
Verdot, Pinot Noir, port, Riesling,
Sauvignon Blanc, Tempranillo, and
dessert wines

WINE CLUB: Yes

TASTING ROOM AMENITIES: Merchandise

REGION: Santa Ynez Valley AVA

Earl W. Brockelsby and Arthur A. White are the driving forces behind the Arthur Earl Winery and what is now Alexander and Wayne. (In this profile I focus on Arthur White, the winemaker at both facilities; I spend more time with Earl Brockelsby in the Arthur Earl profile.) Their friendship and business partnership has endured for almost thirty-five years. Their business relationship began when they were at Ross Perot's Electronic Data Systems Company in San Francisco, and from day one they have put the emphasis on the business side of the corporation. They now have two bonded wineries.

Arthur is originally from Pennsylvania and is a veteran of the Vietnam War era. A graduate of Rutgers University in New Jersey with a degree in Russian studies, he is currently the only Rutgers alumnus who is a winemaker. During the Vietnam War he served in the Air Force and was sent to intelligence school (his degree in Russian studies proved valuable after all); during this training he was introduced to computers and programming. After his service, his experience with computers led him to EDS and friend Earl Brockelsby. Later the two reconnected in New Jersey. Arthur's wife was from Santa Barbara and, tired of the East Coast winters, was ready to move back home when the opportunity presented itself. At that point, Arthur and Earl decided to get into the wine business in California. Their first winery, then called Austin Cellars, was started in 1981 by Tony Austin, the former winemaker at Firestone. Austin was also an associate of the famous André Tchelistcheff, who early in the '70s had already identified Santa Barbara as a region capable of producing excellent wines. In 1992 Austin sold the winery to White and Brockelsby, who renamed it Los Olivos Vintners in 1994. When it became a success, they obtained a second bond and in 1996 established the Arthur Earl Winery. In an effort to make the Los Olivos line more identifiable to the consumer, in 2005 they changed the name to Alexander and Wayne, using their middle names.

The emphasis at Alexander and Wayne is on French and California iterations of Chardonnay, Sauvignon Blanc, Cabernet Sauvignon, Merlot, and Pinot Noir, for example. Arthur makes only as much wine as they can sell, and production is currently about 2,500 cases a year at each winery. Their business model is to sell the wines at true retail, affording the customer a fair value for the wines. This means that almost 98 percent of their wines are sold directly to the consumer; there is little or no distribution involved, with the exception of placing the wines in restaurants in the Santa Barbara area. Nor do Arthur and Earl place their wines in many shows or competitions: for them the consumer is the ultimate arbiter of the taste and quality of the wines they produce.

RECOMMENDED WINES: Arthur suggests the Mille Delices, a reserve blend of Cabernet Sauvignon and Cabernet Franc. The 2002 is opaque in the glass and black cherry in color. The nose is black cherries, raspberries, and chocolate, with some vanilla notes from the oak. This very nice blend is accessible now. Chocolate mocha returns on the fine finish. Drink now and over the next two to three years.

I suggest the excellent Pinot Noir. The 2001 is a reserve wine taken from Careaga Canyon vineyard in Santa Barbara County. The wine is a true burgundy color in the glass and admits light to the stem. The nose is red currants, red cherries, and raspberries, with a touch of earth and bacon below the fruit. The excellent fruit leads to a wonderful middle and a long and fruity finish. The wine exhibits elegance and is a pleasure to drink. It is ready now but will give at least another two to four years of peak drinking.

RATING: Two stars (reserve wines three stars)

Alma Rosa Winery & Vineyards

WINERY OWNERS: Richard and Thekla Sanford

WINEMAKER: Christian Roguenant

TASTING ROOM: Yes

DAYS/HOURS: Daily 11 A.M.–5 P.M.

ADDRESS: 7250 Santa Rosa Rd., Buellton, CA 93427; 805-688-9090; 805-688-9001 (fax); almarosawinery.com

WINES/GRAPE VARIETIES: Chardonnay, Pinot Noir

WINE CLUB: Yes

REGION: Santa Barbara County

Ampelos Cellars and Vineyard

WINERY OWNERS: Rebecca and Peter Work

WINEMAKER: Peter Work

TASTING ROOM: No

DAYS/HOURS: Tuesday–Saturday 10 A.M.– 3 P.M.

ADDRESS: Call for details; 805-736-9957; 805-456-0461 (fax); ampeloscellars.com

WINES/GRAPE VARIETIES: Grenache, Pinot Noir, Syrah, Viognier

WINE CLUB: Yes

REGION: Santa Rita Hills AVA

Andrew Murray Vineyards

WINERY OWNER: Murray family

WINEMAKER: Andrew Murray

TASTING ROOM: Yes

DAYS/HOURS: Daily 11 A.M.–5:30 P.M.

ADDRESS: 2901-A Grand Ave., Los Olivos, CA 93441; 805-693-9644; 805-686-9704 (fax); andrewmurrayvineyards.com

WINES/GRAPE VARIETIES: Enchanté (white blend), Espérance (red blend), Syrah, Viognier

WINE CLUB: Yes

TASTING ROOM AMENITIES: Merchandise

REGION: Santa Ynez Valley AVA

A little bit of serendipity can go a long way, and Andrew Murray admits that he got lucky. His parents, Jim and Fran, got Andrew interested in wines and started in the business. When he was sixteen, they took him along on a family vacation to Condrieu in France's Rhône region. Luckily, young Andy had taken French in grade school. In Condrieu they met Philippe Faury, one of the area's most influential producers of Viognier. He gave them a tour of the vineyard and the family winery and let them taste the new wine. Inspired by this firsthand introduction to wine culture, Andrew's parents came away with a new vision for the family business, then centered on their Mexican restaurants. Back in the States, they bought what is now the vineyard as a getaway property and met other vintners in the area, such as Bill Wathen of Foxen. Bill took on the job of laying out the vineyards on their property. Jim Clendenen of Au Bon Climat told them the history of Rhône vines and taught them about the grape varieties of that region. Bill and Jim convinced the Murrays that they had a wonderful location for Syrah and other Rhône varieties.

Good luck can also turn bad. It turns out that the Viognier cuttings the Murrays received in 1990 were mostly Syrah. Their Roasted Slope vineyard (côte-rôtie in French) still shows evidence of these early plantings, with Syrah intermingled with the newer Viognier plantings.

At nineteen, in 1992, Andrew went to Australia to work for Rob Brown. When they saw how young he was, the Aussies were tempted to put him right back on the plane. Instead they kept him on for a year, taught him to make wine, and gave him the gift of a trained palate. In the meantime, his parents were selling the grapes from the vineyards to Clendenen and Wathen. Ultimately, his dad sold the restaurants, and when Andy returned from Australia, he found that work had begun on a winery. After an initial start at Berkeley, Andy went to Davis and graduated in 1995 with work in fermentation science and viticulture. His wife graduated from Cal Poly, but his dad puts all those degrees in perspective when he states that he earned his doctorate by working in the vineyards day after day. The first vintage was in 1993, and by 1998 the wines were winning the accolades for which Andrew Murray wines are now famous.

RECOMMENDED WINES: Andy recommends the Espérance. The 2003 is a blend of Syrah, Grenache, and Mourvèdre. The wine is black and purple and almost opaque in the glass. The nose is blueberries, spice, vanilla, and baked blueberry pie. The wine fills the mouth, and the wonderful fruit carries over to a long and satisfying finish. This wine will easily last another five to seven years.

I found the Estate Viognier to be outstanding. The 2003 is light green in the glass with a superb nose of pears, honeysuckle, and peaches lying atop a cool layer of minerality. The nose smells sweet thanks to the ripeness of the fruit. The acidity and mineral balance is excellent, supporting the wonderful aromatics. Drinking superbly now, the wine should give another three to four years of pleasure. Philippe Faury and Rob Brown would be proud of both these efforts produced by their young charge.

RATING: Four stars (excellent to outstanding whites and reds)

Arthur Earl

WINERY OWNERS: Earl W. Brockelsby and
 Arthur A. White

WINEMAKER: Arthur A. White

TASTING ROOM: Yes

DAYS/HOURS: Daily 11 A.M.–6 P.M.

ADDRESS: 2921 Grand Ave., Los Olivos,
 CA 93441; 805-693-1771; 805-686-1690
 (fax); arthurearl.com

WINES/GRAPE VARIETIES: À Genoux
 (blend), Barbera, Cinsaut, Counoise,
 Grenache, Il Re (blend), Mourvèdre,
 Nebbiolo, Pinot Grigio, Syrah, Viognier,
 Zinfandel

WINE CLUB: Yes

TASTING ROOM AMENITIES: Merchandise

REGION: Santa Ynez Valley AVA

Earl W. Brockelsby and Arthur A. White are the driving forces behind the Arthur Earl Winery and what is now Alexander and Wayne (formerly Los Olivos Vintners). (In this profile I focus on Earl Brockelsby, and spend more time on Arthur A. White, the winemaker at both companies, in the profile on Alexander and Wayne.) They have developed both a business partnership and a friendship that has lasted for decades.

Earl began his education at Rollins College in Florida but put his studies on hold to work part-time for Eastern Airlines. After only one month in a full-time job in Houston, he moved to Atlanta, where he tested in the new field of computers. On the basis of his scores, he was sent to Miami to write programs for mainframe computers. After six or so years there, he moved back to California and worked at Electronic Data Systems Company in 1969, where he met Arthur White. From there he worked at a bank in New Jersey, but kept in touch with his friend. After Arthur moved back to California, the two started their partnership in the wine business.

The purpose at Arthur Earl is to focus on emerging varieties, particularly those from northern Italy and France's Rhône valley. At any point in time, Arthur and Earl offer the consumer at least eight to ten different wines, though they have produced up to twelve different varieties. With the exception of the Rhône blend, all grapes used at the winery are sourced from single vineyards.

RECOMMENDED WINES: Earl recommends the Nebbiolo, made from grapes sourced from the Stolpman vineyard in the Santa Ynez Valley. The 2002 is light to the stem and a pretty red cherry color in the glass. The nose is red cherries, cedar, sweet tobacco, and a hint of tea. The wine has good levels of fruit, but the tannins are currently dominant; as the wine ages and the tannins drop and resolve, the fine fruit in this wine will emerge. Buy now, but give it a year or two to evolve.

My recommendation is Il Re, a blend of Barbera and Nebbiolo grapes, renowned in Italy's Piedmont region. The 2001, from the Carrari vineyard in Santa Barbara County, is entirely opaque in the glass thanks to the Barbera, and black cherry in color. The nose is cherries, blackberries, plums, and vanilla spice. This is a well-blended and well-balanced wine of excellent mouthfeel. It is ready for drinking now but will give another three to four years of drinking pleasure.

RATING: One star (competently made whites and reds offer good value)

Artiste

WINERY OWNER: Bion Rice and partners

WINEMAKER: Bion Rice

TASTING ROOM: Yes

DAYS/HOURS: Daily 11 A.M.–5 P.M.

ADDRESS: 3569 Sagunto St. Studio 102, Santa Ynez, CA 93460; 805-686-2626; 805-686-2625 (fax); artiste.com

WINES/GRAPE VARIETIES: Nonvintage blended wines

WINE CLUB: Yes

TASTING ROOM AMENITIES: Fine art, art merchandise, packaged food

REGION: Santa Ynez Valley AVA

Artists can take an idea of the mind and creatively express that vision through some external medium such as wood, or dance, or color. Winemakers can elevate their craft to high art in the same sense, though the medium of their expression is the grape. The lucky ones simply take the bountiful fruits of nature, nurture them, gently guide them to artistic expression, and are done. Others face the challenge of blending, where different lots and different varieties serve as the paints on their winemaking palette. Most great French wines are in fact the result of artistic blending. Bion Rice of Artiste chose this path.

Bion, whose family runs Sunstone Vineyards and Winery, saw an opportunity to merge art and wine, as both share a basis in subjectivity and provide participatory opportunities. Bion is intrigued by the different blending styles that have come to represent different regions of the world. Although rules and regulations determine the percentages and the grape varieties depending on the country of origin, the artistry remains in the hands and the palate of the individual blender. The blend is the result of a creative process, and this is Bion's passion. Artiste is also his attempt to make wines that pay homage to old-world appellations while using new-world grapes. Accordingly, he buys the best grapes that he can get for his blends.

Bion is a great admirer of the Impressionists because they were, in their day, the rebels of the art world. He sees himself as an Impressionist, blending wines that become impressions of the great wine styles of the world. He tries first to capture the essence of the grape, and second, through the artistic blending process, to discover the best expression of those grapes as they form a synergy of taste, color, and smell. For that reason, his artistically styled labels do not include the names of the grapes on the front, though you can find them on the back. In order not to influence conceptions of taste, the prices are also listed on the back.

Artiste is a co-venture with his wife and three business partners. The tasting room is set in a gallery that combines their two loves, art and wine. Children can come and paint while the parents taste.

RECOMMENDED WINES: Bion recommends La Malagueña, representative of a Spanish blend. The blend is Tempranillo, Grenache, and some Mourvèdre. It is opaque in the glass and shows the dark purple and black color one expects of a Tempranillo. The nose is cigars, cherries, plums, and blackberries. At present, the wine shows its tannin ahead of the excellent fruit, but over time, as the tannin curtain drops, the fruit will emerge and provide excellent drinking. Buy this one for the cellar and pull it out in two years. It should be fine for another three or four years after that.

I recommend the Canal Follies, Bion's impression of a Châteauneuf-du-Pape, a blend of Grenache, Syrah, Viognier, and a touch of Mourvèdre. The wine is almost opaque in the glass, the color of red cherry with hints of purple. The nose is red currants, raspberries, some spice, and pepper, with an intriguing underlay of smoke and grilled sausages. This is a beautifully balanced wine of fine structure, excellent fruit, and wonderful aromatics. It is ready for drinking now but will reward another two to four years in the bottle.

RATING: Three stars (very good to excellent wines)

Au Bon Climat

WINERY OWNER: Jim Clendenen

WINEMAKERS: Jim Clendenen

TASTING ROOM: At Tastes of the Valleys

DAYS/HOURS: Thursday–Monday 10 A.M.–
  4 P.M.

ADDRESS: Tastes of the Valleys, 1672 Mission
  Dr., Solvang, CA 93463; 805-688-7111;
  805-937-2539 (fax); aubonclimat.com

WINES/GRAPE VARIETIES: Barbera,
  Chardonnay, Pinot Blanc, Pinot Noir, and
  blends

WINE CLUB: Yes

REGION: Santa Ynez Valley AVA

One of the things that I truly appreciate about my European heritage is the sense of place at the table with family. It is still a tradition in German *Gasthäuser* to reserve a *Stammtisch* ("tribal table") for the regulars of the house. Don't sit there, even if it's empty. Some of my fondest memories involve a house full of relatives—uncles and aunts, cousins and nephews—all gathered around the table enjoying good food and good wine. I visited Jim Clendenen at Au Bon Climat and was impressed when he invited me to sit with him and his crew for their noon meal. It sparked those early memories of the importance of people coming together to share food, wine, and conversation. For me, that is the essence of wine culture.

Jim started his journey to wine culture at the relatively young age of twenty-one. A student at UC Santa Barbara, he traveled to France during his junior year abroad in 1974. He enjoyed travel so much that he dropped out of school and lived with his girlfriend in France. He loved to cook even then, and his passion pulled him more deeply into the culture of wine. In a sense, his discovery of Bordeaux provided the direction his life needed. At one point he moved to Spain, then Monaco, living on five bucks a day when you could still do that in Europe and survive. He finished his studies in 1976, graduating with high honors in prelaw, but in 1977 was back on the road, spending more time abroad. He went to Champagne, then Burgundy, and along the way realized that he needed to be self-employed for his personal happiness. His goal was to come home and establish himself. Instead of going on to law school, he took a trip to explore Zaire, and then started in the wine business at Zaca Mesa Winery after returning home.

In 1980, after three years at Zaca Mesa, where he worked as assistant winemaker, Jim, with the help of friend Adam Tolmach, a UC Davis graduate, started to build Au Bon Climat (loosely translated from the French, it means "from a good region") on the Burgundian model. They were interested in producing great Chardonnay and Pinot Noir. One of his fellow employees at Zaca Mesa had been none other than Bob Lindquist of Qupé fame, who worked as a tour guide in the tasting room (Ken Brown was the winemaker at the time). Bob would later join with Jim to form CLV, a holding company for their business interests. The winery, bonded in 1982, sits amid the world-famous Bien Nacido vineyard, owned by the Miller family.

For Jim, the key to good wine is properly farming the ground where the grapes are planted and allowing them to maximize their potential while on the vine. He likes the idea of hierarchical greatness: great vineyards, great ideas, great wines. He and Adam were always great winemakers—there is critical consensus on that point—but now Jim has the great grapes from Bien Nacido. In the early years, they had to use the same grapes most others got, and made wines by intervention and addition. Now the winemaking process is one mostly of reduction that enables finesse, elegance, and greatness to emerge. In this sense, Jim sees Au Bon Climat enjoying a second renaissance of sorts (in 1990, Adam Tolmach departed to pursue other interests in wine). As recently as 2001, *Food & Wine* magazine gave Jim the Winemaker of the Year award.

RECOMMENDED WINES: I had the privilege of doing flighted tastings of both the Chardonnay and the Pinot Noir with Jim. He sees himself primarily as a winemaker of Burgundian influence who has branched out into other varieties. Jim's recommended Pinot Noir is the 2002 vintage, La Bauge Au-dessus. This wine is opaque to the stem, black cherry in color with a touch of purple. The nose is redolent of blackberries, cherry, and spice, with a hint of anise. The tannins are still huge, but the fruit is there ready to emerge. The wine is wonderful in the mouth, and the finish lasted more than a minute. The wine is ready for drinking now, but that would be a shame. In five years it will be sensational.

My pick is the 2003 Chardonnay, grapes from the Clendenen Family Vineyards, tasted in the barrel. The wine was yellow and gold in the tasting glass with a nose of lemons, apples, pears, and tangerines, and a wonderful underlying minerality. The wine carries enough acidity to balance the fruit and the judicious use of oak. I believe this wine has the potential to surpass the great 2001. It should be sensational drinking for the next four years.

RATING: Four stars (excellent to outstanding whites and reds)

Babcock Winery & Vineyards

WINERY OWNERS: Babcock family

WINEMAKER: Bryan Babcock

TASTING ROOM: Yes

DAYS/HOURS: Daily 10:30 A.M.–4 P.M.

ADDRESS: 5175 E. Hwy. 246, Lompoc, CA 93436; 805-736-1455; 805-736-3886 (fax); babcockwinery.com

WINES/GRAPE VARIETIES: Cabernet Franc, Cabernet Sauvignon, Chardonnay, Fathom (Bordeaux blend), Pinot Gris, Pinot Noir, rosé, Sauvignon Blanc, Syrah

WINE CLUB: Yes

TASTING ROOM AMENITIES: Merchandise

REGION: Santa Rita Hills AVA

While studying philosophy on his own after his days as an undergraduate at Occidental College in Los Angeles, Bryan Babcock contemplated returning to school to get an MBA that would somehow link business to ethics. Instead, he wound up at UC Davis working on a master's degree in enology. Sometimes life gets in the way of philosophy and purely educational pursuits, and thanks to his growing obligations at his family's vineyard he was unable to finish the master's. However, after twenty years in the school of hard knocks, Bryan is finally at a point where he feels appropriately educated; or, as he says, "blissfully beat-up."

Bryan's parents, Walter and Mona, bought the current property in 1979 when he was still a sophomore at Occidental College, where he studied biology with a chemistry minor. His father grew up around farming; his grandfather owned a hardware store in Nebraska. When the store burned down the family moved to Southern California. Bryan's father established himself as a dentist in the Long Beach area but never forgot the family's roots in agriculture as he sought a way out of the hustle of metropolitan life. Some twenty years before the creation of the Santa Rita Hills AVA, the Babcocks bought 100 acres near Lompoc. After spending some time with Boyd Bettencourt, a renowned local grower and vintner already established in the interior of the Santa Ynez Valley, Bryan's dad planted the property to grapes, joining Pierre Lafond and Richard Sanford as a winegrowing pioneer in the area. Bettencourt suggested white varieties for the cooler climate, as Riesling and Chenin Blanc grapes were then popular in the Santa Ynez Valley. Of course, the whims of the market changed and

Chardonnay became the popular white wine at the table, so the Babcocks converted the fields, pulled up the Chenin Blanc vines, and replanted to Chardonnay. Then the root louse phylloxera hit and forced the Babcocks to replant again on phylloxera-resistant rootstock. They used the opportunity to add Pinot Noir plantings, a prescient move. By 1994 their Pinot was receiving critical accolades and others jumped on the bandwagon. The mid-1990s thus saw an explosion of interest in Pinot Noir in an area where the conventional wisdom had it that Burgundian grape varieties could not be grown. Bryan found himself converted through "coercion by a bug."

The Santa Rita Hills appellation, which the Babcocks helped define, is an exciting area for the Pinot Noir grape, and this dovetails very nicely with Bryan's passion for what he does. He allows the fundamentals of the *terroir* to shape his vision. But is Bryan done with his study of philosophy? Absolutely not. As he proceeds in life and in wine, he constantly checks his premises, seeing winemaking as a long chain of events that results in wine in the bottle. In this sense, the links are like logical premises: all the links in the chain must be examined or the final product can fail. As Bryan says, "If you are an Aristotelian like me, causality becomes a very important tool."

RECOMMENDED WINES: A great success and a testament to Bryan's abilities as a thinker and winemaker is his recommended wine, the Grand Cuvée Pinot Noir. This is a purple- and red-colored wine, opaque in the glass. The nose has hints of chocolate, black cherry, boysenberry, sweet cigar box, and sizzling bacon. The tannins are supple, supporting the fruit. In the mouth the chocolate is followed by the stone fruit and leads to a finish of almost a minute. This is an excellent example of Pinot Noir and will hold beautifully for another five to seven years, given the ripe, silky tannins in the wine.

I suggest the Grand Cuvée Chardonnay. The 2002 is a lovely gold in the glass with aromatics that remind me of pears, pineapples, and lime, as well as rich buttery flavors from the oak. The excellent acidity provides a tart crispness in the mouth. Vinified from 100 percent estate-grown grapes, this wine is ready for drinking now and over the next two to four years.

RATING: Three stars (four stars for the Grand Cuvée line)

Barnwood

WINERY OWNER: Selim Zilkha

WINEMAKER: Eric Hickey

TASTING ROOM: At Laetitia Winery (see chapter 7)

DAYS/HOURS: Daily 11 A.M.–5 P.M.

ADDRESS: 453 Laetitia Vineyard Dr., Arroyo Grande, CA 93420; 805-481-1772; 805-481-6920 (fax); barnwoodwine.com

WINES/GRAPE VARIETIES: Barnwood Trio (red blend), Cabernet Sauvignon, Grenache, Malbec, Petite Sirah, port, Sauvignon Blanc, Tempranillo

WINE CLUB: Yes

TASTING ROOM AMENITIES: Picnic area, merchandise

REGION: Santa Barbara County

Beckmen Vineyards

WINERY OWNER: Tom Beckmen

WINEMAKER: Steve Beckmen

TASTING ROOM: Yes

DAYS/HOURS: Daily 11 A.M.–5 P.M. (winter Friday–Sunday only)

ADDRESS: 2670 Ontiveros Rd., Los Olivos, CA 93441; 805-688-8664; 805-688-9983 (fax); beckmenvineyards.com

WINES/GRAPE VARIETIES: Cabernet Sauvignon, Grenache, Grenache rosé, Marsanne, Mourvèdre, Roussanne, Sauvignon Blanc, Syrah

WINE CLUB: Yes

TASTING ROOM AMENITIES: Merchandise

REGION: Santa Ynez Valley AVA

The theme of the prodigal son returned home has played out more than once in these profiles, but Steve Beckmen exemplifies the tale. A native of Santa Monica, Steve went north to college and spent a year and a half at Lewis and Clark College before he decided that he wanted the excitement of a larger school. He returned home to California and UCLA. This time the pendulum swung a bit too far, and after two terms as a Bruin he transferred to UC Santa Cruz, where he finished a degree in anthropology and archaeology. His education led him to an archaeological dig in Hawaii, a nice place to do some spade and trowel work. He enjoyed that experience so much that he returned for an additional three months of work on another dig in Maui. After graduation in 1990 he set out for Jackson Hole, Wyoming, but returned to California after one winter. Wyoming will do that to a man used to Hawaiian weather. He next hooked up with a survey company working in the badlands region near Palm Springs. After finding one arrowhead and a lot of angry rattlesnakes, he went back to Jackson Hole, this time to ski and figure out what to do with his life.

When Steve returned home, his father, Tom, offered him an opportunity that changed his life and kept him home. Tom Beckmen had been born to cattle ranching, but when he left the ranch for college, he noticed that the music industry was becoming more and more electronic after the invention of the synthesizer. He founded Roland Corporation and was one of the early pioneers who merged computers with music making. In 1993, after a long and successful career, he looked for other challenges. He sold Roland and undertook extensive research into the potential of the Santa Ynez Valley for growing grapes. He found a 40-acre parcel that already had an established winery (dating to 1982), bought it, and restored it. When Steve came home from his wanderings, Tom offered him the job of overseeing the new operation and, eventually, making the wines. This freed Tom to pursue his first and abiding love, farming. Shortly thereafter, now thoroughly convinced of the area's potential for growing outstanding wine grapes, Steve's parents purchased an additional 365-acre parcel, which became the now-famous Purisima Mountain vineyard, and planted it to Rhône varieties. To learn his new trade, Steve put his degree in archaeology to work digging in the vineyard and then made a pilgrimage to Europe to study winemaking. He met renowned Italian producer Paolo de Marchi in Tuscany, who taught him his trade secrets for outstanding viticulture. Once in the vineyards back home, Steve worked with respected Santa Barbara viticulturist Jeff Newton as he honed his craft. In 1996 Steve and Tom produced their first vintage, and they have never looked back.

RECOMMENDED WINES: Steve recommends the flagship Syrah, known as Clone 1. We tasted the 2002, an opaque wine of black and purple in the glass. The nose is redolent of ripe blackberries, black licorice, black plums, and a hint of smoke. The wine is outstanding in the mouth and is beautifully integrated. This is a seamless wine of rich fruit, a great middle, and a long finish. It is already drinking wonderfully, but it will be even more sensational over the next five to nine years.

My recommendation is the Estate Syrah. The 2001 is more transparent than the Clone 1 but showed nearly the same black cherry and purple colors in the glass. The nose is cherries, ripe blueberries, blackberries, and black currants, earthy tannins, and a hint of truffles. Again, this wine is outstanding in the mouth with excellent integration of all its elements, and shows silky-smooth tannins in the finish. It is superb now but will improve over the next five to seven years. If you love great Syrahs, these two are worth the effort to find.

RATING: Four stars (reds slightly ahead of whites)

Bedford Thompson Winery & Vineyard

WINERY OWNER: Stephan Bedford

WINEMAKER: Stephan Bedford

TASTING ROOM: Yes

DAYS/HOURS: Daily 11 A.M.–5 P.M.

ADDRESS: 448 Bell St., Los Alamos, CA 93440; 805-344-2107; 805-344-2047 (fax); bedfordthompsonwinery.com

WINES/GRAPE VARIETIES: Cabernet Franc, Chardonnay, Gewürztraminer, Grenache, Mourvèdre, Petite Sirah, Pinot Gris, Syrah

WINE CLUB: Yes

TASTING ROOM AMENITIES: Picnic area, merchandise

REGION: Santa Barbara County, Los Alamos area

One of the pleasures of scholarly work is the opportunity to examine, hold, and read old and rare texts. Holding a book is a sensory experience much like drinking wine, and old books, if properly cared for, have a unique smell, weight, and feel. Stephan Bedford shares the same appreciation for books when he noses through classic wine texts. His knowledge of the history of the Santa Barbara wine region is extraordinary, and I came away from our interview with a much better understanding of the county's importance in the Central Coast wine story. This is in part because Stephan is counted among the old hands of the Santa Barbara County wine industry.

His introduction to the wine business began in 1975 when a mutual friend introduced him to Dr. Stanley Hoffman and his family in Paso Robles, where Stephan was visiting on holiday. In 1977 he graduated from UCLA with a degree in life science and began work at Ridge Vineyards in Santa Cruz. There he saw fruit brought in from the famous Tepusquet vineyard and remembers the outstanding Cabernet Franc made from that fruit. It changed his winemaking style. After a stint at Felton-Empire as enologist, he became winemaker at Mount Eden Vineyards in 1982. In 1984 he started as winemaker for Rancho Sisquoc, near Tepusquet vineyard. He stayed with Sisquoc until 1996, working as a consultant to many of the other famous wineries in the region, among them Foley Estates and Lincourt, where he served as winemaker and general manager for two years, bringing both wineries to prominence.

Stephan branched off in 1994, teaming with David Thompson to establish a winery and vineyard. He wanted to do his own thing and control the viticultural practices and selection of the clones planted in the vineyard. In the late 1960s and early 1970s, Stephan acknowledges, not all the winegrowers of the region were doing the best job possible. But by the 1990s growing practices had changed, as a scarcity of grapes resulted when the corporate wineries came south to Santa Barbara County and prices again began to escalate. This gave Stephan and other growers the opportunity to introduce and properly farm varieties best suited to the conditions of the soil and climate. Stephan took the time to travel to Europe, where he learned how the Europeans matched their grapes to their growing conditions and modified their viticultural practices accordingly. The first harvest from David Thompson's vineyard, located in Los Alamos, was in 1994 and featured a Syrah that became the signature wine. By 1997, Stephan's work at Foley and Lincourt concluded, he focused full-time on his partnership with David. In 2003 Stephan became the sole proprietor.

Stephan now knows the soils of his place and has the right grapes in the right places, grown using the right techniques, resulting in the best flavors possible from the grapes. The Thompson vineyard is now planted primarily to Syrah, Chardonnay, and Cabernet Franc, though other varieties are being added as the vineyard expands. A true student and scholar of winemaking, he continues to seek out old books on old-world winemaking in an effort to return to practices that have stood the test of time.

RECOMMENDED WINES: Stephan recommends the Cabernet Franc. The 2000 is opaque in the glass and a deep black cherry color. The nose is blueberries, blackberries, and vanilla spice. The wine has a wonderful mouthfeel and shows a lovely balance among fruit, acidity, and tannin. There is a lush elegance that carries over into the long and satisfying finish. Ready now, the wine should last another three to four years.

I suggest the Petite Sirah. The 2001 is inky black in the glass and opaque to light. The aromatics consist of plums, allspice, blackberries, and an intriguing hint of cloves. The wine lives in the mouth and shows wonderful integration of all its elements. The finish is more than a minute, making this an altogether excellent wine. Drink now and over the next three to five years. If white wines are more your style, do try the excellent Pinot Gris.

RATING: Three stars (reds ahead of whites)

Bernat Vineyards & Winery

WINERY OWNER: Sam Marmorstein

WINEMAKER: Sam Marmorstein

TASTING ROOM: Yes

DAYS/HOURS: Daily 11:30 A.M.–5 P.M.

ADDRESS: Los Olivos Café & Wine Merchant, 2879 Grand Ave., Los Olivos, CA 93441; 805-688-7265; 805-688-5953 (fax); losolivoscafe.com

WINES/GRAPE VARIETIES: Chardonnay, Syrah

WINE CLUB: Yes

TASTING ROOM AMENITIES: Restaurant

REGION: Santa Ynez Valley AVA

If Los Olivos is on your wine-tasting tour, or if you are traveling through on a cycling excursion, do take the time to stop in at the Los Olivos Café, one of the town's most charming restaurants. You'll see there other similarly dressed and like-minded travelers, much to the satisfaction of the proprietor, himself an avid rider. The establishment is owned by Sam Marmorstein (pronounced "-steen"), also the owner of Bernat. Sam grew up in the Bronx and had a typical early experience with wine as a teenager: drinks of Pink Chablis sneaked out of a paper bag. His good friend Andy came from an Italian family who played poker in the basement, where Andy's father made wine. Sam remembers that it was cool to have a friend who made wine, however horrible the taste.

After finishing his degree in accounting at Lehman College in the Bronx, Sam came out to California. He began his working career as an accountant before becoming a stockbroker. A friend at the firm where he worked wanted to make wine, so they bought some Chardonnay and Pinot Noir grapes and vinified them at home. Sam's conception of what wine can be was radically and forever changed. As his career flourished, he purchased and tasted some of the great wines of the world. Making wine that tasted good got him to thinking not only about wine but also about the lifestyle that surrounds winemaking. In 1995 he decided it was time to get out of Los Angeles.

That year he purchased 10 acres in Los Olivos and planted them to Chardonnay and Syrah grapes. Passionate about bicycling, he had cycled through the Santa Ynez Valley on numerous occasions and discovered that little town. About the same time, he saw the former Almendinger's Deli was for sale and bought that too with the expectation of creating a local restaurant featuring local wines and California cuisine with a Mediterranean flair. In 2001 retail space adjoining the restaurant became available, and Sam expanded his operation to start the Los Olivos Wine Merchant. Sam's wife, Shawnda, manages three little ones at home but also helps with label design and marketing of the Bernat line. Bernat is the name of Sam's father, born in Transylvania, of Romanian and Hungarian heritage.

At this point, Sam is interested in planting other varieties to augment his Chardonnay and Syrah. His winemaking approach is to make distinctive, pure wines that reflect the quality of the vineyard and its *terroir*. There is an owlery on the property (hence the owl on the label), and the resident owls help manage the gopher population. Sam has seen as many as five owls at a time working to protect the property. The first wines produced under the Bernat label were harvested in 1999.

RECOMMENDED WINES: Sam recommends the Syrah. We tasted the 2001, an opaque wine of red and purple colors in the glass. The nose shows elements of leather, earth, black cherries, black currants, plums, and a touch of cocoa. The wine is excellent in the mouth and shows lovely ripe, rounded tannins. The aromatics are excellent, the fruit is plentiful and accessible now thanks to the ripe tannins, and I expect that this wine will be drinking even better in three to five years. This release bodes well for the vineyard, the farming practices therein, and the skill of the winemaker.

I suggest the Chardonnay. The 2002, based on a Wente clone, is green and gold in the glass with lovely aromatics that are reminiscent of lemon zest and cream. The wine has a fortifying minerality that supports the fruit. This is a lovely, fruity Chardonnay with enough oak to give complexity and structure. It is huge in the mouth, with a crisp, refreshing finish from the excellent acidity profile. I expect that this wine will drink beautifully for another three to four years.

RATING: Three stars (both wines very good to excellent)

Blackjack Ranch Vineyards & Winery

WINERY OWNER: Roger Wisted

WINEMAKERS: Roger Wisted and Christian Roguenant

TASTING ROOM: Yes

DAYS/HOURS: Thursday–Monday 11 A.M.–5 P.M.

ADDRESS: 2205 Alamo Pintado Rd., Solvang, CA 93463; 805-686-4492; call for fax; blackjackranch.com

WINES/GRAPE VARIETIES: Allusion (blend), Chardonnay, Harmonie (blend), Merlot, Pinot Noir, Syrah

WINE CLUB: Yes

TASTING ROOM AMENITIES: Picnic area, merchandise

REGION: Santa Ynez Valley AVA

Cable television has contributed to the recent proliferation and popularity of televised poker tournaments, and "going all in" has emerged as a metaphor for commitment. Roger Wisted, owner of Blackjack Ranch, knows firsthand what it means to go all in. He began his working life at age fourteen in the produce department of his family's supermarket in Chicago. At that time, he was already studying the wines and winemaking styles of France and California, even as he fermented his first fruit wines at home. At age seventeen he bought his first bottle of the legendary Château d'Yquem (one of my favorite French Sauternes). He stayed with his interest in wine and by age twenty-one had a flourishing wine cellar. He also knew that the logical extension of his passionate hobby was to own a winery. University took him to Illinois Wesleyan, where he earned a degree in business. The fierce Chicago winters, however, blew him to Las Vegas, where he loved to play blackjack. That love, like his passion for wine, eventually turned into a lucrative business interest.

In 1873 the legislature of the state of California enacted section 330 of the penal code, which outlawed the playing of 21, also known as blackjack, because of all the professional gamblers coming into the San Francisco area intent on liberating the miners from their bags of nuggets and gold dust. The statute is still in effect, although Native American casinos are permitted to play 21 under the federal Indian Gaming Regulatory Act. This leaves the more than 235 legal card rooms and casinos not owned by American Indians unable to play 21. Roger, while in Los Angeles in 1989, saw an opportunity in the strict prohibition of the law: he invented, patented, copyrighted, and trademarked a casino card game called California Blackjack. He recodified the game so that two aces constituted a "natural," and this transformed the game into 22, a game with no restrictions under California gambling law. The L.A. County Sheriff's Department approved the game for play in Los Angeles, and the game was licensed to legal card rooms and casinos across the state. It generated hundreds of jobs for casinos and more than $4 million in revenues annually for the municipalities where the game is played. Roger became a very wealthy fellow—an object lesson that it is better to have the intellectual wherewithal to invent a game of chance than actually to play it.

He took his lucrative rewards and spent three years searching for land on which to build a winery and plant a vineyard. In 1995 he found the Blackjack Ranch property, and, as they say, the rest is history, one to which wine critic Robert M. Parker Jr. made a substantial contribution with his favorable reviews of Wisted's wines. In fact, Parker was the first visitor to the Blackjack Ranch tasting room and awarded Roger's first two wines, a red and a white, scores of 90 points. Parker considers the winery to be one of the best run in the Santa Barbara area, and Blackjack Ranch is one of only two wineries outside Napa-Sonoma to receive Parker's coveted five-star rating for the production of Bordeaux varieties. Those early years of reading about, studying, buying, and tasting Bordeaux wines have reaped dividends indeed. The cowinemaker with Roger is Christian Roguenant, of Baileyana and Maison Deutz fame.

RECOMMENDED WINES: Roger recommends the Harmonie Proprietary Red, a blend of 85 percent Cabernet Sauvignon and 15 percent Merlot. I was able to taste this wine in flights going back to 2000, and it is getting better every year. The 2003 is opaque to the stem, of purple and black colors in the glass. The nose is black cherries, black currants, cedar, cassis, and a touch of bay leaf in the soft vanilla-spice bouquet. This is a complex but elegant blend that displays wonderful ripe fruit, a gorgeous middle, and a finish that lies on the tongue for well over a minute. This is a testament to the quality of the wines produced at Blackjack. It has the potential to age at least another ten to fourteen years.

Tongue in cheek, I will take a gamble and recommend the Blackjack Vineyard Reserve Chardonnay. The 2003 shows green and gold in the glass and gives up a heady bouquet of honeysuckle, a medley of tropical fruits, Golden Delicious apples, and butter. The wine is wonderful in the mouth, has an excellent balance of acidity and minerals, and has a long and satisfying finish that lasts nearly a minute. Ready for drinking now, the wine will age beautifully over the next three to five years. I can definitely see Christian Roguenant's influence in this wine.

RATING: Five stars (both reds and whites outstanding to superb)

Brander Vineyard

WINERY OWNER: Fred Brander

WINEMAKER: Fred Brander

TASTING ROOM: Yes

DAYS/HOURS: Daily 10 A.M.–5 P.M. (winter 11 A.M.–4 P.M.)

ADDRESS: 2401 Refugio Rd., Los Olivos, CA 93441; 805-688-2455; 805-688-8010 (fax); brander.com

WINES/GRAPE VARIETIES: Bouchet (blend), Cabernet Sauvignon, Merlot, Sauvignon Blanc, Sauvignon Blanc blends

WINE CLUB: Yes

TASTING ROOM AMENITIES: Picnic area, merchandise

REGION: Santa Ynez Valley AVA

Erik and Virginia Brander bought the property where their vineyards are now established in 1974, making the Brander vineyard one of the oldest in Santa Ynez Valley. Son C. Frederic (Fred) Brander, winemaker and owner of the winery, is the product of two cultures. Erik Brander's father, Fritz, was once the Swedish ambassador to Argentina. Fred was born in Buenos Aires but moved with his family back to the United States and Santa Barbara in 1962. He became acquainted with the Sauvignon Blanc grape in the Graves region of Bordeaux and the Mendoza region of western Argentina, that country's largest and most important winegrowing province. A graduate of Harvey Mudd College, where he took a degree in chemistry, he furthered his studies in enology at UC Davis. During his university studies in Claremont, he opened a business importing French and Argentine wines to the United States. His family's acquisition of the land on which the vineyard is planted allowed him to realize his dream of owning a winery and making his own wines. Over the course of the past thirty years or so, his Sauvignon Blanc wines have gained the reputation of being among the best on the Central Coast, if not all of California.

Domaine Santa Barbara is Brander's label featuring both Burgundian wines and Rhône-style Syrahs. Brander is the winemaker, and the wines are also available in the beautiful château-style tasting room at Brander Vineyard.

RECOMMENDED WINES: Fred makes at least four or five Sauvignon Blancs per vintage, and if you are a fan of the grape, as am I, the nuances and differences he achieves in each of his iterations make for a wonderful tasting experience. Fred's recommendation is the Sauvignon Blanc au Naturel, a wine made in the Loire style from free-run juice. This is an estate-grown 100 percent Sauvignon Blanc that does not see oak. The 2002 is a light green and gold in the glass. The wine presents aromas of grapefruit, gooseberries, pineapple, kiwifruit, sweet lime zest, melon rind, and a hint of grass. The wine presents its excellent fruit to the palate, and a wonderful minerality pervades it. My personal preference is for a touch more acidity; nevertheless, this is an unctuous and complex wine that is a favorite of the wine writers year after year. The consumer who shares my taste for a slightly more acidic wine should try the 2004 made from Beckmen's Purisima Mountain vineyard grapes.

I recommend the Cabernet Sauvignon Reserve. The 2001 has a touch of Merlot and is a black and purple color in the glass and opaque to light. In the nose I found red cherries, red currants, violets, and crème brûlée. The wine is superb in the mouth and has enough ripe tannins to merit a long, healthy life in the bottle. The finish is wonderful and although this wine is drinking splendidly now, it will age another five to ten years.

RATING: Four stars (both reds and whites excellent to outstanding)

Brewer-Clifton

WINERY OWNERS: Greg Brewer and Steve Clifton

WINEMAKERS: Greg Brewer and Steve Clifton

TASTING ROOM: No

ADDRESS: 329 North F Street, Lompoc, CA 93436; 805-735-9184; 805-735-9185 (fax); brewerclifton.com

WINES/GRAPE VARIETIES: Chardonnay, Pinot Noir

WINE CLUB: Mailing list

REGION: Santa Rita Hills AVA

Bridlewood Estate Winery

WINERY OWNER: E. & J. Gallo Winery

WINEMAKER: David Hopkins

TASTING ROOM: Yes

DAYS/HOURS: Daily 10 A.M.–5 P.M.

ADDRESS: 3555 Roblar Ave., Santa Ynez, CA 93460; 805-688-9000; 805-688-2443 (fax); bridlewoodwinery.com

WINES/GRAPE VARIETIES: Arabesque (a blend of seven Rhône grapes), Grenache, rosé, Roussanne, Syrah, Tannat, Viognier

WINE CLUB: Yes

TASTING ROOM AMENITIES: Picnic area, merchandise

REGION: Santa Ynez Valley AVA

When you drive up to Bridlewood you notice immediately that it was at one time a fairly substantial equestrian facility done in impressive Mission-style architecture. In 1998 the facilities were renovated and a winery established on the 80-acre property. The winemaker is David Hopkins, hired in 2001 from Kendall-Jackson.

At the time of his hire, the winery was experiencing financial difficulties, and David had the foresight to ask for a five-year contract. A short time later, Matt Gallo bought the winery sight unseen with the guarantee that David would stay on as winemaker—a good indicator of David's reputation within the industry. He started at Kendall-Jackson's Lakeport facility as cellar master and eventually rose through the ranks to become winemaker. He was in charge of producing the top-line Chardonnay every year at K-J.

A Vietnam veteran originally from Apple Valley, where he began his training with an associate degree in science that reflected his love of chemistry, David transferred to Fresno State and first took a degree in plant science with a minor in botany and chemistry. A former lab partner introduced him to the student winery on campus, where he tasted wines from student projects and realized his calling in life. He greatly enjoyed working with his professors as he explored flavor chemistry, learning to blend chemical analysis and artistry in the process of winemaking. Though ready to graduate, he asked the department chair to allow him to change majors and received permission to do so—one sign of a good department. That department chair became his friend and mentor.

After graduation in 1985, he worked at Paul Masson as a lab technician and after two weeks became lab director. When the cellar supervisor died in a shooting accident on-site, David stepped into that position, albeit with some trepidation. It seems that some shooters using a fully automatic M-16 were firing at targets near the facility, and when the cellar supervisor, in the process of weighing trucks, stood up, he was hit and killed by an errant round.

There followed a short stint in Temecula making Petite Sirah before David returned to the Central Valley for two years as an assistant brandy master. David next went to work at De Loach Vineyards when Cecil De Loach was just starting to produce Zinfandel. After working at Kendall-Jackson he was hired at Bridlewood, and continued with assurances from Matt Gallo that he would have the opportunity to be an artisan winemaker, producing the best-quality wines possible with the purpose of establishing Bridlewood as a premier Rhône-style winery. Over time he has established his style for understated elegance, using old-world winemaking techniques to highlight the lovely fruit flavors manifest in high-quality Central Coast grapes. His style is readily apparent in the wines featured below.

RECOMMENDED WINES: David suggests the Estate Reserve Syrah. The 2002 is a purple-red wine opaque in the glass. The nose shows blackberry fruit, licorice, cedar and vanilla, leather and smoke, with a hint of chocolate powder. The tannins in this wine are huge and need a bit of time yet to resolve and allow the fruit to come forward. Buy it now, lay it down, and your patience will be rewarded.

For more immediate drinking, I recommend the Reserve Syrah, cofermented with 5 percent Viognier. The 2003 shows the same purple-red colors in the glass and is opaque to light. Here the dominant notes are blueberries, purple plums, chocolate, and a hint of violets. The wine lies beautifully in the mouth and the tannins permit the ripe, luscious fruit to come forward. This wine is accessible now but will age beautifully for another three to six years.

RATING: One → two stars (David Hopkins is raising overall quality across the line)

Brophy Clark Cellars

WINERY OWNERS: John and Kelley Clark

WINEMAKER: John Clark

TASTING ROOM: Yes

DAYS/HOURS: By appointment only

ADDRESS: Call for details; 805-929-4830;
805-929-8301 (fax); brophyclarkcellars.com

WINES/GRAPE VARIETIES: Pinot Noir,
Sauvignon Blanc, Syrah, Zinfandel

WINE CLUB: Yes

REGION: Santa Ynez Valley AVA

John Clark met Kelley Brophy while both were in college in San Diego. She comes from a ranching family in Arizona; he from La Jolla, California. After earning their degrees at UC San Diego, both went to Fresno State for master's degrees, his in enology and hers in agricultural science. After his graduation in 1985 and hers in 1986, they moved from Fresno knowing that Corbett Canyon Vineyards had a facility on the Central Coast. They visited the winery across from Kynsi, and John received permission to start as a cellar rat. She got a job working in the lab. From 1986 to 1988 she was Dale Hampton's viticulture technician during the time he managed upwards of 5,000 acres of grape plantings.

Corbett Canyon became very successful, pushing about 2 million cases of wine a year out the door. When Corbett Canyon sold, the new owners asked John to stay on as winemaker and manager. In 1996, as the wine industry was in good shape at the time, they started Brophy Clark with the purpose of making premium Pinot Noir. In 1998 the Miller brothers, whom they knew from their work with the Bien Nacido vineyard, opened their Central Coast Wine Services in Santa Maria, and initially John and Kelley made their wines there. John helped Steve and Bob Miller build the business. Among other duties, he served there as winemaker and general manager in 1998 and 1999, then spent a year as winemaker and redoing the vineyards at Laetitia. In February 2000, the Wine Group (Corbett Canyon Vineyards) invited him to return as vice president of premium wines, overseeing winemaking. Part of his deal involved permission to continue the Brophy Clark line and move its winemaking production from the shared facilities at Wine Services to Corbett Canyon. Brophy Clark now produces about 2,500 cases; he makes the wine and she does the rest. They hand-sell everything through brokers and distributors. The two handle the entire operation.

John's approach is to take the best grapes Kelley can buy and let the fruit express itself. They use only Central Coast grapes and are very excited about the potential for

Sauvignon Blanc and Pinot Noir. Syrah is also a mainstay of their line. Price is an important factor: they want to make wines their friends and professors at state universities can afford, which I certainly appreciate. They are not interested in making wines to appease wine writers' tastes or to achieve numerical ratings. As an interesting aside, Kelley has her own consulting business, Coastal Vineyard Consulting, and in this capacity has helped plant most of the vineyards in the Santa Rita Hills, the AVA quickly becoming famous as a premier Pinot Noir area on the Central Coast. Kelley's mother is a watercolor artist, and the labels are from her paintings; the originals hang in Kelley's house.

RECOMMENDED WINES: Kelley recommends the Pinot Noir. The 2001 is black cherry–colored and opaque in the glass. The nose is cherries, smoke, stone, and boysenberries. The wine is lovely in the mouth and shows a fine balance between the acidity and the tannins. The wonderful fruit leads to a lush middle and a silky finish thanks to the soft, rounded tannins. The wine is ready for drinking now and over the next three to four years.

I was impressed with the Sauvignon Blanc. The 2002 is pale green in the glass and has a nose of vanilla, straw, lemons, orange zest, melons, lychee nuts, and honey. The acidity is just right, and the wine is a distinct pleasure in the mouth. The finish approaches a full minute and brings you back for another whiff of the superb aromatics. This is a fine Sauvignon Blanc from the Louis Lucas vineyards.

RATING: Two stars (very good wines and very good values)

Brucher Winery

WINERY OWNER: Peter Brucher

WINEMAKER: Peter Brucher

TASTING ROOM: No

DAYS/HOURS: By appointment only

ADDRESS: 2115 S. Blosser Rd., #118, Santa
  Maria, CA 93458; 805-347-8720;
  805-347-8782 (fax); brucherwinery.com

WINES/GRAPE VARIETIES: Cabernet
  Sauvignon, Chardonnay, Pinot Noir

WINE CLUB: Yes

REGION: Santa Maria Valley AVA

A good friend who is an excellent attorney once asked me, "What do they call a hundred lawyers at the bottom of the ocean?" I had no idea. "A good start," he said, laughing. Peter Brucher, like Barbara Banke at Cambria Winery and a few other vintners on the Central Coast, is also a lawyer, but he's one I would jump out of the boat to rescue. Pete went to UC Berkeley, graduated from law school in 1962, and began work as a practicing attorney. Shortly thereafter, he managed to straighten his life out and in 1972 began to buy vineyard properties in Napa. He started Vichon Winery and Vineyard in Napa's Oakville area, got through his first crush in 1980, and by 1985 garnered such an excellent reputation for the winery that Robert Mondavi bought it from him. By contract agreement with Mondavi, he stayed on as landlord until 1989 but eventually needed to find other business challenges, so he moved on after taking that enterprise to prominence.

This amicable parting of the ways allowed him to start looking for other proper-ties, and he headed south. When he moved to the Central Coast in 1992, he was as-tounded at the similarities between the wine industry there and that of St. Helena in the early 1970s. He had spent part of Christmas 1989 in Cambria after he sold Vichon, and got to know the Central Coast in his pursuit of new vineyard properties. He thought, given the excellent growing conditions in Edna Valley, the area would take off faster than Paso Robles, but he admits he was wrong in this prediction. Then Santa Barbara hit it big with Chardonnay and Pinot Noir, especially in the Santa Rita Hills, but he is convinced that Edna Valley will get the next big pop, and I believe he is cor-rect in this assessment. In the early '90s when the Central Coast Wine Services facil-ity in Santa Maria was starting, he rented space for his production in what was once a Columbia Records manufacturing plant. In fact, Pete's first office there was formerly a listening booth. He has since moved down the street.

Former wife Gayle's paintings are on some Brucher wine labels. Interestingly, some of his distributors said they didn't like the labels, but Pete keeps them—not for the ob-vious reason, but because so many of his customers appreciate the art.

RECOMMENDED WINES: Although he does use consultants when technical problems emerge from time to time, Pete is proud of the fact that he *designs* his wines. His goal is to produce wines of style and grace. Accordingly, he recommends his award-winning Pinot Noir. The Santa Maria Valley Pinot Noir of 2000 is a bright cherry red and light to the stem of the glass. The nose is reminiscent of ripe cherries baked in a pie crust, red currants, and cranberries. Befitting a true Burgundy-style Pinot Noir, there is an undertone of grilled meat. The tannins are round and soft, giving the wine an additional element of elegance. Beautifully balanced, the wine is drink-ing fine now and will reward another two to four years in the bottle.

The Arroyo Grande Chardonnay is my recommendation, with prodding from my partner, Nancy Clark. The 2001 is a light gold with a nose of sweet butterscotch, Bartlett pears, mango, and lychee nuts. The wine is rich in the mouth and wonderfully balanced between the acidity and the fruit. The finish is nearly a minute long, and the wine will age gracefully for another three to four years.

RATING: Three stars (both reds and whites very good to excellent)

Buttonwood Farm Winery & Vineyard

WINERY OWNERS: Betty Williams and Bret Davenport

WINEMAKER: Michael Brown

TASTING ROOM: Yes

DAYS/HOURS: Daily 11 A.M.–5 P.M.

ADDRESS: 1500 Alamo Pintado Rd., Solvang, CA 93463; 805-688-3032; 805-688-6168 (fax); buttonwoodwinery.com

WINES/GRAPE VARIETIES: Cabernet Franc, Cabernet Sauvignon, Devin (blend), Marsanne, Merlot, Sauvignon Blanc, Syrah, Syrah rosé, Trevin (blend)

WINE CLUB: Yes

TASTING ROOM AMENITIES: Picnic area, merchandise

REGION: Santa Ynez Valley AVA

One of the trees native to Santa Barbara County is the buttonwood, a variety of sycamore with brown ball-like seed clusters (buttons) on long stems. They remind me of cheap earrings. Some buttonwood trees live 600 years. Buttonwood Farm consists of 106 acres, of which 39 are planted to grapes. Betty Williams and son-in-law Bret Davenport began the plantation in 1983. The winery was built on the property in 1989 and the winemaker is Michael Brown, whom I profile under his Kalyra Winery. When Betty Williams, a New Orleans native, bought the property in 1968, she had every intention of starting a horse ranch. But Michael Benedict, of Sanford and Benedict vineyard fame, convinced her that she had an outstanding vineyard site. (The two later partnered to start the Santa Barbara Land Trust.) She asked Bret to help lay out and plant the new vineyard.

A graduate of Sarah Lawrence College and always something of a trailblazing rebel, Betty, with the encouragement of her father, joined the business world in southern Louisiana, establishing interests in sugar and cypress plantations. At one point she ran away to be married and wound up in Pasadena, California. She went back to school, got a law degree, raised three children (one of whom married Bret), and wrote a book of poetry.

Bret, like so many others in the wine industry, did not get his start in wine. He characterizes himself as a "car guy" who ended up in the wine business. Along the way, he graduated with a degree in theater arts from San Francisco State University. After working for a time in a theater commune, Bret put his degree to work as a part-time janitor, as he says tongue-in-cheek. Of course, that kind of training is invaluable when it comes to working at a winery. When Betty called for his help to start the vineyard, he was ready. Over the past five or six years Bret has guided the expansion of the winery from an initial case production of 562 to more than 5,000 a year. Winemaker Mike Brown came aboard in 1989, hired after an interesting initial test. Three winemakers were offered Sauvignon Blanc grapes with the promise that they could keep half of what they produced, Buttonwood retaining the other half. Brown's efforts initially did not taste the best, but surpassed the others over time.

RECOMMENDED WINES: The emphasis at Buttonwood is on producing elegant wines ready for drinking. Not interested in fruit bombs or highly tannic wines, Betty and Bret prefer to offer the consumer wines that are accessible now. Accordingly, Bret recommends the Sauvignon Blanc. We tasted the 2002, which has a touch of Sémillon added in the French fashion. The wine shows a lemon and lime color to the light in the glass. The nose is grapefruit, lemon, lychee nut, and orange peel, with a hint of grassiness. The wine has not seen oak, enabling the fruitiness to come forward and showcase the lovely aromatics. It is ready for drinking now.

I suggest the 2002 Marsanne, a grape variety that probably originated in the northern Rhône and is often a blending partner with Roussanne. In France, if the wine is too low in acidity, it can tend to flabbiness. There is none of that in the muscular Buttonwood. The wine showed lemon and gold colors in the glass. The aromatics are butter from the oak, lime, kiwifruit, and a minerality that contributes to the structure of the wine. The acidity levels are fine, leaving a balanced wine that lies nicely in the mouth. This fine Marsanne will give an additional three to four years of drinking pleasure.

RATING: One star (competently made wines; whites ahead of reds)

Cambria Winery

WINERY OWNER: Barbara Banke

WINEMAKER: Denise Shurtleff

TASTING ROOM: Yes

DAYS/HOURS: Daily 10 A.M.–5 P.M.

ADDRESS: 5475 Chardonnay Ln., Santa
Maria, CA 93454; 888-339-9463;
805-937-8091; 805-934-3589 (fax);
cambriawines.com

WINES/GRAPE VARIETIES: Chardonnay,
Chenin Blanc, late-harvest Viognier,
Pinot Gris, Pinot Noir, Sangiovese, Syrah,
Viognier

WINE CLUB: Yes

TASTING ROOM AMENITIES: Picnic area,
merchandise, food items

REGION: Santa Maria Valley AVA

The vintners profiled in this book are certainly a diverse group, united by their passion for wine. Not all went to Davis or Fresno State or even Cal Poly for wine and viticulture studies; many have degrees in disparate fields, and this is the case with Barbara Banke. Educated as an attorney after graduating from UCLA in 1975, Barbara received her law degree from UC Hastings College of the Law at Berkeley and specialized in land-use and constitutional law. In addition to maintaining her private practice, Barbara argued a number of landmark cases in the United States and other courts of appeal. In 1986 she and husband Jess Jackson bought the famous Tepusquet vineyard. Cambria Winery now sits on more than 1,400 acres of property that includes the Tepusquet land planted in 1970 by the renowned Louis Lucas, now at Lucas & Lewellen, and his partners. In 2002 Barbara announced the appointment of Denise Shurtleff as winemaker.

Denise is a California native and graduate of Cal Poly's dietetics program. In 1983 she started at Corbett Canyon as a lab technician and worked her way up to enologist and, eventually, winemaker. After sixteen years at Corbett Canyon, Cambria winemaker Fred Holloway asked Denise to join him there. With Fred at her side, she worked on award-winning Chardonnays and Pinot Noirs. The vineyards at Cambria, named Katherine and Julia after Barbara's daughters, are capable of producing high-quality grapes. In addition, at Cambria Denise has both the facilities and the scale to maintain excellence across the extensive vineyards. Her goal is to showcase the quality of the grapes grown on the estate and accentuate the inherent quality of the fruit, but not overshadow the wines with too much technical intervention.

RECOMMENDED WINES: Denise recommends the Bench Break Pinot Noir, a blend of Swiss clones selected for the Cambria vineyards. We tasted the 2000, a nearly opaque black cherry–colored wine. The lovely sweet fruit showed itself in the blueberry, blackberry, and black cherry nose. A layer of sweet vanilla cream supports the ripe fruit. Well balanced, the wine is drinking beautifully now but will reward another two to three years in the bottle.

I suggest the Rae's (Barbara's middle name) Pinot Noir, produced from a single Swiss clone. This wine is nearly opaque in the glass and a bright red cherry color reminiscent of a true Burgundy. The nose does not have quite the effulgent qualities of the Bench Break Pinot Noir, but the 2000 shows sweet plum, cherries, and sweet vanilla spice, in addition to an intriguing hint of mint and cinnamon. The wine is silky-smooth in the mouth and has a long, lingering finish.

It's ready for drinking now, but another two to three years in the bottle will reward the patient consumer.

RATING: Three stars (very good to excellent whites and reds across the line)

Carhartt Vineyard & Winery

WINERY OWNERS: Mike and Brooke
  Carhartt

WINEMAKERS: Mike and Brooke Carhartt

TASTING ROOM: Yes

DAYS/HOURS: Wednesday–Sunday 11 A.M.–
  5 P.M.

ADDRESS: 2990 Grand Ave., Los Olivos,
  CA 93441; 805-693-5100; 805-688-3004
  (fax); carharttvineyard.com

WINES/GRAPE VARIETIES: Merlot, rosé,
  Sauvignon Blanc, Syrah

WINE CLUB: Online store

TASTING ROOM AMENITIES: Some
  merchandise

REGION: Santa Ynez Valley AVA

Farming is hard work and requires clothing designed to stand up to the rigors of the job. One of the more famous brands is Carhartt, and students who proudly wear the clothes associated with farm living are called Carhartts. Mike Carhartt, a second-generation farmer, grew up on the 1,500-acre ranch bought by his father in the 1950s. The place was originally a dairy farm founded in the 1920s. In the '60s, Mike helped his father convert the barn to a house. Over the years, the property served as a working cattle ranch, and by age thirteen Mike was custom hay farming. At twenty, Mike moved off the ranch, worked in the agriculture assurance business for a time, helped with vineyard plantations, and became friends with Bill Wathen at Foxen. When Mike's father died in 1990, Mike bought the ranch and took six years redoing the property. In 1996, convinced that it was time to get out of the cattle business, he planted some of the acreage to Syrah and Merlot, intending to sell the grapes to Wathen. In 1998 Mike and Brooke bottled their inaugural vintage.

Brooke does the chemistry and the enology for Carhartt, while Mike takes care of the viticulture. Brooke grew up on a sailboat and fondly remembers sailing trips to Catalina and Mexico. She considers herself a water person and was sailing before she could walk. A graduate of Cal State Los Angeles, she had applied for Ph.D. studies when water met soil and she became a Carhartt. Together, team Carhartt practices sustainable organic farming and has a passion for transforming the best of what the soil gives them into the best wine in the bottle. Brooke, given her academic training, is intrigued by both the science and the art of winemaking. Mike, given his years as an agriculturist, knows what it takes to produce the best possible grapes for their wines. Their combined passions and love for the land give them the lifestyle they now enjoy. Currently producing about 600 cases, production will be ramped up at Carhartt to about 1,000 in the near future.

RECOMMENDED WINES: Brooke and Mike suggest the Syrah. The 2002 is opaque in the glass and shows purple and red colors to the light. The nose is leather, spice, blackberries, figs, and smoke.

The wine is beautifully balanced and shows fine structure. The fruit is lovely, and the finish shows finesse. Accessible now, the wine will give another three to six years of drinking pleasure.

I suggest the Merlot. The 2003, tasted in the barrel, will be a huge wine. It is opaque to the stem and black-purple in color. The nose is cherries, vanilla, cassis, black currants, and leather. Already lovely in the mouth, the wine shows excellent balance among fruit, acidity, and tannins. The finish lasts fully a minute. I expect that this powerful Merlot, given its structure and balance, will easily give ten years of fine drinking.

RATING: Three stars (2003 wines will merit four stars)

Carina Cellars

WINERY OWNER: David Hardee and Joey Tensley

WINEMAKER: Joey Tensley

TASTING ROOM: Yes

DAYS/HOURS: Daily 11 A.M.–5 P.M.

ADDRESS: 2900 Grand Ave., Ste. A, Los Olivos, CA 93441; 805-688-2459; 805-688-0795 (fax); carinacellars.com

WINES/GRAPE VARIETIES: 7 Percent (blend), Cabernet Sauvignon, Iconoclast (blend), Syrah, Viognier

WINE CLUB: Yes

TASTING ROOM AMENITIES: Picnic area, merchandise

REGION: Santa Ynez Valley AVA

General systems theory, the work of biologist Ludwig von Bertalanffy, suggests that the whole is often greater than the sum of its parts. For instance, if you laid all the parts that go into the making of a car on the floor, you would not have a car. Only when those parts are assembled into the system—that is, the whole that becomes the vehicle—do you actually have a car. Carina, too, is the result of a collaboration in which the whole is greater than the sum of its parts. Joey Tensley is the winemaker and co-owner of Carina Cellars, and I spend time with him and his wife, Jennifer, in the profile of Tensley Wines. In fact, when you finish tasting at Carina, turn around, walk across the room, and start tasting at Tensley.

David Hardee, originally from North Carolina, is a retired tax attorney and local businessman. An avid student and collector of fine wines, his dream was to own a winery one day. In 2002 he met Joey, an experienced and well-respected young winemaker in the area, and the two realized that the synergy of their combined interests could far exceed their individual interests. A partnership was born, Carina Cellars was named, David had his winery, and Joey had the security a young man with a young family needed, even as he was trying to establish a name for himself.

At Carina, the emphasis is on Rhône-style wines using the best-quality fruit produced in Santa Barbara County. Joey has distinct ideas about growing grapes and chooses to work only with growers and farmers who share those ideas. For example, he is concerned with proper canopy management, keeping the vines naturally healthy, and keeping yields low. These practices result in rich, flavorful wines true to their varietal characteristics. Joey learned his craft while working for Eli Parker at Fess Parker

Winery as a cellar rat. He moved on to Babcock, where he was mentored by friend Bryan Babcock. There he rose to assistant winemaker. After a stint as assistant winemaker at Beckmen, where he discovered his passion for Syrah, Joey started his eponymous label. His wines for both labels have now achieved high critical success among the nation's best wine writers. Carina Cellars currently produces about 2,000 cases per year, specializing in Syrah and Viognier.

RECOMMENDED WINES: Joey recommends the 7 Percent Syrah. The wine is 93 percent Syrah from the Colson Canyon Vineyards, and the remaining 7 percent is Sanford and Benedict Viognier. It is not uncommon in the Côte-Rôtie region of France's Rhône valley to add a touch of Viognier to the Syrah; this gives the nose a bit more flower and perfume. Even with the addition of the white wine, this Syrah is red and purple in the glass and opaque to light. The lovely nose is boysenberry, red cherries, strawberries, vanilla, and violets. The wine has a wonderful texture thanks to the ripe, supple tannins. The finish approaches a full minute, and this is a fine example of what Joey can do with the Syrah grape. Drink now and over the next seven to eight years.

I suggest the Viognier from the Stolpman vineyard. The 2003 is a green-gold that shines in the glass. This wine shows a touch more oak than the lovely 2002, but it is well integrated with the pears, honey, lemon peel, and guava. The wine has just the right amount of acidity and a fine minerality that lends structure to the fruit. Elegant and lush in the mouth, it has a long, satisfying finish. This is an excellent Viognier and has potential to get even better over the next four to five years.

RATING: Three stars (whites ahead of reds)

Casa Cassara Winery & Vineyard

WINERY OWNERS: Bennie Cassara and Sons

WINEMAKER: John Krska

TASTING ROOM: Yes

DAYS/HOURS: Daily 10 A.M.–5 P.M.

ADDRESS: The Olive House, 1661 Mission Dr., Solvang, CA 93463; 805-686-8691; 805-693-1121 (fax); casacassarawinery.com

WINES/GRAPE VARIETIES: Chardonnay, Pinot Noir, Sauvignon Blanc, Syrah

WINE CLUB: Yes

REGION: Santa Rita Hills AVA

Cellar 205

WINERY OWNERS: Christian Garvin, John Bargiel, and Ryan Carr

WINEMAKERS: Christian Garvin, John Bargiel, and Ryan Carr

TASTING ROOM: Yes

DAYS/HOURS: Daily 11 A.M.–5 P.M.

ADDRESS: 205 Anacapa St., Santa Barbara, CA 93101; 805-962-5857; 805-435-1446 (fax); cellar205.com

WINES/GRAPE VARIETIES: Each winemaker has a label. Oceana label (Garvin): Pinot Noir, sparkling wine, Syrah; Bargiel label: Grenache Noir, Syrah; Carr label: Pinot Grigio, Pinot Noir, Sauvignon Blanc, Syrah

WINE CLUB: Yes

TASTING ROOM AMENITIES: Gourmet shop, merchandise

REGION: Santa Barbara County

Clos Pepe Vineyards

WINERY OWNER: Steve Pepe

WINEMAKER: Wes Hagen

TASTING ROOM: No

DAYS/HOURS: By appointment only

ADDRESS: 4777 Hwy. 246, Lompoc, CA 93436; 805-735-2196; 805-736-5907 (fax); clospepe.com

WINES/GRAPE VARIETIES: Chardonnay, Pinot Noir

WINE CLUB: Allocation and mailing list

REGION: Santa Rita Hills AVA

In 1994 Wes Hagen was teaching at the local community college in Ely, Minnesota. Four or five winters in the Great North Woods are enough to wear down anyone, and by 1998 he was teaching in the more climatically friendly town of Lompoc. In 1994 Steve Pepe, a lawyer and home winemaker, purchased the property for Clos Pepe. Nearing retirement, Steve and his family had been looking for land but found Napa and Sonoma too expensive; Temecula was a possibility but didn't seem right at the time. He ran into Jeff Newton, a well-respected viticulturist, and asked him to come to Santa Ynez Valley. In the early '90s the two found a promising property, but Melville stepped in and bought it. At La Purísima, llama farmers outbid them. When a horse ranch along Highway 246 became available they put in a bid, and it was accepted. The original intent was to use the property merely for growing high-quality Chardonnay and Pinot Noir grapes, and then offer those grapes to good producers. Over time, this practice established the reputation of the vineyard. In fact, data indicate that over the past couple of years, wines produced by the Clos Pepe (pronounced "kloh peppy") vineyard have achieved some of the highest average scores from the *Wine Spectator*.

Once Steve's stepson Wes Hagen had arrived from Minnesota and thawed out sufficiently, he took over the management of the vineyard and planted Pinot Noir vines in 1998. Eventually, the focus shifted to producing their own wines under the Clos Pepe label, and they currently produce about a thousand cases a year. The emphasis at the vineyard and winery is on making great wine using sustainable organic agriculture. They do everything possible to let the diversity in the soil come through to the wine on the table. Yields are deliberately kept low, resulting in elegant wines of intensity and concentration. Much of the work done in the vineyard requires intensive hand-farming. The passion and care taken in the making of Clos Pepe wines extends to the way Steve compensates employees. Workers there receive a salary, health benefits, and vacation and sick leave; they are even paid when it rains, an unusual practice among wineries.

RECOMMENDED WINES: Wes recommends the Estate Pinot Noir. The 2003 is opaque to light and a pretty red and purple color in the glass. The nose is blackberries, blueberries, earth and spice, cassis and a hint of truffles. The wine shows a wonderful balance of acidity and tannin, is seamlessly structured, and has a ripe, fruity elegance in the mouth. Altogether, this is an excellent example of Pinot Noir from an excellent vineyard.

I recommend the Estate Chardonnay. In an homage to the Chablis region in France, the wine is made in small 55-gallon stainless steel "casks" and allowed to age *sur lie* ("on the lees," a practice said to enhance the flavor). The wine is light gold in the glass and has a nose of lemon zest, ki-wifruit, sea spray, and pineapple. The excellent acidity and the underlying minerality carry the fruit. The wine has a creamy and elegant feel in the mouth and is ready for drinking now and over the next three years.

RATING: Three → four stars (both whites and reds excellent to outstanding)

Cold Heaven

WINERY OWNER: Morgan Clendenen

WINEMAKER: Morgan Clendenen

TASTING ROOM: Yes

DAYS/HOURS: Thursday–Monday 11 A.M.–
5 P.M.

ADDRESS: 448-B Bell St., Los Alamos, CA
93440; 805-344-5030; 805-344-3640 (fax);
coldheavencellars.com

WINES/GRAPE VARIETIES: Pinot Noir,
Viognier

WINE CLUB: Yes

REGION: Santa Barbara County

Consilience Wines

WINERY OWNERS: Thomas and Jodie
Daughters, Brett and Monica Escalera

WINEMAKER: Brett Escalera

TASTING ROOM: Yes

DAYS/HOURS: Daily 11 A.M.–5 P.M.

ADDRESS: 2933 Grand Ave., Los Olivos, CA
93441; 805-691-1020; 805-691-1018 (fax);
consiliencewines.com

WINES/GRAPE VARIETIES: Cabernet Sauvignon, Grenache, Grenache Blanc, Roussanne, Petite Sirah, Pinot Noir, Syrah,
Viognier, Zinfandel, Zinfandel port

WINE CLUB: Yes

TASTING ROOM AMENITIES: Merchandise

REGION: Santa Ynez Valley AVA

I first encountered the word *consilience* during my studies in the philosophy of sci-ence. If two inductions from dissimilar phenomena concur or are in agreement, they are said to be consilient. *Consilience* as defined by Harvard University biolo-gist E. O. Wilson is the "unity of knowledge." It is a beautiful word and aptly and creatively describes the winery founded in 1997 by Brett and Monica Escalera and their partners, Tom and Jodie Daughters. They see winemaking as both an art and a science, and the consilience of these two perspectives serves as the inspiration for their wines.

Tom, a radiologist, studied medicine at the University of Minnesota. Jodie is from Circle Pines, Minnesota, about 15 miles north of the Twin Cities. The two met in Min-nesota and moved to California to allow Tom to complete his medical residency at Santa Barbara Cottage Hospital. There Tom met an emergency-room nurse from San Diego named Monica. Monica was dating a paramedic, Brett, who was pursuing a ca-reer in the wine industry. The four, in an act of consilience, formed a lasting friendship based on their trips together through the wine fields. Sharing a dream of making wine together, they formed a business partnership in 1997. In 1998 the first bottles of Consilience appeared, and the group sold their first case to a friend. They were now officially in the wine business.

Brett is a formally educated and trained winemaker and received an early introduction to wine. In the Escalera household, wine was part of everyday living, and young Brett developed his tastes at the family table. When both your grandfathers are home winemakers, chances are fair that at some point in your life you will make wine. He started his university training at Chico State, where he took an introductory course in winemaking. One of his favorite subjects there was an advanced course on the sensory evaluation of wines. After a weeklong trip into different California wine regions, students were required to do presentations on any aspect of the wine industry. As a result the content of the course was different each time, and Brett loved it so much he took it six semesters in a row!

After graduation from CSU Chico, Brett returned to the Santa Barbara area and became a real-estate appraiser. Although he was rather successful, he never gave up his interest in the wine industry. A chance encounter with a former Chico classmate, previously an assistant winemaker at Santa Barbara Winery, led to a harvest position and seasonal work at the winery. After several years of seasonal work, he decided to forgo a career in real estate in order to pursue a graduate education in winemaking. He took prerequisite science courses at Santa Barbara City College and worked as a paramedic to support his education. The paramedic company where he worked sent Brett to Fresno. In the spring of 1992, he saw that Fresno State had a vineyard and money to build a winemaking facility. He applied to and was accepted into the master's program, where he earned a degree in agricultural chemistry. After graduation in 1996 he worked as the enologist at Byron Winery in Santa Maria Valley. Fess Parker offered him a job as production manager after the harvest of 1996. The Parker family graciously offered Brett and his partners the opportunity to crush fruit and launch the Consilience brand in 1997. Prior to the 1999 harvest he was named the winemaker and in 2004 was promoted to director of winemaking and vineyard operations at Fess Parker Winery. In 2005 he briefly served as director of winemaking for Central Coast Wine Services in Santa Maria but returned to the Fess Parker organization that summer as the head winemaker for the Parker Station line of wines. The Consilience lineup of wines, primarily Rhône varieties from Santa Barbara County, is currently produced at the Fess Parker Santa Barbara County Wine Center in Santa Maria.

Brett, Monica, Tom, and Jodie strive to produce wines that are unpretentious and enjoyable. They emphasize the importance of making great wines that are also great values.

RECOMMENDED WINES: Brett recommends the Santa Barbara County Syrah. The 2002 has a splash of Zinfandel and Petite Sirah. The wine is purple-black and opaque to light. The nose is smoke, blackberries, forest floor, mocha, and a touch of blueberry from the Zinfandel. The tannins are ripe and silky, lending the wine a wonderful mouthfeel. This is a refined and elegant Syrah, rather than huge and muscular. It is accessible now thanks to the lovely tannic balance but will age nicely for the next three to five years.

All the Syrahs I tasted at Consilience were excellent, but the Star Lane stood out. The 2001 is again an opaque black-purple wine with a sweet nose of blackberries, cherries, wood smoke, and black currants. The body of the wine is tremendous in the mouth, the finish lasts more than a minute, and the fruit is superb. By any measure, this will be an outstanding Syrah as the elements finish their integration over the next year or two. It should then hold another ten years. The Petite Sirah is also one of the best I've encountered on the Central Coast.

RATING: Four stars (excellent to outstanding across the line)

Costa De Oro Winery

WINERY OWNERS: Burk and Espinola families

WINEMAKER: Gary Burk

TASTING ROOM: Yes

DAYS/HOURS: Daily 11 A.M.–6 P.M.

ADDRESS: 1331 S. Nicholson Ave., Santa Maria, CA 93454; 805-922-1468; 805-925-0980 (fax); cdowinery.com

WINES/GRAPE VARIETIES: Chardonnay, Pinot Noir

WINE CLUB: Yes

TASTING ROOM AMENITIES: Merchandise, gourmet foods

REGION: Santa Maria Valley AVA

Gary Burk is a winemaker and musician, playing blues guitar in his own band when not in the vineyards or making wine. For years the Burk and Espinola families farmed in the Santa Maria Valley, where they met grape grower and pioneer viticulturist Dale Hampton. They received both tutelage and cuttings from Dale's vineyards to get a start in the grape-growing business. Costa De Oro now has a vineyard planted to Chardonnay and Pinot Noir grapes.

Gary is a 1986 graduate of Cal Poly with a degree in business. After graduation, he moved to Los Angeles in 1987 and put his degree and love for music to work at Capitol Records. After a time he left the corporate world to pursue music and songwriting, playing gigs in clubs whenever possible. After he met Dick Doré and Bill Wathen of Foxen Canyon, he became interested in selling grapes. In 1993 his sister married a local chef, and Gary put a band together for the wedding. Jim Clendenen, an extraordinary winemaker and fine cook in his own right, jumped at the chance to jam with the band and sing, and a musical friendship was born. Gary established a relationship with Jim's winery, Au Bon Climat, and Jim bought fruit from the Costa De Oro vineyards in 1993. Gary remembers that he worked the harvest at Au Bon Climat in 1994 and afterward Clendenen offered him a full-time job as a cellar rat. Eight years later, Gary left as sales manager.

Gary learned to make wine under the tutelage of such great winemakers as Clendenen and Bob Lindquist of Qupé, both of whom were named to the list of fifty most influential winemakers by *Wine & Spirits* magazine in fall 2004. The first vintage for Costa De Oro was in 1995 and consisted of one barrel of Chardonnay and one barrel of Pinot Noir. In 1998, after making a barrel of wine here and there, Gary hit the mark with his Pinot Noir. In 2002 he came to Central Coast Wine Services in Santa Maria, and he now has five full vintages under the Costa De Oro label. In 2006 Costa De Oro opened a tasting room on the property where the Burk family used to have their produce stand on the outskirts of Santa Maria.

If you get a chance to hear Gary play onstage, please know that he often donates his time, music, and proceeds from his concerts to children's charities.

RECOMMENDED WINES: The Oro Rojo Pinot Noir is Gary's recommendation. We tasted the outstanding 2002. This is a black cherry–colored wine opaque in the glass. Bacon and plums are in the nose above scents of earth, rose, sandalwood, and a touch of pomegranate. The flavors are ripe, the wine is luscious, and the finish lasts more than a minute. This is a wonderful Santa Maria Valley Pinot Noir and will be even better in five years.

I suggest the Chardonnay. The 2001 Reserva Dorada is a bright gold with butterscotch, caramel, pears, pineapple, and lemon in the nose. This is a beautifully balanced wine with the fruit, acidity, and mineral backbone all in harmony. Lively and lush on the palate, the native yeasts used in fermentation give the wine an additional dimension of creamy texture in the mouth. This altogether excellent Chardonnay will give at least five years of drinking pleasure.

RATING: Four stars (both reds and whites excellent to outstanding)

Cottonwood Canyon Vineyard & Winery

WINERY OWNER: Norman Beko

WINEMAKER: Norman Beko

TASTING ROOM: Yes

DAYS/HOURS: Daily 10 A.M.–5:30 P.M.

ADDRESS: 3940 Dominion Rd., Santa Maria, CA 93454; 805-937-8463; 805-937-8418 (fax); cottonwoodcanyon .com

WINES/GRAPE VARIETIES: Cabernet Franc, Cabernet Sauvignon, Chardonnay, Merlot, Pinot Noir, Synergy Classic (blend), Synthesis (blend), Zinfandel

WINE CLUB: Yes

TASTING ROOM AMENITIES: Wine cave tours, picnic area

REGION: Santa Maria Valley AVA

Norman Beko has had two careers, as have many other vintners profiled in this book. Sometimes, however, the best course of action is to forgo one and pursue the other, as Norm has done. He started as an accountant, hated it, and switched to computer graphics. He was very successful in sales and thought he was wealthy until he got into the wine business. Hailing from Ohio, the Beko family wound up in Orange County and invested in land. With his background in sales, he saw that the wine industry was behind the curve in terms of financial arrangements, customer service, and most of all distribution. Norm saw an opportunity and took advantage of it when a distributor he knew went under. He took over the company and made the transition into the wine industry. He developed a business plan and in the process learned just how arcane and byzantine are the rules for wine distribution in the United States. Unable to fight the state and federal bureaucracies, he got out of distribution and bought the vineyard at Cottonwood in 1988. He immediately made money again, and by 1989 the wineries to which he sold his grapes were winning "top fifty wines" awards.

At the time Norm bought the winery, the vineyard was already 15 years old and planted to 46 acres of Chardonnay grapes. The vineyard at Cottonwood Canyon has the distinction of being one of the first in the region planted in north-south-oriented rows, permitting excellent sun exposure mitigated by cooling afternoon breezes off the nearby Pacific. The 7,000-foot-high San Rafael Mountains to the east trap morning and evening fog, also moderating the heat of the day. These conditions allow the vineyard to achieve physiologically ripe fruit while maintaining the natural acidity crucial for balance and aging.

Norm is now emphasizing Pinot Noir with his recent vintages, taking grapes from as many as six different blocks, with Dijon clones making up the vast majority of the program. He produces small lots of purchased grapes for the other reds. He offers three Chardonnay styles: Bistro, Estate, and Barrel Select.

Given the excellent soils and the climate in which Norm grows the grapes, he is interested in producing long-lived wines. He knows that most of the customers who buy his wines have wine cellars. Although he considers Cottonwood to be a family business—even his grandchildren work at the winery with their grandpa—Norm makes the wines and handles, you guessed it, the distribution.

RECOMMENDED WINES: Norm emphasizes that his wines are designed to complement food at the table. For example, Norm loves his Chardonnay with tomato-based dishes and sauces in addition to spicy foods. Accordingly, he recommends the Estate Chardonnay. The 2000 was aged ten months in the barrel and shows a pale gold color to the light. The nose is evocative of lime, vanilla from the oak, apples, cinnamon, and caramel. The mid-palate is lush and rounded, complementing the wonderful aromatics. The finish is crisp, clean, and tart, and holds on for nearly a minute. The wine is ready for enjoyment now but will give another five years of drinking pleasure.

I suggest the SC Chardonnay: the 2000 received twelve hours of skin contact, contributing to its deep lemon and gold color. Lemon strikes the nose first, followed by buttery toast, pears, and pineapple. The wine is enormous in the mouth, lush and creamy on the tongue. The beautiful balance of fruit, minerality, and acidity will add another five to six years of life to the wine. My colleague and wine aficionado Jim Conway says that Cottonwood Canyon Chardonnays are his favorite.

RATING: Three stars (very good to excellent across the line; four stars white wines)

Curran

WINERY OWNER: Kris Curran

WINEMAKER: Kris Curran

TASTING ROOM: No

ADDRESS: 4457 Santa Rosa Road, Lompoc, CA 93436; 805-588-0152; 805-736-5761 (fax); curranwines.com

WINES/GRAPE VARIETIES: Grenache Blanc, Sangiovese, Syrah

WINE CLUB: Mailing list

REGION: Santa Ynez Valley AVA

Curtis Winery

WINERY OWNER: Firestone family

WINEMAKER: Chuck Carlson

TASTING ROOM: Yes

DAYS/HOURS: Daily 10 A.M.–6 P.M. (winter 5 P.M.)

ADDRESS: 5249 Foxen Canyon Rd., Los Olivos, CA 93441; 805-686-8999; 805-686-9956 (fax); curtiswinery.com

WINES/GRAPE VARIETIES: Grenache, Heritage Blanc (blend), Heritage Cuvée (blend), Heritage Rosé, late-harvest Viognier, Mourvèdre, Roussanne, Syrah, Viognier

WINE CLUB: Yes

TASTING ROOM AMENITIES: Picnic area, merchandise

REGION: Santa Ynez Valley AVA

Sailing is a popular pastime on the Central Coast, with its many fine, protected harbors not too far from the vineyards. Avid sailor Chuck Carlson, the winemaker at Curtis, goes by the nickname Calypso, which is somewhat surprising when you learn that Chuck grew up in Reedley, California, near Fresno, the fruit basket of the San Joaquin Valley. In fact, his family was involved in citrus farming and growing avocados, which nurtured his early love for agriculture and science. At the time, he had friends who worked for the Christian Brothers Winery, and he was intrigued by the possibility of incorporating his two interests by working in the wine business. He went to junior college and then to Fresno State. This was a good move for Chuck because Fresno, like Cal Poly, believes in giving its students hands-on experiences in addition to their theoretical work. It also helped that he was in a class of three. He first discovered Firestone Winery, then in the midst of its start-up phase, and the Santa Ynez Valley while on a viticulture field trip to do research with his professor. After he graduated from Fresno State, Chuck took a lab position at Zaca Mesa Winery in 1981 and stayed for more than a decade. He had the unique experience of being part of Zaca Mesa's rise to prominence, and he believes that you can't buy that kind of work experience.

In 1983, while he was still at Zaca Mesa, the consensus there was that Syrah would become an important grape for the area. They arranged to get cuttings from Gary Eberle's famous "suitcase Syrah" imported from France via nontraditional channels and produced the first Syrah in Santa Barbara County. Chuck, then assistant winemaker, was part of a dynamic group, some of whom would go on to fame in their own right. For example, Bob Lindquist, now at Qupé, ran the tasting room, and Ken Brown was the winemaker, later going to Byron. In 1992 Chuck left Zaca Mesa to help the Miller brothers at their Central Coast Wine Services facility. The Firestones contacted him there and asked him to come aboard as associate winemaker. In 1995 he was responsible for creating the Rhône program at Curtis, just up the road from the Firestone Vineyard.

Firestone purchased the current site of the winery and vineyard from Hollywood producer Douglas Cramer in 1995. Curtis, though owned by Firestone, emphasizes wines of the Rhône such as Syrah, Viognier, Grenache, and Mourvèdre. The intent is to maintain the feel of a boutique winery of handcrafted wines. About one-third of the wines are currently sold through their customer-friendly tasting room.

RECOMMENDED WINES: Chuck recommends the Roussanne. The 2003 is gold and green in the glass with a nose of pears, honeycomb, vanilla oak spices, kiwifruit, lime, and a touch of hazelnut. The grapes show excellent ripeness and are well balanced by the acidity and the minerality in the wine. All combine to provide a sense of richness in the mouth. The finish is nearly a minute long and complements the wonderful aromatics. The wine is accessible now but will hold another three to five years for peak drinking.

I selected the flagship Syrah, the Crossroads. The 2001 is opaque to the stem, purple and black in the glass. The nose is blueberries, blackberries, smoke, spice, and black currants. The wine has a silky texture in the mouth from the ripe tannins. The nose is lovely, the spice is exotic, and the tannic grip of this wine suggests that it will age beautifully over the next five years.

RATING: Two → three stars (Chuck Carlson continues to raise the overall quality of the line)

Daniel Gehrs Wines

WINERY OWNERS: Daniel and Robin Gehrs

WINEMAKER: Daniel Gehrs

TASTING ROOM: Yes

DAYS/HOURS: Daily 11 A.M.–6 P.M. (winter 5 P.M.)

ADDRESS: 2939 Grand Ave., Los Olivos, CA 93441; 800-275-8138; 805-693-0750 (fax); dgwines.com

WINES/GRAPE VARIETIES: Cabernet Sauvignon, Chardonnay, Chenin Blanc, Gewürztraminer, Merlot, Pinot Noir, port, Riesling, Syrah, Tempranillo

WINE CLUB: Yes

TASTING ROOM AMENITIES: Picnic area, merchandise

REGION: Santa Ynez Valley AVA

When Daniel and Robin Gehrs pulled up to their Heather Cottage tasting room in full-dress motorcycle leathers aboard a splendid Harley, I knew we would have a great interview. Dan admits he wasn't born to the business the way so many others were. At Pacific Lutheran University in Washington, where he met his wife, he was a political science major with a minor in history. In the early 1970s, the culture of wine and its important place in Western civilization captured his imagination. During this time the back to the land movement also intrigued him, with its emphasis on organic and biodynamic farming. When a job came along at Paul Masson, near Saratoga, he took it as an opportunity to learn the wine business as opposed to winemaking. Robin, unlike Dan, grew up with wine (her family made wine at home). She was encouraged when Dan made his first wine for them with grapes from La Cresta vineyard at Paul Masson, planted by Masson himself. That property, after changing hands numerous times, is now known as Mount Eden Vineyards.

Dan's knowledge of viticulture is due in part to having rented a house in the Santa Cruz Mountains from a former Iowa pig farmer. That gentleman farmed a property that had been semiabandoned in the 1950s but still included some three acres of seventy-five-year-old Zinfandel vines. He helped the farmer with the grape growing in the vineyard and later named it Congress Springs. He received grapes from the property as compensation and used all his profits from their sale to buy a single book on viticulture. He then approached the owner with an offer to develop a partnership and start a winery. Dan and Robin moved into the house on the property and celebrated their first vintage in 1976. They loaded an old Chevy Malibu station wagon with grapes to haul them to the winery and sold the wines in the little tasting room there.

In 1990 Dan and Robin left Congress Springs Vineyard to start the Daniel Gehrs label. After seeing Silicon Valley's encroachment on the vineyards up in the Santa Cruz Mountains they went south, and he took a job as winemaker at Zaca Mesa Winery. During his five years there, he received permission to make his own wines on the property. At Zaca Mesa he was part of the group who had the foresight to see the potential for Rhône varieties in Santa Ynez Valley. In 1993 his friend Randall Grahm of Bonny Doon gave him cuttings of Roussanne grapevines. The 1996 Zaca Mesa Roussanne won a gold medal and Best of Show for white wines at the San Francisco Wine Fair. Much to his dismay, a genetic analysis of the Roussanne grape later showed it to be Viognier, and this is now called the "R-clone." After the 1997 vintage, while maintaining his label, Dan returned to work as a consultant and designed a "dream winery" at Bridlewood in the tradition of great French estates and châteaus. He started them on the right track with Syrah and other Rhône-style wines. Although Dan is currently the winemaker for the three labels owned by Louis Lucas and Royce Lewellen, he and Robin are now able to focus their considerable experience and knowledge on the Daniel Gehrs label. Daughter Jennifer is often in the tasting room and is already trying her hand at winemaking in the cellar with her new label, Vixen.

RECOMMENDED WINES: Dan recommends the Pinot Noir. The 2001 is light to the stem and a bright red cherry in the glass. The nose shows black cherries, plums, and spiced oak. The wine is well balanced and pleasant in the mouth. It is ready for the table now and should drink nicely over the next two years.

I suggest the Methuselah. The 1999 spent three years in the barrel and is a blend of Merlot, Cabernet Sauvignon, and Cabernet Franc. This black cherry–colored wine is translucent in the glass. The nose is black currants, vanilla cream, cherries, and wild plums. Under the fruit I found red peppers and a hint of black olive. The wine shows fine balance and maintains an excellent tannic grip with a finish of almost 45 seconds. It is ready for the table now but will improve in the bottle over the next three to four years.

RATING: Two stars (wines are consistently very good)

Dierberg/Star Lane Vineyard

WINERY OWNERS: Jim and Mary Dierberg

WINEMAKER: Nicholas G. de Luca

TASTING ROOM: No

DAYS/HOURS: No tasting available

ADDRESS: P.O. Box 1882, Santa Ynez, CA 93460; 805-693-0744; 805-688-1985

(fax); dierbergvineyard.com; starlanevineyard.com; threesaintsvineyard.com

WINES/GRAPE VARIETIES: Cabernet Sauvignon, Chardonnay, Merlot, Pinot Noir, Sauvignon Blanc, Syrah

WINE CLUB: Online store

REGION: Santa Ynez Valley AVA

Many Iowans are still rooted to the rich topsoil that sustains their farms. People of the land tend to be a hospitable group. When I visited Jim and Mary Dierberg, I asked for and received permission to bring along two dear friends visiting from Iowa, Steve Doty and his wife, Marlene Ciorba. After the introductions were made, to our astonishment we learned that Marlene and Mary had grown up not too far from each other in Iowa. Mary's family ran the Bancroft Hatchery where Marlene's father bought chicks for his farm, not twenty miles away. Mary says she probably packed the chicks, one hundred to the cardboard crate, for Marlene's father.

When Jim Dierberg was in the service he went to Paris, where he learned to eat oxtail soup and drink a different wine with each course of his meal. After graduation from Washington University Law School, he went into banking and transformed Creve Coeur Farmers Bank in his Missouri hometown into First Bank, an enterprise that now has more than 150 locations.

In Hermann, Missouri, Jim and Mary bought an old brewery and winery about thirty years ago and founded Hermannhof Winery, one of the first there, and now one of the best known in Missouri. Jim's banking business brought him to California, and after a ten-year search he found the Star Lane Ranch at the eastern end of Santa Ynez Valley in Happy Canyon, an up-and-coming area hot enough to grow Bordeaux varieties successfully. In the 1920s, hotel businessmen owned the property and ran it as a racing-horse ranch. After the Depression, owners of American Standard bought the place and turned it into a working dude ranch. After 1945 it was in the possession of an owner of movie theaters, and Hollywood stars congregated there to preview their movies in private. Luminaries like Roy Rogers and Gary Cooper kept horses at Star Lane. Word has it that Trigger, Roy's famous palomino, came from this ranch. Aeronautical engineer Clarence "Kelly" Johnson, designer of the U2 spy plane and head of the top-secret Skunk Works, was the last owner, and his widow sold the property to the Dierbergs in 1996. The vineyards at Star Lane were planted in 1997; Jim has also acquired vineyards in the Santa Rita Hills and near Santa Maria, all within Santa Barbara County. The winemaker for Dierberg wines is Nicholas G. de Luca, with David Ramey and Paul Hobbs acting as consulting winemakers. Marta Polley, a former professional ballerina, is director of sales and marketing. Dierberg produces wine under the labels Dierberg, Star Lane, and Three Saints.

RECOMMENDED WINES: Jim recommends the Three Saints Pinot Noir. The 2003 is light to the stem and red cherry in the glass. The wonderful nose is cherries, boysenberries, and red currants. The tannins are soft and rounded, and the long, luscious finish shows a touch of chocolate. The wine is ready for drinking now, thanks to the silky tannins, but will continue to improve over the next three years.

I suggest the Three Saints Syrah. The black-purple 2002 is almost opaque in the glass. The lovely aromatics show blackberries, figs, smoke, forest floor, white pepper, and clove, with a touch of violet perfume. The wine is lush in the mouth, and the tannins are ripe and soft, making this wine accessible now. The finish lasts nearly a minute; this wine will continue to age and become even more elegant over the next three to six years.

RATING: Three → four stars (Three Saints line represents fine value; Estate wines four stars)

East Valley Vineyard and Winery

WINERY OWNERS: David and Sharon Dascomb

WINEMAKER: David Dascomb

TASTING ROOM: Yes

DAYS/HOURS: By appointment only

ADDRESS: 4960 Baseline Ave., Santa Ynez, CA 93460; 805-455-1412; no fax; eastvalleywines.com

WINES/GRAPE VARIETIES: Cabernet Sauvignon, Pinot Noir, Sangiovese, Syrah

WINE CLUB: Yes

REGION: Santa Ynez Valley AVA

Weather satellites have proved crucial to farming in general and to grape growing in particular. They provide the meteorological data growers need to help determine such things as when to pick and, as in the case of the winter of 2006, when to protect against subfreezing temperatures. David Dascomb knows a thing or two about weather satellites since he builds them for Raytheon, where he is a project manager. In 1975 his father, Don, planted the family's first vineyard to Cabernet Sauvignon grapes. He sold the fruit from that vineyard to such notable wineries as Beckmen and Babcock. David remembers helping his father plant the vines in the heavy clay of the eastern end of Santa Ynez Valley while still in junior high school. In high school an influential agriculture teacher recommended that David attend Cal Poly if he was accepted to the mechanical engineering program. This made for a difficult decision on David's part because he was also recognized for his talents in viticulture during his involvement in the Future Farmers of America program. David chose to enter Cal Poly, knowing that he would leave the vineyard in his father's capable hands. After university, he moved to Seattle and raised a family in the Pacific Northwest. In 1998 he moved back to the Santa Ynez Valley. He started East Valley as a sideline in 2000, making the wines himself. In 2001 David's Syrah took a bagful of gold medals home from the California State Fair. Don still does the farming and also helps out in the winery.

The emphasis at East Valley is on growing the best possible fruit given the *terroir.* At the vineyard, located about one mile from the Happy Canyon area, the fog burns off relatively early in the day, and temperatures can reach the 90s. On summer evenings, temperatures drop into the mid-50s. David's overarching interest is to make wines that he would be happy to drink, and he prefers to make a softer wine using careful oak management of his French barrels. The key to achieving wines with softer tannins is vineyard management, and David pays attention to trellising practices, vertical shoot positioning, soil preparation, and canopy management. In essence, he is trying to close what he sees as a big disconnect between growers and winemakers. In his case, that problem is solved nicely since he has control over the vineyards. He merely has to yell at his dad on the tractor. Their combined efforts have begun to pay off.

RECOMMENDED WINES: The California State Fair richly honored the 2001 Syrah. The wine won Best of Class in Region, Best Wine in Region, and the high honor of Best Syrah in the state of California. Not surprisingly, this wine is David's recommendation. It is purple and red in the glass and opaque to the stem. The nose is raspberries, plums, and red roses. The spice is black pepper, and there is a hint of earth in the wine. On the mid-palate, cloves appear. The wine shows excellent balance, and the soft tannins add to its elegance. The finish is almost a minute. Drinking beautifully now, the wine should hold another three to four years. If it disappears too quickly, try the 2002. It showed a somewhat lighter color in the glass and white chocolate, figs, cinnamon, and raspberry jam in the nose. It too should develop into a fine Syrah.

I suggest the Cabernet Sauvignon. The 2001 has 20 percent Merlot. This black-purple wine is opaque in the glass and has a wonderful nose of cassis, black currants, black cherry, and vanilla spice. The wine is well balanced and shows fine integration. The ripe fruit is forward, and the soft tannins provide a luscious mouthfeel. The finish lasted over a minute. Drink now and over the next three to six years. In all, an excellent example of what Cabernet Sauvignon can be from this somewhat warmer growing area in Santa Ynez Valley.

RATING: Three → four stars (wines excellent to outstanding)

Epiphany Cellars

WINERY OWNER: Eli Parker

WINEMAKER: Eli Parker

TASTING ROOM: Yes

DAYS/HOURS: Thursday–Monday 11:30 A.M.–
5:30 P.M.

ADDRESS: 2963 Grand Ave., Los Olivos, CA
93441; 805-686-2424; 866-354-9463;
805-686-2634 (fax); epiphanycellars.com

WINES/GRAPE VARIETIES: Grenache Blanc,
Grenache rosé, Gypsy (Grenache Noir),
Petite Syrah, Pinot Gris, Revelation
(blend), Roussanne, Syrah

WINE CLUB: Mailing list, online sales

TASTING ROOM AMENITIES: Merchandise

REGION: Santa Ynez Valley AVA

The original meaning of the Greek word from which *epiphany* derives denoted the manifestation or sudden appearance of something. The English word denotes the appearance of a life-changing thought or idea. Eli Fess Parker uses the word to describe his new line of wines. His father, Fess (profiled under Fess Parker Winery), started a vineyard with the help of Dale Hampton in 1988. Ken Brown came in to consult, and the Parker family's excursion into the wine business nearly ended shortly thereafter when Ken showed them the true costs associated with developing a vineyard, to say nothing of building and starting a winery. Nevertheless, given Dad's success in real-estate development, the Parker family pressed on and saw their first bottling in 1989. Wente Brothers in Livermore was kind enough to handle the first three vintages for the new Fess Parker label. In 1990 they broke ground on the current winery and tasting room.

After an early start in the real-estate business, Eli came back to the vineyards and the tractor. He got hands-on experience working as a cellar rat. In the first days of Fess Parker wines, Riesling was the mainstay, but Mark Shannon of Wente, anticipating the move to Syrah and Rhône varieties in the region, convinced the Parkers to move in that direction too, and this gave Eli his first great wine experience. One might say that he had an epiphany after tasting his first great example of Syrah—a Penfolds Grange, noted as one of Australia's premier wines. After Shannon left for Italy, Eli immersed himself in winemaking. By 1992 he had made friends with some of the region's best winemakers, Stephan Bedford among them. Dale Hampton suggested Jed Steele as a consulting winemaker, but he declined more than once before accepting a three-year contract, with Eli working at first as his apprentice in the spring of 1993. Unfortunately, the 1995 vintage, when yields dropped precipitously, almost put them out of business. The Parkers decided after this near-calamity not to depend on outside fruit sources again and substantially increased their acreage planted to grapes. By 1996 Eli was flying solo and had the good fortune to experience a great harvest that year. In 1995 he had met Brett Escalera, then working at Mondavi, and tried to hire him, but had to wait a year before Brett was able to make the move. In 1996 the Fess Parker Winery named Eli president of the company. Originally Brett was hired to be production manager, but as Eli found himself devoting more and more time to selling the wines and being on the road, Brett took over more winemaking duties. Recently, Eli decided to return to a more active role in the winemaking process, freeing Brett to give more attention to his Consilience line. This move also enabled Eli to start Epiphany, with Brett acting as consulting winemaker. Eli outlines the program at Epiphany, and Brett helps make it happen.

RECOMMENDED WINES: Eli recommends the Syrah. The 2001 is made from grapes grown at the Hampton Vineyard. This black and purple wine is opaque to the stem of the glass and has a nose of cherries, chocolate, black currants, and white pepper spice. The wine shows wonderful balance between the acidity and lovely ripe tannins. Together with the outstanding fruit in this wine, they integrate for a hedonistic mouthfeel and a fine finish. The wine is drinking very nicely now but will hold another five to nine years.

I recommend the Revelation, an aptly named wine. The 2001 is a blend of Syrah, Grenache, and Petite Sirah. This black cherry–colored wine is opaque in the glass. The nose is rich, ripe, and fruity with strawberries, cranberries, smoke, and blueberries. The wine is huge in the mouth and is outstanding in every regard: the aromatics, the middle, and the enormous finish. It is ready now but will hold easily another eight years. This is truly a wine to seek out and enjoy; try it and you might very well experience your own epiphany.

RATING: Four stars (reds ahead of whites)

Fess Parker Winery & Vineyard

WINERY OWNER: Fess Parker

WINEMAKER: Blair Fox

TASTING ROOM: Yes

DAYS/HOURS: Daily 10 A.M.–5 P.M.

ADDRESS: 6200 Foxen Canyon Rd., Los Olivos, CA 93441; 805-688-1545; 805-686-1130 (fax); fessparker.com

WINES/GRAPE VARIETIES: Chardonnay, Frontier Red (blend), Pinot Noir, Syrah, Viognier, White Riesling

WINE CLUB: Yes

TASTING ROOM AMENITIES: Picnic area, merchandise, tours

REGION: Santa Ynez Valley AVA

Many readers will recall with fondness Fess Parker's television work in his roles as Daniel Boone and Davy Crockett. Both he and his Iowan wife, Marcella, were raised on farms and ranches. Born in Texas, Fess grew up during the Great Depression and graduated in 1950 from the University of Texas with a degree in history. He furthered his education with academic work toward a master's degree in drama at the University of Southern California. In 1951 he got work as a professional actor, and in 1954 Walt Disney signed him to the role of Davy Crockett. Ten years later he filmed the *Daniel Boone* series, one of the highest-ranked shows airing at the time. During its six-year run he took on other duties, such as coproducer and director of many of the show's more popular episodes. Even as his television and film career flourished, he embarked on a second career as a real-estate developer. He built a resort hotel in Santa Barbara on 24 acres of oceanfront property and called it the DoubleTree. In 1998 he purchased the Grand Hotel in Los Olivos, a Victorian-style inn with a restaurant where he often dines. Other major projects are currently in the works.

The Parker family, including mom Marcella, son Eli, and daughter Ashley, has a long history of wine appreciation. Throughout the 1960s, Fess's fame permitted the family to buy, taste, and learn about some of the best wines in the world. About 1973 or 1974, already well established as a real-estate tycoon, Fess bought a property near Santa Maria and contemplated planting vineyards there. He went so far as to enlist the help of a Fresno State professor to test the soils, but the project did not work out. In 1987, at the age of sixty-four and contemplating retirement, Fess bought 714 acres of ranchland about 30 miles north of Santa Barbara. Although bought to create a working cattle ranch, the property provided an opportunity for him to establish a vineyard; he originally planted 5 to 10 acres on an experimental basis. In 1988 he hired Ken Brown of Zaca Mesa fame to consult on the selection of varieties and enlisted the help of noted viticulturist Dale Hampton to design the vineyard. Fess Parker thus accomplished what few men have done: he made the transition from playing frontier pioneer to becoming a real-life pioneer on the Santa Barbara County wine country frontier. He took his place alongside such notables as Boyd Bettencourt, Louis Lucas, and the Firestone family, to mention a few. To this day, the six-and-a-half-foot-tall Parker still enjoys working with cattle. His son Eli, now president and director of winemaking and vineyard operations, is profiled under Epiphany Cellars, Eli's other wine enterprise. The winemaker at Fess Parker Winery is Blair Fox.

RECOMMENDED WINES: For the Fess Parker wines, Eli recommends the Pinot Noir from Ashley's vineyard. The 2002 is transparent to the stem and black cherry in color. The nose is blackberries, smoke, leather, forest floor, and cardamom spice. This wine is rich in the mouth and shows a lovely balance among the fruit, tannins, and acidity. An elegant wine, it is vinified in a Burgundian style. The finish is almost a minute, and although this wine is drinking beautifully now, the tannins suggest another eight years of great drinking ahead.

I recommend the Viognier. The 2002 is a steely gold and has a nose of ripe, Rubired grapefruit, sweet Alberta peaches, and honeysuckle perfume. The wine shows an excellent balance of fruit, acidity, and underlying minerality. The wine is creamy in the mouth, and the finish lingers almost a minute. It is a fine Viognier and will last another three to four years.

RATING: Three stars (quality is improving across the line, and there are fine values to be found in both whites and reds)

Fiddlehead Cellars

WINERY OWNER: Kathy Joseph

WINEMAKER: Kathy Joseph

TASTING ROOM: Yes

DAYS/HOURS: By appointment only

ADDRESS: 1597 E. Chestnut Ave., Lompoc,
    CA 93436; 805-742-0204; 805-742-0205
    (fax); fiddleheadcellars.com

WINES/GRAPE VARIETIES: Pinot Noir,
    Sauvignon Blanc

WINE CLUB: Yes

REGION: Santa Rita Hills AVA

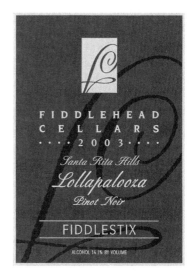

Kathy Joseph grew up in a family that loved food, and she can remember wine served at the supper table. Her mother was an accomplished cook and also a home economist. Raised outside Chicago, Kathy graduated from the University of Wisconsin, where she discovered that she had a talent for microbiology and chemistry, loving the sciences a bit more than the liberal arts. Her studies gave her a first introduction to soil sciences as she unknowingly laid the groundwork for a future move into the wine business. In the meantime, she accepted a research position at the University of Illinois Medical Center. Work there convinced her that she needed to broaden her horizons. Her father persuaded her that she should consider putting all her training in science to work as a winemaker. She had no idea that one could go to graduate school for something that fun!

Certain now that medical research was not the way to go, Kathy next took a job at Simi Winery in the public-relations department and did VIP tours. More important, she had the opportunity there to taste under the tutelage of winemaker Zelma Long, whose artistry drew Kathy away from the hard sciences. Convinced now of the excellent opportunities available in the wine industry, she applied to UC Davis and was accepted in 1981. Nearing graduation, Kathy thought she was best suited to do research at a larger winery instead of owning a winery herself. To that end, she accepted an internship in Napa at Joseph Phelps as a cellar rat in 1982 to get hands-on experience. She learned vineyard management and helped set up a lab at Long Vineyards in 1983.

The next year Bob Long introduced her to Robert Pecota, and she worked for him as full-time winemaker after graduation. The job at Pecota lasted until 1988, and she learned everything it took to run a smaller winery: wine style, equipment choices, employee management, and barrel selection, for example. Pecota even sent her on the road to do marketing. Over the years she directed her passion to the making of Sauvignon Blanc and Pinot Noir. In 1988 she sat down and wrote a business plan that resulted in the creation of Fiddlehead Cellars.

Her extensive tasting experiences led her to believe that Willamette County in Oregon would be excellent for producing Pinot Noir; Santa Barbara County also caught her attention for that grape and Sauvignon Blanc. The White House served her first Pinot Noir, produced in 1989. After her initial success from Santa Barbara County grapes, she needed additional venture capital and in 1991 started a limited partnership wherein she retained complete control over all winemaking and financial decisions. Her operation changed slightly when Mondavi purchased the source of her Pinot Noir grapes in 1993, forcing her to find other sources. Following her palate once again, she discovered the Santa Rita Hills. The quality of the fruit and the wines produced there convinced her it was time to invest in land and develop a vineyard of her own. In 1996 Jeff Newton, the viticulturist from whom she bought her Sauvignon Blanc grapes, helped her find a property along Santa Rosa Road, directly across the street from the famous Sanford and Benedict vineyard. She bought a 133-acre parcel formerly used to grow flowers, and Fiddlestix vineyard was born. Kathy planned to keep the best 15 percent of Fiddlestix for her own small production at Fiddlehead Cellars and sell the remainder of the grapes to other Pinot Noir producers. She quickly learned that selling grapes was a full-time job by itself, so in 2001 Kathy made Fiddlestix into a separate company and sold a 50 percent interest in that property to create an automatic home for half of the grapes. Her friend Chuck Ortman, then at Meridian, introduced her to officials at the corporate level, and they loved her idea of starting a vineyard partnership. She now manages the entire vineyard and sets the standards for farming it. From her half of Fiddlestix, she sells to about ten small producers and keeps the rest for her own label.

RECOMMENDED WINES: Kathy recommends the Sauvignon Blanc from Happy Canyon grapes. The 2001 is lime-colored and shows grapefruit, gooseberry, lemon, stone, and honeyed perfume in the nose. The wine has wonderful balance and great acidity to support the lovely fruit. In addition, the wine displays a silky structure, and its time on oak suggests an aging potential of another five to six years, though it is drinking beautifully now. If the 2001 is sold out, look to the 2005, vinified in a similar style.

I recommend the 728 Pinot Noir. This wine is a dark black cherry color and opaque to light in the glass. The nose is sweet cherry, white chocolate, black currants, black plums, and earth. The body has a silky texture thanks to the ripe, rounded tannins, and the finish lasts nearly a full minute. The wine will hold another eight years, and my notes suggest that this Pinot Noir will develop into an excellent wine if you can keep from drinking it now.

RATING: Four stars (whites and reds are both outstanding)

Firestone Vineyard

WINERY OWNER: Foley Wine Group

WINEMAKER: Kevin Willenborg

TASTING ROOM: Yes

DAYS/HOURS: Daily 10 A.M.–5 P.M.

ADDRESS: 5000 Zaca Station Rd., Los Olivos,
CA 93441; 805-688-3940; 805-686-1256
(fax); firestonewine.com

WINES/GRAPE VARIETIES: The Ambassador
(blend), Cabernet Sauvignon, Chardonnay,
Gewürztraminer, Merlot, Riesling,
Sauvignon Blanc, Syrah

WINE CLUB: Yes

TASTING ROOM AMENITIES: Picnic area,
merchandise, tours

REGION: Santa Ynez Valley AVA

Firestone Vineyard is an icon in the Santa Barbara County wine scene. The property was bought recently by William P. Foley of the Foley Wine Group, a friend and neighbor of the Firestones. He is profiled under Foley Estates. Below I share my interview with Brooks Firestone.

Now in its third generation, with patriarch Leonard, father Brooks, and son Adam comprising the lineage, the Firestone family has been instrumental in starting and developing the worldwide wine reputation of both Santa Barbara County and the Central Coast. When Leonard and Brooks took a chance on planting grapes, most books didn't even list Santa Barbara as a wine region. More than thirty years later, Firestone has become an iconic destination for wine tourism in Santa Barbara County.

Leonard Firestone did his due diligence before putting his money into the ground. A ten-year local weather study showed that almost every year in Santa Ynez Valley was a good year for growing grapes. The climate is moderate enough to permit the grapes to hang until November. Ocean currents and cool water bring fog and cool nights, all adding up to a moderate growing season lasting longer than up in Napa. The right soils were there, and with the right viticulture practices in the vineyard, all the elements for excellent results were in place. In 1972 Leonard gave the go-ahead to break ground. After twelve years in the tire business started by his grandfather, Brooks, Leonard's son, dropped out of corporate life and moved his family from the company's London headquarters to Santa Ynez Valley and the family ranch. But he wasn't much interested in a new life of pruning vines, pulling shoots, or running livestock. Like his father before him, he put his nose into the research and, convinced that they were located in a potentially world-class growing region, set about establishing the area's first estate winery. Japanese brewer Suntory came on as a limited partner in those early days (Firestone bought Suntory out in 1994), and André Tchelistcheff, hired as consultant, oversaw the first harvest in 1975.

Over the years, Firestone winery has brought international renown to the area, particularly with its Chardonnay and Merlot, and yes, Riesling. Sauvignon Blanc, Gewürztraminer, and now Syrah are currently playing pivotal roles in the winery's new direction, guided by winemaker Kevin Willenborg and president Adam Firestone. Kevin, who interned at Château Pétrus, arrives with fourteen years' experience working in Napa, ten of those as winemaker at Louis Martini. The new vineyard manager is Eric Davidian.

RECOMMENDED WINES: Kevin recommends the Reserve Merlot—not surprising considering his time at Pétrus. This wine permits some light to the stem and is a bright red cherry color. There is a wonderful nose of blackberries, violets, vanilla spice, black currants, clove, and anise. This is one of the best Merlots I have tasted from the region. It has excellent ripe fruit, a wonderful balance and plush feel in the mouth, and an elegant and long finish. The wine is ready for drinking now and over the next five years.

My recommendation is the Ambassador, a representative of the new Bordeaux program now at Firestone. Named in honor of Leonard Firestone, the 2001 is opaque to the stem and a classic Cabernet Sauvignon color of black and purple. The nose is a wonderful perfume of cassis, raspberry, black cherry, tobacco, soft vanilla from the oak, and dark chocolate. The excellent fruit is complemented by the ripe, sweet tannins and contributes to a well-integrated and finely textured middle. The finish is nearly a minute and recalls the fruity aromas in the nose. This is an outstanding bottle of wine, ready for drinking now and over the next eight years.

RATING: Two stars (Kevin Willenborg will revitalize the entire line if his Reserves, which merit four stars, are indicative)

Flying Goat Cellars

WINERY OWNERS: Norman and Pam Yost

WINEMAKER: Norman Yost

TASTING ROOM: At Wine Country

DAYS/HOURS: Daily 11 A.M.–5 P.M.

ADDRESS: Wine Country, 2445 Alamo Pintado Ave., Los Olivos, CA 93441;

805-686-9699; 805-688-8603 (fax); flyinggoatcellars.com

WINE/GRAPE VARIETY: Pinot Noir

WINE CLUB: No

REGION: Santa Rita Hills AVA

Norman and Pam Yost are Pacific Northwest natives; Norman is from Seattle and came south to California, where he studied environmental science at UC Davis. His roommate at the time was in the enology program and got him a job in Sonoma. He worked construction at Silver Oak Cellars and spent some time removing gables from old barns. In 1982 he was hired as a cellar rat at Monticello Vineyards, and this job afforded him the opportunity to learn the details of the wine industry. In four years, he helped that winery progress from 20,000 cases a year to 40,000. He then returned to his alma mater and took all the available enology courses. His next job was at Mark West Winery in Sonoma. In 1990 he traveled to Perth, Australia, to learn winemaking techniques there. After returning to the United States he worked again in Oregon, making Pinot Noir. When a job opened up at Foley Estates in 1998, he accepted the offer to be part of a new venture and work in the Santa Rita Hills appellation. He remained at Foley until he and Pam started their own label, convinced of that area's great potential for Pinot Noir.

In 2000 they crushed fruit for their first vintage, with a production of about 250 cases. They needed a name for their label, and Pam, drawing on her expertise in marketing and design at a multinational athletics company, chose the name Flying Goat after the pygmy goats they kept on their land. Their purpose was to produce serious wine behind a fun and whimsical label. After some difficulties obtaining fruit in 2001, Norman contracted with Jim Dierberg to purchase grapes from his vineyard, which was rapidly gaining a reputation for excellence. In 2002 he signed long-term contracts with additional grape growers in the region, assuring a steady stream of high-quality Pinot Noir for his label. Pam and Norman emphasize that they want to offer the consumer wines that first taste good and then give value for the dollar. When Norman is not making wines for Flying Goat or Huber Cellars, he teaches at Allan Hancock College in Santa Maria and, when time permits, pursues his passion for skiing.

RECOMMENDED WINES: Norm suggests the Dierberg Vineyards Pinot Noir. The 2002 is from Dijon clones 115 and 31. The wine is a medium ruby in the glass and opaque to the stem. The lovely aromatics in the nose suggest black cherry, spice, cola, black currants, and black plums. This is a medium-bodied wine that displays its excellent fruit. The finish is soft and luscious; ready for the table now, it should provide another three to four years of fine drinking.

I recommend the Rancho Santa Rosa Pinot Noir. The 2002 is made from Dijon clones 667 and 2A. These two make for a dark cherry-red wine that is opaque in the glass. The nose suggests blueberries, spice, smoke, and plums. The wine has a larger structure than the Dierberg thanks to the greater tannic grip. The fruit is ripe and luscious, leading to a longer finish and a greater potential for aging. The Santa Rosa is the one to buy and lay down for a few years while you are enjoying the Dierberg. And I have to admit that the flying goat on the label has a certain cuteness about it that will appeal to Capricorns.

RATING: Three stars (very good to excellent Pinot)

Foley Estates

WINERY OWNER: William Foley II

WINEMAKER: Alan Phillips

TASTING ROOM: Yes

DAYS/HOURS: Daily 10 A.M.–5 P.M.

ADDRESS: 6121 E. Hwy. 246, Lompoc, CA 93436; 805-737-6222; 805-737-6923 (fax); foleywines.com

WINES/GRAPE VARIETIES: Chardonnay, Pinot Gris, Pinot Noir, rosé, Syrah

REGION: Santa Ynez Valley AVA

WINE CLUB: Yes

TASTING ROOM AMENITIES: Picnic area, merchandise

William Foley II has paid his academic dues. He started at the United States Military Academy, where he took a bachelor of science degree in engineering in 1967. His military career ended on his retirement as captain in the U.S. Air Force. He holds an MBA from Seattle University, where he also earned a law degree. Since 1984 he has served as the chairman of the board and chief executive officer of Fidelity National Financial, Inc., and sits on numerous boards for major corporations.

In 1994 Bill and his wife, Carol, moved their four children out of the Los Angeles area to Santa Barbara County. A great fan of wines with a taste for fine Burgundies, Bill decided to enter the wine business. His initial venture was a partnership in the historic Santa Ynez Valley Winery, one of the first established in the area. In 1997 he purchased the majority share in the partnership and renamed it Lincourt, after his daughters Lindsay and Courtney. In 1998 Bill bought 460 acres of hillside property in the Santa Rita Hills, securing a reliable source of high-quality grapes for both the Foley and the Lincourt lines. The Foley winery and tasting room is located on this property, called Rancho Santa Rosa. Alan Phillips, the winemaker, is discussed in detail in the Lincourt profile.

RECOMMENDED WINES: Alan recommends the Foley Rancho Santa Rosa Syrah from Santa Rita Hills grapes. The 2002 is black-purple in the glass and opaque to the stem. White pepper, black cherry, coffee, cassis, and sweet tobacco show in the aromatics. The pepper returns on the mid-palate, and the finish lasts nearly a minute. This is wonderful cool-climate Syrah and reminded me of a Crozes-Hermitage. Drink now and over the next five or six years.

I recommend the Foley Pommard Clone Pinot Noir from a single hillside block found at the top of the Rancho Santa Rosa vineyard. The 2002 is almost opaque to the stem and a pretty raspberry color. In the nose I find chocolate, blackberry, pomegranate, vanilla, and cinnamon spice. The fruit is excellent, the structure is lovely and layered, and the elegant finish lasts nearly a minute. Drink now and over the next seven to nine years.

RATING: Four stars (both reds and whites excellent to outstanding)

Foxen Winery & Vineyard

WINERY OWNERS: Bill Wathen and Richard Doré

WINEMAKER: Bill Wathen

TASTING ROOM: Yes

DAYS/HOURS: Daily 11 A.M.–4 P.M.

ADDRESS: 7200 Foxen Canyon Rd., Santa Maria, CA 93454; 805-937-4251; 805-937-0415 (fax); foxenvineyard.com

WINES/GRAPE VARIETIES: Cabernet Franc, Cabernet Sauvignon, Chardonnay, Chenin Blanc, Cuvée Jeanne Marie (Rhône blend), Foothills Reserve (blend), late-harvest Viognier, Pinot Noir, Sangiovese, Sangiovese Volpino (blend), Syrah

WINE CLUB: Yes

TASTING ROOM AMENITIES: Picnic area

REGION: Santa Maria Valley AVA

Artists no doubt appreciate the weathered and warped planks of the old smithy at the entrance to the Foxen winery, so easy to drive by if the sign isn't out by the side of the road. There is a fascinating history behind the sun-bleached wood of what was formerly Rancho Tinaquaic. Dick Doré's great-great-grandfather, William Benjamin Foxen, an English sea captain, came ashore to California in the early 1800s. He married a Spanish woman whose father just happened to be the governor of the region. In 1837 William Benjamin Foxen received a Mexican land grant of nearly 9,000 acres in what is now Foxen Canyon—supporting the old dictum that it's all about whom you know—and chose an anchor for his cattle brand, the forebear of Foxen Winery's anchor logo. Of the original acres, 2,000 remain with Foxen's descendants. Dick's great-grandfather once had a small planting of Mission grapes on the property and made small batches of wine for the family. He renovated some of the original buildings, part of a stagecoach stop nearly 150 years old. In fact, the tasting room was previously the old smithy supporting the stagecoach stop.

Dick Doré, a sixth-generation native of Santa Barbara County, left to seek his fortune, much like his Foxen ancestor. He found that fortune, gave much of it away, explored the world, and came back home. A graduate of UC Santa Barbara, he became a successful banker after graduation, but after fifteen years in the business developed banker's disease: boredom! He sold his cars, gave away his stuff, and began a journey across Europe reminiscent of Jason's. With an old VW van as his *Argo,* he set out on a search for his personal golden fleece. Instead, he found some of the great wines of the world. After two years on the road he returned to reestablish himself, and while working one day at Tepusquet Mesa vineyard on the back of a tractor, he met his friend and future partner at Foxen, Bill Wathen.

A San Luis Obispo native, Bill graduated from Cal Poly in 1978 with a specialization in vineyard management. For his first two jobs, he worked for Santa Barbara County viticulture pioneers Dale Hampton and Louis Lucas. After graduation, Chalone hired him as vineyard manager, where he worked with renowned Monterey County winemaker and grower Dick Graff. Graff earned part of his reputation by being one of the first winemakers in the area to import French oak barrels and put his wines through malolactic fermentation. At Chalone, Graff mentored Bill in the French style of winemaking.

Bill and Dick renewed their friendship in 1984 and Foxen Winery was born, receiving its bond in 1987. Their contacts at the world-famous Bien Nacido vineyard, at Sea Smoke (which Bill helped find and develop), and in up-and-coming Happy Canyon for Bordeaux varieties give them top-quality fruit for their wines. In addition, they pull fruit from their estate vineyard.

RECOMMENDED WINES: Bill and Dick suggest the 2001 Foothills Reserve, a blend of 72 percent Merlot and 28 percent Cabernet Franc grapes. The wine is opaque to the stem and black-purple in color, and it has a nose of cherries, cassis, blackberries, anise, tobacco, and mint. This is a ripe, luscious wine, full in the mouth with a finish lasting a whole minute as it recalls the anise. Drink now and over the next three to five years.

I suggest the Pinot Noir, also one of Dick's favorites. The 2002 is from the Sea Smoke vineyard, translucent in the glass with a cherry-red and purple color. The nose is cherries, red currants, vanilla, and smoke. The lovely ripe tannins contribute to the wine's richness on the tongue. This is an elegant and lush Pinot with five years of wonderful drinking ahead of it.

RATING: Three stars (very good to excellent across the line)

Gainey Vineyard

WINERY OWNERS: Dan J. and Dan H. Gainey

WINEMAKER: Kirby Anderson

TASTING ROOM: Yes

DAYS/HOURS: Daily 10 A.M.–5 P.M.

ADDRESS: 3950 E. Hwy. 246, Santa Ynez, CA 93460; 805-688-0558; 805-688-5864 (fax); gaineyvineyard.com

WINES/GRAPE VARIETIES: Chardonnay, Merlot, Riesling, Pinot Noir, Sauvignon Blanc, Syrah

WINE CLUB: Yes

TASTING ROOM AMENITIES: Picnic area, merchandise, tours

REGION: Santa Ynez Valley AVA

The Gainey family has farmed in Santa Barbara County for more than four decades. Over the years, they have produced vegetables, fruits, flowers, and alfalfa. They established a cattle ranch and created a 100-acre Arabian horse facility. It all started in 1962 when Dan C. Gainey and his son Dan J. purchased an 1,800-acre ranch in Santa Ynez Valley. The Gaineys saw the potential of their land for grape growing and planted 50 acres to Burgundian varieties in 1983. They opened a Spanish-style winery a year later, still one of the prettiest in the region. In the 1990s the family expanded its grape-growing operation by purchasing 120 acres in the Santa Rita Hills AVA. This gives the winery access to grapes from the cooler western end of the valley, where Pinot Noir, Chardonnay, and Syrah grow, as well as from the warm eastern end. The vineyard manager is Jeff Newton, and the winemaker is Kirby Anderson.

Many of the winemakers in these profiles have reinvented themselves, moving from an unrelated field into a career in wine. Kirby Anderson is a graduate of UC Santa Barbara, where he took a degree in art. His interests in art, music, and fine dining led to his interest in wine; his busy mother did not always have time for the kitchen, so in his late teens Kirby took it upon himself to learn to cook, making the culinary arts his hobby. He dabbled in a few fields of study at university (he took courses in pharmacology, dentistry, and zoology) until he found the viticulture and enology program at Davis. He is originally from Gilroy (but was born in Iowa), and agriculture is part of his background. In fact, in order to save money for college, he once worked in the research department of an agricultural co-op. After college, he worked as a sommelier and later at Italian Swiss Colony, getting the hands-on training he needed to supplement his theoretical and lab work at Davis. He dropped out of the wine business for ten years to take an acting job with a local theater group, augmenting his salary by waiting tables, as many actors do. He moved to Los Angeles and tried the film industry, working his way up to executive assistant in charge of finding new scripts, but after the Rodney King incident he moved his family out of the fires, the riots, and the floods, leaving his well-paying job for an eight-dollar-an-hour position at Buena Vista Winery. After a move to the Carmel Valley, he worked with French-trained winemaker Don Blackburn at Bernardus, where he rose to assistant winemaker. That got him a job at La Crema, and six months later, a headhunter called. After a series of interviews, he was offered the job at Gainey in July 1997. His first vintage was 1998, and his Riesling won gold medals out of the gate.

RECOMMENDED WINES: The Gainey recommendation is the Chardonnay. The limited-edition 2001 is bright gold in the glass and shows elegant aromatics of apples, pears, tropical fruit, and toast. The acidity balances wonderfully with the oak and contributes to a luscious mouthfeel. The buttered toast shows up on the finish and augments the wonderful fruit in this wine. Drink now and over the next three to or four years.

I suggest the excellent Merlot. The limited-edition 2001 is opaque to the stem and purple-black in color. The nose shows black cherries, plums, figs, and coffee undertones. The acidity in this wine is well integrated with the tannins and the fruit. This is a luscious, ripe wine with a long, smooth finish. The wine is ready now but will hold another three to six years. This is a Merlot to seek out and drink as a counterbalance to watching the movie *Sideways*.

RATING: Three stars (very good wines across the line; whites are excellent)

Great Oaks Ranch and Vineyard

WINERY OWNERS: Michael and Nancy Lippman

WINEMAKER: Nancy Lippman

TASTING ROOM: At Wine Country

DAYS/HOURS: Daily 11 A.M.–5 P.M.

ADDRESS: Wine Country, 2445 Alamo Pintado Ave., Los Olivos, CA 93441; 805-686-9699; 805-686-5866 (fax); greatoaksranch.com

WINES/GRAPE VARIETIES: Bordeaux blend, Sauvignon Blanc, Syrah

WINE CLUB: No

REGION: Santa Ynez Valley AVA

Hartley-Ostini Hitching Post Winery

WINERY OWNERS: Gray Hartley and Frank Ostini

WINEMAKER: Frank Ostini

TASTING ROOM: Yes

DAYS/HOURS: Daily 4–6 P.M.

ADDRESS: Hitching Post II restaurant, 406 E. Hwy. 246, Buellton, CA 93427;

805-688-0676; 805-686-1946 (fax); hitchingpostwines.com

WINES/GRAPE VARIETIES: Generation Red (blend), Pinot Noir, Syrah

WINE CLUB: No

TASTING ROOM AMENITIES: Restaurant

REGION: Santa Ynez Valley AVA

When I interviewed Frank Ostini—owner, chef, and winemaker at the Hitching Post II restaurant—he alerted me to the fact that his restaurant would be prominently featured in the then soon-to-be-released film *Sideways*. That film had an enormous impact on the sales of Pinot Noir in Santa Barbara County, on the Central Coast in general, and on Hartley-Ostini in particular. Even if you haven't seen the film, do take the time to visit the restaurant for a tasting or to try the excellent ostrich steak. It pairs beautifully with Frank's wines. Frank's family traces its restaurant roots back to the Casmalia Hitching Post in 1952, featuring Santa Maria–style barbecue. The restaurant in Buellton is Hitching Post II, which marries the barbecue the Ostini family popularized with contemporary cooking styles. The tasting room–wine bar is located in the restaurant.

When Frank arrived for the interview, his hands were still black from the harvest and crush—no apologies necessary given the time of year. As noted above, Frank was literally born into the restaurant industry, which gave him an early exposure to fine wines. His family worked hard to establish the restaurant so that Frank could choose another line of work, if he so desired. Although Frank is a graduate of UC Davis in business, his father taught him to cook "just in case." He parlayed his skills into an opportunity to cook for winemakers in Napa, Mendocino, and Sonoma, where he was introduced to the romance and lifestyle of the wine industry. Frank started the winery with his longtime friend, professional fisherman Gray Hartley, in 1984, though the two had made wine together at home since 1979, after Frank's excursion to the wine country up north. Frank fell in love with the Pinot Noir grape, fostered to some degree by his friendship with Jim Clendenen at Au Bon Climat. By that time Gray was ready to get out of the fishing industry, and the two put together plans for the restaurant and winery. Gray is in charge of winery logistics and Frank handles the winemaking, a partnership of two distinct personalities: Gray is the romantic and innovator, and Frank is the pragmatist looking after the nuts and bolts. The two want to give their consumers a gustatory experience, pairing the food in the restaurant with the wines they produce, emphasizing, of course, Pinot Noir.

RECOMMENDED WINES: In the lingo of commercial anglers, a highliner is one of the best fishermen in the fleet, something Gray knows well from his twenty-eight years spent in the Alaskan salmon fishery. Frank recommends the Highliner Pinot Noir. The 2001 is almost opaque and one of the darkest of the Pinot Noirs he makes. This is a black cherry–colored wine with a nose of cherries, pepper spice, black currants, and a touch of anise. The body is soft and silky from the ripe, rounded tannins, and the wine shows a wonderful complexity and integration of all its elements. Drinking beautifully now, it will age another three to four years.

If the 2001 is gone, try the excellent 2002 Highliner, my recommendation. This wine is opaque to the stem and black-purple in the glass. It shows many of the same flavor components as the excellent 2001 with its mélange of stone fruit and spice, but this wine has even greater depth and structure. It is soft, lush, and elegant in the mouth, and I predict it will surpass the 2001 in greatness. It will age eight or nine years without problem, if you have the patience to wait that long.

RATING: Three stars (very good to excellent wines across the line)

Huber Cellars

WINERY OWNERS: Norman and Traudl Huber

WINEMAKER: Norman Yost

TASTING ROOM: At Olde Mission Wine Company or Wine Country

DAYS/HOURS: Friday–Sunday 9 A.M.–6 P.M., Monday–Thursday 9:30 A.M.–5:30 P.M. (Olde Mission); daily 11 A.M.–5 P.M. (Wine Country)

ADDRESS: Olde Mission Wine Company (Honeywood Farm), 1539 Mission Dr., #A, Solvang, CA 93436; Wine Country, 2445 Alamo Pintado Ave., Los Olivos, A 93441; 805-686-9323 (Olde Mission), 805-686-9699 (Wine Country); 805-736-7814 (fax); hubercellars.com

WINES/GRAPE VARIETIES: Chardonnay, Dornfelder, Pinot Noir

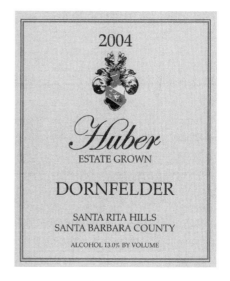

2004

Huber

ESTATE GROWN

DORNFELDER

SANTA RITA HILLS
SANTA BARBARA COUNTY

ALCOHOL 13.0% BY VOLUME

WINE CLUB: Online store

REGION: Santa Rita Hills AVA

In scholarship, as in life, you work an inordinate amount of time to get what you feel is a pretty good grasp on things, until a new discovery or item of information comes along and reintroduces you to humility. This is exactly what happened when I met Traudl and Norman Huber. I live for such moments, because they give me the opportunity to participate in the joy of discovery and learning something new. Norman Huber introduced me to a variety of grape, the Dornfelder, and Traudl provided me with a recipe for *Zopf,* a sweet, braided bread that my grandmother in Germany baked specially for me.

Norman left Canada at age seven when his family moved to Germany. He met Traudl while in school and married her not ten days before they immigrated to the United States in 1953. Norman received formal training as an artisan woodworker in Munich and also learned from his father, who practiced the craft. They started their life in America in Glendale, California, and later moved to Long Beach. You can see elements of Norman's work in the department stores and banks in the area. After he retired from the woodworking business, the Hubers bought their current property in the Santa Rita Hills appellation in 1986, second there only to Walter and Mona Babcock. They made frequent trips through the area to visit their son, then attending Cal Poly, and found a perfect spot for their retirement home. They built a house on the property (the woodwork, all done by Norman, is splendid throughout the house), drilled a well, and discovered water. With encouragement from the Babcocks, they planted a vineyard in 1987. Currently they still sell most of their grapes to outstanding wineries in the area, but a few years ago Norman began to make wine as a hobby. Convinced of the potential of the grapes in his vineyard, Huber has brought in Norman Yost of Flying Goat Cellars to make the wines professionally.

RECOMMENDED WINES: Norman Huber recommends the Chardonnay. The 2002 is straw-colored with golden highlights. The nose has honey, butter, apples, pears, and crème fraîche. The lovely nose is complemented by the luscious mouthfeel, which speaks to the wonderful balance of fruit, acidity, and minerality in the wine. The finish is nearly a minute long. In every regard this wine is, as the Germans say, *ausgezeichnet* ("excellent")!

I recommend the Estate Dornfelder. After a recent trip back to Europe I was embarrassed to see that the Dornfelder grape is fairly well known in Germany's Rheinhessen and Pfalz wine regions. The Dornfelder is the result of a cross by German viticulturist August Herold in 1956; according to Jancis Robinson, the grape "incorporates every important red wine vine grown in Germany somewhere in its genealogy and happily seems to have inherited many more of their good points than their bad." I tasted both the 2002 and the 2003, the '03 capable of surpassing the excellence of the '02. The 2003 is so dark and black in the glass that it is like looking down into the back of a cave. This black-purple wine has a perfumed nose of cassis, smoke, earth, leather, blackberries, and black cherries. The wine is beautifully balanced among the sweet perfume of the fruit, the acidity, and the soft tannins. It already shows excellent structure and complexity. It is accessible now but will certainly age another ten to fourteen years. The wine is a fantastic find, and if you enjoy discovering varieties far off the beaten track, the Huber Dornfelder will not disappoint. Be warned: it will stain your tongue a delicious black and purple for a time, but half the fun is showing and sharing the stain with friends. I am pleased to report that the 2003 recently won a gold medal and the Chairman's Best of Class award at the Grand Cru tasting competition in Long Beach, California.

RATING: Three → four stars (whites and reds very good to excellent; Dornfelder is outstanding)

J. Kerr Wines

WINERY OWNERS: John Kerr and Joan Brandoff-Kerr

WINEMAKER: John Kerr

TASTING ROOM: At Los Olivos Tasting Room & Wine Shop

DAYS/HOURS: Daily 11 A.M.–6 P.M.

ADDRESS: Los Olivos Tasting Room & Wine Shop, 2905 Grand Ave., Los Olivos, CA

93441; 805-688-7406; 805-688-0906 (fax); jkerrwines.com

WINES/GRAPE VARIETIES: Cambodian Red (blend), Chardonnay, Syrah, Zinfandel

WINE CLUB: No

REGION: Santa Barbara County

John Kerr was born in Oakland, California, the son of a career Navy "top gun" pilot. While he was in junior college the Army called him to duty, and as the son in a service family, he joined without hesitation. He shared his father's love for flying, but his eyes weren't good enough to qualify; the Army offered him an appointment to West Point, but he wanted to stay in aviation, so he reenlisted and spent the next two years of his life in Vietnam as a helicopter weapons specialist and door gunner. He served as a gunsmith working on the heavy machine guns and got the flight time he wanted as a door gunner. John has the dubious honor of having been aboard the first helicopter officially shot down while flying over Cambodia. Thought to be dead on rescue, he managed a remarkable recovery and eventually rotated back to the United States. In recognition of these experiences John produces a wine called Cambodian Red, a Syrah blend of different vintages. A percentage of John's profits from the sale of this wine goes into a fund he has established for Vietnam veterans, a noble cause indeed.

His service completed, he returned home a decorated veteran and went to work at Brookside Winery in Ventura in 1972. His family served wine at the dinner table, and his father's postings all over the world afforded John the chance to try a wide variety of wines. In Vietnam he often used his ration card to trade for French wines. While at Brookside, where he helped in the tasting room and ran the tractor, he made wines at home. In 1973 John's wife, Joan Brandoff-Kerr, received her bachelor's degree and starting working for the Forest Service in Los Padres National Forest. In 1978 she was assigned to the Monterey Ranger District and began work on her master's degree, which she completed in 1982. In 1980, she and John moved to Monterey County where he began working for Chalone, then Jekel, eventually spending four years at Ventana Vineyards, where he was in charge of production. In 1984 they moved back to Santa Barbara County, where John became a consulting winemaker and Joan became the lead archaeologist for the Forest Service in the Santa Barbara Ranger District.

In addition to making his own wines, John has had a very successful career as an independent consulting winemaker. He had the pleasure of assisting Bryan Babcock with the first crush at Babcock Winery. All seven wines produced during that first crush won medals. He also assisted Fred Brander in 1985 and 1986 and later worked at Byron. In early 1987 John made wines at Houtz Winery, which later became Beckmen

Vineyards. In the meantime, he produced wines for his own label, launched in 1986. When Byron became part of Mondavi in 1990, he took the position of assistant winemaker, and 1995 saw him working for the Firestone family at J. Carey Cellars. Firestone changed the name to Curtis but sold the facility to William Foley and transferred the Curtis name to a facility near the Firestone Winery, with John continuing to make the wines until 1998. He then dedicated his time to the development of his label, J. Kerr Wines.

RECOMMENDED WINES: John recommends the Reserve Chardonnay from Bien Nacido grapes. The 1999 is green-gold in the glass with a complex nose of pears, apples, quince, a dab of butter, orange zest, honey, apricot, and pineapple. The wine has a lovely acidity to balance the ripe fruit, and the mouthfeel is rich and luscious. The finish is long and smooth, lasting nearly a minute. The wine is ready for drinking now, but this beauty should last another eight or nine years. It is excellent in every regard.

I suggest the Syrah. I tasted a sample pulled from the barrel of the 2003 vintage. The red-purple wine is almost opaque in the glass and has a nose of blackberries, cloves, red currants, and cherries. The oak gives the wine a vanilla creaminess, and the wine will receive another year in the barrel before bottling. The components for an excellent wine are in place.

RATING: Three stars (both reds and whites are very good to excellent)

J. Wilkes

WINERY OWNERS: Jeff and Kimberly Wilkes

WINEMAKER: Jeff Wilkes

TASTING ROOM: No

DAYS/HOURS: By appointment only

ADDRESS: 2717 Aviation Way, Santa Maria, CA 93455; 805-899-2845; 805-957-0101 (fax); jwilkes.com

WINES/GRAPE VARIETIES: Pinot Blanc, Pinot Noir

WINE CLUB: Online sales

REGION: Santa Barbara County

Jaffurs Wine Cellars

WINERY OWNER: Craig Jaffurs

WINEMAKER: Craig Jaffurs

TASTING ROOM: Yes

DAYS/HOURS: Friday–Sunday 12–4 P.M.

ADDRESS: 819 E. Montecito St., Santa Barbara, CA 93103; 805-962-7003; 805-962-7003 (fax); jaffurswine.com

WINES/GRAPE VARIETIES: Grenache, Petite Sirah, Roussanne, Syrah, Viognier

WINE CLUB: Yes

REGION: Santa Barbara County

Kalyra Winery / M. Brown

WINERY OWNER: Mike Brown

WINEMAKER: Mike Brown

TASTING ROOM: Yes

DAYS/HOURS: Saturday–Sunday 10 A.M.–4:45 P.M., Monday–Friday 11 A.M.–4:45 P.M.

ADDRESS: 343 N. Refugio Rd., Santa Ynez, CA 93460; 805-693-8864; 805-693-8865 (fax); kalyrawinery.com

WINES/GRAPE VARIETIES: Black Muscat, Cabernet Franc rosé, Cabernet Sauvignon, Cashmere (blend), Chardonnay, dessert wines, eiswein, Gewürztraminer, Merlot, Nebbiolo, Orange Muscat, Pinot Grigio, port, Riesling, Sangiovese, Sémillon, Sauvignon Blanc, Syrah

WINE CLUB: Yes

TASTING ROOM AMENITIES: Merchandise

REGION: Santa Ynez Valley AVA

Mike Brown, the owner and winemaker of Kalyra, hails from Australia and travels frequently back home from Santa Barbara County, where he now surfs and makes wine. Originally from South Australia's Riverland region, where his father owned a vineyard, Mike got his start working for his dad. After pulling shoots in the heat and humidity of the Australian climate, Mike quickly decided to try another line of work. He graduated from the University of Adelaide with degrees in microbiology and pharmacology. In the United States, he finished a master's degree in enology at UC Davis in 1981. On a tour through Napa he came south, discovered the beaches and surfing of Santa Barbara County, and looked for a place to hang his surfboard. His first job was at Los Vineros in Santa Maria. He traveled back to Australia in the off-season for work experience to augment his training at Davis. Done with so much continent-hopping, he took a job at Zaca Mesa Winery in 1983, where he worked with Bob Lindquist. His next job was making wines at the historic Santa Ynez Valley Winery.

In 1989 Mike started the Kalyra label. That same year, the Santa Ynez Valley Winery label was sold, and Mike left. In 1989 Betty Williams of Buttonwood Farm Winery offered him the job of head winemaker even as he continued to grow his own line. In 1997, using his contacts and expertise with Australian grapes, Mike started the M. Brown label, designed to feature the best of Australia's finest wine-producing regions.

The Kalyra name has an interesting genesis. In addition to owning a vineyard, Mike's father was a thoracic surgeon. During his work with tribal people in New Guinea, he was stationed at a sanatorium called Kalyra, a native word for a flowering plant that grows there. It is also the Aborigines' word for a "wild and pleasant place," which fits perfectly the theme that Mike and his brother Martin present at their tasting room, opened in 2002 on the site of the former Santa Ynez Valley Winery. Over the years that property did not receive the care it deserved, and Mike has revitalized the vineyards and the winery. If you visit the tasting room, seen in the movie *Sideways,* you'll see the surfboard and the Australian themes that mark this interesting and decidedly unsnobbish winery.

RECOMMENDED WINES: Mike has had great success with both port and late-harvest dessert wines. In fact, he is one of the few winemakers I know who has ever made a port from the Gewürztraminer grape. Mike recommends Cashmere, a blend of Cabernet Franc, Shiraz, and Merlot that combines wines from Australia's renowned Barossa Valley with ones from the Santa Ynez Valley. The wine is opaque to the stem and black cherry in color. The nose is blackberries, plums, chocolate, black currants, and black cherries. The tannins are soft now and resolved, displaying the excellent fruit. A wine ready for the table, it should be drunk over the next two to three years.

In keeping with Mike's excellent reputation for dessert wines (also among my favorites), I'm pleased to recommend his Orange Muscat. The 2003 is lightly fortified and a pretty tangerine color. The nose is redolent of orange blossoms, lemon zest, apricots, and crème fraîche. The wine has a residual sugar of 8.5 percent, and the natural acidity nicely balances the sweetness. The nose is lovely, the middle is rich and luscious on the palate, and the acidity leads to a clean, satisfying finish. Drink now and over the next five years. If the 2003 is gone, look for the 2005.

RATING: Two stars (three stars for dessert wines)

Ken Brown Wines

WINERY OWNER: Ken Brown

WINEMAKER: Ken Brown

TASTING ROOM: No

DAYS/HOURS: By appointment only

ADDRESS: 2025 Still Meadows Rd., Solvang,
  CA 93463; 805-688-4482; 805-456-0656
  (fax); kenbrownwines.com

WINES/GRAPE VARIETIES: Chardonnay,
  Pinot Noir, Syrah

WINE CLUB: Mailing list

REGION: Santa Rita Hills AVA

Kenneth Volk Vineyards

WINERY OWNER: Ken Volk

WINEMAKER: Ken Volk

TASTING ROOM: Yes

DAYS/HOURS: Daily 10:30 A.M.–4:30 P.M.

ADDRESS: 5230 Tepusquet Rd., Santa Maria,
  CA 93454; 805-938-7896; 805-938-1324
  (fax); volkwines.com

WINES/GRAPE VARIETIES: Cabernet Sauvignon, Chardonnay, Merlot, Pinot Noir

WINE CLUB: Mailing list

REGION: Santa Maria Valley AVA

Ken Volk was the owner and winemaker at Wild Horse Winery & Vineyards for many years and has the distinction of being—along with Jerry Lohr, Gary Eberle, Justin Baldwin, Chuck Ortman, and John Alban—one of the great contributors to the establishment and acceptance of San Luis Obispo County wines in particular and, indirectly, the wines of the Central Coast. His importance, like Eberle's, is also rooted in his mentoring some of the Central Coast's most famous winemakers. He takes pride in the fact that more than a dozen wineries are now staffed, owned, or managed by his former employees. Such notables as Neil Collins, Matt Trevisan, John Priest, and Terry Culton, to name a few, worked with Ken at one time or another. He was instrumental in founding the Paso Robles Grape Growers Association in 1982, and served as its president and later as an officer of the Paso Robles Wine Growers Association. After the sale of Wild Horse in 2003 he took some time for himself, and is now ready to move back into grape growing and winemaking, albeit on a smaller scale.

Ken Volk's father was a builder-developer near San Ramon, and when a cellar was part of one of the family's purchases, Ken received his first exposure to wine culture. Ken grew up in Southern California where he developed first an interest in horticulture, then grape growing. His family had orchards on their property, and when Ken graduated from high school he thought about going into orchard management as a career. He started at the University of Arizona, came back to California after a semester, and finished an associate degree before going to Cal Poly to study fruit science in 1977. While at Poly, he came to know and enjoy the area and began making wine at home. In 1978 he took an internship at Edna Valley Vineyards, where he was given the title "You"—You get this, You do that, and so on. After discussing with his family the possibility of starting a vineyard-winery investment on the Central Coast, he almost bought land near Prunedale, but in November 1981 purchased 64 acres outside Templeton. He planted the vineyard on that property the next year and acquired a bond for the winery in 1983. He grew Wild Horse from an initial production of 600 cases to more than 120,000 cases of wine a year.

Ken stayed busy during the time his noncompete clause was in effect with the new owners of Wild Horse. Ken had his eye on the Byron Vineyard and Winery, founded by Kent Byron Brown in 1984. Brown brought that label to national prominence. In 1990 he sold to Mondavi but remained as winemaker and general manager, working with Tim Mondavi. Volk purchased the "original" Byron Winery facility in Santa Barbara County from Mondavi in 2004 and did winemaking for Mirasol Wine LLC. The Byron label and the "new" Byron Winery, Ken's next-door neighbor, were acquired by the Legacy Group in 2005, and I hope to include them in the next edition of this book. Kent Brown, Byron Winery's founder, is making wines in Lompoc under the Ken Brown Wines label. Volk established Kenneth Volk Vineyards at his new Santa Maria Valley winery in Santa Barbara County in 2004 and is featuring Pinot Noir and Chardonnay from Santa Maria Valley vineyards as well as Bordeaux varieties from Paso Robles. We welcome his return.

RECOMMENDED WINES: I recommend the Kenneth Volk Cabernet Sauvignon, made from Paso Robles grapes. The 2003 is a classic claret color and opaque to light. The nose is chocolate, leather, vanilla cookies, blackberries, candied cherries, anise, and ginger spice. The ripe fruit makes for a complex and well-integrated structure, which shows beautifully in the mouth. The persistent finish is more than a minute long. The wine is drinking beautifully now but will benefit from another seven to ten years of age. This bottle takes Volk's Cabernet up to the next level.

RATING: Ken has informed me that the Cab was released as of March 2006. Until I have the opportunity to taste his other releases, I will reserve my rating for the new winery.

Koehler Winery

WINERY OWNER: Kory Koehler

WINEMAKER: Chris Stanton

TASTING ROOM: Yes

DAYS/HOURS: Daily 10 A.M.–5 P.M.

ADDRESS: 5360 Foxen Canyon Rd., Los Olivos, CA 93441; 805-693-8384; 805-693-8383 (fax); koehlerwinery.com

WINES/GRAPE VARIETIES: Cabernet Sauvignon, Chardonnay, Pinot Noir, Riesling, Sangiovese, Sauvignon Blanc, Syrah, Twisted Tuscan (blend), Viognier

WINE CLUB: Yes

TASTING ROOM AMENITIES: Picnic area, merchandise

REGION: Santa Ynez Valley AVA

Wine and art are inextricably linked when it comes to the Central Coast. Some winemakers are artists, such as Gary Conway in Paso Robles and Ardison Phillips in Santa Maria; others have hired artists to produce their labels in the style of Mouton-Rothschild. In some instances, an artist is in the family, and in a few cases, all of the above applies. Some owner-vintners were at one time celebrities from Hollywood, as in the case of the gregarious Fess Parker. Douglas S. Cramer—a Hollywood producer who worked on such television series as *The Love Boat, Dynasty,* and others—originally owned the vineyard where Koehler Winery now sits. Cramer was also part-owner of the Sierra Madre vineyard, one of the pioneer vineyards planted in the area in 1973. That 750-acre property was sold to Mondavi in 1996. Cramer is noted as one of this country's leading collectors of contemporary art, some of which he stored in the building that later became the Curtis Winery tasting room. Cramer moved back to the East Coast in 1997 and sold the 100-acre estate to Kory Koehler. Dan Zurliene is the tasting-room manager, and the winemaker is Chris Stanton. Stanton is interested in making fruit-forward wines from estate fruit grown on one of the oldest vineyards in the region.

RECOMMENDED WINES: Dan recommends the Twisted Tuscan. The 2002, a blend of Sangiovese, Syrah, and Cabernet Sauvignon, is translucent and a red cherry color in the glass. The nose shows cherries, blackberries, white pepper, and a trace of sweetness. The wine is well balanced with sufficient acidity and tannin to support the ripe fruit. It has a ripe and rounded feel on the palate and a nice lively finish. The wine is ready for drinking now and over the next two years.

I suggest the Winemaker Select Cabernet Sauvignon. The 2000 spent three full years in the barrel. It too is translucent in the glass and red-purple in color. The dominant notes in the nose are cherries, chocolate, and cassis. There are enough tannins present to reward aging, but the wine is drinking well now. The ripeness of the fruit and the long time on the wood give the wine a lush finish. A hint of bell pepper appears at the end.

RATING: One star (well-made wines with reds ahead of whites)

Labyrinth

WINERY OWNER: Ariki Hill

WINEMAKER: Ariki Hill

TASTING ROOM: At Wine Country

DAYS/HOURS: Daily 11 A.M.–5 P.M.

ADDRESS: Wine Country, 2445 Alamo Pintado Ave., Los Olivos, CA 93441;

805-686-9699; 805-929-8534 (fax); labyrinthwine.com

WINE/GRAPE VARIETY: Pinot Noir

WINE CLUB: Yes

REGION: Santa Barbara County

Lafond Winery and Vineyards

WINERY OWNER: Pierre Lafond

WINEMAKER: Bruce McGuire

TASTING ROOM: Yes

DAYS/HOURS: Daily 10 A.M.–5 P.M.

ADDRESS: 6855 Santa Rosa Rd., Buellton, CA 93427; 805-688-7921; 805-693-1524 (fax); lafondwinery.com

WINES/GRAPE VARIETIES: Chardonnay, Pinot Noir, Syrah

WINE CLUB: Yes

TASTING ROOM AMENITIES: Picnic area, merchandise

REGION: Santa Rita Hills AVA

Pierre Lafond, an architecture graduate of Montreal's McGill University, came to Santa Barbara in 1957. At that time, there were no commercial wineries in Santa Barbara County. In 1962 Lafond changed the course of Santa Barbara's post-Prohibition wine history when he established Santa Barbara Winery (originally called El Paseo Cellars). Two years later, the facility still used by Santa Barbara Winery (see that profile for more of its history) opened. For the next ten years he was the only player on the board. During the early years of the winery, Pierre purchased his grapes from Bill York of the historic York Brothers Winery west of Paso Robles. In 1971, because the high-quality grapes produced in Santa Barbara were being sold to major wineries in Northern California, Pierre planted 65 acres in the Santa Rita Hills at the western tip of the Santa Ynez Valley. Bruce McGuire came aboard as winemaker ten years later. In 1998 Pierre Lafond, architect, designed the Lafond Winery, built by his son David, who served as the general contractor for the project. This facility, which emphasizes wine made exclusively from grapes grown in the Santa Rita Hills appellation, opened in the spring of 2001.

When Bruce McGuire arrived in 1981, he elevated the quality of the winemaking from amateur to professional status, according to Pierre, but even Bruce started as an amateur winemaker. As a precocious tenth grader, he received a home winemaking kit for Christmas in Long Island, New York. His uncle, a competent home winemaker, helped tutor his nephew. Bruce remembers with a certain fondness those early attempts at making rhubarb wine. At the University of New Hampshire, he earned a degree in entomology—perhaps a prescient choice given the current threat of the glassy-winged sharpshooter, a dangerous pest that, if not properly contained, threatens California's viticultural areas. After graduation, he pursued a career in winemaking and set out for California in 1979 to get firsthand experience working the harvest. He worked for a year at Chateau Souverain before a friend introduced him to Bill Arbios at Field Stone Winery. Shortly thereafter, he moved to Clarksburg, near Sacramento, to work at the now-defunct R & J Cook Winery. Bruce consulted for Pierre Lafond, who hired him as the full-time winemaker in 1981.

Bruce McGuire, nationally regarded and one of the first winemakers to explore and emphasize Pinot Noir and Syrah in Santa Barbara County, has the benefit of perspective as he looks over the Santa Rita Hills where his grapes are planted. He convinced Pierre and David, now general manager, to spend the money and take the time to grow the right varieties in the right places for the best possible results. He watched and contributed to the evolution of winemaking in Santa Barbara as it grew from largely amateur mom-and-pop operations to corporations run by such wine industry giants as Beringer, Kendall-Jackson, and Mondavi. Thanks to Pierre Lafond's foresight more than forty years ago, they will never again have to worry about getting high-quality grapes to make their award-winning wines.

RECOMMENDED WINES: Bruce recommends the Lafond Syrah. The 2001 is black and purple in color and almost opaque to the stem of the glass. The nose is sweet tobacco, strawberries, red currants, and white pepper spice. The wine comes alive in the mid-palate, showcasing the wonderful fruit and judicious use of oak. The white pepper reemerges on the finish. This wine is drinking very nicely now and should hold another five to six years.

I had the pleasure of tasting the 2000 Lafond Chardonnay and offer it as my recommendation. This is a golden Chardonnay with pineapple, pears, kiwifruit, and a drizzle of butter in the nose. This is a well-balanced, lively wine with excellent fruit, a lush middle, and a smooth finish. Drink it now and over the next three to four years.

RATING: Three stars (consistently excellent across the line)

Lane Tanner Winery

WINERY OWNER: Lane Tanner

WINEMAKER: Lane Tanner

TASTING ROOM: No

ADDRESS: P.O. Box 286, Santa Maria, CA 93456; no phone or fax; lanetanner.com

WINES/GRAPE VARIETIES: Pinot Noir, Syrah

WINE CLUB: Online sales

REGION: Santa Barbara County

Lincourt Vineyards

WINERY OWNER: William Foley II

WINEMAKER: Alan Phillips

TASTING ROOM: Yes

DAYS/HOURS: Daily 10 A.M.–5 P.M.

ADDRESS: 1711 Alamo Pintado Rd., Solvang, CA 93463; 805-688-8554; 805-688-9327 (fax); lincourtwines.com

WINES/GRAPE VARIETIES: Cabernet Sauvignon, Chardonnay, Merlot, Pinot Noir, rosé, Sauvignon Blanc, Syrah

WINE CLUB: Yes

TASTING ROOM AMENITIES: Picnic area, merchandise

REGION: Santa Ynez Valley AVA

No matter where you find yourself on the Central Coast, you are more than likely to find an outstanding golf course. Many of the visitors to the region spend the morning playing eighteen and the afternoon touring wineries. In 1994 avid golfer William Foley II (discussed in the profile of Foley Estates) and his wife, Carol, moved their four children out of the Los Angeles area to Santa Barbara County. A great fan of wines with a taste for fine Burgundies, Foley decided to enter the wine business. His initial venture was a partnership in the historic Santa Ynez Valley Winery, one of the earliest established in Santa Barbara County. In 1997 he purchased the majority share in the partnership and renamed it Lincourt, after his daughters Lindsay and Courtney.

The property where Lincourt wines are now offered was a dairy farm until the 1950s. Some of the original buildings still standing date from 1913. In the early '70s, Dr. Jim Carey purchased the place and started a winery, J. Carey Cellars. The Firestone family purchased the property from Carey and changed the name to Curtis with the intent to establish the label as a superpremium line. In 1997 Bill Foley bought the property, but the Firestones kept the Curtis name and reestablished it with a tasting room closer to the main Firestone facility. The next year, Foley bought 460 acres of hillside property in the Santa Rita Hills, securing a reliable source of high-quality grapes for both the Foley and the Lincourt lines. Because Bill loves golf, he often played with the Miller brothers of Bien Nacido. This afforded him access to their premium grapes as well. Bill built a brand-new facility on the Santa Rita Hills land near Babcock and Melville, which now houses the Foley tasting room; the original Foley tasting room on Alamo Pintado Road is now the Lincourt tasting room. (The only facility to predate Lincourt in the area—that is, the Santa Ynez Valley Winery—is now Kalyra.)

Alan Phillips grew up in the Bay Area, went to Davis to become a veterinarian, and got hooked on chemistry. He took a job as a chemist at a winery to help pay his way through college. Working in the Central Valley, he sampled and checked the sugars and acidity in the grapes to determine picking times. Unfortunately, he almost died from pesticide-related illnesses, so he moved on to Rutherford Hill Winery, where the chemist had just left. At Davis he switched to a chemistry major and got credit for his work in the field. He eventually graduated with a degree in enology and a minor in chemistry. In 1978 he became the assistant winemaker at Rutherford, though he was still working on his degree. He graduated in 1979 and after two years went to work for Monticello Vineyards in Napa, where he helped build the winery and was the winemaker for nine years. In the meantime, he started a consulting company for new wineries starting up and needing a one-stop shop for their business venture. After a stint as winemaker and general manager for a winery in Santa Cruz, he became the director of winemaking at both Lincourt and Foley in 1998.

RECOMMENDED WINES: Alan recommends the Chardonnay, for which Lincourt gained its first accolades; this wine from his inaugural 1997 vintage was named one of *Wine Spectator's* top 100 wines. The 2002 is butter-yellow with a nose of pears, apples, butter, mango, and honeysuckle. The wine has excellent acidity to balance the voluptuous fruit. The finish is long and satisfying and plays up the ripe, luscious fruit. Drink now and over the next three to four years.

I recommend the Pinot Noir. The 2002 is cherry-red and light to the stem. The aromatics are reminiscent of boysenberry, cherry, chocolate, and vanilla spice. The wine is nicely balanced and has a velvety texture in the mouth. Drink now and over the next three to four years.

RATING: Three stars (whites ahead of reds)

Lions Peak Vineyards

WINERY OWNERS: Ken and Jennifer Soni

WINEMAKERS: Ken and Jennifer Soni

TASTING ROOM: Yes

DAYS/HOURS: Friday–Monday 11 A.M.–7 P.M., Tuesday–Thursday by appointment only

ADDRESS: 1659 Copenhagen Dr., Solvang, CA 93463; 805-693-5466; 805-467-3436 (fax); lionspeakwine.com

WINES/GRAPE VARIETIES: Barbera, Bon Courage (red blend), Cabernet Franc, Cabernet Sauvignon, Cabernet Sauvignon port, Chardonnay, late-harvest Viognier, Lionnesse (red blend), LuLu (white blend), Marsanne, Merlot, Mourvèdre, Petite Sirah, Sangiovese, The Sisters (white blend), Syrah, Viognier, Zinfandel

WINE CLUB: Yes

TASTING ROOM AMENITIES: Merchandise

REGION: San Luis Obispo County

As a young man, Ken Soni escaped the apartheid of South Africa to start a new life in the United States. He arrived in New York with less than a hundred dollars in his pocket. After one of his good friends back in South Africa, a dentist, was tortured to death, Soni went to dental school in his honor and built a successful practice in cosmetic dentistry. Jennifer Soni, already a successful interior designer, escaped the heat of Texas by accepting a position with a design firm in Southern California. In 1971 an acquaintance, Philip Doub, a professor at Cal Poly, bought land in San Miguel and planted a vineyard. Ken and Jennifer often traveled to the Central Coast from Long Beach to visit and taste wine, and at one point Ken decided he wanted to own a vineyard and make wines. On Valentine's Day 1991 they visited Doub's vineyard north of Paso Robles, which was for sale. The Sonis bought the place, and Jennifer went to work decorating the Victorian house on the property while Ken started on the vineyard and later made his first batch of wine.

After favorable feedback on his early efforts, the Sonis searched for an appropriate label. Jennifer had selected a famous painting by the Swiss-born painter Jacques-Laurent Agasse as a birthday gift for Ken and learned that the rights to Agasse's painting *Lion and Lioness* were available. The theme in the painting remains central to the winery as Ken is a Leo and the couple work together like a lion and a lioness to make the winery successful. A few years ago, they debated whether they should first release a 1994 vintage or the 1995 Cabernet Sauvignon. Unable to reach a decision, they turned to chef-owner Laurent Grangien at Bistro Laurent in Paso Robles. Ken set up a blind tasting, and Chef Grangien selected the 1995. When Grangien asked where he could acquire the wine for his restaurant, Soni told him that they had made it and thus made his first sale. The results of their passion for wine were realized when they saw Lions Peak featured on the wine list at the restaurant.

RECOMMENDED WINES: Not surprisingly, Ken recommends the Reserve Cabernet Sauvignon while Jennifer suggests the Lionnesse, a Bordeaux blend of Cabernet Sauvignon, Merlot, and Cabernet Franc. The Reserve is opaque to the stem and a classic black-purple wine of cedar, tobacco, cherries, and black currants. The wine is well integrated, with the fruit in harmony with the French oak. The finish is long; this wine will age another five years.

The 2000 Lionnesse is slightly less concentrated than the 1999 and black cherry in color. The nose is plum, black cherry, and a hint of mocha. The tannins are softer and more resolved than the Reserve because of the blend, and there is excellent fruit in the middle. The finish is long and satisfying, and the wine is ready for drinking now.

My recommendation is the Late Harvest Viognier. I tried the 2001, barrel-aged. The wine shows gold and the first note is crème brûlée, followed by hazelnut, butterscotch, apricot, and honeysuckle. This is a relatively sweet, complex wine with enough acidity to balance the sugars. The finish is somewhat nutty (almonds), and the wine will easily reward four years of aging.

RATING: Three stars (very good to excellent whites and reds)

Longoria Wines

WINERY OWNERS: Rick and Diana Longoria

WINEMAKER: Rick Longoria

TASTING ROOM: Yes

DAYS/HOURS: Friday–Sunday 11 A.M.–4:30 P.M.; Monday, Wednesday, and Thursday 12–4:30 P.M.

ADDRESS: 2935 Grand Ave., Los Olivos, CA 93441; 805-688-0305; 805-688-2676 (fax); longoriawine.com

WINES/GRAPE VARIETIES: Cabernet Franc, Chardonnay, Pinot Grigio, Pinot Noir, Syrah, Tempranillo

WINE CLUB: Yes

TASTING ROOM AMENITIES: Picnic area, merchandise

REGION: Santa Ynez Valley AVA

André Tchelistcheff is a true icon of the wine world and is considered an important contributor to the overall quality and growth of California winemaking. Though thought primarily to have influenced winemaking in Northern California, he also had a lasting influence on the Central Coast region. He advised, among others, Stanley Hoffman at Paso Robles; consulted for the Firestones; and was a close friend of Richard and Diana Longoria. He died in 1994 at the age of ninety-two, passing on his legacy to the many California winemakers he taught, nurtured, and befriended.

Rick's father was in the Air Force, and the family traveled around the United States. While his father was based at Vandenberg Air Force Base, Rick went to Cabrillo High in Lompoc. He started his university education at UC Santa Barbara but transferred to Berkeley at a time when the counterculture revolution was in full force. Rick took part in the protests, ran in the riots, and got tear gas in his nose. His appreciation for the classical and traditional tempered his love of the new and radical when he and friends traveled to Napa to sample and taste the free wines. After graduation in 1973 he thought he was destined for law school but took a year off to see the world. He went to Colombia, a rough and tough place to live even today, but fell in love with the people there, despite being robbed on a train and forced to return home. He dropped his plans for law school, thought working in a winery would be a better way to live, and sent out his résumé. He got two responses: Pedroncelli Winery said no; Buena Vista said yes.

Buena Vista hired him as a cellar rat, and he loved it, but the staff tested the new guy. They put him on the bottling line and for an entire week he ran the corking machine until his arm swelled so badly that he had to take a week off before it returned to normal size. At Buena Vista Rick started his long relationship with Tchelistcheff, then working at Beaulieu Vineyards. Rick remembers the great man as barely five feet two inches tall, but every inch of him a cordial and class act. After about five months, Buena Vista promoted Rick to senior cellar master and allowed him to taste with the great Tchelistcheff, who took an immediate liking to the young man. André informed him that he had started working for the Firestone family, who needed a cellar master. Not willing to pass up an opportunity to return home, Rick applied for the job, was hired in 1976, and helped bottle Firestone's first vintage. At that time, Pierre Lafond had established Santa Barbara Winery, Sanford and Benedict had produced a vintage, Fred Brander was working at Santa Ynez Winery, Ken Brown was a new graduate from Fresno State working at Zaca Mesa, Harold Pfeiffer was at Rancho Sisquoc—and that was pretty much it for the Santa Barbara County wine scene, as Rick remembers it. He stayed at Firestone for two years, where he met his wife, Diana, Firestone's first tour guide.

Rick moved to Chappellet Winery, but decided that life in the wine business back home was better and that the wines there had the potential to become world-class. His buddy Fred Brander recommended him to J. Carey Cellars. Jim Carey and his son, both medical doctors, were at a crossroads: the father wanted to sell grapes, but the son wanted a winery and hired Rick in 1979. Unfortunately, they wanted him only two or three days a week, but this became an advantage when Pfeiffer at Sisquoc needed a part-time winemaker for the 1979 vintage. Rick stayed at Carey five years, and then worked for Gainey Vineyards in 1985. He greatly enjoyed his twelve years there, blossoming as a winemaker. He started Gainey's Reserve program and built the Chardonnay and Pinot Noir offerings, advising Gainey to focus on the Pinot Noir. In 1997 he moved on, ready to give his time to his own label, launched during his tenure at J. Carey in 1982. The tasting room in Los Olivos opened in 1998. As a side note, Rick also consulted on one of my favorite wines, Huber's Dornfelder.

RECOMMENDED WINES: Rick recommends the Blues Cuvée, an artist series he initiated to popularize Cabernet Franc from the area. The 2001 is a blend of Cab Franc and Malbec, making the wine opaque in the glass and black cherry in color. The nose is redolent of cherries, sherried oak, vanilla, and crème de cassis. The wine is full and round on the palate, and the great fruit comes through on the attack and again at the finish. This is a wonderful blend and points to the potential of Cabernet Franc from this region. Drink now and over the next five to eight years.

My personal favorite among Rick's excellent portfolio of Pinot Noirs is the 2002 Mt. Carmel Vineyard, the fruit taken from fourteen-year-old vines. The wine is ruby-red and opaque in the glass. The nose is cinnamon spice, earth, cherries, plums, loganberries, and a hint of caramel. The wine is outstanding on the tongue; it has extraordinary structure and balance and a wonderful complexity. The finish is luscious and rich. In all, these wines are outstanding examples of Rick's talent as winemaker. Drink now and over the next five years.

RATING: Four stars (consistently excellent to outstanding across the line)

Lucas & Lewellen Vineyards

WINERY OWNERS: Louis Lucas and Royce Lewellen

WINEMAKER: Daniel Gehrs

TASTING ROOM: Yes

DAYS/HOURS: Daily 11 A.M.–5:30 P.M.

ADDRESS: 1645 Copenhagen Dr., Solvang, CA 93463; 805-686-9336; 805-686-1081 (fax); llwine.com

WINES/GRAPE VARIETIES: Cabernet Franc, Cabernet Sauvignon, Chardonnay, Merlot, Pinot Noir, Petite Sirah, Petit Verdot, port, Riesling, Sauvignon Blanc, sparkling wine, Syrah, Viognier

WINE CLUB: Yes

TASTING ROOM AMENITIES: Merchandise

REGION: Santa Ynez Valley AVA

Over the past thirty years, Louis Lucas has been one of the principal driving forces behind Santa Barbara County's rise to worldwide recognition for the quality of its grapes and wines. Notable companies such as Sebastiani, Kendall-Jackson, Mondavi, Parker, and others have made their reputations to a significant degree through the purchase and use of grapes from the Lucas and later (Lucas & Lewellen) vineyards. Louis teamed up with Judge Royce Lewellen in 1996 to start Lucas & Lewellen Vineyards and wines. (Because Lucas is also co-owner in the Mandolina venture, I discuss him in that profile and in the "Wine History" section of this chapter, featuring Judge Lewellen here.)

Royce Lewellen is a native of St. Louis, Missouri, and received his undergraduate degree from the University of Missouri in 1952. He came to California to pursue a degree in law at UC Berkeley after his service in the Air Force. His distinguished law career began in 1957. He established himself in a civil practice in Solvang and served as the Solvang Justice Court judge from 1969 to 1975. Interestingly, he once represented the Firestone family during his civil practice. He later received an appointment as judge of the Superior Court in Santa Maria. On his retirement the court complex where he worked was renamed the Lewellen Justice Center in his honor. Judge Lewellen also has a long and distinguished record of service to his community. Royce and his wife, Ann, reside in Santa Ynez.

In order to accomplish a vertical integration of their substantial viticultural interests, Royce and Louis became partners. They now own vineyards in the three principal microclimates for wine-grape growing in Santa Barbara County: Goodchild vineyard in the Santa Maria Valley, notable for Pinot Noir and Chardonnay; Los Alamos vineyards in Los Alamos, where the Italian varieties for the Mandolina program thrive; and Solvang's Valley View vineyard, best known for Cabernet and Sauvignon Blanc. Wines made from these grapes bear one of three proprietary labels: Lucas & Lewellen (focus on Rhône, Bordeaux, and Burgundy grapes), Queen of Hearts (focus on affordable reds and whites), and Mandolina (focus on Italian-style wines). The winemaker is Daniel Gehrs, formerly of Zaca Mesa Winery.

RECOMMENDED WINES: Judge Lewellen recommends the Côte del Sol Cabernet Sauvignon. The 2003 was cofermented with a touch of Syrah. The wine is an opaque black cherry color in the glass. The nose shows cherries, chocolate, black currants, and a hint of anise. The wine has a lovely ripeness and soft, rounded tannins that lead to an excellent feel in the mouth. The lush finish lasts almost a minute. Drink now and over the next five to seven years.

I recommend the 2002 Viognier. This lovely gold-colored wine has a nose of honey, apricots, and grapefruit to go with its spice and excellent minerality. The acidity is sufficient to balance the ripe fruit and leads the wine to a refreshing finish. Drink now and over the next three to four years. If the 2002 is gone, the 2004 is vinified in a similar style.

RATING: Two stars (some very good values to be found)

Mandolina

WINERY OWNERS: Louis Lucas and Royce
   Lewellen

WINEMAKER: Daniel Gehrs

TASTING ROOM: Yes

DAYS/HOURS: Daily 11 A.M.–6 P.M.

ADDRESS: 1665 Copenhagen Dr., Solvang,
   CA 93463; 805-686-5506; 805-686-1081
   (fax); llwine.com

WINES/GRAPE VARIETIES: Barbera,
   Dolcetto, Malvasia Bianca, Moscato,
   Nebbiolo, Pinot Grigio, Pinot Nero,
   rosato, Sangiovese, sparkling wine, Super
   Tuscan blends, Toccata (blend)

WINE CLUB: Yes

TASTING ROOM AMENITIES: Merchandise

REGION: Santa Ynez Valley AVA

The mandolin is a small, short-necked musical instrument with eight strings. It is the descendant of the lute, whose history can be traced back to Mesopotamia about 2000 B.C.E. In Latin, a smaller version of the lute is called a *mandora*. The Italians called the miniature version of this instrument a *mandolina.* Mandolina is also part of a venture started by Louis Lucas and Royce Lewellen in 1996.

Louis Lucas has been instrumental in establishing the Santa Barbara County wine industry and propelling it to prominence. Louis's father, the son of Croatian immigrants, was a leading grower of table grapes in the Central Valley. Louis went east for his university education, and he is a 1963 graduate of Notre Dame with a degree in finance and business economics. After graduation he returned to California to help with his father's agricultural business. Shortly thereafter, he embarked on a viticultural odyssey with his brother George and partner Al Gagnon that would shape many of the Central Coast's great vineyards. The three planted the now-famous Tepusquet vineyard in 1970; Dale Hampton was then their equipment foreman. At the time, the only other two locals engaged in planting grapes were Bill Nielsen and Boyd Bettencourt. In 1971 Louis planted a vineyard in Paso Robles. Prior to the '70s Pesenti, Rotta, Hoffman, and York were about the extent of the wine business in San Luis Obispo County. In 1971–72 he planted grapes in Shandon, east of Paso. He also put in vineyards at Firestone and planted Bien Nacido. It was during these years that Louis challenged the conventional viticultural wisdom and began testing his own theories. He also spent several summers touring the wine regions of France, Italy, Spain, and Germany to study their methods and growing systems. In 1972–73, he planted with Jack Niven at the Paragon vineyard in the Edna Valley, a property that Louis and Al helped Niven select. It was none other than Louis Lucas who went north to Napa, met with Brother Timothy at Christian Brothers, and convinced him that the grapes grown in Santa Barbara County had potential. This single event, perhaps more than any other, put the Central Coast wine industry on the map. In 1996 he partnered with Royce Lewellen, and the two now produce their own wines. Daniel Gehrs (who also has his own label) is the winemaker. Mandolina is the third label from the Lucas-Lewellen partnership and offers wines made from Italian grape varieties.

RECOMMENDED WINES: Louis recommends the Nebbiolo, whose grapes are orange-colored at the time of harvest. The wine permits light to the stem and is cough-drop red in the glass. The 2000 has a nose of cherries, tea, roses, and crème fraîche. The wine is lovely in the mouth, with great ripeness in the fruit to supplement the excellent balance. The finish is long and lush and lasts a minute. This wine reminded me very much of a classic Barolo. It is ready for drinking now and over the next three or four years.

I recommend the Toccata Riserva, a blend of Cabernet Sauvignon, Sangiovese, Merlot, Cabernet Franc, and Freisa (a little-known grape grown near the town of Asti in Italy; often used for blending, it has a raspberry nose). The beautiful 2001 is opaque in the glass and black cherry in color. It shows cherries in the nose, along with raspberries, black currants, smoke, leather, some cedar notes, and a hint of mocha. The tannins are lush and silky, leading to a plush feel on the tongue. The finish is fully a minute in length and recalls the wonderful balance and integration of this wine. It is both elegant and refined and one of the best examples of a Super Tuscan wine that I have tasted in the region. Drink now and over the next seven to nine years.

RATING: Three → four stars (reds ahead of whites)

Margerum Wine Company

WINERY OWNER: Douglas Margerum

WINEMAKER: Douglas Margerum

TASTING ROOM: Yes

DAYS/HOURS: Daily 11 A.M.–3 P.M.

ADDRESS: Wine Cask restaurant, 813 Anacapa St., Santa Barbara, CA 93101; 805-966-9463; 805-892-9611 (fax); margerumwinecompany.com

WINES/GRAPE VARIETIES: M5 (blend), Pinot Gris, Pinot Noir, Riesling, rosé, Sauvignon Blanc, Syrah

WINE CLUB: Yes

TASTING ROOM AMENITIES: Restaurant

REGION: Santa Ynez Valley AVA

Doug Margerum got interested in wine culture at age thirteen when he spent a summer vacation with his parents in Avignon and visited the famous Châteauneuf-du-Pape. He toured the caves, saw the equipment, and was exposed to life in the *vignobles*. When he came of age in Woodland Hills, California, of course, the first wines he bought for the family's Thanksgiving table were from Châteauneuf-du-Pape.

His first jobs were in restaurants, employment that he maintained while working his way through college. While at UC Santa Barbara studying for his bachelor's degree in economics he met a French foreign exchange student, and the two traveled to the south of France. By then, he was convinced that he wanted to work in the wine industry, if only on the business side. It happened that he knew the person who owned the Wine Cask restaurant in Santa Barbara and when informed that it was for sale, his family bought it and opened a wine bar next to it. He ran that restaurant and wine bar for more than twenty years and now owns it outright, doing his tasting there.

In 2001 he decided to make his own wine. He turned over the management of the restaurant to good and capable people and set about learning the craft, using his experience and perspective gleaned from visiting wineries around the world. He makes wines he likes to drink and emphasizes the wines he knew as a young man growing up, namely, the Rhône varieties and Sauvignon Blanc. Doug leases facilities above the Curtis Winery tasting room and for the first three years did everything by himself. Now that his line has been well received, he is taking on some additional help in the cellar. Doug's mentor is Jim Clendenen of Au Bon Climat, a great winemaker himself and a fine cook to boot; in fact, the two co-owned a restaurant named Vina Nova from 1986 to 1998.

RECOMMENDED WINES: Doug recommends the M5, his homage to the great Rhône wines he tasted in France. He blends the five principal grapes: Syrah, Grenache, Mourvèdre, Cinsaut, and Counoise. The 2003 is translucent in the glass and a deep purple-red color. The nose is blueberries, chocolate, leather, smoke, cassis, and red licorice. The ripe, opulent fruit leads to a huge presence on the palate and a long, intense finish that lasts a minute. The wine shows great complexity and integration of all its elements. Already drinking wonderfully now, it should be even better over the next seven to eight years. We tasted the 2004 from the barrel, and although it may not be as great as the 2003, this wine shows substantial potential this early in its life.

I suggest the 2004 single-vineyard Sauvignon Blanc. The wine is a pale lemon color, attesting to its youth. Grapefruit, melon, passion fruit, and kiwifruit linger in the bouquet. The wine has very good acidity to balance the fine fruit. An intriguing steeliness underlies the fruit. This is a well-made wine ready for drinking now and over the next three or four years.

RATING: Three stars (both reds and whites are consistently very good to excellent across the line)

McKeon-Phillips Winery

WINERY OWNERS: Susan McKeon and Ardison Phillips

WINEMAKER: Ardison Phillips

TASTING ROOM: Yes

DAYS/HOURS: Daily 11 A.M.–6 P.M.

ADDRESS: 2115 S. Blosser Rd., #114, Santa Maria, CA 93458; 805-928-3025; 805-928-0902 (fax); mckeonphillipswinery.com

WINES/GRAPE VARIETIES: Cabernet Franc, Cabernet Sauvignon, Ceazar (blend), Chardonnay, Leonardo (red blend), Leopoldo's Cub (blend), Leopoldo's Lair (blend), Merlot, Pinot Noir, port, Sangiovese, Sauvignon Blanc, Syrah

WINE CLUB: Yes

TASTING ROOM AMENITIES: Art and merchandise

REGION: Santa Maria Valley AVA

Ardison Phillips embodies many attributes of great teachers: he loves to teach, he knows his subject thoroughly, and he is not above challenging his students to push themselves and learn more. Perhaps most important, he genuinely loves what he does. Phillips is the only winemaker-educator I know who has drunk a 1789 Madeira and pulled the corks of more than 250,000 wines. A graduate of New York State University with a bachelor's degree in fine arts (1964), Ardison went on to take a master's in 1968 from the Otis Art Institute of Los Angeles County. One of his professors sparked his early interest that developed into a passion for art, food, and wine. Ardison made a splash in the art world by producing holographic Mylar mirror images for an architecture group, a project that Andy Warhol also participated in. Ardison's experiences with the project are detailed in his book, *Pavilion,* published by Dutton.

After working for a time in Japan, he returned to Hollywood and opened the renowned West Hollywood Studio Grill. By 1975 he was making a house wine for the restaurant featuring his artwork on the label, à la Mouton-Rothschild. At one time, the restaurant featured a cellar of more than 13,000 wines. Under the Studio Grill label he produced by customer demand a Black Muscat, a Cabernet Sauvignon, and a Pinot Noir, to mention a few. Today even French vintners are featuring his art on their labels. After he created the label for Qupé's Black Muscat, sales skyrocketed from 600 to 9,000 cases.

In 1982 Phillips and his wife, Susan McKeon, started the winery to feature his art, his winemaking skills (with the assistance of son Bailey), and his passion for food. Ardison is not interested in producing trophy wines sold only to collectors or traded as the value increases. He makes wines that pair well with food, are complex and multistructured, and represent good value for the quality of the wine. In the finest and most noble tradition of giving back, he is opening a cooking school in addition to teaching courses in the certificate program at Santa Maria's Allan Hancock College. You can also hear him on the radio in the area when he does his wine show.

RECOMMENDED WINES: Ardison suggests the 2002 Chardonnay, a wine with twenty-four months in French oak. A pretty bright gold color, it has a lovely nose of butterscotch, pears, and vanilla spice above an excellent layer of minerality. The wine is beautifully balanced by an acidity that will give it an additional nine to ten years of age. Altogether, this is a luscious and creamy wine of excellent Chardonnay fruit with a finish that lasts a full sixty seconds.

I suggest the Bailey's Private Reserve Cabernet Sauvignon, a wine that local wine entrepreneur Archie McLaren says is the Mouton-Rothschild of California. There is much to support Archie's enthusiasm for this wine. It is stygian black and opaque in the glass. The wonderful aromatics suggest semisweet chocolate, anise, black currants, and ripe blackberries. Everything about the wine is superb: the balance, the middle, and a finish that lasts well over a minute. Drink now and over the next ten years or so. As you taste Ardison's handcrafted vinous creations, take the time to try his first port-style wine too, as you enjoy his art featured in the tasting room.

RATING: Four stars (whites are excellent but slightly behind outstanding reds)

Melville Vineyards & Winery

WINERY OWNER: Ron Melville

WINEMAKER: Greg Brewer

TASTING ROOM: Yes

DAYS/HOURS: Daily 11 A.M.–4 P.M.

ADDRESS: 5185 E. Hwy. 246, Lompoc, CA 93436; 805-735-7030; 805-735-5310 (fax); melvillewinery.com

WINES/GRAPE VARIETIES: Chardonnay, Pinot Noir, Syrah

WINE CLUB: No

TASTING ROOM AMENITIES: Picnic area, merchandise

REGION: Santa Rita Hills AVA

Ron Melville began collecting wines during his college days. He has a particular passion for the wines of Burgundy. After graduating from college, he started a successful thirty-year career in finance as a member of the Pacific Stock Exchange. He estimates that during the great crash of 1987 he lost nearly 40 percent of his holdings in one day and knew it was time to diversify. In 1989 he looked north to Sonoma and bought a 153-acre ranch in Knight's Valley near Calistoga. There he indulged a passion for gardening, shared with his father, and planted Cabernet Sauvignon, Merlot, and Chardonnay grapes, which gave him his start in the viticulture business. Ron tells the wonderful story of dining in a local Napa restaurant where the wine list was limited mostly to Santa Barbara County wines. He almost left in despair, but grudgingly ordered an Au Bon Climat Pinot Noir at the last moment. Because of tasting that one wine, he made a point of exploring and trying more Pinot. In fact, he became something of a Pinot Noir fan and was frustrated that Calistoga was too hot to grow it.

Ron attended seminars and learned that growing Pinot Noir is a difficult enterprise, to say the least. He did research at UC Davis and learned everything he could about the grape and the best growing practices for it. By then he considered himself ready to take on the challenge of growing Pinot Noir: he had the right clones, he had the knowledge, all he needed was the right climate and place. He sold his interest in the Calistoga vineyard and moved down to Cambria. On one trip south he passed twenty-two trucks heading north with Chardonnay from the Bien Nacido vineyard. He called a winemaker he knew back in Napa and asked what they were paying for Santa Barbara County fruit. He was stunned when he heard the high prices Napa vintners were paying, and learned that the natural acidity level in Central Coast fruit did not require the addition of tartaric acid.

After talking to Bryan Babcock, Richard Sanford, and Bruce McGuire at Lafond, he knew he had to buy his next property in Santa Barbara County. He met Greg Brewer, a fellow Pinot Noir aficionado, and asked him if he would build a winery and become the winemaker. In 1996 they planted vineyards in the Santa Rita Hills outside Lompoc and opened the winery in 1999. Greg, who is also a partner with Steve Clifton at Brewer-Clifton, graduated from UC Santa Barbara at age twenty, with the hope of being a professor of French. He did additional study at the University of Lyon, met a girl, and taught in Burgundy. When he returned to the United States, Bruce McGuire offered him a job. He also worked at Sunstone before starting Brewer-Clifton in 1997. Currently, Ron's two sons are integral members of the team at Melville. Brent is a vineyard manager, and Chad is an assistant winemaker and vineyard manager.

RECOMMENDED WINES: Ron recommends the Terraces Pinot Noir. The 2002 is a sensational wine almost opaque to the stem, black cherry in the glass. The nose is ripe currants, cherries, strawberries, and cranberries atop a layer of earth and smoke. The wine is huge in the mouth but the ripe tannins give it a silky-smooth elegance. The finish on this muscular Pinot lasted more than a minute. It is accessible now but will drink beautifully for another five to six years.

I suggest the Santa Rita Hills Syrah. The 2002 reminds me of a Côte-Rôtie. The wine is opaque in the glass and purple-black in color. The nose is white pepper, vanilla, blackberries, and boysenberry. The mouthfeel is superb, and the wine shows excellent structure and balance. The finish on this one also exceeds a minute. Not only is this wine a top-flight Syrah, it represents a great value. Drink it now and over the next four to six years.

RATING: Five stars (both whites and reds are outstanding to superb)

Michael Grace Wines

WINERY OWNERS: Michael and Grace McIntosh

WINEMAKER: Michael McIntosh

TASTING ROOM: Yes

DAYS/HOURS: Friday–Sunday 11 A.M.–5 P.M. by appointment only

ADDRESS: 2717 Aviation Way, Santa Maria, CA 93454; 805-291-1008; 805-456-3903 (fax); michaelgracewine.com

WINES/GRAPE VARIETIES: Cabernet Sauvignon, Chardonnay, Grenache, Mourvèdre, Syrah

WINE CLUB: Yes

REGION: Santa Barbara County

Morovino

WINERY OWNERS: David and Andrea Bradford

WINEMAKER: Guerrino Moro

TASTING ROOM: Yes

DAYS/HOURS: Thursday–Sunday 10 A.M.– 5 P.M.

ADDRESS: 550 First St., Avila Beach, CA; 805-693-8466; no fax; morovino.com

WINES/GRAPE VARIETIES: Ambrato, Barbera, Cosa Dolce (dessert wine), Pinot Grigio, Sangiovese, Syrah, Tango (red blend), Zinfandel

WINE CLUB: Yes

TASTING ROOM AMENITIES: Merchandise

REGION: Santa Barbara County

Guerrino "Gerry" Moro has been a fixture on the Santa Barbara County wine scene since 1994 when he opened Morovino Winery. He recently sold the winery to David and Andrea Bradford but will stay on as winemaker. Born in Italy, Gerry was an athlete who represented Canada in the 1964 and 1972 Olympic Games in both the pole vault and the decathlon. He is a graduate of the University of Oregon and holds a master's degree from Cal Poly.

Gerry's interest in wine runs long and deep. His family immigrated to British Columbia, a wine region of some potential. At the time, however, it was nearly impossible there for an Italian family who wanted to do what many Italian families enjoy doing: get grapes for making wine at home. They did the next best thing: they shipped grapes in, and Gerry remembers lugging around heavy crates of Zinfandel, which might help explain his upper-body strength, so necessary for a pole vaulter. At the end of his athletic career, he moved to Santa Barbara and taught for a time at UC Santa Barbara. Living in the region re-enlivened his love of all things related to wine, especially when he saw that Louis Lucas was planting the Tepusquet Bench and Boyd Bettencourt was starting his wine enterprise.

In those early days, because he knew most of the winemakers, including Jim Clendenen and Lane Tanner, he took his truck and, with permission, drove into the fields to harvest whatever was left over for his homemade wine. In 1994 he started the Morovino label. Gerry knows what it takes to be a world-class athlete, and he applies that same passion and work ethic to his winemaking. Although he would rather focus on making the wines, he knows that the hard work is in the selling. Not surprisingly, Gerry emphasizes Italian varieties at Morovino.

RECOMMENDED WINES: Gerry recommends the Sangiovese. The 2001 is light in the glass and cherry-colored. The wine presents blackberries, cherries, plums, and a hint of loganberries above the toasty oak spice. It has fine balance and is luscious in the mouth. The tannins are sufficient for another three to four years of aging, and in many regards this wine reminds me of a fine Chianti Riserva. I tasted the 2003 out of the barrel, and it too is a lovely example likely to surpass the 2001 in quality, given the excellent ripeness of the grapes.

My recommendation is the Tango, a blend of Zinfandel and Merlot that was started by his mother, Elsa. The 1999 is a black-purple wine opaque in the glass and has a fine nose of sweet plums, cherries, figs, and cinnamon spice. Although the wine is well integrated now, the tannic grip suggests another two to four years of aging ahead before it peaks. The wine has a long and smooth finish and is ready for drinking at the table.

RATING: One → two stars (quality improving across the line)

Mosby Winery & Vineyards

WINERY OWNERS: Bill and Jeri Mosby

WINEMAKER: Bill Mosby

TASTING ROOM: Yes

DAYS/HOURS: Saturday–Sunday 10 A.M.–5 P.M.,
Monday–Friday 10 A.M.–4 P.M.

ADDRESS: 9496 Santa Rosa Rd., Buellton, CA
93427; 805-688-2415; 805-686-4288 (fax);
mosbywines.com

WINES/GRAPE VARIETIES: Cortese, Dolcetto,
grappa, Lagrein, Nebbiolo, Pinot Grigio, Roc
Michel (blend), Sangiovese, Teroldego

WINE CLUB: Yes

TASTING ROOM AMENITIES: Picnic area

REGION: Santa Ynez Valley AVA

Bill Mosby was one of the first to settle in Santa Barbara County and start a vineyard. He came out of Klamath Falls, Oregon, from a deeply religious family in which not even wine vinegar was permitted in the house. During those days, the Native Americans in town would buy cheap port to drink, and young Bill collected the empty wine bottles for a penny apiece and sometimes a taste. This whetted his appetite for something better. He loved biology and was accepted to Oregon State; later he became a nationally ranked wrestler. His grandma had a ranch at Cottage Grove, Oregon, where he helped make apple cider from the time he was seventeen years old. Then he moved to California and learned to make wine out of grapes near Lompoc. A dentist, his practice put him in touch with the Italian farmers working in the region. It was standard practice then to give wine to the field hands, so everyone made wine. In 1969 he bought a place for himself, his wife, Jeri, and his two sons, Gary and Mike, and grew alfalfa. The Bank of America lent money in the early 1970s for vineyards and grape production, but he decided not to take on the debt burden. Lafond had opened a winery in Santa Barbara in the early '60s, Nielsen was growing grapes at Rancho Sisquoc, Sanford and Benedict had started their vineyard up the road, and Firestone was planting about the same time Bill put in his first Riesling grapes. In 1976 he bought the land at his current location and began building the winery in 1978. He included in the design the original carriage house with its wood floors, dating from the 1853 Spanish land grant of Rancho de la Vega. A hundred-mile-per-hour wind unfortunately leveled the structure one day and folks got upset at the loss, so Bill had the house rebuilt. At the time he also kept the name Vega for his label, but changed it to Mosby in the mid-1980s.

Although his early efforts were with Riesling and Gewürztraminer and he was well known for his Chardonnay and Pinot Noir, Bill decided after some visits to *bella Italia* to replant and refocus his vineyards and winemaking on Italian varieties. In fact, he brought the first Pinot Grigio and Sangiovese grapevines to the area. His son Gary helps sell the wines, and the famous artist Robert Scherer does his labels. Bill retired from his dental practice in 1998, and is now able to give his wines the full attention they deserve. He is also a member of the Consorzio Cal-Italia, an association of winemakers and grape growers in the region who feature Italian varieties. If you are a fan of award-winning grappa, and if you are interested in less-known cultivars such as Cortese, the traditional white grape of Piedmont, or even Teroldego, a red grape that grows north of Trentino, then Mosby is your place. (Grappa is the name of a spirit the French call *marc* and the Germans call *Testerbranntwein;* it is high in alcohol, clear, and less sweet than brandy. Usually it is distilled from the remains of wine production, that is, the remnants of pomace, fresh fruit skins, and stems.)

RECOMMENDED WINES: Bill recommends the Lagrein, native to the Alto Adige and so obscure here that the TTB does not yet recognize the grape variety. For this reason Bill is not permitted to use the grape's name; he calls it La Seduzione ("the seduction") instead. The 2001 is opaque to the stem and a black-red color. The nose shows black currants, raspberries, vanilla, black cherries, and violet perfume. The wine is nicely balanced between the tannins and the lovely ripe fruit. The mid-palate shows the sweetness of the ripe grapes and the long, pleasing finish recalls the fine aromatics. This is definitely one to seek out and try if you are tired of the same old varieties. It is ready for consumption now but will hold another three to four years.

I recommend the 2002 Estate Cortese. This is a pale, lemon-colored wine with a citrusy nose of lime, lemon, and some pineapple. It is a medium-bodied wine with the fruit supported by the lively acidity, contributing to an attractive mouthfeel. The wine has a clean, fresh finish and is ready for drinking now.

RATING: Two → three stars (whites catching up to reds)

Oak Savanna Wines

WINERY OWNER: Sandy Hill

WINEMAKER: Andrew Murray

TASTING ROOM: Yes

DAYS/HOURS: Daily 11 A.M.–5:30 P.M.

ADDRESS: 2901 Grand Ave., #A, Los Olivos, CA 93441; 805-693-9644; 805-686-9704 (fax); oaksavannawine.com

WINES/GRAPE VARIETIES: Chardonnay, Pinot Noir, One Thousand Hills (blend), Syrah

WINE CLUB: Online sales

REGION: Santa Ynez Valley AVA

Ovene Winery

WINERY OWNER: Jeff White

WINEMAKER: Jeff White

TASTING ROOM: Shared tasting at Wines on Pine

DAYS/HOURS: Wednesday–Sunday 11 A.M.–7 P.M.

ADDRESS: Wines on Pine, 1244 Pine St., Paso Robles, CA 93446; 714-420-2525; 714-970-8174 (fax); ovenewinery.com

WINES/GRAPE VARIETIES: Cabernet Sauvignon, Chardonnay, Pinot Noir, Syrah, Syrah rosé

WINE CLUB: Yes

REGION: Santa Barbara County

Paige 23

WINERY OWNERS: Joe and Jackie Kalina

WINEMAKERS: Joe Kalina and Chris Keller

TASTING ROOM: Vinhus in Solvang

DAYS/HOURS: Daily 10 A.M.–7 P.M.

ADDRESS: Vinhus, 440 Alisal Rd., Solvang, CA 93463; 805-686-0015; 805-693-9325 (fax); paige23wines.com

WINES/GRAPE VARIETIES: Chardonnay, Pinot Noir, Sauvignon Blanc, Syrah, Syrah Noir

WINE CLUB: Online sales

REGION: Santa Barbara County

Palmina

WINERY OWNERS: Chrystal and Steve Clifton

WINEMAKER: Steve Clifton

TASTING ROOM: No

DAYS/HOURS: By appointment only

ADDRESS: 1520 E. Chestnut Court, Lompoc, CA 93436; 805-735-2030; 805-735-2693 (fax); palminawines.com

WINES/GRAPE VARIETIES: Alisos (blend), Barbera, Botasea (blend), Dolcetto, Malvasia Bianca, Mattia (blend), Nebbiolo, Pinot Grigio, Sauvignon, Tocai Friulano

WINE CLUB: Yes

REGION: Santa Barbara County

Presidio Vineyard & Winery

WINERY OWNERS: Braun family

WINEMAKER: Douglas Braun

TASTING ROOM: Yes

DAYS/HOURS: Daily 11 A.M.–6 P.M.

ADDRESS: 1603 Copenhagen Dr., #1 (corner of Atterdag and Mission), Solvang, CA 93463; 888-930-9463; 805-740-1720 (fax); presidiowinery.com

WINES/GRAPE VARIETIES: Chardonnay, Pinot Noir, port, Syrah, Syrah rosé

WINE CLUB: Yes

TASTING ROOM AMENITIES: Merchandise

REGION: Santa Barbara County

There is an appreciable irony in the house if one is a winemaker and one's spouse comes from a family of non–wine drinkers. Such is the case of Douglas and Angela Braun of Presidio. Doug got his start in the restaurant management business in the 1970s. He worked for Justine's at Pacific Beach, which specialized in fresh seafood, and was responsible for ordering wines that complemented the restaurant's menu. This afforded him the opportunity to learn about and taste many different wines. He also worked for a time as the food and beverage manager at a golf club's restaurant but found himself drifting away from food toward wine. One of Doug's other great passions is surfing, so he moved to Hawaii. Somehow, he managed to lose his return ticket and had to stay and surf. During his time at an upscale restaurant called Horatio's the place needed a sommelier, and he rode that wave into a career turning point.

Once back on the mainland, he returned to school, taking every wine course available to him in San Diego. A relative was a professor at Fresno State, so he furthered his education there, earning a degree in enology. He also took a degree in viticulture at Davis. To gain experience he worked for Cribari, then the tenth largest winery in California, and rode a bicycle among the tanks, taking samples for quality analysis. He went north to Livermore and worked as assistant winemaker to Don Blackburn, who had a European education. Doug found Don's style revolutionary and changed his view of making wine. He came back to the south and Temecula, where he consulted for small wineries in that area. About 1991 he created the Presidio label.

His mom was a history teacher, and she taught him that presidios were outposts or garrisons used to protect the Spanish missionaries during the early history of California. It seemed the perfect name for a winery. While consulting at Sunstone and Santa Ynez Winery, Doug was given permission to share their facilities to make Presidio wines. He next established a partnership and searched for a suitable property. His father found the current location, everything that Doug wanted and needed. On the day he closed on the property he met Angela, who was working with Elderhostel out of Arizona. Doug taught wine education at Allan Hancock College, and the two happened to talk on the phone. He invited her out to see his place when she was in town, and a relationship developed. She moved to California to be with Doug, found a job in her field, and to help out started to work in the tasting room.

Doug now has 100 acres near Lompoc, 30 planted to grapes in 1999–2000 and entirely under his control. He maintains a focus on biodynamics in the vineyard and emphasizes the creation of healthy soils that produce healthy vines, thus limiting his need for chemical fertilizers. For instance, to get his plants the nitrogen they need, he grows legumes between the vines. The vineyard is now certified organic and biodynamic. The next step for Presidio is to build a winery on the property and a tasting room. The tasting room, managed by Angela, is currently in Solvang.

RECOMMENDED WINES: Doug recommends the Pinot Noir. The 2003 is almost opaque to the stem and a pretty red cherry in the glass. The nose shows spice, cherries, raspberries, red currants, and a perfume of violets and heather. The wine is well integrated and lush in the mouth, and it resolves to a long, smooth finish. This is a lovely Pinot Noir. Drink now and over the next three to five years.

My recommendation is the 2003 Chardonnay. Bright gold in the glass, the wine's nose is vanilla spice and butter, apples, pears, and a touch of tropical fruit. The body is smooth and lush in the mouth, leading to a sense of elegance. The wonderful aromatics integrate beautifully with the excellent acidity and give the wine a tart, crisp finish. Drink now and over the next two to four years.

RATING: Four stars (reds and whites are both excellent to outstanding)

Qupé

WINERY OWNERS: Bob and Louisa Lindquist

WINEMAKER: Bob Lindquist

TASTING ROOM: At Wine Country

DAYS/HOURS: Daily 11 A.M.–5 P.M.

ADDRESS: Wine Country, 2445 Alamo
  Pintado Ave., Los Olivos, CA 93441;
  805-686-9699; 805-937-2539 (fax); qupe
  .com

WINES/GRAPE VARIETIES: Bien Nacido
  Cuvée (white blend), Chardonnay,
  Grenache, Los Olivos Cuvée (red blend),
  Marsanne, Mourvèdre, Roussanne, Syrah,
  Viognier

WINE CLUB: Yes

REGION: Santa Maria Valley AVA

Bob Lindquist is one of the more familiar names you hear in any discussion of the history of Santa Barbara County wines. He also has the distinction of being one of the original Rhône Rangers of the region. He is a die-hard baseball fan and has a passion for rock music. He started his university education at UC Irvine but dropped out to move to the Santa Clara Valley and live with an uncle in Hollister. Even then Bob enjoyed wine and wanted to learn more about the business rather than pursue it merely as a hobby. In 1975, after he moved in with his uncle, he got a job at Fortino, where he started by working in the vineyards. From there he moved to San Martine and managed a tasting room. This move brought him to Ventura County, closer to the wines of the Central Coast. He visited the most famous of the wineries and vineyards and decided he wanted to be in the Santa Ynez Valley. He managed a retail shop in Los Olivos, but was fired when he took off to attend a Kinks concert. Luckily, Zaca Mesa Winery immediately hired him as its first tour guide.

For up-and-coming winemakers, Zaca Mesa in 1979 was a wonderful place to work. Ken Brown was the winemaker at the time and Jim Clendenen the assistant. Bob's job included work as a cellar rat, so he learned the day-to-day operations within a winery under the tutelage of Ken and Jim as well as Adam Tolmach, the enologist. In 1982 he made his first bottle of Qupé at the Zaca Mesa facilities by trading his services for equipment and space. *Qupé* is the Chumash word for the California poppy that adorns the label. Bob left Zaca Mesa about 1983 and went out on his own. He rented some space from Los Vineros, where he produced his 1984 and 1985 vintages. When Los Vineros went out of business, Bob was forced to move again. Richard Sanford invited him to share his space and make wines at Sanford in '86 and '87. At this point, the owners of Bien Nacido approached him with a proposal to set up a winery at the vineyard. He contacted his old friend Jim Clendenen, and the two formed a partnership. They incorporated as the Clendenen Lindquist Vintners (CLV), a holding company, and Jim started Au Bon Climat while Bob launched Qupé, both housed in the current winery facility at Bien Nacido. Bob's first vintage on that property was 1989.

At Qupé, Bob is interested in advancing the Rhône varieties such as Syrah, Viognier, Roussanne, and Marsanne, but also makes some Chardonnay. He is most famous for his fine Syrahs. Bob sources most of his fruit from Bien Nacido, where the vines are farmed to his specifications, and from a 14-acre vineyard in Los Olivos. In the spring of 2004 Bob and his wife, Louisa, purchased an 80-acre parcel in the Edna Valley, where they have planted 40 acres to vine.

RECOMMENDED WINES: Bob recommends the Bien Nacido Hillside Estate Syrah. I tasted the 2002, a real stunner. The color is as black as the underside of a flat rock in a dense forest. The wonderful aromatics suggest cherries covered with dark chocolate, blackberries, black currants, black licorice, and wood smoke. This is a mouth-filling Syrah, with tannins that coat the tongue. In spite of a few rough edges that will disappear in a year's time, this is a well-balanced and well-integrated wine. The long, pleasing finish lasts more than a minute and speaks to the wine's future elegance. Give this wine a year to knit and it should provide another eight to nine years of outstanding drinking.

I recommend the Bien Nacido Hillside Estate Roussanne. The 2002 is a brilliant gold in the glass. The nose is ripe honeydew melon, butterscotch, hazelnuts, and tea leaves, all floating atop a mineral layer of crushed stone. The wine is round and full in the mouth, showing both excellent balance and marvelous integration of all its elements. The finish persists more than a minute. In sum, this is a testament to the skill of Bob Lindquist and his handling of a very difficult grape variety. He has fashioned a wine that is both elegant and refined. It is drinking beautifully now, but I predict this wine will give an additional seven to nine years of drinking pleasure ahead. My partner, Nancy, proclaims Lindquist's Roussanne one of the finest she has tasted from Santa Barbara County.

RATING: Four stars (consistently excellent to outstanding across the line)

Rancho Sisquoc Winery

WINERY OWNER: Flood Ranch Company

WINEMAKER: Alec Franks

TASTING ROOM: Yes

DAYS/HOURS: Daily 10 A.M.–4 P.M.

ADDRESS: 6600 Foxen Canyon Rd., Santa
Maria, CA 93454; 805-934-4332;
805-937-6601 (fax); ranchosisquoc.com

WINES/GRAPE VARIETIES: Cabernet Franc,
Cabernet Sauvignon, Chardonnay,
Malbec, Meritage (blend), Merlot, Pinot
Noir, Riesling, Sangiovese, Sauvignon
Blanc, Sisquoc River Red (blend),
Sylvaner, Syrah, Tre Vini (blend)

WINE CLUB: Yes

TASTING ROOM AMENITIES: Picnic area,
merchandise

REGION: Santa Maria Valley AVA

Sisquoc is the Chumash Indian word for "gathering place" and was part of an 1852 Mexican land grant that was awarded to a woman, unusual for the time. She graciously gave the land to her husband. James Flood purchased the 37,000-acre ranch in 1952 with the intent of running a cattle operation on the land. In 1968 Harold Pfeiffer, then ranch manager, noticed a neighbor across the fence, Uriel Nielsen, planting grapes and decided that wasn't such a bad idea. After a test plot of Riesling and Sylvaner (a cool-climate grape originally from Austria but also popular in Germany for white wine) fared well in 1970, the first grapes were pressed in 1972 and a winery was bonded and opened to the public in 1977. During the early years Pfeiffer sold the wines on the weekend or by appointment only. Production was about 200 cases, mostly of the Riesling and Sylvaner, with some Cabernet Sauvignon.

Edward A. Holt was just a young feller in the Ozark Mountains of Missouri when he got his first taste of wine. Made from local grapes, it wasn't much to holler about, but the fact that grapes were growing where he lived allowed him to learn a new skill: pruning. He made extra money as a youngster working the vineyard and, while pulling leaves and pruning vines, discovered his passion: growing grapes. In 1976 Ed came west to Rancho Sisquoc, where he helped design the winery. Eventually, he rose to vice president and general manager, but his first and abiding love has always been the vineyard. It is his job to make certain that his winemaker, Alec Franks, gets the best possible fruit for his wines.

In 1986, after Harold retired, Ed took control of the operation for the Flood family and brought on Alec as the winemaker. The emphasis now is on making excellent wines from excellent grapes, and Ed has an intimate knowledge of the soils atop the alluvial fan that was once part of the Sisquoc riverbed. He is convinced that Bordeaux varieties will prosper, but there is Chardonnay now and Syrah. All the grapes are estate grown and are vinified for consumers to enjoy.

You don't have to worry about being intimidated at the tasting room. Ed maintains his Ozark charm and hospitality, making the tasting room a wonderful place to gather. After my interview with him, I tasted through the Sisquoc line. An older couple came in and informed the young woman helping them that they had been coming to

Sisquoc to sample and buy the wines since before she was born. That tells you something about the wines and people at Rancho Sisquoc, who complement its history as one of the first wineries in the region.

RECOMMENDED WINES: Ed recommends the Malbec (also known in Cahors, France, as Côt). The 2001 is almost opaque in the glass and a pretty brick-red color (in Cahors, the wine is almost black). The nose shows tomato purée, black currants, damson plums, tobacco smoke, and black pepper. The tannins are full and rounded, making for an excellent mouthfeel. The finish lasts nearly a minute. Given the intriguing aromatics and the ripe, lush fruit, this is a fine alternative to a Merlot. It is ready for drinking now but should last another three to four years.

I suggest the Chardonnay. The 2001 is a pretty gold and yellow in the glass. The nose is butter, apples, quince, and Anjou pears. The fruit is wonderful in the mouth, and the oak contributes a creamy feel on the tongue. The finish is long and smooth, lasting nearly a minute. This wine is ready for the table but will hold another four years or so.

RATING: Three stars (reds are ahead of whites)

Rideau Vineyard

WINERY OWNER: Iris C. Rideau

WINEMAKER: Andrés Ibarra

TASTING ROOM: Yes

DAYS/HOURS: Daily 11 A.M.–5 P.M.

ADDRESS: 1562 Alamo Pintado Rd., Solvang, CA 93463; 805-688-0717; 805-688-8048 (fax); rideauvineyard.com

WINES/GRAPE VARIETIES: Chardonnay, Chateau Duplantier (red blend), Fleur Blanche (white blend), Grenache, Grenache Blanc, Lagniappe (white blend), Mourvèdre, Petite Sirah, Pinot Noir, Riesling, Roussanne, Sangiovese, Sauvignon Blanc, Syrah rosé, Tempranillo, Viognier, White Riesling

WINE CLUB: Yes

TASTING ROOM AMENITIES: Picnic area, merchandise

REGION: Santa Ynez Valley AVA

Over the past thirty years New Orleans native Iris C. Rideau (family name Duplantier) has owned three businesses, two of which she sold to former employees. She is the only woman in Santa Barbara County who owns both a vineyard and a winery with tasting room. Nearing retirement in 1989, she bought 5 acres in Santa Barbara County. Next to her property stood 25 acres and an old adobe house. Once a famous inn, it is now a historical landmark. In 1995 she bought that property too, with the intention of restoring the old abandoned inn and opening a bed-and-breakfast. The Alamo Pintado Adobe, built in 1884, is reputed to have been the first guest ranch in the Santa Ynez Valley. *El alamo pintado* means "painted cottonwood," and the inn was named after a giant cottonwood tree that grew on the property when the adobe was built, and which was painted with Indian symbols. Because of zoning restrictions Iris was unable to make it a bed-and-breakfast, but she renovated the adobe and turned it into a tasting room to go with her planned winery and vineyard. She brought in partner Rick Longoria to help establish the winery and vineyard in 1996, and in 1997 Rideau Vineyard opened for business, an expression of Rideau's passion for producing fine wines.

Longoria left in 1998 to focus on his own line of wines, and the current winemaker is Andrés Ibarra. Andrés came to the United States from Mexico and at the early age of sixteen got his first job in 1980 working in the vineyards and cellar for Fred Brander. In 1985 Mike Brown of Kalyra hired him as his assistant winemaker. In fact, it was Mike who was responsible for introducing Andrés to Iris. Before she hired him, Andrés worked at Fess Parker with Eli Parker and Brett Escalera, both of whom mentored him and guided his winemaking philosophy. The emphasis at Rideau is on producing premium-quality Rhône-style wines.

RECOMMENDED WINES: The Rideau recommendation is the Chateau Duplantier. The 2004 is a Syrah-based Rhône blend. This is a red cherry–colored wine, translucent in the glass. In the nose it shows cedar, black cherries, truffles, and a hint of forest floor. The wine is well balanced between the fruit and the tannins and lasts nearly a minute on the tongue. Rideau staff suggest decanting the wine before drinking. It will also benefit from an additional three to five years of bottle age.

My recommendation is the Estate Syrah. I tasted the 2002 and the 2003—both excellent wines, but the 2003 has the edge. The wine is almost opaque in the glass and black cherry in color. The nose shows blackberries, mocha, black currants, and blueberries. This is a well-balanced and well-integrated Syrah with wonderfully ripe and sweet fruit on the tongue. The soft tannins lend elegance to the wine, and the finish lasts nearly a minute. Drink this beauty now and over the next four to five years.

RATING: Three stars (reds ahead of whites)

Royal Oaks Winery

MANAGEMENT TEAM: John Leggat, Richard Foster, Berna Arnold, and Larry Dutra

TASTING ROOM: Yes

DAYS/HOURS: Daily 10 A.M.–5:30 P.M.

ADDRESS: 1651 Copenhagen Dr., Solvang, CA 93463; 805-693-1740; 805-693-1568 (fax); royaloakswinery.com

WINES/GRAPE VARIETIES: Chardonnay, Concord, Muscat Canelli, Niagara, Noir Blanc (Pinot Noir–black currant essence), Pinot Noir, Riesling, Sauvignon Blanc, Sémillon, Syrah

WINE CLUB: Yes

TASTING ROOM AMENITIES: Merchandise

REGION: Santa Ynez Valley AVA

Rusack Vineyards

WINERY OWNERS: Geoff and Alison Rusack

WINEMAKERS: John and Helen Falcone

TASTING ROOM: Yes

DAYS/HOURS: Daily 11 A.M.–5 P.M.

ADDRESS: 1819 Ballard Canyon Rd.,
Solvang, CA 93463; 805-688-1278;
805-686-1508 (fax); rusackvineyards.com

WINES/GRAPE VARIETIES: Anacapa
(Bordeaux blend), Chardonnay, Pinot
Noir, rosé, Sangiovese, Sauvignon Blanc,
Syrah

WINE CLUB: Yes

TASTING ROOM AMENITIES: Picnic area,
merchandise

REGION: Santa Ynez Valley AVA

Geoff Rusack's family enjoyed wine at the dinner table when he was growing up in Los Angeles, and this instilled in him a curiosity about the beverage at an early age. He went back east for his university studies at Bowdoin College in Maine. He returned to California, and during his law studies at Pepperdine he dated Alexa Chappellet of Napa. Her family's background in the wine industry enhanced his curiosity. They went their separate ways but remain good friends. He was also a classmate of Adam Firestone. Through these relationships with his fellow students, Geoff gained valuable insight into family-run wineries. In his last year of law school he met Alison, whose family was involved not with grapes but with a 640-acre Arabian horse ranch located on Catalina Island. This got him thinking about the possibility of putting in a vineyard there (a project on which they have recently broken ground). In the meantime, he started his practice as a defense lawyer in Santa Monica while Alison worked for the Walt Disney Company. In the early 1990s, the two were tasting wine in the Santa Ynez area and wound up at Jim Carey's winery, then owned by the Firestones. Kate Firestone was working in the tasting room, and Geoff asked her if she knew of any properties in the area for sale. She said, "Yes, the old Ballard Canyon Winery!" At that time, the property was closed and in need of revitalization; the house on the land needed a complete renovation. Initially, the Rusacks said "No, thanks," but it was 48 acres in beautiful Ballard Canyon, and they finally said yes and bought the property.

A ninety-day escrow took seven months, as there were no permits even though it had been the Ballard Canyon Winery for twenty years. All the hurdles discovered in escrow were eventually resolved, and 1995 became the first vintage for Rusack Vineyards. The tasting room opened in 1997. Because the estate vineyards were planted more than thirty years ago, 2001 saw a replanting using the most up-to-date vineyard techniques. Even though Alison and Geoff saw to all aspects of the business in those early days, they now have John Falcone and his wife, Helen, aboard as winemakers. John had spent seven years at Atlas Peak; when he met the Rusacks the chemistry was right across the board, and the Falcones were hired in 2001. Originally from Gilroy, where he still has Italian relatives in the wine business, John started his wine career at Monterey Vineyard in 1976, the sole facility in the area at the time. In 1992 he moved to Columbia Crest, helping to run production. He returned to Monterey for four years and thereafter was hired as Atlas Peak's winemaker in Napa before moving to Rusack.

Helen, previously assistant winemaker at Paul Hobbs, William Hill, and Chimney Rock, works with John as the assistant winemaker at Rusack.

RECOMMENDED WINES: Geoff recommends the Syrah. The 2002 follows the wonderful prizewinning 2001 and is translucent in the glass. The color is black cherry and the nose is blackberries, black currants, anise, and white pepper. The body is full and round in the mouth, with a fine tannic grip. Well integrated and showing fine balance, the wine resolves to a long, chewy finish that recalls the cherries in the bouquet. The wine is ready now and will last another five to six years.

I suggest the Anacapa, a Bordeaux blend of Cabernet Franc, Merlot, and Cabernet Sauvignon. Named after the smallest of the Channel Islands, the word *anacapa* is derived from the Chumash Indian word *eneepah,* which means "island of deception" or "mirage." I tasted Cuvée II from the 2002 vintage. The color is black-purple, and the wine is opaque in the glass. The nose is cherries, blackberries, roses, tobacco leaf, and red currants. The wine is excellent in the mouth, showing both elegance and finesse. Its finish is nearly a minute and evokes the lovely ripe fruit in the nose. This wonderful blend is drinking beautifully now but should hold another five to six years.

RATING: Three → four stars (quality rising across the line)

Sanford Winery

WINERY OWNER: Terlato Wine Group

WINEMAKER: Steve Fennell

TASTING ROOM: Yes

DAYS/HOURS: Daily 11 A.M.–5 P.M.

ADDRESS: 5010 Santa Rosa Rd., Lompoc, CA 93436; 805-735-5900; 805-735-3800 (fax); sanfordwinery.com

WINES/GRAPE VARIETIES: Chardonnay, Pinot Noir, Pinot Grigio, rosé, Sauvignon Blanc

WINE CLUB: Yes

TASTING ROOM AMENITIES: Picnic area, merchandise

REGION: Santa Rita Hills AVA

After the profile for Sanford was written, I learned that Richard Sanford had ended his relationship with both Sanford Winery and Sanford and Benedict vineyard, citing philosophical differences with the majority owners of the former, Terlato Wine Group. Longtime winemaker Bruno D'Alfonso has also moved on. Richard is launching a new brand called Alma Rosa, focused on Pinot Noir. I look forward to including a profile of his new winery in a future edition of this book.

Sanford Winery is now under the guidance of Doug Fletcher, director of winemaking for Terlato Wine Group, and the winemaker is Steve Fennell. The profile that follows was taken from my interview with both Richard Sanford and Bruno D'Alfonso and is included here as historical context for the winery.

Imagine returning home across the distant wine-dark seas only to discover that your country no longer welcomes your service. This was the situation facing the young naval officer J. Richard Sanford, home from Vietnam. A 1965 graduate of UC Berkeley with a degree in geography, Sanford had joined the Navy and served in Vietnam, following in the honorable footsteps of his father, a graduate of the United States Naval Academy. Deeply troubled by the political and cultural chaos engendered by the war, Richard set out on an inland adventure to find sustenance in the earth and, literally and figuratively, returned to ground. He gave up the status quo, sought a new philosophy and a new way to live and make sense of his life. Taoism guided his spiritual quest, and you see it manifested in the way he lives his life. In the transverse Santa Ynez Valley that is part of the ancient Monterey deposit, he and partner Michael Benedict established the now-famous Sanford and Benedict vineyard in 1971.

In 1980 Michael left the partnership and went a separate way; this afforded Richard the opportunity to begin Sanford Winery in 1981, traveling to Edna Valley Winery to make his wines. There he met Bruno D'Alfonso, and asked Bruno to become his winemaker in 1983. In 1990 Londoners Robert and Janice Atkin purchased the Sanford and Benedict vineyard and asked Richard to manage the property he knows intimately. He acquired other properties and returned to the work of not merely farming the land and taking from it but establishing a sustainable harmony with the land. By 1997, work had begun on an adobe winery, each of the more than 100,000 bricks handcrafted on the site. A statue of the Buddha smiles over it. By 2001 his La Rinconada vineyard was certified organic, following the lead of the Rancho El Jabali and Sanford and Benedict vineyards, the first to be so designated in Santa Barbara County.

Winemaker—or, more appropriately, designer of wines and then-partner Bruno D'Alfonso—first met Richard Sanford when Richard went to the Edna Valley Winery to make his wines. Then an assistant winemaker, Bruno had been mentored by Dick Graff of Chalone. Bruno graduated from Cal Poly in soil science and took an enology degree at Davis in 1980. While at Edna Valley, he worked for Richard on Fridays until the two decided to work together full-time at Sanford.

RECOMMENDED WINES: Richard suggests the La Rinconada Pinot Noir. The 2001 is translucent in the glass and a pretty red cherry color. The nose is blackberries, cherries, and vanilla. The tannins are rounded and soft, leading to silkiness in the mouth. The finish is nearly a minute long, and the wonderful, ripe fruit in this wine makes it a joy to drink. I see four to seven years of pleasurable drinking ahead for it.

I recommend the La Rinconada Chardonnay. The 2002 is a bright yellow with butter, hazelnuts, lemon, pear, and mango in the nose. The wine shows a wonderful balance of acidity and minerality, leading to fine structure and complexity. The finish is nearly a minute and is a fine complement to the intriguing aromatics of the wine. Drink now and over the next three to four years.

RATING: Three stars (this rating is based on the wines made by Bruno D'Alfonso)

Santa Barbara Winery

WINERY OWNER: Pierre Lafond

WINEMAKER: Bruce McGuire

TASTING ROOM: Yes

DAYS/HOURS: Daily 10 A.M.–5 P.M.

ADDRESS: 202 Anacapa St., Santa Barbara, CA 93101; 805-963-3633; 805-963-0104 (fax); sbwinery.com

WINES/GRAPE VARIETIES: Cabernet Sauvignon, Chardonnay, Grenache, Lagrein, late-harvest Zinfandel Essence, Negrette, Pinot Noir, Primitivo, Riesling (dry and sweet), Sangiovese, Sauvignon Blanc, Syrah, Syrah rosé, ZCS (red blend)

WINE CLUB: Yes

TASTING ROOM AMENITIES: Merchandise

REGION: Santa Barbara County

A graduate of Montreal's prestigious McGill University, Pierre Lafond is an architect by profession, but long ago transcended the ordinary working life of an architect. After graduation in 1957 he came from Canada to Santa Barbara, received his architect's license the next year, and went to work for a local firm. After three years or so he began work for himself, but two events conspired to draw him away from his chosen métier and into a life that, on the surface at least, does not require the education and training of an architect. First, he inherited a liquor store from a relative. Second, he read John Melville's *Guide to California Wines,* first published in 1955. Book in hand, Pierre traveled north to Napa and Sonoma, eager to seek out and taste some of the wines featured in the guide. In the course of his travels he had the pleasure of meeting Joe Heitz and then discovered the wines of Zellerbach during a time before Robert Mondavi became the driving force in Napa. He stocked his van with case purchases, and the liquor store morphed into a wine store and delicatessen featuring California boutique wines for sale in Santa Barbara.

Well established in Santa Barbara and now tapped into the California wine scene, Pierre decided to build a winery. The year 1962 saw the completion and establishment of Santa Barbara County's first commercial winery since the 1930s, El Paseo Cellars. However, as Richard Sanford, Michael Benedict, Brooks Firestone, Fred Brander, Louis Lucas, and others planted vineyards and started their own labels, the wine industry in Santa Barbara took off and Lafond lost access to his grape sources. Conversations with Sanford convinced him that Santa Barbara County was conducive to growing premium grapes (the Christian Brothers were already buying grapes grown there by the ton for transport north), and in 1972 he bought land and planted the first of his vineyards. In so doing, he guaranteed his winery a reliable and steady source for its grapes and would no longer have to depend on the vagaries of a cyclical market or other grape growers.

Pierre readily admits that those first efforts were not worth writing home to Canada about, but that all changed when he hired Bruce McGuire as the full-time winemaker in 1981 (for his story, please see the profile of Lafond Winery). The wines are now produced in two facilities: the original Santa Barbara complex, where the whites are made, and the new Lafond Winery complex on Santa Rosa Road, opened with tasting room in 2001, where the reds are stored. In total, production is now about 40,000 cases a year with distribution reaching from California to Japan. The primary grape varieties are Chardonnay, Pinot Noir, and Syrah. Interestingly, Riesling clones grafted to nematode-resistant rootstock will be planted soon, harking back to the early days in 1972 when Pierre's first vineyard received plantings of Riesling vines. When you visit the Web site for Lafond Winery you might be surprised to learn that Pierre created and designed it himself.

RECOMMENDED WINES: Pierre recommends the late-harvest Zinfandel Essence. The 2000 is light to the stem and a pretty cherry-red color. The nose is a panoply of plums, black currants, and golden raisins. The sugar is an astounding 27 percent, but the excellent acidity in the wine prevents it from being cloying. The wine has a huge finish that lasts over a minute and recalls the wonderful stone fruit. This wine will easily last another eight to ten years. It is a wonderful late-harvest Zin.

In keeping with the theme, I recommend the late-harvest Lafond Vineyard Sauvignon Blanc. The 1999 was not affected by botrytis and saw no oak. The color is pure butterscotch. The nose is apricots, honeyed Bartlett pears, nectarines, and peaches. The residual sugar goes off the scale at 34 percent. Sip this one after dinner in a small glass or it will overpower the palate. The finish lasts more than a minute, and the aromatics linger long after that in the glass. I love dessert wines, and this one will no doubt live another ten to fourteen years in the bottle. What a treat it would be to try it then.

RATING: Three stars (consistently well-made wines across the line)

Sea Smoke Cellars

WINERY OWNER: Bob Davids

WINEMAKER: Kris Curran

TASTING ROOM: No

DAYS/HOURS: By appointment for mailing list members only

ADDRESS: P.O. Box 1953, Lompoc, CA 93436; 805-737-1600; 805-737-1620 (fax); seasmokecellars.com

WINES/GRAPE VARIETIES: Pinot Noir

WINE CLUB: Mailing list

REGION: Santa Rita Hills AVA

Bob Davids is the owner of Sea Smoke, one of the prettiest names for a winery on the Central Coast. The general manager is Victor Gallegos, one of the most knowledgeable I have met, and the winemaker is Kris Curran, one of the best in Santa Barbara County. Victor is a viticulturist and a graduate of both Davis and Berkeley. In addition to working at Sea Smoke, he has a winery in Spain's distinguished Priorat wine region. Kris grew up in Santa Ynez and raised animals through her high school year and she was a member of the FFA, the Pony Club, and 4-H. She worked in restaurants to make money, and her interest in wines started there. She used to play polo with the Firestones (Brooks Firestone is an avid polo player) and thought one had to be born into wine culture. But then she met Bruno D'Alfonso after working a harvest at Sanford and Benedict. Bruno showed her the possibilities and suggested that she go to school. She knew he had a degree in enology and after a quarter at Davis she transferred to Cal Poly, where she finished a degree in animal science and pre-vet studies. She was among the top fifty students accepted for veterinary school at Davis but went to Fresno State instead. She loved the hands-on experience there and finished her second degree. After she left Fresno State, she had a friend who worked at Cambria, and since she loved the Central Coast, her friend invited her to meet Dave Guffy there. In 1997 she became Cambria's assistant winemaker and stayed until 1999.

Kris was offered a wonderful opportunity to start a new winery from scratch and became the head winemaker for Koehler Winery, from whose vineyard Firestone used to buy some of its fruit. The original building was once a horse barn, and she transformed it into a winery and a tasting room. She and Bruno met Bob Davids when all three were looking for properties; Kris already had her eye on some beautiful riverbench land across the valley from Sanford and Benedict. Bob offered her the job of starting Sea Smoke in 2000, a year before the first harvest. Kris already knew about the horrors of the permitting process from her time at Koehler. She suggested using the "wine ghetto" in Lompoc as a possible backup for the winemaking just in case and, of course, they were unable to get permits on time. This gave them the opportunity to put their money into the wine and not the winery—a real boon for fans and consumers of Sea Smoke wines. There is currently no tasting room at the ghetto, but members of the mailing list are welcome to visit the facility by appointment. There is no wine club per se. Kris has also started her own label, called Curran Wines.

RECOMMENDED WINES: Kris recommends the Southing Pinot Noir. The 2002 is red cherry in the glass and opaque to the stem. The nose is smoke and earth, pomegranate, and baked cherries. The tannins are ripe and rounded, leading to a lush, full taste in the mouth. This is a silky and sophisticated Pinot Noir with excellent ripe fruit and a long, lush finish. The wine is ready for drinking but will hold another eight years or so.

I recommend the Ten Pinot Noir. The 2002 is also opaque in the glass but has more black cherry behind the red color. This wine has wonderful aromatics of cherries, cranberries, raspberry fruit preserves, cinnamon and cardamom spice, smoke, earth, violets, and crème de cassis. The wine is superb on the tongue, rich and lush with enough tannins to last another eight to ten years. This is one of the best Pinots I have tasted in the region. Moreover, I tasted the 2003 for each of the recommendations, and they were already showing beautifully. The 2003 Ten may be better than the 2002—wonderful news for lovers of fine Pinot Noir.

RATING: Five stars (outstanding to superb Pinot Noir)

Shoestring Vineyard & Winery

WINERY OWNERS: Bill and Roswitha Craig

WINEMAKER: Bill Craig

TASTING ROOM: Yes

DAYS/HOURS: Daily 10 A.M.–5 P.M.

ADDRESS: 800 E. Hwy. 246, Solvang, CA 93463; 805-693-1795; 805-693-8512 (fax); shoestringwinery.com

WINES/GRAPE VARIETIES: Cabernet Sauvignon, Pinot Grigio, Sangiovese, Syrah

WINE CLUB: Yes

TASTING ROOM AMENITIES: Picnic area

REGION: Santa Ynez Valley AVA

Silver Wines

WINERY OWNER: Benjamin Silver

WINEMAKER: Benjamin Silver

TASTING ROOM: At Wine Country

DAYS/HOURS: Daily 11 A.M.–5 P.M.

ADDRESS: Wine Country, 2445 Alamo Pintado Ave., Los Olivos, CA; 805-686-9699; 805-963-3052 (fax); silverwines.com

WINES/GRAPE VARIETIES: Cabernet Sauvignon, I Tre Figli (red blend), Nebbiolo, Pinot Noir, Sangiovese, Sangiovese-Mourvèdre, Syrah, Viognier

WINE CLUB: Yes

REGION: Santa Barbara County

Stolpman Vineyards and Winery

WINERY OWNERS: Tom and Marilyn Stolpman

WINEMAKER: Sashi Moorman

TASTING ROOM: Yes

DAYS/HOURS: Daily 11 A.M.–5 P.M.

ADDRESS: 1659 Copenhagen Dr., #C, Solvang, CA 93463; 805-688-0400; 805-688-0436 (fax); stolpmanvineyards .com

WINES/GRAPE VARIETIES: Gli Angeli (best of vineyard), L'Avion (blend), Lacroce (blend), Limestone Hill Cuvée (blend), Nebbiolo, Poetry in Red, Poetry in White, Sangiovese, Syrah

WINE CLUB: Yes

TASTING ROOM AMENITIES: Merchandise

REGION: Santa Ynez Valley AVA

In the late 1980s attorney Tom Stolpman was searching for a vineyard property to purchase. After looking north to Paso Robles, he enlisted the help of viticulturist Jeff Newton, who showed him a ranch in Ballard Canyon near Rusack and Beckmen vineyards. In 1990 Tom and his wife, Marilyn, purchased the 220-acre ranch in the Santa Ynez Valley. Two years later they planted the first grapevines on the property under the direction of Jeff Newton and Larry Finkle, a top vineyard consulting team. By 1997 more than 100 acres of vines were in production, featuring as many as fifteen different varieties from Bordeaux, the Rhône, and Italy.

Stolpman Vineyards now has some 120 acres planted, and in 2001 winemaker Sashi Moorman joined the team. The vineyard is currently undergoing significant renovation to increase the density of plantings in the European style. Where 720 vines per acre were formerly planted, there will be a doubling to 1,440, with some acres receiving as many as 3,000 Syrah vines. At these densities each plant supports less fruit, resulting in a higher intensity of flavors in the fruit. Tom also stresses the vines by limiting the amount of irrigation done in the vineyard. This results in smaller berries with more concentrated flavors.

Tom emphasizes the importance of his crew in the vineyards. Each year every crew member gets to select a few rows of grapes. They are given the freedom to farm those grapes as they choose and to call the shots at harvest. Those grapes are turned over to winemakers Sashi Moorman and Peter Hunken and at the end of the process, each of the thirteen crew members receives at least two cases of La Quadria wine, translated as "the team."

Another interesting note is that Tom was responsible for naming the Lompoc "wine ghetto," a series of buildings given over to wine production on the outskirts of Lompoc. Rick Longoria was there making wine for him at the time, and as more and more winemakers moved in to take advantage of the space, it became a little wine ghetto. And for those of you who are olive fanatics, in 2002 Tom planted 5 acres of olive trees on the property. The fruit from these trees is pressed and made into extra-virgin olive oil. The year 2004 saw the opening of the new tasting room in Solvang, where you can also purchase bottles of the estate olive oil.

RECOMMENDED WINES: Tom recommends the Sangiovese. The 2002 is red and purple in the glass and translucent to the stem. The nose shows plums, cherries, cinnamon, red currants, and white chocolate. The wine has a full and rounded body with excellent balance of all its elements. The lovely fruit, excellent middle, and fine finish will be even better after another year in the bottle. Buy it, hold it another year, and then drink over the next three to four years.

I suggest the Rhône Ridge Cuvée of 2001, a blend of Syrah, Grenache, and Mourvèdre. This red and purple wine is darker in the glass than the Sangiovese and shows a lovely nose of blackberries, black currants, white pepper, cherries, and leather. It is a fine blend with the ripe fruit forward and all its elements well integrated. The finish recalls the sweet, ripe fruit. Drink now and over the next three to four years. A red wine called Poetry in Red replaces the Rhône Ridge Cuvée in the lineup.

RATING: Three stars (quality continues to improve as the lineup narrows)

Summerland Winery

WINERY OWNER: Nebil Zarif

WINEMAKER: Etienne Terlinden

TASTING ROOM: Yes

DAYS/HOURS: Friday–Sunday 11 A.M.–7 P.M., Tuesday–Thursday 11 A.M.–5 P.M.

ADDRESS: 2330 Lillie Ave., Summerland, CA 93067; 805-565-9463; 805-695-0300 (fax); summerlandwine.com

WINES/GRAPE VARIETIES: Cabernet Sauvignon, Chardonnay, Grenache, Merlot, Orange Muscat, Petite Sirah, Pinot Noir, Sauvignon Blanc, Syrah, Viognier, Zinfandel

WINE CLUB: Yes

TASTING ROOM AMENITIES: Picnic area, merchandise

REGION: Santa Barbara County

Turkey has a long and interesting history and culture of wine, and is in fact the world's fourth most important grower of grapes. Some scholars claim that the region of Mount Ararat is one of the areas where viticulture originated. We do know that wine was produced in that region at least six thousand years ago. Not surprisingly, Turkish native Nebil "Bilo" Zarif was born into a culture in which wine is a celebration of life and is usually served at every meal. Most of his early schooling took place in France, but his university degree includes master's work at the University of Denver. In 1979 he founded Rock Oil, an independent oil and gas company. Sometime later he founded Zarif Companies. His work in the energy field provided him the opportunity to visit Napa often, and he fell in love with the wines and the natural beauty of the place, reminiscent of his home in Iskenderun, Turkey. Convinced of the potential for Central Coast wine after visits there, he bought 30 acres of land in the Cuyama Valley of Santa Barbara County in 1994. These were the old Barnwood vineyards, and they required revitalization and replanting. During the '90s he acquired a total of 2,000 acres of land, 800 planted to grapes. He also bought the Maison Deutz (now Laetitia) winery. His plantings of Pinot Noir grapes elevated Laetitia to world-class rank when the 1999 Laetitia Pinot Noir Reserve won the silver medal at the prestigious Challenge du Vin. In 2001 Bilo sold his holdings in Barnwood/Laetitia and Avila Winery and turned his attention to establishing Summerland Winery, started in 2002.

Etienne Terlinden is the winemaker. His heritage is Belgian, and his grandfather was a wine collector who imported wines from Pomerol in France. Etienne's two uncles were also in the wine business, and he often worked with them, starting as a twelve-year-old. His father came to the United States to teach French. After spending time at a military academy, Etienne spent five years in the Navy. He then went to UC Santa Barbara to study geography. He went to work for Turbodyne after college, but when the company downsized he was out a job. He called his father and got a new job working at Laetitia with Bilo. In the meantime, he took courses at Allan Hancock College to round out his knowledge of viticulture and *terroir*. After working with other winemakers in the region he got a job at the Central Coast Co-op, and when Bilo called with news of his new start-up at Summerland, Etienne answered the phone. Bilo offered him the opportunity to become the full-time winemaker and he accepted, producing his first vintage for Summerland in 2002.

RECOMMENDED WINES: Etienne recommends the Bien Nacido Pinot Noir. The 2002 is an outstanding example, translucent in the glass and black cherry in color. The nose is elegant and shows black currants, blackberry, spice, earth, and chocolate truffles. The wine is full and round in the mouth, where the ripe fruit is showcased. The wonderful aromatics and the elegant and sustained finish combine to make this an excellent Pinot Noir. Drink now and over the next eight to nine years, thanks to the excellent tannins in the wine.

I recommend the fine Estate Chardonnay. The 2002 was made from Bien Nacido grapes and is lemon-yellow in color. The nose is perfumed oak, lemon, pears, apples, and mangoes. The wine is well structured with fine acidity to support the luscious fruit and the aromatics. The finish lasts nearly a minute. This wine is drinking beautifully now but will last another four years or so.

RATING: Three stars (reds are slightly ahead of whites)

Sunstone Vineyards and Winery

WINERY OWNER: Fred Rice

WINEMAKERS: Fred Rice and Daniel Gehrs

TASTING ROOM: Yes

DAYS/HOURS: Daily 10 A.M.–4 P.M.

ADDRESS: 125 Refugio Rd., Santa Ynez, CA 93460; 805-688-9463; 805-686-1881 (fax); sunstonewinery.com

WINES/GRAPE VARIETIES: Cabernet Franc, Cabernet Sauvignon, Chardonnay, Eros (blend), Fred's Red, Merlot, Pinot Grigio, Rapsodie du Soleil (blend), Sauvignon Blanc, Syrah, Syrah rosé, Viognier

WINE CLUB: Yes

TASTING ROOM AMENITIES: Picnic area, merchandise

REGION: Santa Ynez Valley AVA

Fred Rice can trace his family's interest in viticulture and wine back to his great-grandfather, who moved to Napa to grow grapes for Inglenook Winery in the early 1900s. In 1988 Fred and Linda Rice were interested in moving from Santa Barbara to Santa Ynez and the quiet of the country. At the time, they had a horse ranch in mind for themselves and their three children, son Bion and daughters Ashley and Brittany, as the girls in particular loved to ride. Fess Parker and his family also convinced them that a property suitable for growing grapes was not such a bad idea, and suggested that they would buy the grapes. As the Rices drove down Refugio Road, they saw the owner hammering in a for-sale sign at a 55-acre horse ranch, and they slammed on the brakes. A deal was done, and in the spring of 1989, on her birthday, daughter Brittany planted the first vine. The estate has grown to just over 100 acres, most of which are planted to Bordeaux and Rhône varietal grapes. The vineyard meets all California Certified Organic Farmer standards.

The vineyard and winery operation is very much a family business. Fred oversees the winemaking and viticulture with consultant Daniel Gehrs. Linda is the marketing director; Bion sees to wholesaling (he also has his own line of wines, Artiste); Brittany is the director of winemaking and is a chef; cousin Cara, formerly the events coordinator, is traveling the world; and Ashley is the operations manager. The beautiful tasting room is the result of a trip to Europe: the architecture is designed to recall images of wineries in Provence. The building opened to the public in 1994.

The Rice family thought long and hard about a name for their wines. The obvious wouldn't do: Rice Wine? Linda came up with thirty possible names, and the family selected one that evoked elements of the property: sun and sandstone merged to become Sunstone. With the vineyard planted, a name selected, and a winery and tasting room in place, in 2000 they asked Daniel Gehrs to become the consulting winemaker. Dan has the distinction of having produced a 1993 Syrah that was selected as one of the top ten wines in the world by the *Wine Spectator*. (He is discussed in detail in the profile of his eponymous winery.) He appreciates the fact that he gets to work with fruit that contains no residue of herbicide, fungicide, or pesticide, thanks to the Rice family's dedication to organic farming in the vineyard.

RECOMMENDED WINES: Ashley recommends the Reserve Estate Syrah. The 2001 is purple and red to the stem. The aromatics are licorice, plums, misted tobacco leaf, blackberry, and clove spice. The wine shows an interesting complexity of elements and is large and plush in the mouth. The finish lasts nearly a minute and recalls the fruit and spice in the lovely nose. This wine is ready for drinking now but has enough tannic structure to reward another three to four years in the bottle. If the 2001 is sold out, try the 2003, which recently won a silver medal from the Grand Harvest Award competition.

I recommend the Estate Merlot. The 2001 is opaque to the stem and a pretty black cherry color in the glass. The nose is plums, cherries, anise, blackberry, and some black pepper spice. The wine shows excellent balance and is fine in the mouth from the soft and rounded tannins; the finish is just short of a minute. This is an elegant Merlot ready for drinking now and over the next two or three years.

RATING: Three stars (both reds and whites consistently excellent across the line)

Tantara Winery

WINERY OWNERS: Bill Cates and Jeff Fink

WINEMAKERS: Bill Cates and Jeff Fink

TASTING ROOM: Yes

DAYS/HOURS: By appointment only

ADDRESS: 4747 Ontiveros Ln., Santa Maria, CA 93454; 805-938-5051; 805-938-5050; 805-937-1363 (fax); tantarawinery.com

WINES/GRAPE VARIETIES: Chardonnay, Pinot Noir, Syrah

WINE CLUB: Mailing list

REGION: Santa Maria Valley AVA

Bill Cates and Jeff Fink have been friends for more than twenty-five years, and Bill is responsible for helping Jeff discover his appreciation for fine wines back in 1980. In Virginia at the time, Jeff dated Bill's oldest daughter, and his experience with wine was centered pretty much on the cheap stuff. She brought an expensive bottle of Mondavi to one of their dates and the light bulb went off for Jeff, his first wine epiphany. In that instant he realized why people sought out fine wine instead of the plonk he drank.

His younger brother David moved to California to manage the Highlands Inn in Monterey from 1986 to 1999, and Jeff followed to study architecture. Although his appetite for finer wines had been whetted back in Virginia, his brother kept the attention going by exposing Jeff to better and better wines, specifically the Pinots. In fact, on a visit back to Virginia, he treated Bill to a 1975 Mount Eden Pinot Noir, made by Merry Edwards, which they drank in 1988. His relationship with Bill's daughter ended, but he stayed in touch with Bill in Roanoke. He graduated from UCLA in 1988 in architecture and designed a winery as his thesis project. That project turned out successfully and pushed him to think more deeply about the process for building wineries.

As a graduate student, Fink built a house for a client in Topanga Canyon, after which the two made wine together in 1991–92. They wanted to make only one barrel, but that takes about a ton of grapes. Jeff put a couple of guys together in a van; they drove north to the Russian River and got to harvest and destem the Pinot Noir then and there. This was his second epiphany: tapping into the historical and communal activity of harvesting fruit. He was now convinced that wine culture was the place to be because he likes to make things: music, architecture, and wine. His road crew got the sloshing grapes back to Topanga and made their wine. In 1994 Bryan Babcock befriended him and put Jeff in touch with noted grower and viticulturist Dale Hampton. In turn, Hampton put Jeff in touch with Laetitia for fruit from its vineyards. The Central Coast fruit was much better than what Jeff was used to and made a far better wine than previous efforts.

In 1997 he made an important contact with Jeff Wilkes and managed to get some Bien Nacido fruit. Wilkes was trying to put a series of wineries on the property. He told Jeff that an old rundown barn was available and was probably the right project for a guy with Jeff's training. This resulted in a third epiphany. Jeff called Bill Cates and asked if he wanted to move his family out west and make Pinot Noir. Bill agreed. The new partners moved into the renovated building on the Bien Nacido property in 1999 and produced wines under the Tantara label, launched in 1997 and named after a long-lived horse Bill once owned. The name also means a fanfare and flourish of trumpets or a celebration about to begin.

RECOMMENDED WINES: Jeff recommends the Garys' Vineyard Pinot Noir. The 2002 is light to the stem and a classic red cherry color. The nose is cherries, coffee, red currants, and plums, with earth, smoke, and vanilla spice. The tannins are ripe and rounded, leading to a silky feel on the tongue. The acidity is fine, and the wine shows great structure and complexity. The finish is nearly a minute. The wine is ready now but will show at its best in about four years. In all, this is a wonderful bottle of Pinot Noir.

I recommend the Evelyn Pinot Noir (named after Bill's mom), a luxury cuvée that is a blend of Pinot Noir grapes. It is translucent and black cherry in color. The fine aromatics recall wild plums, blackberries, black cherry, earth, and clove spice. The blend is seamless and well integrated, leading to a superb mouthfeel and a finish of nearly a minute. The ripe fruit and fine tannic structure suggest great drinking over the next six to seven years. This is one of the best Pinots I have tasted from the region.

RATING: Four stars (might be my next five-star-rated winery in Santa Barbara County)

Taz Vineyards

WINERY OWNER: Beringer Blass Wine Estates

WINEMAKER: Jon Priest

TASTING ROOM: No

DAYS/HOURS: No tasting available

ADDRESS: 2717 Aviation Way, Santa Maria, CA 93455; beringerwineestates.com/wineries/taz

WINES/GRAPE VARIETIES: Chardonnay, Merlot, Pinot Gris, Pinot Noir, Syrah

WINE CLUB: Online sales

REGION: Santa Barbara County

Tensley Wines

WINERY OWNERS: Joey and Jennifer Tensley

WINEMAKER: Joey Tensley

TASTING ROOM: Yes

DAYS/HOURS: Friday–Sunday 11 A.M.–5 P.M.

ADDRESS: 2900 Grand Ave., Ste. A, Los Olivos, CA 93441; 805-688-6761; 805-688-0591 (fax); tensleywines.com

WINES/GRAPE VARIETIES: Camp 4 Blanc (blend), Grenache Blanc, Pinot Noir, Syrah, Syrah rosé

WINE CLUB: Yes

TASTING ROOM AMENITIES: Picnic area, merchandise

REGION: Santa Ynez Valley AVA

New Orleans is the hometown of Jennifer Tensley, who with her husband, Joey, is one of the driving forces behind Tensley Wines. Joey is also the winemaker at Carina Cellars, which is literally across the rug in the shared tasting room. He grew up in Bakersfield, but his first exposure to wine culture came about when as a young man he traveled to France to play soccer. He stayed in Bordeaux, known to produce some pretty good wines from time to time. Back in the United States, he worked in a deli and was intrigued by that shop's selection of wines. When he first tasted a Zaca Mesa Syrah, he dropped out of school and went to work there. He was there only a couple of months before he moved on to Fess Parker, working for Fess's son Eli and living on the property for three years. His next transition was to Babcock, where he became a mentee of Bryan Babcock and eventually assistant winemaker through 1998. He worked at Beckmen for a time and then started his own label in 1998. When he met David Hardee in 2002, the two combined their respective talents and joined in a partnership to launch Carina.

Joey's other partnership is with Jennifer, and hers is an interesting story indeed. Jennifer is a graduate of the University of Florida, where she took a major in communications. She got her professional start as a radio broadcaster and then became a news anchor in Biloxi, Mississippi. Having had her fill of the airwaves as a radio and TV professional, she moved to Los Angeles, where her mother lived, using the transition to pursue her love of creative writing. She took classes in screenwriting, got an agent and a manager, and became the head writer for *Love Connection*. At one point she wrote for the Jim Henson Group and the television show *Witchblade*. When her mother decided to buy a home in Los Olivos, Jennifer started working in the wine business for fun while writing for a children's Web site called myhero.com. Then one day Joey walked into the tasting room, and ever since the two have worked collaboratively on their life scripts.

Joey adopted a European style of winemaking—that is, very little manipulation of the juice with the emphasis squarely focused on what goes on in the vineyard. For Joey, important factors are *terroir*, selection of the correct clones, and the best farming practices possible. His focus is paying dividends in that his wines have caught the attention of Robert M. Parker Jr., one of the most influential wine critics writing today.

RECOMMENDED WINES: Joey recommends the Syrah from Thompson Vineyards. The 2003 is an inky black-purple in the glass and permits no light to the stem. The nose is black currants, blackberries, cola, and spice. The wine explodes in the mouth, lovely and supple, showing a wonderful balance and excellent structure. It is drinking sensationally now but will continue its integration and improvement over the next seven to nine years.

Another outstanding example of what Tensley can do with Syrah is the 2003 Colson Canyon. Again, the color is an inky black-purple that reflects light like a mirror. The nose is leather, boysenberry, ripe sweet blackberries, earth, and cigar. This is a slightly more flamboyant wine, with similar structure and integration of all the elements. At this time, I believe the wine is slightly farther along in its development, as noted in the lovely aromatics. The lovely ripe finish reflects the wonderful maturation of the fruit, which also speaks to a slightly higher but unobtrusive alcohol percentage. This wine is splendid now but will improve over the next five to six years. You simply cannot go wrong with these two superb examples of Syrah.

RATING: Five stars (outstanding to superb Syrah)

Vandale Vineyards

WINERY OWNERS: Bruce and Beth Vandale

WINEMAKER: Bruno D'Alfonso

TASTING ROOM: At Wine Country

DAYS/HOURS: Daily 11 A.M.–5 P.M.

ADDRESS: Wine Country, 2445 Alamo Pintado Ave., Los Olivos, CA 93441;

805-686-9699; 805-686-4560 (fax); no Web site

WINE/GRAPE VARIETY: Sangiovese

WINE CLUB: No

REGION: Santa Ynez Valley AVA

Verdad

WINERY OWNER: Louisa Sawyer Lindquist

WINEMAKERS: Louisa and Bob Lindquist

TASTING ROOM: At Wine Country

DAYS/HOURS: Daily 11 A.M.–5 P.M.

ADDRESS: Wine Country, 2445 Alamo Pintado Ave., Los Olivos, CA 93441; 805-

686-9699; 805-784-0785 (fax); verdadwines.com

WINES/GRAPE VARIETIES: Albariño, rosé, Tempranillo blend

WINE CLUB: Mailing list

REGION: Santa Barbara County

Westerly Vineyards

WINERY OWNERS: Neil and Francine Afromsky

WINEMAKER: Seth Kunin

TASTING ROOM: No

DAYS/HOURS: No tasting available

ADDRESS: 690 Alamo Pintado Rd., Solvang, CA 94363; 805-686-9558; 805-686-1347 (fax); westerlyvineyards.com

WINES/GRAPE VARIETIES: Après (dessert wine), Merlot, Sauvignon Blanc, Syrah, Viognier, W (blend), W Blanc (blend)

WINE CLUB: Yes

REGION: Santa Ynez Valley AVA

Whitcraft Winery

WINERY OWNER: Chris Whitcraft

...AKER: Chris Whitcraft

......G ROOM: Yes

.......OURS: Daily 11 A.M.–6 P.M.

.......ss: Call for details; 805-965-0956; ... 962-5655 (fax); whitcraftwinery.com

WINES/GRAPE VARIETIES: Chardonnay, Lagrein, Pinot Noir

WINE CLUB: Mailing list

REGION: Santa Barbara County

Zaca Mesa Winery

WINERY OWNERS: John and Lou Cushman

WINEMAKER: Clay Brock

TASTING ROOM: Yes

DAYS/HOURS: Daily 10 A.M.–4 P.M.

ADDRESS: 6905 Foxen Canyon Rd., Los Olivos, CA 93441; 805-688-9339; 805-688-8796 (fax); zacamesa.com

WINES/GRAPE VARIETIES: Grenache, Mourvèdre, Syrah, Viognier, Z Cuvée (blend)

WINE CLUB: Yes

TASTING ROOM AMENITIES: Picnic area, life-size chessboard, merchandise, walking trail

REGION: Santa Ynez Valley AVA

Zaca Mesa, which means "restful or peaceful place," was founded in 1972 by a consortium of six businessmen, some of whom were executives from large oil companies. John Cushman, one of the original six, now owns Zaca Mesa with his wife, Louise Cushman. The winery started life as a barn, and this theme is continued today in the rough-sawn timbers used to construct the spacious tasting room and other facilities on the grounds. The vineyards truly are on a mesa, 1,500 feet above sea level and 28 miles from the ocean, that was once part of the ocean floor. Three feet of topsoil cap a bed of well-drained gravel. The Zaca Mesa outfit struggled a bit during the early years as it tried to find the proper direction and focus for the vineyard and winery. Over time, this resulted in narrowing the winery's production, from as many as twenty-eight grape varieties and a production total that at times reached more than 100,000 cases to its current focus on Rhône varieties such as Syrah, Roussanne, and Viognier.

Over the years, the winery reduced its holdings from the original 1,500 acres to about 750. In fact, actor James Garner once bought a section of the vineyard and built a house, but never moved in. Because the first vines were planted in 1973, the estate vineyards are being renovated and replanted with an emphasis on putting the right grapes into the right soils on the property. For example, acres of thirty-year-old Chardonnay vines now at the end of their economically viable life are being torn out, and Viognier is being replanted. Syrah, successfully planted in 1978, is again emphasized. The Syrah vineyard has the distinction of being the oldest of that variety in the region. The plan now, according to winery president Brook Williams, formerly of Beringer and Kendall-Jackson, is to produce about 30,000 cases of wine per year.

Zaca Mesa enjoys the distinction of being an incubator of some of the finest winemaking talent in Santa Barbara County. Among others, Ken Brown worked there as the first winemaker (he recently sold Byron and has his own line of wines); other former employees include Jim Clendenen of Au Bon Climat and Bob Lindquist of Qupé, to mention but two. The winery came into prominence when the 1993 Syrah was ranked sixth among the *Wine Spectator's* top 100 wines of 1995. The Syrah vines planted in the famous Black Bear block came from Gary Eberle, then at Estrella River Winery, who imported cuttings from Chapoutier in the northern Rhône valley. This famous Estrella clone is known as the "suitcase Syrah cutting."

The current winemaker is Clay Brock, a graduate of Cal Poly and former resident of Napa. He worked four years as assistant winemaker at Byron in Santa Maria and in 1997 became the winemaker at Edna Valley Vineyard. He came to Zaca Mesa in 2001, where he works with a crew, some of whom have been at the winery more than twenty years.

RECOMMENDED WINES: Brook suggests the Z Cuvée, an estate-bottled blend of five grapes: Grenache, Mourvèdre, Counoise, Syrah, and Cinsaut, Zaca Mesa's Châteauneuf-du-Pape homage. This red and purple wine is almost opaque in the glass, with a nose of raspberries, mocha, red currants, strawberries, and a whiff of roses. Well balanced and nicely integrated, it also has a finish that is long and luscious. The wine is ready now but will improve over the next three to four years.

My recommendation is the Black Bear Syrah, named after the black bears that often visited the vineyard. In fact, the small windows of the adobes built in the early days were designed to keep those bears out. I tasted the 2001, a black-purple and opaque wine that is a real beauty. The nose is ripe, sweet blackberries (just the sort black bears love), crème de cassis, vanilla from nearly two years in the barrel, sage, and white pepper spice. The wine is wonderful and grand in the mouth, showing excellent balance and integration of all its elements. The finish on this black beauty lasts nearly a minute. It is drinkable now, but if you can hold off two years, you will have a superb wine at the table. It should last another five to six years beyond that.

RATING: Three → four stars (quality once again improving at Zaca Mesa)

CURRENT CENTRAL COAST AMERICAN
VITICULTURAL AREAS BY COUNTY

This book covers the three Central Coast counties of Monterey, San Luis Obispo, and Santa Barbara (in contrast to the Tobacco Tax and Trade Bureau, which includes ten counties in the Central Coast AVA; see appendix B). The profiles and nonprofiled listings are organized alphabetically according to the county in which they are located. I provide below a list of the AVAs by county, noting the year in which each AVA was approved.

MONTEREY COUNTY

Arroyo Seco AVA 1983
Carmel Valley AVA 1983
Chalone AVA 1982
Hames Valley AVA 1994
Monterey AVA 1984

San Antonio Valley AVA 2006
San Bernabe AVA 2004
San Lucas AVA 1987
Santa Lucia Highlands AVA 1992

SAN LUIS OBISPO COUNTY

Arroyo Grande Valley AVA 1990
Edna Valley AVA 1987

Paso Robles AVA 1983
York Mountain AVA 1983

SANTA BARBARA COUNTY

Santa Maria Valley AVA 1981
Santa Rita Hills AVA 2001

Santa Ynez Valley AVA 1983

THE CENTRAL COAST
AMERICAN VITICULTURAL AREA
ACCORDING TO THE ALCOHOL AND
TOBACCO TAX AND TRADE BUREAU

The Central Coast AVA as defined by the Alcohol and Tobacco Tax and Trade Bureau at present comprises the following ten counties: Alameda, Contra Costa, Monterey, San Benito, San Francisco, San Luis Obispo, San Mateo, Santa Barbara, Santa Clara, and Santa Cruz. Below I list the counties and areas granted appellation of origin status within the Central Coast AVA and their subappellations, if any.

CENTRAL COAST AMERICAN VITICULTURAL AREA 1985

San Francisco Bay AVA 1999

Alameda County
    Livermore Valley AVA 1982
Contra Costa County
San Benito County
    Cienega Valley AVA 1982
    Lime Kiln Valley AVA 1982
    Mount Harlan AVA 1990
    Paicines AVA 1982
    San Benito AVA 1987
San Francisco County
San Mateo County
Santa Clara County
    Pacheco Pass AVA 1984
    San Ysidro District AVA 1990
    Santa Clara Valley AVA 1989

Santa Cruz County
    Ben Lomond Mountain AVA 1988
    Santa Cruz Mountains AVA 1982
    (NOTE: According to 46 FR 59239 Santa Cruz Mountains Viticultural Area Final Rule, the Santa Cruz Mountains AVA, with its subappellation Ben Lomond Mountain AVA, is distinctively different in geography, soils, and climate from the San Francisco Bay AVA and is therefore considered a "distinct and recognizable area." This area includes portions of San Mateo, Santa Clara, and Santa Cruz counties. The petition for this change was offered by Paul Draper of Ridge Vineyards and thirty-two others.)

Monterey County

Arroyo Seco AVA 1983	San Antonio Valley AVA 2006
Carmel Valley AVA 1983	San Bernabe AVA 2004
Chalone AVA 1982	San Lucas AVA 1987
Hames Valley AVA 1994	Santa Lucia Highlands AVA 1992
Monterey AVA 1984	

San Luis Obispo County

Arroyo Grande Valley AVA 1990	Paso Robles AVA 1983
Edna Valley AVA 1987	York Mountain AVA 1983

Santa Barbara County

Santa Maria Valley AVA 1981	Santa Ynez Valley AVA 1983
Santa Rita Hills AVA 2001	

ALPHABETICAL LISTING BY COUNTY AVA

Alameda County (San Francisco Bay)

Livermore Valley AVA 1982

Contra Costa County (San Francisco Bay)

Monterey County

Arroyo Seco AVA 1983	San Antonio Valley AVA 2006
Carmel Valley AVA 1983	San Bernabe AVA 2004
Chalone AVA 1982	San Lucas AVA 1987
Hames Valley AVA 1994	Santa Lucia Highlands AVA 1992
Monterey AVA 1984	

San Benito County (San Francisco Bay)

Cienega Valley AVA 1982	Paicines AVA 1982
Lime Kiln Valley AVA 1982	San Benito AVA 1987
Mount Harlan AVA 1990	

San Francisco County (San Francisco Bay)

San Luis Obispo County

Arroyo Grande Valley AVA 1990	Paso Robles AVA 1983
Edna Valley AVA 1987	York Mountain AVA 1983

San Mateo County (San Francisco Bay)

Santa Barbara County

Santa Maria Valley AVA 1981	Santa Ynez Valley AVA 1983
Santa Rita Hills AVA 2001	

Santa Clara County (San Francisco Bay)

Pacheco Pass AVA 1984

San Ysidro District AVA 1990

Santa Clara Valley AVA 1989

Santa Cruz County (San Francisco Bay)

Ben Lomond Mountain AVA 1988

Santa Cruz Mountains AVA 1982

(See note under Santa Cruz County in the previous list)

Amerine, Maynard A., and Vernon L. Singleton. 1976. *Wine: An Introduction.* 2nd ed. Berkeley: University of California Press.

Appellationamerica.com. n.d. Central Coast AVA. Retrieved November 20, 2005, from www.appellationamerica.com/appellationPage.

Broadbent, Michael. 1982. *Michael Broadbent's Pocket Guide to Wine Tasting.* New York: Simon & Schuster.

Catholic University of America. 2002. *New Catholic Encyclopedia.* Vol. 13. New York: Thomson Gale.

Clarke, Oz. 2002. *Oz Clarke's New Wine Atlas.* New York: Harcourt.

Clarke, Oz, and Margaret Rand. 2001. *Oz Clarke's Encyclopedia of Grapes.* New York: Harcourt.

Daily, Marla. 1989. "Santa Cruz Island Anthology." *Noticias: Quarterly Magazine of the Santa Barbara Historical Society* 35 (1,2): 1–161.

Geraci, Victor W. 2004. *Salud! The Rise of Santa Barbara's Wine Industry.* Reno: University of Nevada Press.

Graham, Otis L. Jr., et al. 1998. *Aged in Oak: The Story of the Santa Barbara County Wine Industry.* Santa Barbara, CA: Cachuma Press.

Haeger, John W. 2004. *North American Pinot Noir.* Berkeley: University of California Press.

Hinkle, Richard P., and William H. Gibbs III. 1977. *Central Coast Wine Tour from San Francisco to Santa Barbara.* St. Helena, CA: Vintage Image.

Johnson, Hugh, and Jancis Robinson. 2001. *The World Atlas of Wine.* 5th ed. London: Mitchell Beazley.

Kocher, Paul H. 1976. *California's Old Missions: The Story of the Founding of the 21 Franciscan Missions in Spanish Alta California, 1769–1823.* Chicago: Franciscan Herald Press.

Krieger, Dan. 2004. "Vino de los Californios." Unpublished manuscript.

Kroeber, A. L. 1976. *Handbook of the Indians of California.* New York: Dover.

Laube, James. 1999. *Wine Spectator's California Wine: A Comprehensive Guide to the Wineries, Wines, Vintages and Vineyards, with Ratings and Tasting Notes for 5000 Wines.* 2nd ed. New York: Wine Spectator Press.

Laville, P. 1990. "Le terroir, un concept indispensible à l'élaboration et à la protection des appellations d'origine comme à la question des vignobles: Le cas de la France." *Bulletin de l'OIV* 709–10: 217–41.

Millner, Cork. 1983. *Vintage Valley: The Wineries of Santa Barbara County.* Santa Barbara, CA: McNally & Loftin.

Ontiveros, Erlinda P. 1990. *San Ramon Chapel Pioneers and Their California Heritage.* Los Olivos, CA: Olive Press.

Paderewski, Ignace Jan, and Mary Lawton. 1938. *The Paderewski Memoirs.* New York: Charles Scribner's Sons.

Parker, Robert M. Jr. 2004. "California's Rhône Rangers." *The Wine Advocate,* no. 154 (August 31): 2–24.

Penimore, Ernest P., and Sidney S. Greenleaf. 1967. *A Directory of California Wine Growers and Wine Makers in 1860: With Biographical and Historical Notes and Index.* Berkeley, CA: Tamalpais Press.

Peynaud, Émile. 1987. *The Taste of Wine: The Art and Science of Wine Appreciation.* Michael Schuster, trans. San Francisco: Wine Appreciation Guild.

Pinney, Thomas. 1994. *The Wine of Santa Cruz Island.* San Fernando, CA: Nut-Quad Press.

Press, Frank, Raymond Siever, John Grotzinger, and Thomas H. Jordan. 2004. *Understanding Earth.* 4th ed. New York: W. H. Freeman.

Rankin, Cindy. 1989. *A History and Tour Guide of the Paso Robles Wine Country.* Paso Robles, CA: Paso Robles Chamber of Commerce.

Robinson, Jancis, ed. 1999. *The Oxford Companion to Wine.* New York: Oxford University Press.

Sullivan, Charles, L. 1998. *A Companion to California Wine: An Encyclopedia of Wine and Winemaking from the Mission Period to the Present.* Berkeley, CA: University of California Press.

Volk, Kenneth. 2000. "Making Sense of the Central Coast." Presentation to the Epcot International Food and Wine Festival 2000, Orlando, FL.

Wasserman, Sheldon, and Pauline Wasserman. 1985. *Italy's Noble Red Wines.* El Monte, CA: New Century Publishers.

Wine Style Monterey County. 2005. Monterey, CA: Bay Publishing.

Woodward, W. Philip, and Gregory S. Walter. 2000. *Chalone: A Journey on the Wine Frontier.* Sonoma, CA: Carneros Press.

MAPS

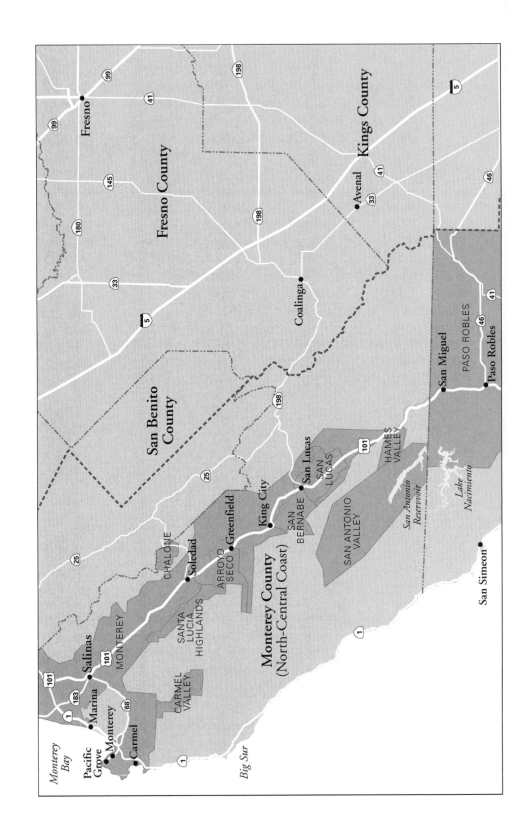

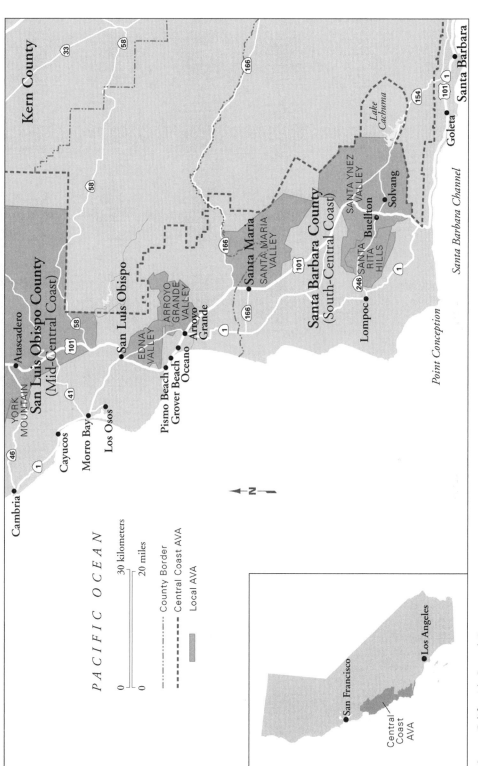

Map 1. California's Central Coast

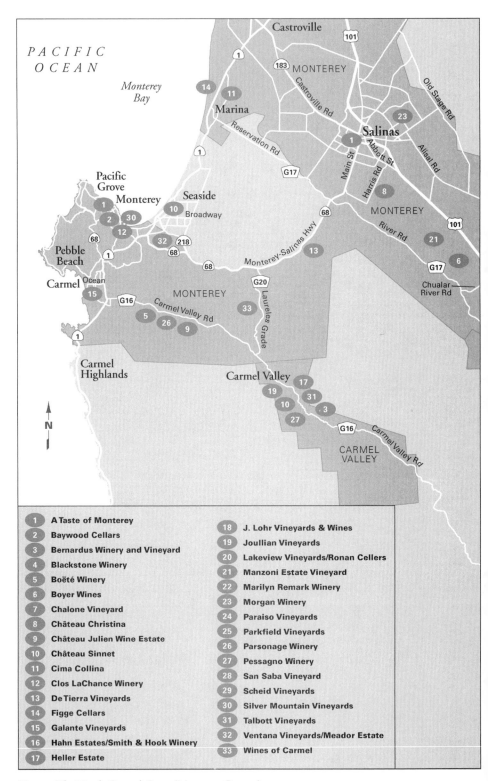

Map 2. The North-Central Coast (Monterey County)

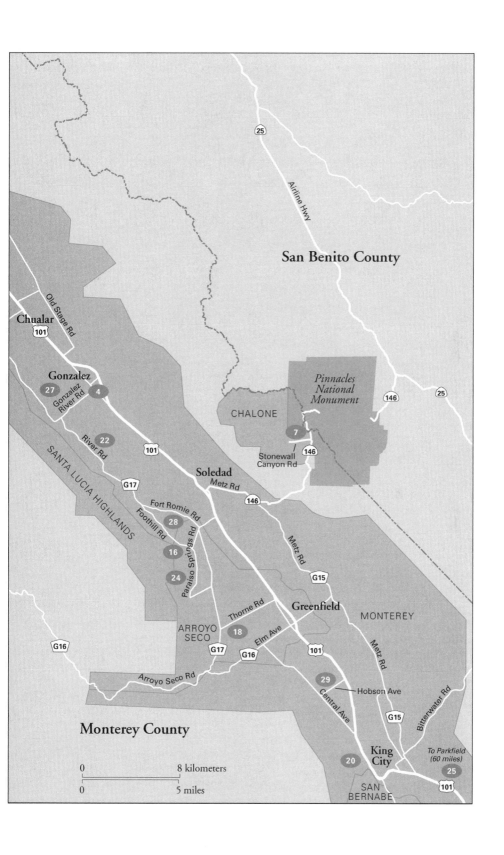

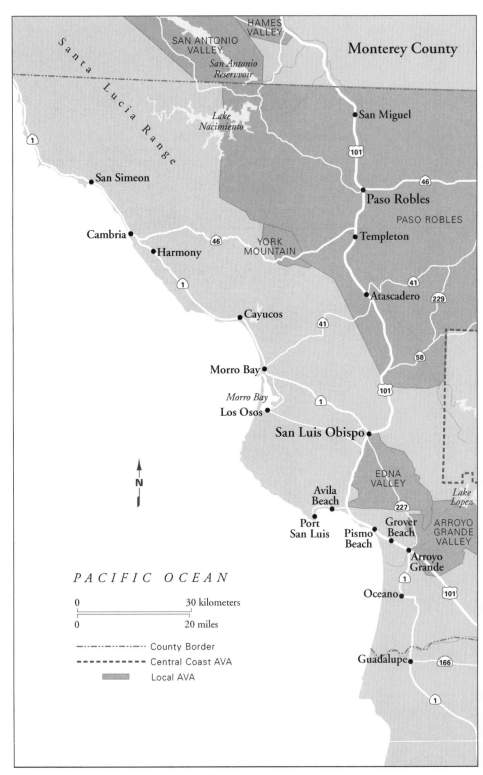

Map 3. The Mid-Central Coast (San Luis Obispo County)

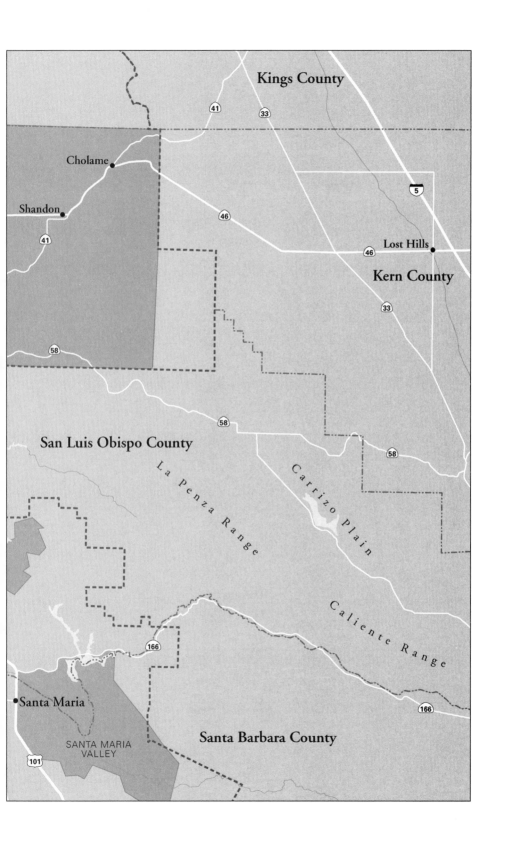

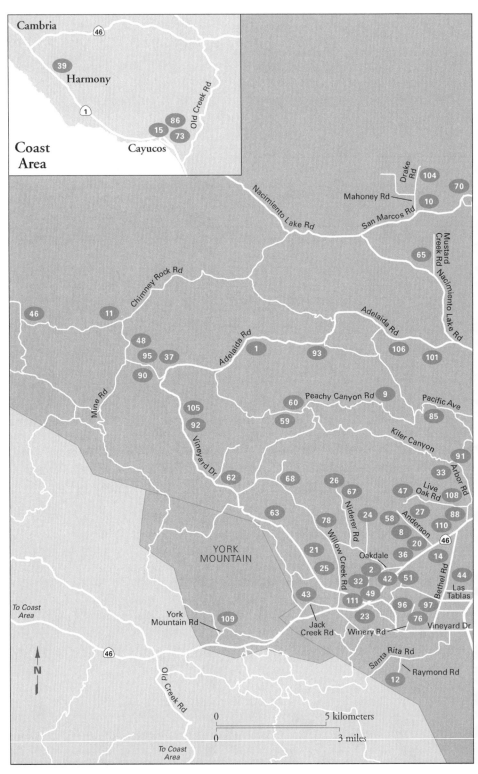

Map 4. Paso Robles

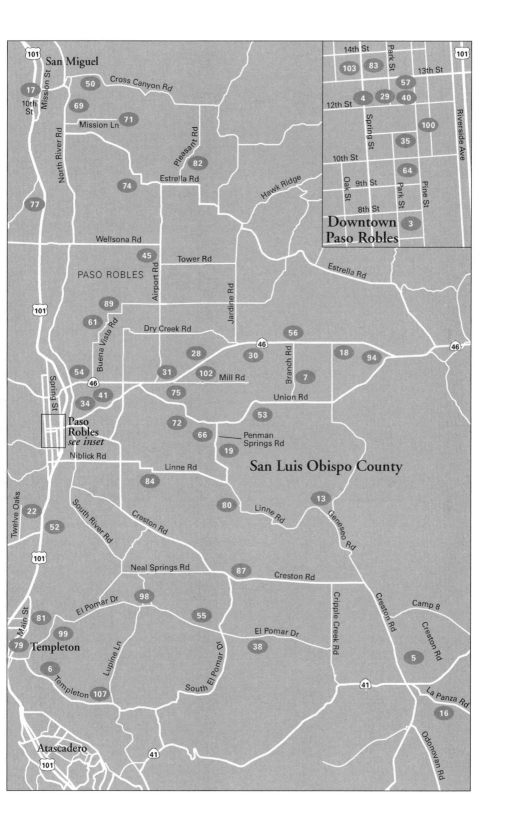

San Miguel

101

17

10th St

50 Cross Canyon Rd

Mission St

69

North River Rd

Mission Ln 71

Pleasant Rd

82

74 Estrella Rd

Hawk Ridge

77

Wellsona Rd

45 Tower Rd

PASO ROBLES

Airport Rd

Jardine Rd

Estrella Rd

89

61

Dry Creek Rd

Buena Vista Rd

56

46

28 30

Branch Rd

18 94

46

101

54

Spring St

46

31 102 Mill Rd

7

41

34

75 Union Rd

53

72

66 Penman Springs Rd

19

San Luis Obispo County

Paso Robles *see inset*

Niblick Rd

Linne Rd

84

Twelve Oaks

22

80 Linne Rd

13

52

Geneseo Rd

Neal Springs Rd 87 Creston Rd

Cripple Creek Rd

Creston Rd

Camp 8

98

El Pomar Dr

Main St

81

55

Creston Rd

99

El Pomar Dr

79 **Templeton**

38

5

6

Lupine Ln

South El Pomar Dr

Templeton 107

South El Pomar Dr

41

La Panza Rd

16

Atascadero

41

101

Odonovan Rd

Downtown Paso Robles

14th St

Park St

103 83

13th St

57

4 29 40

12th St

Spring St

100

10th St

35

Riverside Ave

64

Oak St

9th St

Park St

Pine St

8th St

3

101

Key to Map 4 (The Paso Robles Area)

1	Adelaida Cellars	29	Edward Sellers Vineyards & Wines
2	AJB Vineyards	30	Eos Estate Winery
3	Anglim Winery	31	Firestone Vineyard (Paso Robles)
4	Arroyo Robles Winery	32	Four Vines Winery
5	B & E Vineyard/Winery	33	Fratelli Perata
6	Bella Luna Winery	34	Garretson Wine Company
7	Bianchi	35	Gelfand Vineyards
8	Brian Benson Cellars	36	Grey Wolf Cellars
9	Calcareous Vineyard	37	Halter Ranch Vineyard
10	Caparone Winery	38	Hansen Vineyards
11	Carmody McKnight Estate Wines	39	Harmony Cellars
12	Casa de Caballos Vineyards	40	Hice Cellars
13	Cass Wines	41	Hug Cellars
14	Castoro Cellars	42	Hunt Cellars
15	Cayucos Cellars	43	Jack Creek Cellars
16	Chateau Margene	44	JanKris Winery
17	Christian Lazo Winery	45	J. Lohr Vineyards & Wines
18	Chumeia Vineyards	46	Justin Vineyards & Winery
19	Clautiere Vineyard	47	L'Aventure Winery
20	Dark Star Cellars	48	Le Cuvier Winery
21	Denner Vineyards & Winery	49	Linne Calodo Cellars
22	Doce Robles Winery & Vineyard	50	Locatelli Vineyards & Winery
23	Donati Family Vineyard	51	Lone Madrone
24	Donatoni Winery	52	Madison Cellars
25	Dover Canyon Winery	53	Maloy O'Neill Vineyards
26	Dunning Vineyards	54	Martin & Weyrich Winery
27	Eagle Castle Winery	55	McClean Vineyards
28	Eberle Winery	56	Meridian Vineyards

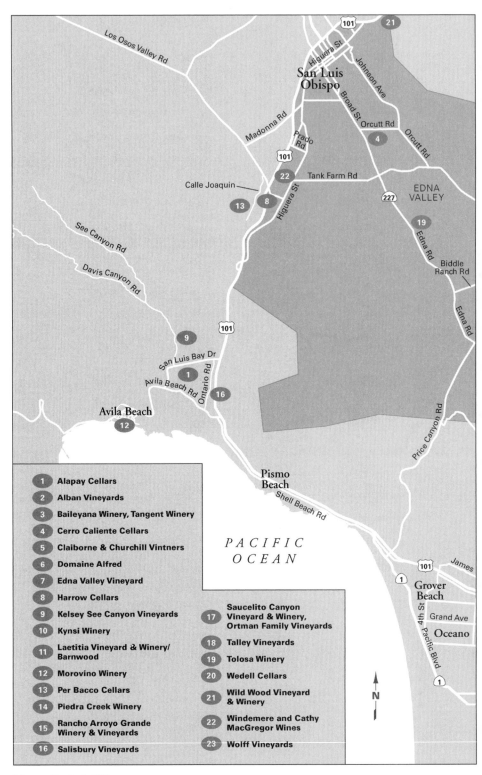

Los Osos Valley Rd

Higuera St

San Luis
Obispo

Johnson Ave

[101] 21

Madonna Rd

Broad St

Prado Rd

Orcutt Rd

Orcutt Rd

4

[101]

22

Tank Farm Rd

Calle Joaquin

13   8

Higuera St

EDNA
VALLEY

[227]

19

Edna Rd

Biddle
Ranch Rd

See Canyon Rd

Davis Canyon Rd

Edna Rd

[101]

9

San Luis Bay Dr

1

Avila Beach Rd

Ontario Rd

16

Price Canyon Rd

Avila Beach

12

Pismo
Beach

Shell Beach Rd

1	Alapay Cellars
2	Alban Vineyards
3	Baileyana Winery, Tangent Winery
4	Cerro Caliente Cellars
5	Claiborne & Churchill Vintners
6	Domaine Alfred
7	Edna Valley Vineyard
8	Harrow Cellars
9	Kelsey See Canyon Vineyards
10	Kynsi Winery
11	Laetitia Vineyard & Winery/ Barnwood
12	Morovino Winery
13	Per Bacco Cellars
14	Piedra Creek Winery
15	Rancho Arroyo Grande Winery & Vineyards
16	Salisbury Vineyards

17	Saucelito Canyon Vineyard & Winery, Ortman Family Vineyards
18	Talley Vineyards
19	Tolosa Winery
20	Wedell Cellars
21	Wild Wood Vineyard & Winery
22	Windemere and Cathy MacGregor Wines
23	Wolff Vineyards

PACIFIC
OCEAN

[101]   James

1   Grover
        Beach

4th St

Grand Ave

Pacific Blvd

Oceano

1

N

Map 5. San Luis Obispo

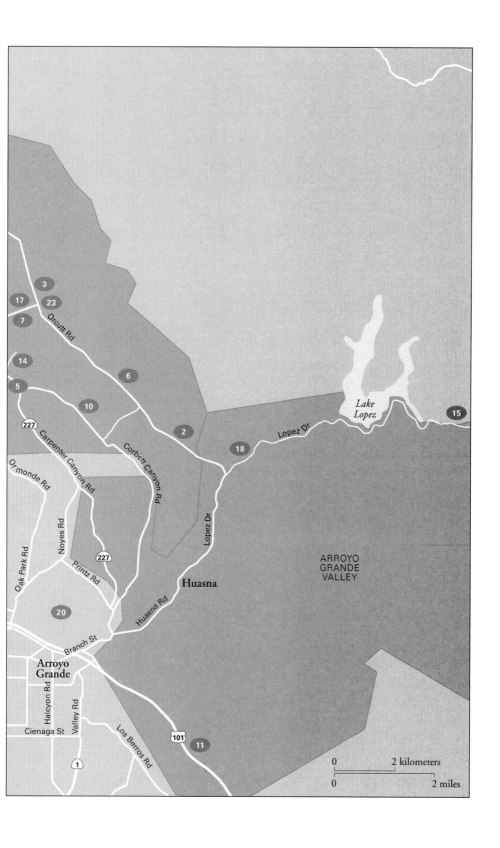

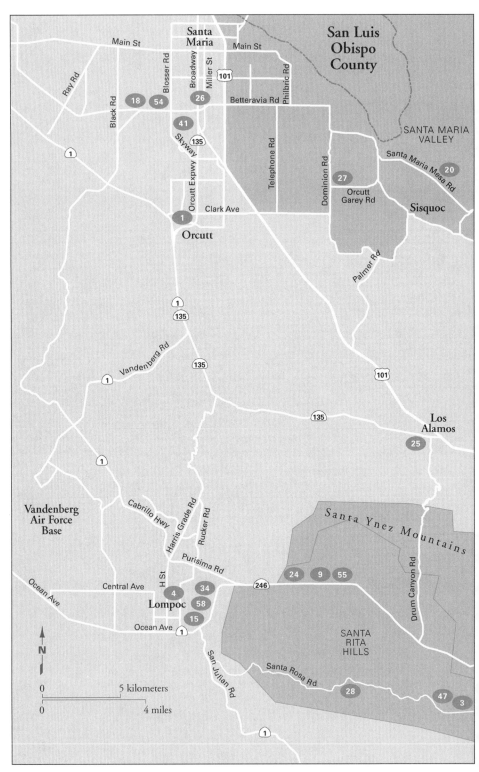

Map 6. The South-Central Coast (Santa Barbara County)

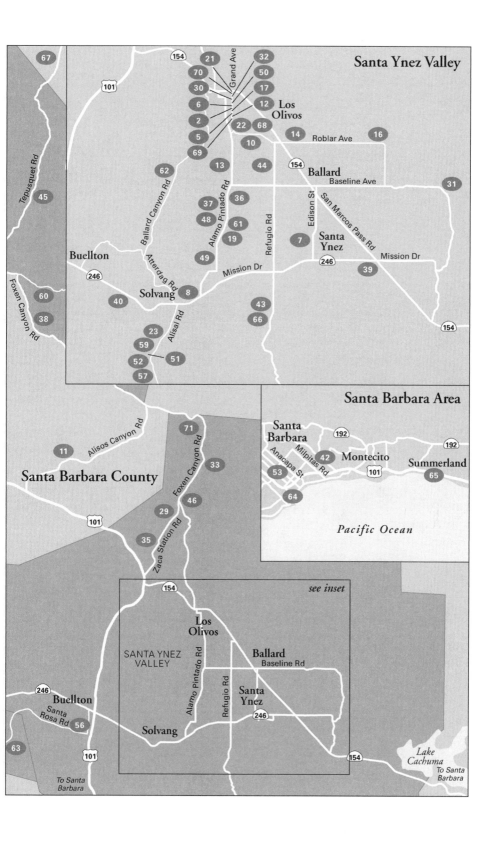

Key to Map 6 (The South-Central Coast)

1 Addamo Vineyards

2 Alexander & Wayne

3 Alma Rosa Winery & Vineyards

4 Ampelos Cellars & Vineyard

5 Andrew Murray Vineyards,
J. Kerr Wines, Oak Savanna Wines

6 Arthur Earl

7 Artiste

8 Au Bon Climat

9 Babcock Winery & Vineyards

10 Beckmen Vineyards

11 Bedford Thompson Winery & Vineyard

12 Bernat Vineyards & Winery

13 Blackjack Ranch Vineyards & Winery

14 Brander Vineyard

15 Brewer-Clifton

16 Bridlewood Estate Winery

17 Brophy Clark Cellars

18 Brucher Winery

19 Buttonwood Farm Winery & Vineyard

20 Cambria Winery

21 Carhartt Vineyard & Winery

22 Carina Cellars

23 Casa Cassara Winery & Vineyard

24 Clos Pepe Vineyards

25 Cold Heaven

26 Costa De Oro Winery

27 Cottonwood Canyon Vineyard & Winery

28 Curran

29 Curtis Winery

30 Daniel Gehrs Wines

31 East Valley Vineyard and Winery

32 Epiphany Cellars

33 Fess Parker Winery & Vineyard

34 Fiddlehead Cellars

35 Firestone Vineyard

36 Flying Goat Cellars

37 Foley Estates

38 Foxen Winery & Vineyard

INDEX OF WINERIES

Page numbers in italics indicate Wineries and Profiles listings.

DESIGNER: SANDY DROOKER
CARTOGRAPHER: LOHNES+WRIGHT
INDEXER: RUTH ELWELL
TEXT: 11/14 ADOBE GARAMOND
DISPLAY: ADOBE GARAMOND, SACKERS GOTHIC
COMPOSITOR: BINGHAMTON VALLEY COMPOSITION
PRINTER AND BINDER: SHERIDAN BOOK & JOURNAL SERVICES